Skill and Education:
Reflection and Experience

ARTIFICIAL INTELLIGENCE AND SOCIETY

Series Editor: KARAMJIT S. GILL

Knowledge, Skill and Artificial Intelligence
Bo Göranzon and Ingela Josefson (Eds.)

Artificial Intelligence, Culture and Language: On Education and Work
Bo Göranzon and Magnus Florins (Eds.)

Designing Human-centred Technology: A Cross-disciplinary Project in Computer-aided Manufacturing
H.H. Rosenbrock (Ed.)

The Shape of Future Technology: The Anthropocentric Alternative
Peter Brödner

Crossing the Border: The Social and Engineering Design of Computer Integrated Manufacturing Systems
J. Martin Corbett, Lauge Baungaard Rasmussen and Felix Rauner

Artificial Intelligence and Human Institutions
Richard Ennals

Dialogue and Technology: Art and Knowledge
Bo Göranzon and Magnus Florin (Eds.)

Understanding the Artificial: On the Future Shape of Artificial Intelligence
Massimo Negrotti (Ed.)

Computer-aided Manufacturing and Women's Employment: The Clothing Industry in Four EC Countries
Swaski Mitter (Ed.)

Connectionism in Context
Andy Clark and Rudi Lutz (Eds.)

Human-Centered Systems in the Global Economy
Yuji Masuda (Ed.)

Bo Göranzon and Magnus Florin (Eds.)

Skill and Education: Reflection and Experience

Springer-Verlag
London Berlin Heidelberg New York
Paris Tokyo Hong Kong
Barcelona Budapest

Bo Göranzon, PhD
Professor,
The Royal Institute of Technology,
S-100 44 Stockholm, Sweden

Magnus Florin
Dramaturg, The Royal Dramatic Theatre,
PO Box 5037, S-102 41 Stockholm, Sweden

Cover illustration: Lennart Mörk, *Ramanujan*

ISBN 3-540-19758-3 Springer-Verlag Berlin Heidelberg New York
ISBN 0-387-19758-3 Springer-Verlag New York Berlin Heidelberg

British Library Cataloguing in Publication Data
Skill and Education: Reflection and
Experience. – (Artificial Intelligence & Society Series)
I. Goranzon, Bo II. Florin, Magnus
III. Series
006.3
ISBN 3-540-19758-3

Library of Congress Cataloging-in-Publication Data
Skill and education : reflection and experience / Bo Göranzon and
Magnus Florin, eds.
p. cm. – (Artificial intelligence and society)
Includes bibliographical references and index.
ISBN 3-540-19758-3 (Berlin : alk. paper). – ISBN 0-387-19758-3
(alk. paper)
1. Artificial intelligence–Congresses. 2. Knowledge, Theory of–
Congresses. 3. Linguistics–Data processing–Congresses.
I. Göranzon, Bo, 1941– . II. Florin, Magnus, 1955– . III. Series.
Q334.S55 1992 92-16598
001–dc20 CIP

Typeset by Fox Design, Surbiton, Surrey
Printed and bound at Page Bros Ltd, Norwich
34/3830-543210 Printed on acid-free paper

Preface

This book has an important starting point in the conference held in Stockholm in May–June 1988 on Culture, Language and Artificial Intelligence. It assembled more than 300 researchers and practitioners in the fields of technology, philosophy, history of ideas, literature, linguistics, social science etc. The conference was an initiative from the Swedish Center for Working Life, based on the project *AI-Based Systems and the Future of Language, Knowledge and Responsibility in Professions* within the COST 13 programme of the European Commission. Participants in the conference and researchers related to its aims were chosen to contribute to this book.

It is preceded by *Knowledge, Skill and Artificial Intelligence* (ed. B. Göranzon and I. Josefson, Springer-Verlag, 1988), *Artificial Intelligence, Culture and Language* (ed. B. Göranzon and M. Florin, Springer-Verlag, 1990) and *Dialogue and Technology: Art and Knowledge* (ed. B. Göranzon and M. Florin, Springer-Verlag, 1991). The two latter books have the same conference connection as this one, and their aim is to present the contours of a research field with a multitude of issues that demands thorough investigation.

The contributors' thinking in this field varies greatly; so do their styles of writing. For example: contributors have varied in their choice of "he" or "he/she" for the third person. No distinction is intended, but chapters have been left with the original usage to avoid extensive changes. Similarly, individual contributor's preference as to notes or reference lists have been followed.

We want to thank Jon Cook for his support and his contribution to the editorial shaping. We also thank Rolf Hughes for his eminent chapter summaries.

Stockholm
June 1992

Bo Göranzon
Magnus Florin

Contents

Contributors

Jon Bing
Professor dr juris, Norwegian Research Center for Computers and Law, Oslo University, Niels Juels gate 16, N-0272 Oslo 2, Norway

Malcolm Bolton
Consultant, Technology Art Information, Hi Tech House, 10 Blackfriars Street, Norwich, NR3 1SF, UK

Joseph Cannataci
Director dr juris, Research Centre for Law and Information Technology, University of Malta, Malta

Jon Cook
Director, Centre for Creative and Performing Arts, University of East Anglia, Norwich, NR4 7TJ, UK

Albert Danielsson
Professor, Department of Industrial Economics and Management, Royal Institute of Technology, S-100 44 Stockholm, Sweden

Richard Ennals
Professor, Head of School, Operations Management and Quantitative Methods, Kingston Polytechnic, Kingston Hill, Kingston upon Thames, Surrey, KT2 7LB, UK

Magnus Florin
Dramaturg, The Royal Dramatic Theatre, Box 5037, S-102 41 Stockholm, Sweden

Bo Göranzon
Doctor of Technology, Swedish Center for Working Life, Box 5606, S-11486 Stockholm, Sweden and Adjunct Professor, Skill and Technology, Royal Polytechnic, S-100 44 Stockholm, Sweden

Rolf Hughes
Author and Researcher, Centre for Creative and Performing Arts, University of East Anglia, Norwich, NR4 7TJ, UK

Allan Janik
Professor, Brenner Archive, Innsbruck University, A-6020 Innsbruck, Austria

Kjell S. Johannessen
Doctor, Lecturer, Department of Philosophy, University of Bergen, N-5000 Bergen, Norway

Ingela Josefson
Doctor, Linguist, Swedish Center for Working Life, Box 5606, S-114 86 Stockholm, Sweden

Herbert Josephs
Professor, Department of Romance and Classical Languages, 342 Old Horticulture Building, Michigan State University, East Lansing, Michigan 48824, USA

Lars Kleberg
Assistant Professor, Culture Councellor, Swedish Embassy, Ulitsja Mosfilmovskaya 60, 119 590 Moscow, USSR

Francesco Lerda
Professor, Department of Mathematics, University of Turin, via Carlo Alberto 10, Torina 10123, Italy

Olov Östberg
Professor, The Swedish Agency for Administrative Development, Box 34107, S-100 26 Stockholm, Sweden

Michael Robinson
Professor, Department of Drama and Theatre Arts, University of Birmingham, Edgbaston, Birmingham B15 2TT, UK

Mike Sharples
Doctor, School of Cognitive and Computing Sciences, University of Sussex, Falmer, Brighton BN1 9QN, UK

David Smith
Research and Consultancy in Education and Training, 29 Milner Road, Burnham, Slough, SL1 7PA, UK

Per Sörbom
PhD, Östra Tulegatan 26, 733 33 Sala, Sweden

Stephen Toulmin
Professor, Department of Philosophy, Northwestern University, Bretano Hall, Evanston, Illinois 60208, USA

Randall Whitaker
Doctor, The Swedish Agency for Administrative Development, Box 34107, S-100 26 Stockholm, Sweden

Summaries

Chapter 2. Tacit Knowledge and Silenced Knowledge: Fundamental Problems and Controversies

Bengt Molander

During the 1980s the concept of "tacit knowledge" became the central theme in discussions about professional skills and expertise in Sweden. This chapter discusses the reason for its popularity and investigates the most important underlying issues and controversies. Essentially, there seem to be two different knowledge traditions: a "scientific" tradition with the emphasis on articulated theories and descriptions, and a "practical" knowledge tradition with the emphasis on training and apprenticeship. It is argued that the expression "tacit knowledge" is misleading if it is taken as referring to a particular type of knowledge because, on the one hand, all knowledge is in a way tacit, and on the other, verbal expression plays an important role in all kinds of professional knowledge and expertise. In various attempts to explain the nature of "practical" knowledge, three strands can be distinguished, related to the view of knowledge as inherent in, respectively, a human body, a social community, and human actions. It is also argued that the main problem in trying to develop an explanation of "practical" knowledge is the tension between knowledge as an essentially critical enterprise, emphasized in science, on the one hand, and confidence in action, which is the hallmark of practical skills on the other. Finally, some outlines for a future epistemology of practical knowledge are proposed, suggesting that knowledge is never ending but always "moving", and that people do not "have" but rather "participate in" knowledge.

Chapter 3. Why is Wittgenstein Important?

Allan Janik

To understand the importance of Wittgenstein we must examine language as an *ensemble* of strategies for weaving together words and actions. A failure to grasp the workings of language is at the root of our philosophical problems. Wittgenstein's approach to philosophy, investigating both the formation and transference of skill and the notion of rule-following, was that of a craftsman. A craft embodies "tacit knowing" in that it is learned through the repetition of a specified action until it becomes second nature. Skills cannot be learned from books because they cannot be described literally, although description can play a role in reminding the apprentice of the different stages through which (s)he must pass in order to master the craft. There is no single or fixed application of any rule. In his work on skill-acquisition Wittgenstein articulates what it means to learn on the basis of practical experience alone. Words, symbols, and sentences are only *part* of language, meaningful only to the extent that they are embedded in actions (or what Heidegger termed a *situation*). Through his study of language games, Wittgenstein shows how the whole range of human activities is constituted in changing alliances between words and actions. Wittgenstein's mature philosophy is therefore vitally important for understanding the relation between artificial and natural intelligence, and the dependence of the new technology on human modes of learning (rather than vice versa).

Chapter 4. Rule-Following, Intransitive Understanding and Tacit Knowledge

Kjell S. Johannessen

If a scientist is incapable of articulating the precise nature of an important discovery in chemistry, how can we consider the legitimacy of his/her claim? Traditionally, we demand that knowledge be capable of formulation in some form of language and that it be supported by experience or proven by formal means. We should also, however, examine the ways we use the terms of knowledge in different contexts, such as those informed by moral, aesthetic, legal and religious values. The concept of an exact language, in which all scientific knowledge can be articulated in an unambiguous way, is thus limited. From the tradition of propositional knowledge emerges the possibility of tacit knowledge, a form of knowledge which for logical reasons cannot be adequately articulated by linguistic means. Drawing on Wittgenstein's theories of practice and intransitive understanding in *Philosophical Investigations*, the chapter explores the concept of rule-following as a practice and, by extension, the roles of analogy and performance in our linguistic grasp of reality.

Chapter 5. On Creativity and Development

Albert Danielsson

This chapter argues that creativity, far from being uniform or simplistic, is an even more complex and exciting phenomenon than is usually conceived. The gist of creativity may correspond to the following seven stages:

1 An individual
2 has the ability to
3 invent and develop something new, or
2a–3a applies something in a new way
4 which generally consists of ideas,
5 which especially are artistic, and
6 which give rise to interesting and unusual results.

The chapter examines the influence of Thomas S. Kuhn on the posthumous reputation of the Polish microbiologist Ludwick Fleck, and the role of the apostles in the rapid spread of Christianity under the Roman Empire. It is argued that the development of an idea may be conceived as the following sequence of stages: birth, development and spread, penetration, regulation – and, possibly, death. We need to consider the social context of creativity; alongside our observation of creativity as an individual endeavour, we should examine creativity and its immediate group of peers and followers (the profession), creativity and the surrounding society (the scientific community at large), and creativity and the recipients-receivers. The chapter advocates a conception of creativity which enables us to express the contribution of an individual within a "creative" situation, and an inclusion of what might be termed "creativity-in-use" and/or "creativity-in-invention". We need a family of concepts, a series of new terms or categories which are related to each other and to creativity.

Chapter 6. Language and Experience

Ingela Josefson

What does a "good" nurse need to know? How does (s)he acquire this knowledge? Can all the knowledge required to nurse people be acquired by theoretical study alone? If so, this knowledge must be susceptible to formulation in a scientific language. Experienced nurses, however, stress that the ability to "see" unusual symptoms and developments in the condition of their patients is an ability which can only be acquired from direct experience and with practice. Thus, although a scientific language may engender greater respect for the nursing profession than it currently enjoys, one runs the risk of placing greater value on the knowledge which can be expressed in precise theoretical terms than the knowledge discussed in an everyday language or that which simply manifests itself in actions. A great deal of nursing knowledge is passed on in a kind of master-apprentice relationship; the experienced nurse teaches the less experienced nurse to "see" unusual symptoms or changes in a patient's health. Many nurses emphasize how important this period of apprenticeship was to them at the start of their professional careers. In seeking to design expert computer systems for nursing care, advances in technology should therefore take seriously ethical values integral to the profession such as the "experience", "devotion" and "patience" of which Florence Nightingale wrote.

Chapter 7. The Psychology of Apprenticeship: a Discussion Paper

David Smith

The meritocratic cult of the "expert"and the rise of "training" and the professional trainer have contributed to the discrediting of apprenticeship and its perception as an "unprofessional", inefficient and irrelevant anachronism. This chapter calls for a positive revaluation of the role and possibilities of apprenticeship in educational and vocational development. The chapter traces the history and evolution of apprenticeship in England, from its origins in mediaeval craft guilds to the present day. A series of anecdotes from former apprentices illustrates some of the beneficial and potentially harmful aspects of the experience of apprenticeship in developing skills. If learning is an essentially social activity, the "apprentice" in education must not only make a body of knowledge his/her own, but must do so in a community which shares a sense of belonging to a culture. The idea of acculturation into a specific working life environment is, in fact, at the very heart of apprenticeship. Formal education is now an integral part of most apprenticeships, but no less important is the tacit knowledge immanent in an emotional engagement with the task in hand, allowing a crafts worker, for example, to operate creatively at one of the interfaces between conscious and subconscious thought. Finally, the chapter examines the persistence of male, youth-based apprenticeships, the issue of how to evaluate, economically and politically, the effectiveness of existing apprenticeship schemes, and the largely unexplored potential of these schemes in terms of both the communication of skills and their transfer from a specific context to new fields. Apprenticeship at its best, the article concludes, conforms with many current ideas about optimum conditions for effective learning and, unlike the current orientation of much UK "training", may provide many key components for learning for the quality era.

Chapter 8. The Introduction of Information Technology into the Work-place: Some Practical Considerations

Malcolm Bolton

Why do highly regarded and initially cost-effective computer systems fall into disrepute? Why do staff become disaffected and blame "the computer" when difficulties occur in producing time critical information? The chapter argues for the need to view the information requirements of an organisation as a whole rather than adopting the often disparate, reductionist view of knowledge and education of traditional systems analysis. The information culture of any organisation is generally heuristic or even holistic. Each part of the organization informs each other part, even though there is not necessarily any direct transfer of information. The combination of all this information, the values attached to the information and the personnel who have control over the information constitute the information culture. Between departments various epistemologies will have been developed depending upon the use to which the information is to be put. Determining these epistemologies, through a process of dialogue with employees and management alike, will help to establish the topology of the Information Culture. The concept of dialogue is integral to the methodology adopted by Technology Arts Information and essential for the effective implementation of an information technology system within an organization. Dialogue, the article concludes, should be ongoing if the information technology systems and the corporate Information Culture is not to become unmanageable.

Chapter 9. Expert Systems: Channels for Dialogue

Randall Whitaker and Olov Östberg

The chapter examines biases underlying current expert systems (ESs) characterizations. These biases concern direction of knowledge flows in a consultation, the communicational competence of the consultee, the nature of the knowledge transferred, and the accuracy with which an ES mimics the expert. The chapter then discusses information loss in the ES channel. By showing that such losses occur from the consultee to the consultant, the authors argue that consultation is a bidirectional process; the consultee provides notification and description, and the consultant provides advice or answers. The consultative process can therefore be described in terms of conversational interaction between consultee and consultant, and insights into this form of interaction – or consultative dialogue – can be gained from analysis of existing models of conversational interaction (e.g. from linguistics). Only by considering such models can we arrive at a serious, unbiased appraisal of ES value and their impact within workplace settings.

Chapter 10. Controlling the Application of Knowledge-Based Systems

Mike Sharples

This chapter aims to indicate some of the potential benefits and dangers inherent in the technology of Knowledge-Based Systems

(KBSs) and to suggest courses of action that would both minimize risk and promote social benefit in future developments. KBSs offer cheap and ready access to knowledge, efficient management and organization of information, conversion of information into usable knowledge to guide human action, knowledge and advice relevant to the context in which it is needed. There are, however, potential dangers if a user is unfamiliar with the assumptions underlying KBS structures of reasoning and representing knowledge; the danger of a program becoming incomprehensible or unreliable in an emergency; the possibility of placing too much faith in the abilities of KBS and thereby losing the capacity for critical evaluation of its judgments; the inevitable uncertainty or inexactitude programmed into KBS; the economic implications of an uneven distribution of new technology; and the likelihood of misinterpretation or technical failure when autonomous systems are automatically activating machinery (e.g. military/defence systems). The chapter argues for the regulation of KBS construction, particularly for those systems designed for public or "non-expert" use. Suggestions include programming into each system a clear qualification of answers and requests for data, setting up a workable Code of Conduct for AI practitioners, and constant supervision of the assumptions and activities of each computerized system. Since KBS work by consulting an internal model of the world (supplied to them by a human programmer), their decisions must be challenged or ignored when necessary and always treated with an appropriate degree of scepticism.

Chapter 11. Law and Expert Systems

Joseph A. Cannataci

How may a lawyer define an "expert system"? In considering the implications of defining expert systems for the law of liability, this chapter raises both the role of language in the construction of expert systems and the effect of expert systems on language. The paradox of a law is that its language must be both extremely vague and simultaneously specific. A definition must be elastic enough to cover all possible situations covered by the legislator's intentions and at the same time narrow enough to exclude situations extraneous to the legislator's intentions. This paradox recurs when one examines the problems of knowledge acquisition and representation in creating and defining KBS. How does one represent not only the concept behind, for example, "stealing" but also the host of related concepts such as "fraud", "embezzlement" or "misappropriation"? If we are to participate in shaping the future of the society we live in, we should endeavour to ensure that our legal systems provide the right infrastructure and sense of direction for our efforts. This entails, amongst other things, carefully monitoring the language our legislators use in the laws governing behaviour in a computerized society.

Chapter 12. The Image of the Intelligent Machine in Science Fiction

Jon Bing

Fiction picked up man's dependency on machines at an early stage; the work of both H.G. Wells and E.M. Forster, for example, indicates that the presence of the intelligent machine was felt long before the emergence of the modern computer. Mary Shelley's *Frankenstein* had earlier explored a central dilemma of the industrial revolution, namely how, in exploiting the possibilities offered by science and technology, man is to be responsible to both his creator, or to basic ethical principles, and to the use and implications of what he has created. *Frankenstein,* the chapter argues, embodies the spirit of the industrial revolution and reflects on the ethical issues involved in developing an artificial and intelligent being. The chapter traces other instances of the intelligent machine in fiction, from Daedalus' sculptured nymphs which came to life, to Asimov's modern robot, Qutie, which claimed, convincingly enough, to be superior to its human creators. Science fiction, however, has still to explore adequately the issues and dilemmas which haunt AI-research, such as the question of whether a computer can be constructed to become aware of itself or to meet an acceptable test for human intelligence. Science fiction, in other words, has yet to discover myths and symbols appropriate to recent developments in AI research.

Chapter 13. Computers and Thought: A Modern Version of Old Illusions

Francesco Lerda

Computer Science and Artificial Intelligence will gain ever increasing importance in our society. Such disciplines are continually expanding with reference to component technology, system architecture, operational approach, programming languages, man – machine interaction, applications, methodological impact. This chapter emphasizes the possibilities opened by the new instruments and methodologies, but also draws attention to the potential for incorrect utilization, unexpected breakdowns, and control complexity, amongst other risks. Computer science developments give rise to complex cultural, political, social and ethical problems. New foundations are needed for the school organization at any level and for research programming. Information science and artificial intelligence possess fundamental cultural and methodological characteristics: they give systematic form to the structural and hierarchical nature of problems, provide scientifically operational bases to the notion of algorithm, facilitate the research stage, allowing actual as well as illustrative exemplifications, and increase the possibilities for operational experimentation in the didactic environment.

Chapter 14. Concluding Remarks Part I: Towards Human-Centred Systems

Richard Ennals

This chapter celebrates the new synthesis of ideas and experience evident in recent work, such as that contained in the present volume, and seeks to clarify the implications of moving towards human-centred systems. The tendency is towards a combination of interests; practical experience of technology and of working life as well as philosophical and educational concepts. There is a renewed interest in the culture of work and of the workplace as a learning environment in which technology should be deployed to meet human needs. Out of this is emerging a newly coherent perspective of human-centred systems, sometimes described as anthropocentric systems, which in turn have radical implications for both education and work. There is a new audience for radical alternatives, with human needs as the focus of attention. A shift from a technocentric to a human-centred approach in education requires a fundamental reappraisal of curriculum and teaching method. Philosophy, personal experience of work and social action, and the concept of tacit knowledge are accorded greater significance than they have held in recent years. Imaginative uses of the computer will re-unite practical and theoretical knowledge, thereby allowing us to dispense with many inauthentic forms of division of labour. Participation in the design process and the enhancement of the quality of work should be encouraged. Individual skills have to be seen in the context of the needs of the group, placing new emphasis on skills in communication and collaboration. External events are accelerating the process of change. The human-centred design process, where participation is encouraged and valued, lies at the heart of a modern approach to democracy. In order to counter the mystique and disillusionment often associated with expert systems, artificial intelligence and information technology, the chapter stresses the need for acceptable working models of people assisted by technology in productive activity; there are many opportunities for the realization of such models, it is suggested, in current European developments.

Chapter 15 Remarks on the Diderot Project

Lars Kleberg

What is the role of the aesthetic in our search for theoretical and practical knowledge? Why is the most beautiful form also the most durable, from an engineer's point of view, in Michelangelo's dome? The chapter raises the concepts of *heterodoxy* (multi-perspectivity) and *heteroglossy* (multilingualism) and their implications for the Diderot Project. As a translator and a creative artist in the field of scientific problems, Diderot exemplifies the importance of heteroglossy or multilingualism and syncretism, not only for a writer but for the survival and dynamic evolution of a culture. The quest for an exact language ironically seems to accompany an increase in what cannot be said in language. Yuri Lotman, the Soviet semiotician and historian of culture, has argued that heteroglossy and the process of translating the *Unknown* is crucial to the dynamic functioning of culture. We should therefore avoid a forced synthesis of the Project's many discussions and it is for this reason that *Rameau's Nephew* serves as a useful emblem for the Diderot Project.

Chapter 16. Caliban's Revenge

Allan Janik

How can we employ our knowledge justly and humanely? How can we develop teaching techniques that conform to actual modes of learning? What does a worker with skill actually know? The Diderot Project poses questions about the social consequences of the implementation of computer technology in the workplace, starting from a series of informed studies of the internal – or epistemological – structure of work and drawing heavily upon such diverse disciplines as economic history, linguistics, mathematics and literary criticism as well as classical and contemporary philosophy. Enlightenment, skill and education have emerged as the pivotal issues around which a humanized and productive discussion of the new technology must be shaped. Diderot's *Rameau's Nephew* questions the limits of the Enlightenment, offering a trenchant analysis of the relationship of teleology to instrumentality, and, in doing so, challenges a central tenet in modern philosophy – namely, that practical knowledge ultimately has a theoretical basis. In Diderot's view, the forms of knowledge we might label practical and theoretical, experiential and propositional, are not only incompatible, but actually in competition with one another in the social world. His use of the dialogue form, moreover, induces a form of reflective tension in the reader, who is thereby invited to actively participate in the textual debates. The chapter discusses the power of the hypocrite – or counter-example – with reference to both *Rameau's Nephew* and Shakespeare's *The Tempest*. The success of "lui" as a parasite depends upon his ability to act or imitate; his knowledge entails knowing the appropriate gesture in any given social situation – a matter of skill, a "knowing how" rather than a "knowing that". He cannot articulate in words this form of knowledge and thus the reflections of the philosopher mediate for the reader: words are explained by gestures and gestures by words. The dialogue form thus intersects two different modes of expression and thereby makes communication, if not resolution, possible.

Chapter 17. The Dome of Michelangelo

Magnus Florin

What does *instinct* mean to Diderot? His entry in the Encyclopaedia is a critique of Descartes' notion of instinct as the mechanistic, automatic, and uniform nature of the animal (an argument used to support Descarte's case for a fundamental separation of mind and body, man and beast). For Diderot, instinct is rooted in experience; it is a series of engravings in the memory of reflections and sensations. The training of animals is possible due to their memories. Remembered responses, reinforced by repetition, become habitual responses. La Hire has shown by the use of geometry that the vault of Michelangelo's dome, aside from its aesthetic qualities, also had the curvature of the highest supporting capacity. How, wonders Diderot, could Michelangelo choose from all his sketches precisely the one that combined elegance and solidity, without the help of La Hire's geometry? His answer cites calculation and experience as of equal importance in solving the problem: "If the one is well-founded it must correspond to the other." The conflict in Bo Göranzon's project Education–Work–Technology is between calculation and work or practice; the transfer of skills in the process of doing or making something. In *Rameau's Nephew* Diderot moves us from the completed into the coming-into-being. The conversation between moi and lui becomes a play of possible meanings and directions; unable to hide behind calculation from the outside, we participate in this ongoing play and become subjects of continuous experience.

Chapter 18. Diderot's Russian University

Per Sörbom

This chapter chronicles Diderot's detailed proposals to Catherine II on the best way to organize education in Russia. The aim of education over the centuries, Diderot argues, has been, and continues to be, to make people virtuous and enlightened. Education must be designed to meet the needs of the majority. We must adapt the teaching to suit both the age of the students and their ability to understand. In order to attain these objectives, Diderot, writes, we should proceed from the simple to the complicated, from the first stage to the last, from what is most useful to what is least useful, from what is essential to all to what is essential to only a few. There are two sorts of knowledge, Diderot states: elementary knowledge which is essential to everyone, and secondary or conventional knowledge which is needed only for the particular path we have chosen in life. Not every occupation requires the measure of essential or elementary knowledge which a full university education requires. The volume and diversity of knowledge taught is to be determined by its benefit to society. Diderot would classify the sciences in the same way as his fellow countryman and contemporary Georges-Louis Leclerc Buffon, classified minerals and plants in the 36 volumes of his *Histoire Naturelle*. According to this method, animals and plants are classified according to their usefulness and proximity to us in nature; the more remote the type of animal, the more obscure its place in science. An ox or a horse are therefore scientifically important, a hyena or a wolf rather less so. Diderot's pyramid-shaped blueprint of knowledge may seem hierarchical to us, but it encompasses and involves all individuals, equips them with what they need and thereby makes them both happier people and more useful citizens. It is therefore, the chapter concludes, wholly in the spirit of the Encyclopaedia, that handbook for a better, more practical and enlightened world.

Chapter 19. Diderot and the Dramatization of Philosophical Thought

Herbert Josephs

Diderot's use of the dialogue form necessitated the invention of an "other", a narrative figure in whom was inscribed values and attitudes frequently resistant to those of the narrating subject. The figure of the "other" in Diderot serves various narrative functions in relation to the philosopher's ideas, from affirmation and validation to criticism, counter-argument and scepticism. The literary form of the dialogue reflected in its own structures the shape of a dramatic encounter between some part of the self that *experienced* and another to which was usually assigned the function of active spectator and creative observer. The chapter discusses Diderot's practice and theory of drama, and his representation of mental activity as a process of division and dialectics which dispersed, multiplied and integrated into literary dialogue a subjective intelligence that had hitherto been constructed as a unified entity. The drama of human intelligence was likened in Diderot's imagination to an interactive encounter between sensation and reflection. With the transposition of philosophical inquiry into the pluralized discourse of literature, it is no longer possible to isolate and identify any solitary voice of authority to which we might attach a sense of stable truth. Thus, by relinquishing claims to absolute authority in his narration and by allowing and even obliging his reader increasingly to become the author, Diderot provides an eloquent illustration of the larger Enlightenment project that implicitly structures and determines all his writing: not to propagate ideas but to encourage and make possible the continuous activity of critical thinking.

Chapter 20. The Translator as Actor

Lars Kleberg

Is the literary translation an independent creation or, at best, a faithful reproduction? Is the translator an artist or a craftsman?

This chapter compares the translator to other interpretative artists, such as the classical musician or actor. Both the actor and the translator break down structures into smaller units and then reassemble them, using building blocks from other languages. In the process, the personality of the translator/actor is explored and restructured by the original text. A key concept to be considered in both an actor's and a translator's work, is the *subtext*. The subtext is all that is not explicitly said in the dialogue: the underlying motivations (the situation, psychology, story) for the words, the web of significance to be found between the lines. The translator's presence in the text – unlike the actor's double presence (physical and fictional) on the stage – is in effect theoretical and almost invisible; a successful rendition of another text means that the translation itself appears completely transparent. The chapter speculates on the motivations behind the desire to become a translator or an actor. It is said, for example, that Diderot, forever vacillating between submission and rebellion finally "became himself" by hiding behind other people's speech. In order to extend the limits of culture, the translator/actor begins by exploring his/her own limitations. The resulting sense of freedom is at once the motor of creativity as well as its goal.

Chapter 21. Translating the Self

Michael Robinson

This chapter examines the paradox of autobiography, a genre which attempts to construct a single, authoritative narrative by translating a multiplicity of past selves into the language of the present. Individual, lived experience passes into language and is mediated by the interrelationship between the signifiers, which stand in for the experience itself. The writer becomes a figure of the text, his past rooted in the present of its recall. Autobiographical story-telling elevates a temporal sequence into a causal one through the chronological enchainment of the text in which the writer inscribes himself. The narrative takes on the attributes of a plot which confers a line of intention and a portent of design upon the data it is processing. Identity is adapted from a plurality of texts and structured within and around the discourses available to it at any one moment in time. The autobiographer *is* his text, and as such constituted by the complex intertextuality of the discourses through which his identity is assembled. Like a good translation, an autobiography may resemble its primary text but cannot reproduce it exactly. This accounts for the self-reflexive nature of so many autobiographies. What an autobiographer writes supplements what he has lived and yet is an event in the life he is recounting. Like the actor, the writer has a capacity for the *dédoublement* of experience, for assuming, dissembling, or "representing" emotion in a manner that subverts the idea of a fixed, inviolable selfhood and the moral order with which it is often associated. In this, as someone who is his own spectator, he resembles Diderot's actor, at once his own subject and object, the player and first audience of his many roles.

Chapter 22. One Culture, Two Cultures, Three Cultures

Jon Cook

The university's corporate culture is conditioned by the duality of its intellectual culture. The opposition of science and the humanities fuels a logic of "either/or" rather than "both/and", and encourages the two disciplines to compete for authority within the university's authoritative structure. A university's importance is defined by its exclusiveness, an exclusiveness maintained, historically, by the exclusion of different social groups. This attitude is mirrored in an attitude towards knowledge – the cult of the expert and of specialization, the belief that specialized forms of knowledge require esoteric codes and, therefore, that any advance in knowledge will be expressed in such codes. Distinguishing between the informal, practical and collaborative practices of "community knowledge" and their negation in the formal structures of "university knowledge", the chapter argues that the interactions across this boundary are an important concern for any group considering the future of universities. The sciences and the humanities share a capacity for problem-solving. Problem-solving is not a skill that can be learnt in isolation from the historical and philosophical context which is its necessary condition, nor is it a skill that can be taught by learning a set of specific rules. Problem-solving is an attempt to mediate between skill and knowledge. Narrative may be seen as one form of problem-solving which pervades social life. The chapter advocates a history of knowledge as an integral subject, available to students in both the humanities and the sciences and thereby holding the two cultures in a single frame. The history of knowledge stimulates intellectual curiosity by rejecting the idea that knowledge is monolithic. The sciences and the humanities can also be held in the same frame by the study of information theory, a subject which may provide the component of a common language for the exchange of experience and ideas across the boundaries of the two cultures. The chapter argues for a form of intellectual opportunism, for cultivating the capacity to experiment with a difficult language in a way that produces a hypothesis useful to the learner. For these proposals to be effective, we need to revise the metaphor of the university itself. The metaphor of the university as an encyclopaedia is suggested, a metaphor intended to evoke "the whole circle of learning", an environment, the play of chance and invention, consultation and participation. The technological basis for this new encyclopaedia would be the computer as an instrument capable of providing an arbitrary, flexible system of classification which would offer large-scale access to – and rapid updating of – the knowledge base of the encyclopaedia. The encyclopaedia would develop the potential of its eighteenth century forbear as a focus for information, debate, group thinking, and reflection.

Chapter 23. On From "The Two Cultures"

Stephen Toulmin

How do we establish cross links between the cultures of science and the humanities in the world of learning and the professions? Why did the "Two Cultures" division, as identified by C.P. Snow in his Rede Lecture, play an unusually large part in English society? Why is English higher education unusually elitist and exclusive? The chapter argues that European culture had *two* separate and distinct origins, and our two sets of contemporary disciplines (humanistic and scientific) derive from, and look back to, either the sixteenth century Renaissance Humanists or the seventeenth century Natural Philosophers. Today, however, with all of industry and engineering open to environmental criticism and control, and all of medicine to a parallel critique in ethical terms, humanist and scientific disciplines will start to enjoy equal status. Matters of theory can no longer be wholly self-justifying. Theoretical explanations and concepts (*episteme*) will increasingly be exposed to a wider analysis, in terms of their general practical efficacy (*techne*) and the prudence (*phronesis*) of putting them to use in particular real life situations. It is one task of the Diderot Project to characterize the confluence, or union, of the two branches of Modern European culture, the "reasonable" Humanities and the "rational" Sciences. The author questions the viability of pursuing the "Encyclopaedia" project within the context of the university, as advocated in the preceding chapter. It is suggested that the greatest power of the Encyclopaedia might lie in its ability to work *outside* specific academic institutions, its potential to form "invisible" patterns of learning by means of electronic information networks. An Encyclopaedia for the third millennium, the chapter concludes, may well become a major intellectual force, but only if it circumvents the orthodox academic world, instead of trying to work within it.

Chapter 24. The Metaphor of Caliban in Our Technological Culture

Bo Göranzon

The meeting of Prospero and Caliban in *The Tempest* depicts a contrast between the abstract and the practical intellect. Prospero was partly modelled on Giordana Bruno (1548–1600), an Italian philosopher who wanted to create a universal language which contained not only an encyclopaedic knowledge but which also thought for itself. Prospero's knowledge is abstract – based on book learning – whereas Caliban's is practical and therefore essential for Prospero's survival on the island. Prospero and Caliban become dependent upon one another; Prospero struggles for 12 years to realize the ambiguous, intuitive qualities of Caliban in his own character, while Caliban in turn learns Prospero's language and is thereby forced into a new way of thinking. The relationship is thus simultaneously creative and riven with conflict and violence. Knowledge requires that one becomes familiar enough with one's area of skills in order to be able to formulate rules and interpret them. Johan Gottlieb Fichte maintained that the man of learning (and the student) must "come through" concepts, form them from himself and for himself, thereby to arrive at an insight, and develop and form the self. The chapter concludes by citing Hojer, who argues for mastering concepts, rather than being mastered by them, for describing one's system and concepts, rather than submitting to the mentorship of others.

Chapter 25. Leadership and Character, or A Little Touch of Harry

Allan Janik

What can we learn from Shakespeare's *Henry V* concerning the nature of leadership in business studies? According to Albert Danielsson, contemporary discussions of leadership tend to view the subject almost exclusively from below – i.e. from the perspective of the led – an attitude which obscures the challenges of leadership, especially in an age of high technology. Leadership must involve guidance through coordination based on trust. Paradoxically, leadership is therefore institutionalized and yet requires individuals in order to institutionalize the requisite confidence in established procedures. Since the maintenance of credibility and trust is essential to leadership, it is argued that leadership cannot be institutionalized without qualities of character. This leads the author to identify elements relevant to the role of character in leadership in Shakespeare's tetralogy, *Richard II, Henry IV Parts 1 and 2, and Henry V*. The tetralogy, it is argued, can be taken as an epic of leadership to the extent that Henry comes to embody the virtues that were so clearly lacking in Richard and his father. His character incorporates the public and the private, the institutional and the personal in a seamless unity. Shakespeare presents us with an ensemble of example and counter-example for distinguishing real leadership from its counterfeits. The chapter contends that literary modes of presentation such as the tetralogy play an important role in showing us how to understand and represent such a nebulous phenomenon as character. The result of an absence of leadership/character qualities may be seen in certain damaging practices of the "post-business" society, such as the hostile take-over.

Chapter 26. Concluding Remarks Part II

Jon Cook

The chapters in Part II are connected by three main themes: Diderot, dialogue and translation. Diderot is discussed in terms of his exemplary force as a non-specialist, encyclopaedic intellectual. The importance of his contributions to an epistomology of skill and to an understanding of dialogue is stressed. The present chapter goes on to summarize the value of dialogue as a form which can tolerate incompatible perspectives in a way that deepens reflective understanding of why we have the beliefs we do. This has both political and educational consequences. Dialogue is presented as a basic form of democracy and as a crucial metaphor for understanding the nature of skills. The discussion of translation extends these themes, giving an example of the relationship between identity and skill, both for the translator of texts and for the other kinds of "translation" involved in acting. These are issues which are contributing to the development of an international PhD programme in Culture and Technology.

Section I:

Introduction

Chapter 1

Introduction

Bo Göranzon and Magnus Florin

A poster at a Swedish work place announces: "Practice is when everybody does everything right, but nobody knows why. Theory is when everything is done wrong, and everybody knows why. In this establishment we try to combine the two: We do everything wrong, and nobody knows why."

So, what is knowledge? Does the baker know what he is doing? Does the carpenter know what he is doing? Put in this naive way, these questions may be simply answered "Yes, of course!". However, epistemology has often tended to respond with a firm "No!" – if the notion of "knowledge" inherent in the question is defined as philosophical and scientific knowledge, marked by independence from practice.

The opposition between "practice" and "theory" has its roots in Plato and has been consolidated to the point that we may be blind to what it conceals. Denis Diderot said: "To know what it is to bake, one must put one's hands in the dough".

During the 1980s the concept of "tacit knowledge" became central to discussions about professional skills and expertise in Sweden. The rapid development of technology that affected professional skills demanded serious reflection on the relations between theory and experience, education and practice, skill and knowledge.

The research in "artificial intelligence" has been characterized by a dangerous limited perspective, where methods have been sought to "drain" professionals of their knowledge. The tendency of experienced professionals to be unwilling to expound their knowledge has been seen as an irritating problem.

In *Artificial Intelligence, Culture and Language* (Springer-Verlag, 1990), the issue of "tacit knowledge" was dealt with in a special section. In this book the topic is further developed. Through disagreement and different perspectives the three contributions in Section II by Molander, Janik and Johannessen reach a qualification of this important concept. It is striking how the educational relationship between master and apprentice, originating in the medieval craft guilds, has gained new attention in our society of highly developed technology. The experienced professional has acquired a knowledge of skill that can be transferred through example and through the relationship between an expert and a novice (and not through mere articulation). Danielsson, Josefson and Smith cast light on the phenomenon of knowledge at work.

This book is turned towards practice also by investigating actual developments in relationships between information technology and professional skills. It is the view of the editors that the concept of "dialogue" must be continuously returned to in this area, philosophically, as in the preceding volume *Dialogue and Technology* (Springer-Verlag, 1991), and more pragmatically, as in the two chapters by Bolton and Whitaker and Östberg (Section IV). The problem of education versus computers seems to bring out fundamental questions.

A knowledge-based system or expert system is certainly derived from reality. But as with any model these systems in their turn act back on reality – defining it. Sharples and Cannatacci make crucial and specific points on the difficult relationships between system and reality – and, in the editors' view, the importance of remembering that they are different things. For the society of computers – the "information society" – has, as Allan Janik has stated, a tendency to be "pornographic" in the sense that it promises easy solutions where there are none to be found, thereby placing reality at a distance. King Lear, forcing answers from his daughters as to which of them loved him most, met a tragic end. The "information society" has certainly the mark of "fiction", as the reader will find investigated in the thought-provoking perspectives given by Bing and Lerda (Section VI).

The people responsible for the conference "Culture, Language and Artificial Intelligence" (Stockholm, May–June 1988) are now involved in Project Diderot, an international research programme exploring the social impact of technology. In Bo Göranzon's research at the Swedish Center for Working Life there has been continuous attention to the highly interesting tensions between the different views of knowledge held by the Enlightenment philosophers. Denis Diderot had, alongside with the ambitions of the Encyclopaedia, a unique sense for ambiguity, paradox and uncertainty, resisting abstract finalism and beliefs in absolute knowledge. With key texts as *The Paradox of the Actor* and *Rameau's Nephew*, Diderot's work has an emblematic status for the research programme. A collection of papers from its participants – Janik, Göranzon, Florin, Sörbom, Josephs, Cook, Toulmin, Robinson and Kleberg (Sections VII–VIII) – presents a spectrum of the Diderot Project: aesthetics versus theory of knowledge, cultural analysis, problems of mathematics and epistemology, translation as existential metaphor, etc.

In his introduction to Part II Lars Kleberg sees Diderot's *Rameau's Nephew* as emblematic for the dynamics of human culture. Concepts such as dialogism and multilingualism shed light on the close relation between Diderot's thinking and twentieth century thought on modern mind and culture. Diderot's "dramatization of philosophical thought" (Josephs) is a challenge

We also want to point out the focusing on the phenomenon of *translation* in this volume and in *Dialogue and Technology*. To the Project Diderot, translation is certainly one of the key words, with great metaphorical reach.

The research programme will work internationally and locally for some years ahead; and Autumn 1993 a new conference is planned in Stockholm to continue and bring forward what was achieved at the 1988 conference.

Part I:
Reflection and Experience

Section II:

Tacit Knowledge

Chapter 2

Tacit Knowledge and Silenced Knowledge: Fundamental Problems and Controversies[1]

Bengt Molander

During the 1980s the concept of "tacit knowledge" became the central theme in discussions about professional skills and expertise in Sweden. This chapter discusses the reason for its popularity and investigates the most important underlying issues and controversies. Essentially, there seem to be two different knowledge traditions: a "scientific" one with the emphasis on articulated theories and descriptions, and a "practical" knowledge tradition with the emphasis on training and apprenticeship. It is argued that the expression "tacit knowledge" is misleading if it is taken as referring to a particular type of knowledge because, on the one hand, all knowledge is in a way tacit, and on the other, verbal expression plays an important role in all kinds of professional knowledge and expertise. In various attempts to explain the nature of "practical" knowledge, three strands can be distinguished, related to the view of knowledge as inherent in, respectively, a human body, a social community, and human actions. It is also argued that the main problem in trying to develop an explanation of "practical" knowledge is the tension between knowledge as an essentially critical enterprise, emphasized in science, on the one hand, and confidence in action, which is the hallmark of practical skills on the other. Finally, some outlines for a future epistemology of practical knowledge are proposed, suggesting that knowledge is never ending but always "moving", and that people do not "have" but rather "participate in" knowledge.

Introduction

Knowledge, insight and skill are to be found in many forms: the insight which an experienced mother practices in her contact with her child, the skill which a craftsperson exhibits in the exercise of her craft and the knowledge expressed in scientific theories, just to give a few examples. In this paper I use "knowledge" as a comprehensive umbrella term to cover also what would more commonly be referred to as insight, skill, understanding, etc.

In Sweden "tacit knowledge" has been a key expression in discussions about the nature of professional skills since the beginning of the 1980s. As far as I can judge this was due to a breakthrough in research carried out by the Center for Working Life in Stockholm.[2] I will return to these research results. First a reminder about some earlier discussions.

In *The Tacit Dimension* (1966), Michael Polanyi takes as his starting point the statement that "we can know more than we can tell".[3] Polanyi generally uses the expression "tacit knowing", where the verb form is essential because he wants to emphasize the active, personal aspect of knowledge. We can recognize many things, for example, faces, without being able to tell how we recognize them; in this sense, we "tacitly know" faces and many other things. "The art of tacit knowing" also includes practical skills, which are manifested, for example, in the use of tools: we can perform skilfully without being able to tell exactly how we do things.[4]

The widespread interest in Polanyi's ideas was in great part due to Thomas Kuhn referring in his *The Structure of Scientific Revolutions* to Polanyi's book, *Personal Knowledge*. When Kuhn says that a "paradigm" can guide research without formulated rules and assumptions and that "the existence of a paradigm need not even imply that any full set of rules exists",[5] he adds: "Michael Polanyi has brilliantly developed a very similar theme, arguing that much of the scientist's success depends upon "tacit knowledge," i.e. upon knowledge that is acquired through practice and cannot be articulated explicitly".[6]

Kuhn's book was much discussed in the 1960s and 1970s. The book points to the research practice as central, thereby directing people's attention to those sides of science which are difficult, and perhaps impossible, to articulate verbally.

The problem area "unarticulated and inarticulate aspects of knowledge" is by no means new: at its root lies the question of how one could and should use various forms of *presentation, exposition, theory, instruction, and training* to learn, to maintain knowledge, and to teach. In short: the whole problem of "theory" and "practice".

A key problem concerning "unarticulated knowledge" is the growth of knowledge, especially how one could combine a critical stance towards knowledge with the protection and cultivation of "tacit" aspects of knowledge, if this is at all possible.[7]

Three factors seem to be particularly important as part of an explanation why the concept "tacit knowledge" became so important – and controversial – in Sweden during the 1980s:

A growing insight that many kinds of knowledge based on practice erode and are difficult or impossible to replace.

A new organization of universities and colleges in Sweden, as institution and ideology.

The "computerization of knowledge" project, as industry and ideology.

Some profound issues are hidden behind the disputes about "tacit knowledge": the relationship between "practical" and "scientific" knowledge, and different conceptions of the human being inherent in various perspectives on knowledge. The following is a broad overview.

In Sweden there has been, and still is, a strong belief in "science-based" knowledge and scientific rationality as important factors in the continued *enlightenment* of people and the continued modernization of society. A new organization of Swedish tertiary education, the so-called "new university", was introduced in 1977. It can be seen as the ideological crown of the belief in "scientific rationality". One formulation in the law of universities and colleges is the following: "Research in universities and colleges should aim at attaining further knowledge and achieving a scientific basis for education and other kinds of practice".[8] This apparently presupposes that trying to find or create such a "scientific basis" is always a sensible objective. Indeed, one aspect of the ideology of the "new" organization of universities and colleges is that work with this aim has been encouraged within all areas except the fine arts.

Verbalization and *theoretical transparency* are essential to scientific rationality and scientific knowledge, according to the prevailing conception of science. Attempts to transpose knowledge based on practice into scientific or scientific-like knowledge – which is an aim of science-inspired modernization – have led to an erosion of practically based knowledge. I like the term "erosion" because it indicates a slow process of thinning out and impoverishment.[9]

The modernization process has a material and economic basis. For some time now the computer industry and computer systems work have been central components of this basis. These businesses have also managed to sell a certain ideology of knowledge, which I will come to shortly. The applications of this modern technology in society have in some cases caused so much erosion of the traditional professional skills that the computerized system cannot receive the "input" of human knowledge required to make the *system* work as an support of the very same *human* knowledge.[10]

Beneath both the idea of modernization through scientific rationality and the attempts to let computers "take care of" knowledge lies a deep-seated problem of genuinely different conceptions of knowledge compared with other "cognitive cultures".

There exist knowledge traditions of which an *essential* part of the insights and skills depend upon knowledge based on and matured through practice, first-hand experience, and training. They are to be found in the care sector, architecture, practical pedagogics (teaching skills) and statistical applications, just to mention a few areas I have come across in my own epistemological studies. It is in no way clear *whether*, and if so *how*, such traditions can be reconciled with "scientific rationality and knowledge". The science-inspired modernization process involves a shift from practice-based knowledge to *applied theory*, which means that theory and not practice comes to be regarded as the very basis of knowledge. In the following I shall address *practical knowledge traditions* as distinct from *scientific traditions*. This is a crude distinction, but nevertheless it captures something of importance.

Knowledge transmitted through models or *exemplars* – through exemplary action, as in the master–apprentice relationship – and knowledge which is attained through *training* and *personal experience* may be called "tacit knowledge". This is a good label because the core of such knowledge does not consist of verbal or mathematical formulations, it consists of abilities to *make judgments* and to *do things* in practice, skilfully and with insight. The knowledge is *in* the judging and the doing.

Practically based kinds of knowledge have often been referred to as *arts*, as in expressions like "the art of cooking", "the art of bookbinding" and "the art of teaching" – though unfortunately the use of "arts" as a label in such cases seems to be increasingly rare. *Art* signifies that the knowledge is in what is done, *in the doing* and in the judgments made *in doing* something. The focus is on the body: the *right movement* of the hand, having a *good eye* for what is to be done, and when.

Many insights are shared and transmitted *bodily*, words are not always necessary. To become live knowledge, theoretical insights must be *incarnated* in human practice. This means also that "application" can never build upon theory alone. Or, in other words, live knowledge has always a tacit side. The research of the Center for Working Life has been important in making incarnated knowledge, the "practical intellect", to borrow an excellent term from Thomas Tempte, the cabinet maker, visible.[11]

It is live knowledge, as it is carried and manifested in human life and commitments, that is at the centre of "tacit knowledge", and not the written symbols, the abstract, the distanced.

The "computerization of knowledge" project – as industry and ideology – has made different conceptions of knowledge, and the different perceptions of the human being that are related to them, clearly visible. Let me begin with an illustration.

> It is becoming increasingly common for key people, before they retire, to record in a computer memory the unique experience they possess.
>
> This is referred to as "draining" their brains.
>
> A computer like the one in Skellefteå takes only a minute or so to retrieve an important passage in, for example, the "testament" left by a miner or a physician.[12]

The person interviewed obviously could not imagine that certain pieces of knowledge can remain "tacit", nor that knowledge could exist in some other place than the brain. Now there also exists a profession, that of the knowledge engineer, whose task it is to "drain" the knowledge of experts and transfer it to computer systems.

Those who believe in the possibility of total "drainage" generally think that the human brain is precisely analogous to a computer.[13] At least they think that the brain carries information and theory which can be reproduced or represented as statements and theories, *formulated* in a suitable language and a suitable mathematical symbolism. Moreover, they believe that what we human beings know and are able to do emanates from the theory in the brain (and *its* data sources). That means, for example, that our actions as functioning human beings are basically "applied theory". This is a way of perceiving the human being and an ideology of knowledge.[14] There is virtually no human experience to support this perception; it is "pure theory".

In view of what I have said so far it is not at all surprising that "tacit knowledge" became a key expression in the discussion of professional knowledge. It was something many people identified themselves with and they began to feel they could stand for their experience and knowledge without being forced to express that experience and knowledge in words. But others could not conceive of knowledge that is impossible to articulate verbally. Defenders of modernization through scientific rationality cannot accept tacit knowledge as real knowledge. For these reasons there occurred a polarization, for and against "tacit knowledge" as a real and fundamental phenomenon.

The "Tacit" Is Everywhere and Nowhere

The expression "tacit knowledge" has had an epistemologically emancipating power. It is a good starting point from which to open up a number of related problems, though it does not take us very far in the direction of solutions; and it is used in several different ways.

The main theme of this section is the, to my mind, strange views of language and knowledge that lie behind a division into "tacit" and "articulated" kinds of knowledge. These views, which are deep-seated, also show themselves when many people who "know better" write about "description" and "articulation".

This strange view of language shows itself in, for example, expressions such as "thoughts can only be incompletely described in words".[15] A variant of the same type of thinking is the idea that there is a "gap" between a description and the reality it describes.[16] In such expressions "description" appears, misleadingly, to be something well defined without any (explicit or implicitly presupposed) reference to methods of description, the "language", and, not least, the purpose. And we are often trapped by a false conception of "thoughts" or "ideas" as something existing independently, which one tries to "describe with" or "fit to" words and expressions as if it were a matter of trying to make a painting or a photograph as "true to nature" as possible.

In a paper presenting "computer system development in a pragmatic perspective"[17] Tore Nordenstam describes a tripartite division of knowledge. Both the perspective and the division have been very influential in the research at the Center for Working Life, and they still are.[18] Nordenstam talks about "propositional knowledge", "practical knowledge", and "knowledge of familiarity".[19] Roughly speaking this means that one distinguishes: (1) knowledge in the form of (articulated) *statements, rules and theories*; (2) knowledge in the form of *skills* and *skilful performance* – the ability to *do* things; and (3) knowledge in the form of *familiarity* with phenomena and practices. Behind this distinction there are many important insights, not least the emphasis put on familiarity.[20]

Now I want, however, primarily to draw attention to the *division*, where "propositional or theoretical knowledge" equals *articulated* or *verbalized* knowledge, while the two other kinds are forms of tacit knowledge. Is it fruitful to draw a borderline in this way?

The answer is yes, but only if the tripartite division is not seen as a division of distinct kinds of knowledge but of different *aspects* of knowledge. Because one can argue both that no knowledge is "purely tacit" and that all knowledge is, at bottom, tacit. I sketch both of these arguments.

I begin with the argument that all knowledge is, *au fond*, tacit. Clearly, there are many things one can *do* without being in a position to give an "exhaustive description" of how or why one does what one does – what is needed is practical skill, proficiency and sound judgment. All this is, basically, tacit.

The statements "mass equals energy" and "each transformational rule is defined by a *structural analysis* stating a condition on the class of phrase-markers to which it applies and specifying an analysis of the terminal string of this phrase-marker into successive parts" are not particularly difficult to read out loud and learn by heart. I can do that as well or as badly as anyone who has learnt to read English fairly well. However, I understand the first sentence but not the second since I have acquired an understanding of physics but not of linguistics (here transformational grammar).

It is obvious that no knowledge is contained in the sentences taken by themselves. There is a possibility of knowledge only if one *understands the concepts* used and the contexts in which the sentences are normally used, and that is not the same as having the ability to repeat the sentences parrot-fashion. This is valid for all sentences. What I have said here about "knowledge in sentences", taken together with what I said about doing things and performing actions shows that all knowledge is, at bottom, tacit. The tacit – our understanding and our actions – gives meaning to the words we use. Polanyi regards this as one example of the "personal" side of knowledge.[21]

The attraction of "propositional knowledge" as a particular category of knowledge thereby disappears. Such "knowledge" presupposes and is permeated by "tacit knowledge".[22]

I shall now turn to the other half of my argument, which intends to show that no knowledge is "purely tacit".

Too many discussions about knowledge have taken their starting point in what it means to "have knowledge" as a human *state*. Polanyi, however, constantly stresses the active side of knowledge, *knowing* rather than knowledge. This seems to be the right perspective; we should think about knowledge primarily as something dynamic and in movement all the time. One could say that only knowledge in use *is* knowledge.

Two typical and often cited examples of tacit knowledge are "cycling" and "face recognition". It is clear that no one can give a "complete description" of the knowledge involved in cycling in the sense that it would provide an instruction which anyone who can read could take in and then ride a bike with reasonable success straight away. It is also clear that one can learn to cycle without being able to give even an approximately accurate description of what happens *from the point of view of physics* – and *that* point of view is often taken as the standard! It is easy to say similar things about face recognition (though it seems that we cannot avoid learning that): to be able to recognize a face is quite another thing than to describe it so another person can recognize it or know who is described.

However "descriptions" (including remarks about what happens, pieces of advice to do certain things and not others, etc.) are often important when learning something (apply steady pressure to the pedals, keep up the speed, do not look down at your legs, focus on where you want to go ... !) as well as when improving a skill by training, which is possible both in cycling and in face recognition. No activity involving knowledge is carried out without any words. Even if one could *imagine* completely wordless skill acquisition and skill improvement it would normally seem pointless to try to realize it. Sometimes nothing can replace words, the right words.[23]

Cycling and face recognition are normally meaningless activities in themselves. They are, however, integral parts of many meaningful activities (getting out of the city, for example, or greeting people); they serve certain purposes. What we do forms part of complex systems of actions with a variety of objectives, purposes and functions. That is obvious in, for example, professional skills of various kinds. It is, however, sometimes far from clear exactly what the tasks and the objectives are, and it is often disputable how they should best be accomplished. Here, language plays a decisive, even an irreplaceable, role in gaining knowledge, *within* a certain activity or profession.

In every profession, and in every branch of knowledge, one gives and takes *advice*, doubts and uncertainties occur where *reasons* must be found for doing one thing rather than another, and there is thus often a need for *discussion* and *argumentation*. If we do not take into account artificial or isolated examples – like cycling and face recognition taken by themselves – it is easy to see that there are no "purely tacit" activities, nor, then, any "purely tacit" knowledge.[24]

The conclusion so far is that the "tacit" is everywhere and nowhere. Notwithstanding all I have said there may of course be some point in talking about "tacit knowledge," "tacit sides" of knowledge, phenomena that are "not possible to describe", etc., in certain contexts. I will conclude this section by distinguishing three different senses of "tacit" or "inarticulate" knowledge. To distinguish exactly *three* senses is fairly arbitrary. However, the three I focus on seem to me to have been the most central ones in discussions about professional knowledge.

The *first* sense of "tacit" knowledge is knowledge that it is impossible to describe or articulate in words and formulae. The questions "what is describable?" and "what is indescribable?" without any reference to a context seem to me to be utterly meaningless. That should be clear from what I have already said in this section – "description" by whom, by which means, for what purpose? I want, however, to add some remarks about the "indescribable" or "inarticulate", to change the angle of perception.

A description of something is normally not identical with what is described: an action is not the same thing as a description of it; description of a sound is not the same thing as the sound itself, and so on.

It can be quite correct to *say* that "I cannot describe how one does this", even though the person himself *can* do it. What the person most probably means is that she cannot describe it in such a way that the person she addresses *understands* and *can do the same*. Rarely can one learn to do something entirely by description. In a similar way, one can often interpret statements of the type "I cannot describe my feelings for ...". The point is that words are usually insufficient to *convey adequate understanding* to the other person. However, it is always *possible* to describe, and by other means, through artistic expressions for example, *present* actions, feelings, etc.

The possibilities of description and presentation are unlimited. Instead of talking about impossibility of description or articulation, it seems to me generally better to talk about the *inexhaustibility* of reality – and knowledge is part of reality. No description and no presentation *exhausts* a particular body of professional knowledge, for example.[25]

The *second* sense of "tacit" knowledge, or rather the "tacit" side of knowledge, is the "tacitly presupposed" or the "taken for granted". There are many kinds of presuppositions and implications which are, or can be, "tacit". I shall mention a few which are essential for the understanding of the "tacit" sides of professional knowledge.

Training is necessary to become a skilled craftsperson, and this involves training in "how to do things" in a sense that includes both the physical aspects and judgment.[26] One could say that all professions, even the most "intellectual" ones, have a craft side. Arithmetic requires training in counting and calculation; it is not possible to learn arithmetic "purely theoretically". Certain *habits* are important prerequisites for most kinds of knowledge.

Many convictions that we take for granted about the world and ourselves are not true or false taken by themselves, they constitute neither knowledge nor ignorance; rather they constitute a frame which is a *condition for* the formation of knowledge. (Cf. the last section below.)

Concrete models and paradigms – exemplary attempts and achievements – are important in all kinds of knowledge formation, often much more important than any particular "description" of them.[27] Practice-based knowledge acquisition, for example through apprenticeship, relies essentially on concrete examples; those that show what to do and those that show what one should at all costs avoid doing.

Polanyi includes in the tacitly presupposed things which we have only indirect or "subsidiary" awareness of, we have and cannot avoid having our *attention* directed to something else. For example, when we see a face, we are normally not aware of the individual details but of the face as a whole, as a *gestalt*. When a blind person has learned to use her stick she does not feel the stick, she feels what the stick touches. This can be generalized: when one has learned to use a tool it feels, as it were, as a part of one's body. Acquired knowledge in the form of skills becomes part of what one "naturally does" it becomes "tacit", as it were automatic. However, in the examples mentioned we are, Polanyi says, "subsidiary aware" of the details of the face, and the feel of the stick or the tool in the hand.[28]

It seems to me that while some people who talk about "tacit knowledge" regard more or less all "tacit" presuppositions of knowledge as part of the knowledge, others do not. This often results in mutual misunderstandings.

The *third*, and last, sense of "tacit" knowledge is the "silenced" knowledge: the knowledge of people who have not been given a voice or have not been allowed to use their own voice. I think not only of the right to "describe" or tell what one knows but also of the possibility to "stand up" for what one is capable of doing and what one believes to be right *as* knowledge. In some cases, "silenced" knowledge refers back to the presuppositions for knowledge. If one is not, for example, allowed and encouraged to focus one's attention on one's own knowledge, nor allowed and encouraged to maintain a language, with concepts that are *rooted in* and *fit into* a particular professional activity, then that knowledge will erode.

The field of "silenced knowledge" can be expanded on in any directions. Some "languages" can silence knowledge. The *posing of questions* to a person is often taken by that person to indicate that her knowledge, and thereby her identity as a skilled person, is *put in question* – in many cases quite rightly so. Remaining silent can be a form of resistance – sometimes to *protect* knowledge, sometimes to *obstruct* knowledge. Social status, power relations and other social structures can "silence" the knowledge which certain groups or individuals have, and in some cases thereby even destroy it. Generally, oppression of people means suppression of their knowledge;

but some knowledge may be favoured, namely that used in resisting oppression.

The subject of "silenced" knowledge has no limits. I have made a few points and suggestions here; let that suffice here.

Reactions Against the Authority of the Articulated

Our western philosophical and scientific tradition has to a very high degree focused on the articulated side of knowledge: statements and theories of various kinds. I assume that the outlines of this history are well known. What I want to do now is to describe some of the reactions *against* this tradition; there are insights to be gained from them.[29] But before going into that, it should to be pointed out that the demand for *articulated* theories and hypotheses *and* the demand for evidence from observation and experiment, which are the demands of the Age of Enlightenment and of modern science, implied an emancipation from the authority of the tradition and from the demand for "truth by insight". It was a radical step.

In this section I present three main lines of thought in the reactions against the scientific tradition that gives articulated and articulable knowledge the most prominent place. This is not an attempt to write an historical account; my aim is to provide a systematic account, or at least its outlines.The three lines of thought are not clearly separated as a matter of empirical fact. Their centre points are, however, different: The first line of thought places the centre point of knowledge (still in a very wide sense) in the *individual's body*; the second places it in the *culture* or the *social community*; the third places it in *human actions*. In none of the three cases is it easy to know where the centre point of ignorance and folly is to be found; I leave that tricky question aside here.

Both Michael Polanyi and Hubert Dreyfus could be used to illustrate the *first line of thought*, with *the body* as the epistemological centre. Dreyfus's approach is, however, a better illustration because it focuses almost exclusively on the body, while Polanyi works with a blend of different approaches. Dreyfus's approach means here the theory about skill acquisitions which is also a theory about a hierarchy of levels within a skill, that Hubert Dreyfus presented in collaboration with his brother Stuart Dreyfus in *Mind over Machine.* I call this theory "the Dreyfus scheme".

According to the Dreyfus scheme, there are five stages of skill acquisition.[30] I will only say something about the fifth, the final and highest, stage, the level of expertise, and about the difference between the skill and knowledge of the expert and that of lower levels.

Normally, Dreyfus says, "an expert does not *reason.* He does not *solve problems.* He does not *think.* That is what makes him an expert. He does what normally works and, of course, it normally works".[31] Only a person that is not (yet) an expert must think and analyse a situation.

The expert *reacts* immediately in a situation. Dreyfus and Dreyfus call the relationship between the type of situation and an appropriate expert response a "holistic pairing". This means, if I have understood it correctly, that the expert immediately, without any analysis or reasoning, *recognizes a whole situation*, and then reacts, as it were, by instinct. It could, however, take years of training and experience to acquire the right instinct. I should like to borrow Harald Grimen's cogent metaphor and say that situations have faces.[32] We learn to recognize faces without analysing their features.

Dreyfus and Dreyfus turn against a fairly common view, viz. that the development to expert means that the person has learnt and interiorized a more and more advanced *system of rules* or a more and more advanced *theory* of the activity and subject matter in question.

Dreyfus and Dreyfus say that rules and theories can be useful, even necessary, in the learning process but once somebody has become an expert she does not follow rules and apply theories when she acts, she acts directly – reacts intuitively. The belief that there exist rules or theories which the expert follows continues to be held because, according to Dreyfus and Dreyfus, if an expert is *asked to explain* what she does she will mention rules and theories. But these are the rules and theories she learnt and used *before* becoming an expert. There are no other rules and theories that the expert could articulate.

So much for the Dreyfus scheme. It sketches a possible account. The theory and the empirical evidence offered by Dreyfus and Dreyfus have, however, considerable lacunae – they build quite a lot on armchair reflection about chess and car driving.[33] I shall bring up only one point here, but it is a crucial one.

The philosopher Gilbert Ryle has written with insight about "knowing that" and "knowing how". He stresses the role of thinking and learning in connection with skills.[34] Ryle talks in terms of "intelligent performance" and "intelligent practice". One important aspect is that in intelligent practice one consciously controls and is responsible for what one does. It is not a matter of mere reaction: "to regulate one's actions and not merely to be well-regulated".[35] Moreover:

> It is of the essence of merely habitual practices that one performance is a replica of its predecessors. It is of the essence of intelligent practices that one performance is modified by its predecessors. The agent is still learning.[36]

This is, I think, crucial: it is not sufficient for a good expert to know a lot; *she must not have ceased to learn*. This seems impossible to fit into the Dreyfus scheme without causing its breakdown.

Now let us turn to the *second* line of thought, with the *culture* or the *social community* as the centre of knowledge. Here, knowledge formation and education are seen as essentially collective enterprises, built upon and inseparable from the processes of "enculturation" and socialization, in which the elements of a culture are transmitted and transformed. The background of this line of thought is essentially the same as that of the first line, viz. (1) observations of the nature of practice-based knowledge acquisition and knowledge transfer, from master to apprentice for example; and (2) the observation that the skilled practitioner "uncritically" takes much for granted in carrying out her tasks in her area of competence. However, the body is not now the centre, the most central aspects in the second line of thought is the social and communicative sides of the formation of knowledge, or with a slightly different emphasis: the *hermeneutic* side of knowledge and science.

As my main illustration I choose Thomas Kuhn's paradigm theory in *The Structure of Scientific Revolutions*, partly because it is so well known that I do not have to explain very much. Kuhn's theory is not the best choice to illustrate a hermeneutic perspective, but it will do.

Scientific work, according to Kuhn, is characterized by fairly long stable periods of "normal science", during which the scientists' work in a community is held together, and to a large extent determined, by one "paradigm" (in a wider sense). A paradigm contains basic convictions about the world and about human beings; it contains basic convictions about the science in question, what good research is and which theories are acceptable. It also includes paradigmatic examples of good research work, good problem solutions, etc. Such *concrete examples* constitute "paradigms" in a narrower sense, *exemplars*. The scientific enterprise is regarded as a culture, a collective into which members are socialized and which is preserved by a common practice and a common language, *with* shared exemplars (a "paradigm" is immersed in a wider practice and language).

Such a culture is constituted by, among other things, the things people work with, ways of posing questions, the criteria used for judging answers to the questions, habitual procedures and norms of action – all these things are parts of the cultural and linguistic *community*. Our understanding – in scientific and other forms of knowledge formation – presupposes that we have learnt to take much for granted. Our understanding always builds upon a pre-understanding, our judgments always build upon prejudgments, as it is usually expressed in the hermeneutic tradition. We never begin from zero and we can never completely free ourselves from the "horizon" given by our own tradition.

A culture *is* a collective phenomenon, a community. Kuhn stresses the collective in the second edition of *The Structure of Scientific Revolutions*, for example when he talks about the shared paradigms of a research community and the "intuitions" scientists have and use in the community.[37] The intuitions are not individual, he says. Kuhn focuses on scientific communities. The second line of thought about "tacit knowledge", with culture as epistemological centre, is, however, in no way limited to scientific contexts.

Kuhn underlines that paradigms – in the sense of shared exemplars – are essential when one learns to recognize two situations as similar, as exemplifying the same type of situation. Moreover, we should, he says, resist the temptation to assume that when two situations are similar, the question "similar respect to what?" is answerable through a general rule or (a full set of) criteria. Reference to the concrete paradigms is necessary. Such knowledge is "embedded in shared exemplars".[38] Judgments about similarity, as well as other judgments, *work* all right in the community, in a common practice with a common language and shared exemplars. Exactly analogous things can be said, I think, about the "holistic pairing" Dreyfus and Dreyfus talk about.

I put forward this "cultural perspective" as an alternative to a view of science and knowledge which places the articulated and articulable side of knowledge at the centre. Of course one can *discuss* and *describe* various aspects of a culture in all kinds of ways, for various purposes. However, any such "description" presupposes that one takes much of the culture (tacitly) for granted (or: in the *cultures*, in the case where somebody describes a culture other than her own). A culture must, to a high degree, be understood by *acritical participation* in it, such understanding cannot be reduced to articulated knowledge. What the "limits" of articulation are is a meaningful question only when a clear problem exists.[39]

I have placed *human action* as the epistemological centre in the third line of thought which I distinguish. Let us now turn to that. Here we can talk about a "pragmatic perspective", meaning that human actions, rules and habits are primary, not beliefs, thoughts and theories "in themselves". Under this broad heading of "pragmatic" exist various, some quite different, approaches and theories. I shall indicate a few.

Behind the Center for Working Life's approach to professional knowledge, with the tripartite division of knowledge I discussed in the previous section, there is a pragmatic perspective which above all emanates from Kjell Johannessen's interpretation of Ludwig Wittgenstein's later philosophy.[40,41] It is not possible to present this perspective, where the concepts of "practice" and "following a rule" are fundamental, in any detail here. I shall give a couple of illustrations.

In his important book *On Certainty* Wittgenstein asks: "'An empirical proposition can be tested' (we say). But how? and through what?"[42] He continues:

> What *counts* as its test? – "But is this an adequate test? And, if so, must it not be recognizable as such in logic?" – as if giving grounds did not come to an end sometime. By the end is not an ungrounded presupposition: it is an ungrounded way of acting.[43]

Many of Wittgenstein's insights concern the central position of *human actions* in our lives: we cannot justify our theories and what we believe by reference to some kind of *basic assumptions* or *basic truths*. Our arguments come to an end somewhere, and what remains is: we *act* in some way. The practice "has to speak for itself", he says.[44]

One can build a pragmatic – or pragmaticist – perspective from other points of departure, through the American pragmatism for example, with Charles S. Peirce, William James, and John Dewey as philosophical leaders. However, these three are very different as personalities and thinkers. Here I want to put forward just one important thought from Peirce and one from James. That should give a flavour of American pragmatism.

A main point in American pragmatism is that people's *ideas* and *theories* of reality are empty in themselves as it were; they have their primary meaning through their consequences in and for human actions, "Bare thoughts" are conceptions removed from their primary life history, one might say.

Peirce's "pragmatic principle" has been a guiding idea in the tradition. There are several formulations. The following is one of them:

> The essence of belief is the establishment of a habit; and different beliefs are distinguished by the different modes of action to which they give rise.[45]

Another formulation which Peirce uses in the same paper is that a belief is "a rule for action".[46] This can be interpreted in many ways, but I leave it without further comments as an illustration of a fairly open-ended line of thinking.

William James sides with something like Peirce's pragmatic principle, at least according to his own interpretation.[47] An interesting, but too often ridiculed, thought in James's writings is that "the true" is what is, in the long run and on the whole, "the expedient in the way of our thinking".[48] This should not be seen as a strict definition and it must be interpreted together with other things he says.[49] His ideas about "truth" amounts to both an ethical theory and a theory of knowledge.

James, like the other American pragmatists and the later Wittgenstein, repudiates all ideas to the effect that true ideas and theories are somehow copies or pictures of, or are tied by a unique correspondence to, "the world as it is in itself". Truths are what lead us successfully (in the long run and on the whole) through the world. We must accept truths in the *plural*, James says![50] He then consistently says that truth is "made", it is made through verification processes in the multifarious world we inhabit and experience.[51] There is no *one* way we can be led successfully through this world.

I shall conclude my account of this third line of thought by mentioning another approach within an American pragmatic tradition, viz. Donald Schön's theory of "knowing-in-action" and "reflection-in-action".[52] A working practitioner, for example an architect, is not primarily a problem solver, she has her starting point in a "mess" which she tries to shape or *design* in order to find or create a problem, this in turn should lead to a continued fruitful or successful change of the situation. A "researcher in practice" is *in* the situation she is trying to understand and which in some measure she changes. Understanding and change build partly upon representations of reality, but such representations are not pictures of reality independent of action but parts of the process of changing reality through action. The knowledge is *in* the actions and one could well say that truths are "made" or "constructed".

The skilful practitioner is, fairly literally, a designer.[53] Schön often refers to John Dewey. It is also easy to see many parallels between Schön and William James. Knowledge from a pragmatic – or pragmatist – point of view is a part of a continuing creation of the world, as are ignorance and prejudices too, unfortunately (see the next section).

Some brief words of conclusion remain in this section. Action seems to be central in all of the three lines of thought I have mentioned, but that is at least partly because I accept a "pragmatic perspective" as the most fundamental one, and that is mirrored in the text. However, *culture* need not be seen as having action as its centre; in Kuhn's' theory the human action is only one component – theoretical beliefs are as important. Dreyfus emphasizes the body, above all bodily *reactions* and *intuitions* rather than actions. The three main lines I have tried to distinguish put forward three *aspects*, three ways of *approaching* "tacit" knowledge. None of the three aspects is wholly independent of the others, but the thinkers I have presented regard one aspect as being more *fundamental* than the other two.

Why All This Talk about "Knowledge"?

I have talked about "tacit knowledge", and I have used compounds like "propositional knowledge", and "knowledge of familiarity"; I do not know how many times I have used the word knowledge and related expressions so far in this paper. However, "tacit knowledge", "professional knowledge", and "skill" are not just matters of knowledge. That is the topic of this section.

In many cases the phenomena we call instances of "tacit knowledge" could be referred to just as well, or even better, in other terms:

understanding, skill, confidence, security in performance, mastery of an art, judgment, ability, talent, attentiveness, familiarity, experience, commitment...

The list may be unending. In a job or profession it is essential to get the right things done at the right time, which is something more than just "the sum of all special competences". For example, a farmer must make his farm work as a whole. It is also important to know (understand, be clear about ...) which tasks one has mastered and which one has not mastered. One should trust one's own knowledge and experience, but at the same time "know" (recognize, be aware of ...) its limits. It is important to be able to change perspective, since if one is not aware of alternatives one does not know (much about) what one does.

Lack of self-confidence is an obstacle to knowledge acquisition and an obstacle to letting the knowledge one possesses come to expression. A personal commitment is often needed to carry out tasks in a successful way. Sometimes a personal involvement, an emotional commitment, is necessary. The possibilities of commitment, personal involvement, etc., depend heavily on personal talents and dispositions, character traits, attitudes, etc., which could not be equated with knowledge but are necessary to bring (and keep) knowledge alive when facing reality.

On the other hand, too much self-confidence is an obstacle to (further) knowledge acquisition. An emotional involvement can place some kinds of knowledge beyond our reach. There is no *one* kind of involvement, attitude or stance which is requested in all kinds of knowledge.

I could continue for a long time to list features which could be counted as parts of professional knowledge and skill, and continue to list features needed in the creation and maintenance of active, live knowledge. However, without going into specific areas and without concrete examples, such a list tends to become like a list of wishes for all good things: openness, responsibility, attentiveness, etc. Nevertheless, such things *are* important.

"Why all this talk about knowledge?" Is it good that the word "knowledge", and its compounds, like "tacit knowledge", is used in this broad sense in this chapter and even more in other discussions about "tacit knowledge"? I think one should be careful. The conceptual richness of our language should be used and explored. There may, however, be reason to talk about knowledge in a very wide sense, including, for example, understanding and judgment, namely in cases where we can talk about (more or less) *correct* or *valid* understanding, (more or less) *correct* judgment, etc.; and that is possible in many cases, in all professional areas. We should, however, always be aware of the risk of merely apparent unity – the issue of knowledge and ignorance is many-sided.

Something may be labelled as "knowledge" to enhance the social and political – and epistemological – status of a certain type of activity or a certain idea. Obviously the expression "tacit knowledge" has sometimes been used in that way.

One consequence of the extensive use of "knowledge", not least in compounds like "tacit knowledge", is that not enough attention has been given to what is *not* knowledge, may it be *lack of knowledge, ignorance* or what is *neither* knowledge *nor* a lack of knowledge.[54] For example, a generous, indeed too generous, use of "tacit knowledge" includes much of the "wisdom" of our ancestors that is tradition and time-honoured custom but nonetheless builds on false conceptions or plain ignorance. Petrified rituals do not express or yield knowledge. The history of science, not least medicine, is a rich source of examples of the prevalence of both time-honoured customs based on false beliefs and petrified rituals. Thus there exist things like "tacit ignorance" and "tacit prejudices". There is also much in life that constitutes neither examples of knowledge nor of ignorance (or lack of knowledge), for example, a set of habits of doing things in certain ways (this includes fundamental language use) (Cf. the second section above, about presuppositions of knowledge, and the final section below.)

The tensions between knowledge and tradition, between empathic understanding and critical investigation, just to give a few examples show how difficult it is to reach anything like a thorough understanding of the concept of tacit knowledge and ignorance. I see these tensions as aspect of what in the next section I call the main problem.

The Main Problem: What Is Knowledge in Action? Confidence and/or Critical Consciousness?

What is knowledge in action? If we do not want to get stuck in a blind alley straight away we must accept that there exist a multitude of forms of knowledge and a multitude of ways to approach them. I consider trying to capture in a handy formula what knowledge in action *is* to be a hopeless task.

I will not, then, try to answer the question, "what is knowledge in action?" Rather, it provides a problem setting. And given that question, I think that we can discern a problem centre, which may be represented by the tension, or conflict, between *confidence in the exercise of knowledge* on the one hand and *critical knowledge formation* on the other.[55] The term "confidence" covers the idea of a unification of self-confidence, acting without doubt, and reliably producing (by and large) successful results. This confidence is the hallmark of the practical knowledge tradition. The question is, then, whether such confidence is compatible with critical knowledge formation, i.e. critical knowledge acquisition and a critical justification of knowledge claims; and if they are compatible, how could they be joined or combined? Calling this a *problem centre* means, firstly, that it lies behind many other tensions and conflicts, and secondly, that it is crucial to attempts to construct a convincing theory of knowledge.

The relation between confidence and a critical stance is a many faceted problem. One of Polanyi's main points in *Personal Knowledge* – with the subtitle *Towards a Post Critical Philosophy* – is that the personal knowledge, "tacit knowing", cannot be critical, at least not fully. Polanyi says that "systematic forms of criticism can be applied only to articulate forms",[56] and it is clear from the context that he thinks of assertions as the subjects of systematic criticism. I don't think he is quite right. Not only assertions may be criticized, though systematic critique without any articulation seems impossible. The question of *what* needs to be articulated to make systematic critique possible is not easy to answer. I leave this open

Polanyi does not regard personal knowledge as uncritical; rather it is neither critical nor uncritical. It is *a-critical*, he says.[57] Personal knowledge builds upon another form of knowledge formation than critically judged knowledge. The personal in knowledge – understanding, passion, commitment, responsibility – is not compatible with doubt and critical questioning. The personal aspect of knowledge is knowledge-in-life, which requires one to, as it were, enter and live *in* the knowledge, *in* one's skills, theories and beliefs.[58]

In the third section above, concerning the reactions against the tradition of articulated knowledge, I quoted Wittgenstein. The most important message was that justifications, "giving grounds", must come to an end and that we stand upon a "ground" of ungrounded ways of acting. When we learn a skill by training, at the same time we learn confidence, we learn to trust in what we do. Skilful acting and confident acting are inseparable in practice. One of the insights Wittgenstein most convincing brings to the fore in his late reflections (in *On Certainty*) is that it is sometimes not a belief or a trust that requires justification; *doubt* and *distrust* would need reasons or grounds to become justified.

Hubert Dreyfus underlines the intuitive *reaction* in the expert's exercise of knowledge. But it is typical that he has virtually nothing to say about how the expert could continue to learn, especially to learn critically. That is a lacuna in his (and his brother's) theory.

Donald Schön wants to put to the fore "reflection-in-action", i.e. the agent's reflections while she acts – she reflects "on line" as Schön expresses it somewhere. However, as far as I know he never takes up knowledge as a critical enterprise as a theme for discussion; validity problems fall outside his discussions. He could, for example, equally well talk about "believing-in-action" instead of "knowing-in-action".[59] Whether his theory could be supplemented with a critical perspective or not is difficult to judge.

Typically, then, when practice dominates, it does so at the expense of the critical aspect of knowledge – and vice versa; but I have not gone into that here.

In Plato's dialogue, *Gorgias*, an important part of the discussion is about the difference between a (genuine) art, like medicine, and what is only "a habitude or knack", like cookery.[60] For something to count as an art it must be done with *insight* into what one is doing. An art is *rational*, performed with knowledge and reason, and it is exercised for the sake of the *good* or the *best*, not for the sake of, say, mere pleasure. It is not sufficient that people have the *feeling* that something is good for them. To exercise an art one has to have *knowledge* of what the good and the bad is, or at least about what is *better* and *worse* for the human body and soul. Knowledge and rationality thus have an inseparable ethical side. Even though Plato is, I think, unfair to cookery – he calls it an irrational "flattery" – the requirements he sets for (genuine) art have not lost any of their topicality.[61]

The demand for insight and enlightenment that Plato has Socrates express in *Gorgias* seems to me still to be valid, not least for "knowledge in action". The demand that an art shall be for the sake of the good, or the best, is also fully defensible today. One can find it in the American pragmatist tradition, it is clearly present in James's and Dewey's Works. One can also find it in Thomas Tempte, the cabinet maker's account of his own practice.[62] It is a matter of "the honour of work": "The piece of furniture must be imbued with every care, with a sense of responsibility and a sense of honour, in such a way that others can experience it ... Moderation, discretion, good sense and care should be imprinted on the things that serve people in their living".[63]

The main question, and it is worth repeating, is whether critical knowledge formation and confidence in acting can be reconciled, without either of the two swallowing up and destroying the other.[64] All simple formulae, like "first make a critical investigation, then act with confidence", give a misleading picture of practical knowledge traditions. However, the reconciliation seems possible "in practice". Is this answer sufficient?

I make no attempt to provide an answer in this chapter.

Knowledge is Always on the Way ...

"Genuine communication always contains genuine uncertainty I do not know what I have said before you have answered and you do not know what you have said before I have answered. You *show me* what I have said and *I show you* what you have said".[65] These words by Johan Asplund express in a nutshell an important side of language: it is always moving. The uncertainty mentioned may exist without any lack of confidence in action (communication *is* a form of action). Instead of talking about uncertainty we can put Asplund's point this way: what somebody has said is never finished.

In this last section I sketch my own conception of knowledge. I describe a perspective that is far from complete and I continue to struggle with the problems I touch on.[66] "My" epistemological perspective is unfinished. However, we should not try to remove all uncertainty about the meaning of "knowledge" and "skill"; the concepts are in various ways open. And we shall be open-minded about the limits of knowledge.

What a person says is unfinished. This means, among other things, that our concepts are unfinished. Many other actions are also always unfinished. The unfinished character of communication, concepts and actions has consequences for our conception of knowledge in various professions and activities. Strictly speaking, knowledge can never be finished, nor can our understanding of knowledge.

"Knowledge *formation*", in a sense which does not presuppose knowledge as a final state, is therefore more fundamental than "knowledge". I do not, however, propose that our ordinary use of language should be changed, all of us *have* knowledge in an ordinary sense: we can do things, we know things because we saw them, etc. I propose a partial restructuring of the ways we think about "knowledge".

It seems to me inappropriate to call pure copying or imitation of an action knowledge, even if what is copied is knowledge, for the same reason that makes it inappropriate to say that somebody has knowledge of a theory just because she can state the articulated side of the theory (cf. the second section above). Only if we *understand* what a theory says and is about can we have theoretical knowledge. Only if a person *understands* what she does and why can she have knowledge in action, for example in a profession. There are, of course, varying degrees of understanding and insight – as is the case with knowledge; the foregoing makes it plain that knowledge and understanding stand and fall together. Understanding is, like knowledge, always unfinished.

To say that utterances and concepts are (in principle) always unfinished, always awaiting an answer, as it were, means that the idea of a correct or better understanding refers to a collective, a community with a common language and common practices. For the same reason knowledge – or more correctly, the "formation of knowledge" – is something essentially collective. It is therefore slightly misleading to say that somebody "has" or "has not" knowledge of one kind or another. It would be more to the point to say that a person "participates" or "does not participate" in knowledge of some kind. A "knowledge community" is often characterized by a extensive division of labour, which does not imply that the individuals are unimportant. I am convinced, like Polanyi, that participation in knowledge requires individual commitment. Not least, individual action is required.

We need pictures, perspectives and models to be able to reflect. Through expressions like "unfinished utterances", "unfinished knowledge" and "participation in knowledge" I attempt to produce a picture, or the outlines of one. I think the picture brings to the fore important insights and issues, and is therefore worth further exploration. The picture in itself does not solve any problems, it creates a frame for the formulation and fruitful discussions of important problems.

In particular, I have not suggested a solution to or dissolution of the main problem, as formulated in the preceding section. The tension between confidence and critique remains the main problem. This becomes even clearer when we address the issue of the justification of knowledge: must what purports to be knowledge be *justified* before it may be counted as knowledge? This is the problem of validation. A few reflections about that conclude this section, and thereby this chapter.

It is a classical idea that only *justified* beliefs, theories, etc. could be serious candidates for knowledge. Justification is then taken as a necessary condition for knowledge. One has to have *good reasons* to believe a statement, a theory, etc. This seems to be reasonable requirement and I think it is correct in *many* cases. I do not want to open a discussion here about what "good reasons" or "sufficiently good reasons" are. It is sufficient to say here that it has *something* to do with what stands up to critical questioning and critical investigation. For example, a mere reference to an authority or a certain tradition is not in itself sufficient.

The following may be advanced *against* the idea that justification through reasons is a necessary condition for knowledge: when we grow up in or grow into a certain culture or community we come to accept many beliefs and ideas without any doubt or critical investigation. We adopt, moreover, uncritically or at least a-critically, many methods of knowledge acquisition. It is, in many cases, perfectly correct to say that I know something because I was present and *saw* this and that. As I said earlier, we would often need reason *not* to believe or to *doubt* something. Justification by reasons *cannot* be generally valid as a condition for knowledge.

From a certain point of view it also seems to me reasonable to require that a claim to exercise *knowledge in action* is valid only if the agent has *good reasons* for acting the way she does, which would mean that the agent must act with insight about what she does, she must *know* what she does and why. We see once more the demands from Plato's *Gorgias* come to the surface. But again we meet obvious problems. I have mentioned them earlier, so I can be brief here: we become skilful through training. In this training, reasons cannot be given for everything; "at bottom" there are no reasons – this is done *like this*! Again, it is *doubt*, not trust and confidence, that would require reasons.

However, in all professions, and most other activities, reasons are as a matter of fact often given, in the "native language" of the profession or activity. Reasons are also "stated" partly through other means than language – people *show* or *demonstrate* in one way or another why one way of doing something is better than another. One difficult question is, then, how we could find, if possible, a balance between reasons that are given "naturally" within an activity and critical questions and demands for reasons from "the outside". Knowledge in an Enlightenment perspective must be open to critical questions from, in principle, anybody; this is important because sometimes external critique is necessary to prevent a practice where people participate in knowledge from turning into a mere ritual.

There exists in some sense false ideology, prejudices, silliness, etc., in actions, not only in beliefs and ideas. If we want to have (further) knowledge such things must be counteracted. However, what is and what is not knowledge is often controversial; conflicts and disputes occur – and that is exactly as it should be, given the idea of Enlightenment and the conviction that knowledge is always unfinished. Or am I, when I put it that way, still stuck in "the old" Enlightenment ideal which again and again has misrepresented and devalued "the practical intellect"? But what is the alternative? A belief that the "invisible hand" will lead to the best knowledge? Is the hand, then, a market mechanism, social acceptance, biological adaptation or something else?

Notes

1 This paper is a slightly revised English version of my "Kunskapers tysta och tystade sidor – ett försök till översikt" (*Nordisk pedagogik* 10 (3), 1990). The work was carried out as part of my research project "Acting with good Reason", supported by the Swedish Council for Research on Higher Education. I am grateful to Struan Robertson, who did the basic English editing, and to Paul Needham, who helped me to bring many of my thoughts together with suitable English expressions.

2 The research is presented in Göranzon (ed) (1983).

3 Polanyi (1966), p 4.

4 Cf Polanyi (1966), chap 1, and Polanyi (1978), which I use as my main source.

5 Kuhn (1970), p 44. The first edition of Kuhn's book, in which this is included, was published in 1962.

6 Kuhn (1970), p 44, n1. Kuhn refers to Polanyi 's *Personal Knowledge*, first published in 1958. Kuhn focuses on *one* side of Polanyi' s many faceted concept "tacit knowing".

7 Bo Göranzon (1990) has stressed that this is a central area of dispute and unresolved tension in the Encyclopaedia project of the Age of Enlightenment.

8 The Swedish Higher Education Act (SFS 1977:218, §3). This is difficult to translate. I have translated "vetenskaplig" as "scientific", even though the Swedish "vetenskaplig" is semantically closer to the German "wiessenschaftlich" than to the English "scientific". The Swedish "vetenskap" also includes history and the arts although "vetenskaplig rationalitet" ("scientific rationality") is heavily influenced by an idea of the natural sciences as the most developed examples of "vetenskap".

9 This process has been evidenced in studies carried out at the Swedish Center for Working Life. Cf Göranzon (ed) (1983), which emphasizes the long term, "third order", consequences; Göranzon (1990) and Section II of Göranzon and Josefson (eds) (1988).

10 Cf the literature mentioned in the preceding note.

11 Cf Göranzon and Josefson (eds) (1988); Göranzon (1990); Tempte (1982).

12 Statements made by Roland Fastberg in an interview with Caj Norén (1987).

13 "The most amazing computer of all is born, not made", reads the caption below a picture of a child's face in an advertisement from Control Data. *New York Times*, 12 October 1988.

14 Cf the critique in Dreyfus (1979) and in Dreyfus and Dreyfus (1986).

15 At times Polanyi expresses such a conception of language, though it does not fit in with other things he says (cf Polanyi 1978, chap 5).

16 Cf e.g. Schön (1983), p 276. Of course this can be given an "innocent" interpretation too, making it a trivial truth.

17 Nordenstam (1983).

18 For reasons yet to be discussed in this section, the division has sometimes been taken too literally, as a division into three distinct kinds of knowledge. In Göranzon (1990) the division is used essentially *within* a certain practice. And I think it is justified *only* within a certain practice.

19 Nordenstam (1983), pp 20–21. In English, good sources are the papers by Göranzon, Josefson, Gullers and Perby in Göranzon and Josefson (eds) (1988).

20 The source of this concept is Kjell S. Johannessen; and he has continued to develop the idea of "knowledge of familiarity". Cf. Johannessen (1988, 1990).

21 Cf, for example, Polanyi (1978), pp 27–30.

22 This has consistently been argued by both Nordenstam and Johannessen. My criticism is that they, and to a greater extent some of their followers, have been careless in talking about distinct kinds of knowledge.

23 I write throughout as if ordinary verbal language were the only means of expression. Of course I also include, tacitly as it were, other kinds of sign language.

24 Language and action are tied to each other in a hermeneutic circle. For an introduction to hermeneutics from an analytical point of view, see Taylor (1985), first published in 1971.

25 This is not to deny that the "indescribable" or "ineffable" can be treated as a serious and important topic in, for example, the philosophy of language and the philosophy of religion. "What cannot be said" is a main theme in Wittgenstein's writings, both in *Tractatus* (1961) and *Philosophical Investigations* (1972). However, such themes are far outside my ambitions in this chapter.

26 Donald Schön has said (somewhere) that in many cases one must first learn to *do* things and only later one can begin to understand *what* one is doing.

27 Kuhn stresses this in the area of (normal) science, cf "Postscript-1969" in Kuhn (1970).

28 Cf. Polanyi (1978), pp 55–63, 92; Polanyi (1966), pp 10–11, 16–17.

29 I want, however, to defend and keep part of the tradition; cf Molander (1989b, 1990).

30 Cf Dreyfus and Dreyfus (1986), chap 1; also Molander (1989b), sect 4.

31 Dreyfus (1990), p 224; almost the same formulation occurs in Dreyfus (1988), p 106.

32 Grimen (1987), p 188.

33 Cf Molander (1989b), sect 4.

34 Ryle (1949), chap 2.

35 Ryle (1949), p 28.

36 *Ibid*, p 42.

37 Cf Kuhn (1970), pp 191–192..

38 Kuhn (1970), p 192. cf the discussion about "intersubjective meanings" in Taylor (1985).

39 This is one of several reasons which demonstrate why all attempts to represent "common sense" in expert systems are doomed to fail.

40 Cf Johannessen (1988).

41 Cf Johannessen (1990).

42 Wittgenstein (1974), sect 109.

43 *Ibid*, sect 110.

44 *Ibid*, sect 139.

45 Peirce (1955), p 29.

46 *Ibid* , p 28.

47 Cf James (1978), pp 28–29.

48 *Ibid*, p 106

49 *Ibid*, p 42.

50 *Ibid*, p 104.

51 *Ibid*, p 104.

52 Schön (1983, 1987)

53 Cf for example Schön (1987), p 42.

54 The English language does not contain any *one* direct general opposite or antithesis to "knowledge", and neither does Swedish for that matter. There are no simple opposites to be found related to the concept of knowledge.

55 Magnus Florin and Bo Göranzon talk about "security in one's praxis" in their introduction in Göranzon and Florin (eds) (1990).

56 Polanyi (1978), p 264.

57 *Ibid*, p 245.

58 Cf Polanyi (1978), chaps 9–10.

59 In conversations we had 1989 he seemed to agree that this was a defect of his writings so far.

60 Cf *Gorgias* 462–465, 500–501. I use Lamb's translation, though I have compared it with Jowett's. A more detailed discussion is to be found in Molander (1989b), sect 3.

61 Cf Göranzon (1990), p 142.

62 Tempte (1982), p 76–79, especially p 79.

63 *Ibid*, p 77.

64 Bo Göranzon leaves them facing each other in a artistically conscious way in Göranzon (1990).

65 Asplund (1987), p 45.

66 This is ongoing work in my research project "Acting with Good Reason. Knowledge and Ignorance in Human Action", which is described in Molander (1989a).

References

(Quotations from Swedish sources in the text are translated by me unless otherwise stated in the notes.)

Asplund, Johan (1987) *Om hälsningscermonier, mikromakt och asocial pratsamhet*. Korpen, Gothenburg.

Dreyfus, Hubert (1979) *What computers can't do. The limits of artificial intelligence*, revised ed. Harper & Row, New York.

Dreyfus, Hubert and Dreyfus, Stuart (1986) *Mind over machine. The power of human intuition and expertise in the era of the computer*. The Free Press, New York.

Dreyfus, Hubert (1988) The Socratic and Platonic basis of cognitivism. *AI and Society* 2 (2): 99–112.

Dreyfus. Hubert (1990) Is Socrates to blame for cognitivism? In: Göranzon B,Florin M (eds), pp 219–228.

Grimen, Harald (1987) *Aspects of act-identification and intention-identification. An essay on identificatory practices in human life*. Vitskapsteoretisk Forum, The University of Bergen, Bergen.

Göranzon, Bo (ed) (1983) *Datautvecklingens filosofi.Tyst kunskap och ny teknik*. Carlsson & Jönsson Bokförlag, Stockholm.

Göranzon, Bo (1990) *Det praktiska intellektet. Datoranvändning och yrkeskunnande*. Carlssons, Stockholm (published in English, as *The practical intellect*, by UNESCO and Springer-Verlag,1992.)

Göranzon, Bo and Josefson, Ingela (eds) (1988) *Knowledge, skill and artificial intelligence*. Springer-Verlag, London.

Göranzon, Bo and Florin, Magnus (eds) (1990) *Artificial intelligence, culture and language: on education and work*. Springer-Verlag, London.

James, William (1978) *Pragmatism and the meaning of truth* Harvard University Press, Cambridge, MA.

Johannessen, Kjell S. (1988) Rule-following and tacit knowledge. *AI and Society* 2: 287–302.

Johannessen, Kjell S. (1990) *Rule-following and intransitive understanding*. In: Göranzon B, Florin M (eds), pp 37–44

Kuhn, Thomas S. (1970) *The Structure of scientific revolutions*, 2nd edn. University of Chicago Press, Chicago.

Molander, Bengt (1989a) Acting with good reason. Knowledge and ignorance in human action. *Studies of Higher Education and Research* 1989:1.

Molander, Bengt (1989b) What do you think you are doing? Reflections on justification and knowledge in action. In: Lindstöm S, Rabinowicz W (eds) *In so many words. Philosophical Essays dedicated to Sven Danielsson*. Philosophical Studies, Uppsala pp 249–284.

Molander, Bengt (1990) Socratic dialogue. On dialogue and discussion in the formation of knowledge. In Göranzon B, Florin M (eds), pp 229–243.

Nordenstam, Tore (1983) Ett pragmatiskt perspektiv på dautvecklingen. In: Göranzon B, pp 17–27.

Norén, Caj (1987) Superdatorn lyfter glesbygden. *Dagens Nyheter* 28 December.

Peirce, Charles S. (1955) How to make our ideas clear. In: Buchler J (ed): *Philosophical writings of Peirce*. Dover, New York, pp 23–41. (originally published 1878.)

Plato *Gorgias*.Transl Lamb R M (Loeb Classical Library, 1983); transl Jowett B 3rd edn, in *Plato, The Dialogues* (Clarendon Press, 1924).

Polanyi, Michael (1978) *Personal knowledge towards a post-critical philosophy*. Routledge & Kegan Paul, London.

Polanyi, Michael (1966) *The tacit dimension*. Routledge & Kegan Paul, London.

Ryle, Gilbert (1949) *The concept of mind*, Hutchinson's University Library, London.
Schön, Donald A. (1983) *The reflective practitioner. How professionals think in action*. Basic Books, New York.
Schön, Donald A. (1987) *Educating the reflective practitioner*. Jossey-Bass, San Fransisco.
Taylor, Charles (1985) Interpretation and the sciences of man. In: *Philosophy and the Human Sciences*. Philosophical Papers 2. Cambridge University Press, Cambridge pp 15–57.
Tempte, Thomas (1982) *Arbetets Ära. Om hantverk, arbete, några rekonstruerade verktyg och maskiner*.The Center for Working Life, Stockholm.
Wittgenstein, Ludwig (1961) *Tictatus logico-philosophicus*. Transl Pears DF and McGuiness BF. Routledge & Kegan Paul, London. (Originally published 1921.)
Wittgenstein, Ludwig (1972) *Philosophical investigations*. Transl Anscombe GEM. Basil Blackwell, Oxford. (Originally published 1953.)
Wittgenstein, Ludwig (1974) *On certainty*. Transl Paul D, Anscombe GEM. Basil Blackwell, Oxford.

Chapter 3

Why is Wittgenstein Important?

Allan Janik

For Gustave Kars

To understand the importance of Wittgenstein we must examine language as an *ensemble* of strategies for weaving together words and actions. A failure to grasp the workings of language is at the root of our philosophical problems. Wittgenstein's approach to philosophy, investigating both the formation and transference. of skill and the notion of rule-following, was that of a craftsman. A craft embodies "tacit knowing" in that it is learned through the repetition of a specified action until it becomes second nature. Skills cannot be learned from books because they cannot be described literally, although description can play a role in reminding the apprentice of the different stages through which (s)he must pass in order to master the craft. There is no single or fixed application of any rule. In his work on skill-acquisition Wittgenstein articulates what it means to learn on the basis of practical experience alone. Words, symbols, and sentences are only *part* of language, meaningful only to the extent that they are embedded in actions (or what Heidegger termed a *situation*). Through his study of language games, Wittgenstein shows how the whole range of human activities is constituted in changing alliances between words and actions. Wittgenstein's mature philosophy is therefore vitally important for understanding the relation between artificial and natural intelligence, and the dependence of the new technology on human modes of learning (rather than vice versa).

Why is Wittgenstein important? The question is stupefyingly simple – or at least it stupefied me when the distinguished French Germanist to whom this paper is dedicated put it to me a couple of years ago at a Kraus symposium in Paris. I would have been less taken aback by having to answer the question in a few words were it not for the fact that it genuinely troubled a sophisticated, erudite scholar. However, he is by no means alone in his inability to grasp the significance of Wittgenstein's mature philosophizing. The question is raised continually in circles concerned with language, especially where that concern is related to attempts to produce a *theory* language. In such groups Wittgenstein's achievements tend to look naive or primitive; they are hardly that. All that has a way of showing how little that academic Krupp works, the international Wittgenstein industry, has done to articulate the broader implications of Wittgenstein's mature philosophy to the intellectual community at large. Thus here in Austria on the occasion of Wittgenstein's hundredth birthday a commemorative television broadcast was announced in a leading Austrian newspaper with the words: "Although Wittgenstein never formulated a clear thesis and during his life only published two books the *Tractatus* and the *Philosophical Investigations*, he is considered to be the most radical language researcher, whose teaching was more deeply determined by mathematical logic than the philosophy of a Martin Heidegger". I find this statement remarkable because almost nothing in this brief description is simply and unqualifiedly true. No, we who write about Wittgenstein still have a huge task before us. So I propose to consider this question afresh with a view to illuminating the broader significance of his philosophy.

One reason for taking this question seriously is the very disarming naiveté by which it dazzles the professional. As such it is akin to the problems which the question "What is time?" generated for St. Augustine, whose perplexing character Wittgenstein himself found so deep. Like Strindberg's naval officer in the *Dream Play*, we know the answer but we cannot somehow say it. Of course, any answer to the question "Why is Wittgenstein important?" will depend above all upon who poses the question as well as how it is posed and why the interested party wants to know the answer. In short, the question will have many different answers; yet, I think that there will have to be certain minimal features that any answer will have to contain. I propose to concentrate upon those considerations which bear principally upon Wittgenstein's uniqueness in twentieth century thought.

Since this is not only Wittgenstein's centenary year but also that of a number of other influential philosophers, not to mention those two great actors Charlie Chaplin and Adolf Hitler, one way to approach our question is to look at Wittgenstein in relation to those other figures. I refer to R.G. Collingwood, Gabriel Marcel and above all Martin Heidegger. I suggest that what historians of ideas ought to find noteworthy here is the deep philosophical similarities which lie concealed by the superficial differences between these thinkers (which is by no means to minimize their differences). I refer to the common insistence of all four that philosophy cannot be a body of scientific knowledge, precisely because the way that the subject is involved in posing questions systematically prevents it from itself being an object of knowledge (to use the quaint vocabulary of a previous generation). I take this notion that philosophy must be "above or below" science, in the words of the early Wittgenstein, to be no less the point of Marcel's distinction between problems and mysteries, Heidegger's notion of a conceptual "horizon" that is part and parcel of all seeing on the part of that being-which-is-always-me and Collingwood's emphasis upon the "uncanny" character of that which must be unquestioned if we are to formulate scientific questions at all, than it is of Wittgenstein's analysis of how philosophical questioning terminates in silence as we run up against the limits of language. Moreover, I take it that what these thinkers share with Wittgenstein with respect to their conception of the role of philosophy is at least indirectly connected to a certain quasi-idealist, pragmatist thread that runs through their thought. If we need speak of "influences" here we need only think of Royce's influence upon Marcel, Hegel's influence upon Collingwood, James's influence upon Heidegger via Husserl, as well as James's influence upon Wittgenstein himself.

Be that as it may, I propose to begin by briefly considering some of the consequences of pragmatism for our conception or philosophizing. That means taking a look at the much neglected William James, whose importance as a predecessor of Wittgensteln and Heidegger can scarcely be overestimated; for, as I see it, the Heidegger of *Being and Time* is carrying through a critique of the more Kantian later Husserl on the basis of cues implicit in the more Jamesian early Husserl; while Wittgenstein's insistence that the resolution of the problems that have traditionally tormented philosophers in terms of "showing" rather then "saying", i.e., reflective insight "rather than theory, is no less indebted to James. If this insistence upon the paramount importance of James seems surprising, it is probably because we are all-too inclined to dismiss James as a thinker more vigorous that rigorous in favour of the more serious logician Peirce in discussing the significance of pragmatism for the development of twentieth century thought. This is a serious mistake. James's enormous worldwide popularity before 1914 apart, it is usually ignored that James solved the most vexing issue in the Peircean philosophy when Peirce himself could not. I refer to the question of whether Peirce was a realist or a nominalist. James resolved it implicitly in *Pragmatism* simply by asking whether the answer to that question makes a difference. However fascinating in itself, the question is only important to the extent that our answer to it makes a difference with respect to understanding our epistemological enterprises. In his usual self-deprecating way James was telling Peirce that a pragmatist ought to know better that to take that sort of question seriously. We are all-too inclined to forget, as Richard Rorty does, that pragmatism should be understood first and foremost as a means of solving philosophical disputes by asking what difference the answer makes in the first place. If the answer has no consequences for practice, then the whole business is a waste of time. This pragmatist disciplining of philosophers is frequently ignored but certainly not by Wittgenstein. By concentrating overly upon the so-called "pragmatic theory of truth" the role of pragmatism as a critique of traditional philosophy in all its forms, rationalist and empiricist, metaphysical and scientific, has been overlooked. Thus we can begin to see why Wittgenstein is most important by considering how, following James, he was capable of calling what is generally taken to be the whole of the western philosophical tradition into question in a way that Heidegger would like to have done but never really was able to. Thus one way of explaining Wittgenstein's importance is to say that in a number or crucial respects he managed to cast light upon problems that a philosophical radical like Heidegger only partially and inadequately managed to illuminate.

Clearly enough, if there is any truth at all in this last assertion, it would require a substantial book to explain how Wittgenstein surpassed Heidegger in solving the problems that he set for himself in *Being and Time* – a book which in the final analysis would be of considerable importance *inter alia* in explaining what is alive and what was stillborn in the so- called "postmodern" movement, which owes so much to Heidegger. Here I can say even less about that; at best I can make a few relevant observations about what is absolutely central to that task.

It may not be easy to see, indeed, it may be that it only be seen in terms that are fundamentally foreign to Heidegger, i.e., after Wittgenstein's *Philosophical Investigations* or Austin's "A Plea for Excuses" and, paradoxically, it may be that Heidegger himself did not realize that one of his most startling achievements in *Being and Time* was the identification of the true unit of reference: *the situation,* i.e., that reference is a human practice rather then the property of a proposition. This emerged from his transformation of Diltheyan text hermeneutics into the hermeneutics of action in the exploration of the fundamental ontology, the exploration of the conditions of the possibility, or purposive action. Crucial to this undertaking was a reversal or traditional epistemological priorities according to which scientific knowledge was seen as prior to action. This was rightly seen as a challenge to mainstream philosophy from Aristotle to Kant. In order to accomplish this Heidegger invites us to contrast the way we consider objects that we contemplate or "think" about from objects that we use. I refer to his distinction between those objects which are *vorhanden* and those which are *zuhanden.* The former appear to have a contextless existence; whereas the latter are enmeshed in a nest of psychological and corporal presuppositions from which they cannot be grasped except in terms of the contexts or situations in which they are employed and logically embedded. Briefly, this is a matter of distinguishing between describing a tool, say, a screwdriver in the abstract and using one. Contrasting these two ways of "thinking" about the same screwdriver brings out the fact that the require ment for an abstract theory of reference by its very nature could only be a theory of the *vorhanden* and therefore had to be self-defeating. This is because the most important part of the "meaning"of the tool, i.e., its employment could not be captured in a theory about it. In fact, the use of tools is a set of activities in which the word plays a very small role. Here the similarities with Wittgenstein's builders at the beginning of the *Investigations* are too often commented upon to require mentioning. A theory of reference could not possible deal universally with the subjects of reference for our acquaintance with them is as much a part of their meaning as their description. Thus reflection on what we actually *do* with tools has a way of showing how deficient a theoretical account of their meaning must be. After the fashion or the best pragmatist analysis we come to see the superfluousness of a theory that has no consequences for practice. As Wittgenstein put it, the demand for theory here is merely a matter or ornamental coping; or as James was wont to make the point, theorizing here is holiday activity with no cash value no matter how refreshing the holiday might turn out to be.

In fact, what Heidegger was doing amounted to little less than depsychologization of Jamesian pragmatism. And in this he and the mature Wittgenstein were involved in a common undertaking albeit in quite different ways. However, this enterprise, which amounted to little less then the paradoxical task of supplying the logic and ontology lacking in James, would also serve the critical function of severing pragmatism as a philosophical position from pragmatism as a programme for personal and social edification. Briefly, the optimism of James (but also Dewey and Neurath) would give way to the scepticism or even outright pessimism of Wittgenstein and Heidegger with respect to philosophy's ability to improve the indivldual or the society. For the consistent pragmatist the question as to the improvement of the individual or society must be an open one, which philosophy by its very nature can do nothing to solve. To the extent that philosophers get involved in that task they cease *eo ipso* to be philosophers; to be a philosopher and a social reformer is a pragmatic contradiction like wanting to print money that would be of value to yourself alone or initiating a programme to destroy your successor: no matter how much you try you cannot succeed. But, however interesting, that is another story. What I allege here is that in *Being and Time* Heidegger was consciously or not making a contribution to that logic and ontology in analysing the phenomenological "moments" through which our positive action must pass. The basic problem with all of this was that Heidegger's analysis remained at an all-too abstract level in that he failed to consider (1) how that skill which enables us to use the tool fruitfully is formed and (2) how language constitutes action. Both of these matters are intimately related and it is precisely at these points that Wittgenstein immensely deepens and broadens Heideger's phenomenological critique of pragmatism.

Already in Gilbert Ryle's very detailed, often perceptive and not altogether unsympathetic review of *Being and Time*, Ryle pointed out a certain tendency to mysticism in Heidegger. To the extent that this tendency, which would later come to the fore in his thinking, is rooted in the philosophical position developed in that path-breaking book (rather than, say, pure mystagoguery or even a fundamental change of heart philosophically) I take it to be at least in part rooted in Heidegger's approach to the *zuhanden*. In the favoured terms of Ryle himself and of Clifford Geertz after him, Heidegger failed to deliver a sufficiently "thick" description of what it means for something to be *zuhhanden*. Although Heidegger nowhere says so explicitly, his view of the matter seems to be that the kind of acquaintance that we have with the tools we use is something that we cannot put into words, using tools is a wetter of experiencing them in a peculiar way as opposed to their scientific description. Like Russell, he seems to think that we cannot describe that with which we are acquainted; with Lévy-Bruhl he seems to associate the former with a certain inarticulate, intuitive pre-scientific knowledge. Put differently, description is a matter of discursive knowing whereas acquaintance is a matter of practical experience and as such defies scientific analysis. We might be able to gesture at that experience with language but we should not hope to make it articulate, i.e., discursive. For that reason in the early work of Heidegger, like that of Michael Polanyi later, everyday experience and pre-theoretical knowledge seem to take on an ineffable character which itself is foreign to everyday life. It was Wittgenstein's merit to have shown that this view is at once right and wrong.

Brian McGuinness has rightly emphasized something of the utmost importance here, namely, that Wittgenstein's attitude to philosophy was that or a *craftsman*. Unlike Heidegger, Wittgenstein never saw himself as a seeker after "deep" truths; rather, his aim was to expose the confusions implicit in traditional philosophical questioning such that the very need to question finally becomes superfluous. It was very much a matter of getting a job done in a business-like way. However much Heidegger may have admired craftsmen, he never took his interest far enough to raise the crucial epistemological questions about just how skill is formed, i.e., he never asked about how one *learns* a craft. In short, Heidegger's analysis of *Zuhandenheit* Is defective precisely because he never bothered to ask how skills are transferred. This brings us smack up against the most central insight in Wittgenstein's later philosophy, namely, the notion of following a rule.

To be sure, the crafts embody what Michael Polanyi called "tacit knowing" in that they have to be learned through repeating a specified action till it becomes "second nature". There is no algorithm for this, no short cut, no recipes in order to become, say, a master cabinet maker one must learn from someone who is already master of the skill; it cannot be learned from books alone. Written instruction is only of value after you have received a certain amount of coaching with respect to the most basic techniques that the trade requires. These skills cannot be described literally because they include things such as, say, the machinist's acquaintance with the various smells that an engine makes in various states simply have to be learned from experience. On the other hand, these skills can be described in the sense that it is possible to remind ourselves of the stages through which you have to pass if you are to master them: the novice simply does what he is told; the advanced beginner gets the job done, but awkwardly and often sloppily; the competent craftsman is no longer awkward and his product has a uniform quality; the proficient craftsman produces articles of consistently high quality; finally, the expert is the one who knows what to do when the usual methods by which high quality is produced no longer function. The whole process defies formulation in terms of precise descriptions, although there will be points at which they will play a role. However, at the high end of the scale, proficiency and expertise, the most crucial aspects of what the craftsmen know defy formulation inasmuch as they turn on sensitivity to problems as well as upon a refined sense of the distinction between those situations when the rule obtains and those which are exceptional. In explaining how it is of the essence of rule following that the rule can be followed in many different ways Wittgenstein *inter alia* helps to articulate when it in fact means to learn on the basis of practical experience alone, i.e., on the basis of being shown what action to perform and repeating it. Having developed techniques for reminding us of how human beings learn the most basic skills, Wittgenstein in fact filled in a large stretch of philosophical terrain whose outer edges had been roughly mapped by Heidegger but whose hinterland Wittgenstein was among the very first to explore. Thus one reason why Wittgenstein is important is for the value of his mature philosophy in helping us to articulate vague notions like skill and experience which in fact refer to wholly disparate sets of highly precise, often sophisticated techniques, upon which not only the crafts but natural science itself, as the brilliant analysis of Ludwig Fleck has shown rests. What this all comes down to is saying that Wittgenstein is vitally important for understanding the relationship between artificial and natural intelligence in such a way as to clarify why, for example there should be serious problems when we attempt to implement computer technology on a large scale at the workplace without first seeing to the education of those who shall employ it. Put differently, new technology Is radically dependent upon its compatibility with human modes of learning end not *vice versa*, as the Swedish Center for Working Life's "Technology, Work, Education" project has well documented over the last fifteen years. This too is a subject for a study of its own. Suffice to say that Wittgenstein's mature philosophy has been the corner stone of this research.

If Wittgenstein's later philosophy makes a crucial contribution to the "pragmatic turn" in philosophy initiated by Peirce and James, it was most explicitly in the broader context of a "linguistic turn" that Wittgenstein for the most part initiated himself. In the face of much misunderstanding this should be emphasised alongside the early Heidegger, Wittgenstein was convinced that human action is constituted through language. It is the consequences of this view of language rather than some mere interest in one subject among others that made language important for Wittgenstein. Language is important for Wittgenstein because it permeates *all* aspects of human action as well as because failure to see *how* that is the case gives rise to philosophical problems. In short, our task of explaining why Wittgenstein is important requires nothing more urgently than a discussion of the most crucial features of languages and the roots of our philosophical problems in our failure to grasp its workings.

Our starting point here has to be recognition of the revolutionary character of his mature conception or language as an *ensemble* of loosely related ways of weaving words and actions together. The first point to make about the revolutionary character of Wittgenstein's conception of language thus bears upon the idea that words, symbols and sentences are only *part* of language. Moreover, his second example of a language game, the revered builders, which we have already encountered, would seem to emphasize that they are perhaps the smallest and *least* significant part of language; for those words, symbols and sentences are only meaningful to the extent that they are embedded in actions, i.e., precisely what Heidegger termed a situation. Thus our first big philosophical mistake consists in confusing constituents of language with language itself. The second mistake is to think that there is only one way that words function, i.e., typically as representing something or other. From the very start, Wittgenstein emphasizes that the most primary linguistic function – the one upon which the others are built – is the command, i.e., learning to obey an order. Even an apparently non-linguistic procedure like learning to walk is suffused with language as the child's parent of guardian uses words and actions to order, guide, control, encourage and congratulate the child. Thus my behaviour is constituted by language even before I myself have mastered language: I learn through experience but in the first instance through the experience of others. But commanding and its cognate activities do not represent the only way of interweaving words and actions apart from representing. Take the case of pain language. Wittgenstein insists that if we take a close look at what we actually do with words when we use a phrase like "it hurts!" we discover that it functions less to express an idea than as a substitute for the cry of pain itself. This use of words involves disciplining ourselves with respect to pain in a particular way. First, we instinctively cry when we experience pain. Then we learn exclamations like "ow!" or "ouch". Finally, we learn to replace the cry of pain with conventional sentences. Thus it is contrary to Saussure that the conventional word is and is not arbitrary. In any case, no less than Heidegger, Wittgenstein insists human action is constituted through language; but unlike the mystical Heidegger, the craftsman Wittgenstein delves deeply into the question of just *how* that constituting occurs, only to discover that we play the most disparate games with language. Furthermore, the fact that the word "games" in the phrase "language games" is almost always misunderstood in that it is taken to be exclusively metaphorical, when it is in fact only partly metaphorical; for Wittgenstein emphasizes that many of our linguistic skills are first learned through playing games. Thus the very notion of language games implies that human activity is constituted linguistically – in Heidegger's phrase, speech and action are *gleichursprunglich*: you cannot expect to analyse one in terms of the other as both mentalists and behaviourists would; they are essentially, internally, and grammatically (in Wittgenstein's sense) linked to one another.

All of this brings us to the final point in this exposition, namely that the converse of the fact: (Wittgenstein himself would say it was a basic, even trivial fact) of our natural history that human action is *constituted* through language in *various* ways – is that we are constantly tempted to forget these trivia when we think about thought and action. Certain quasi-transcendental features of language, for example its surface grammar, tempts us to forget about its logical grammar, which is "deeper" (although not in the Saussure – Chomsky sense. Thus language at once constitutes our ability to act and tempts us to misunderstand ourselves when language itself becomes the object of investigation. This brings us to the crucial part of my answer to the question "Why is Wittgenstein important?". I refer to what he himself termed his ability to make thought, fly; to show us, by discovering *and inventing* language games, how the whole range of human activities is constituted by weaving words and actions together in various ways. To concentrate, therefore, upon words alone only obscures the issue. It seems that the idea of inventing fictional natural histories became increasingly the form that Wittgenstein preferred for laying bare the actual structures of our language games. It is no less clear that he took this to be a curious kind of literary activity but one whose point was clearly and exactly determined by the structure of traditional philosophical problems. Thus Wittgenstein's later philosophy in fully sundering the logic of life (logical grammar) from formal logic indicates that rational creatures are not trapped in an "iron cage" (to use Max Weber's metaphor) at the same time as insisting that our linguistic practices are anything but arbitrary. As such the mature Wittgenstein's language games with the metaphorical notion of reference they contain is an implicit critique of both Carnap *and* Quine, Chomsky *and* Skinner, Habermas *and* Derrida. This is why Wittgenstein is important.

Chapter 4

Rule-Following, Intransitive Understanding and Tacit Knowledge. An Investigation of the Wittgensteinian Concept of Practice as Regards Tacit Knowing

Kjell S. Johannessen

If a scientist is incapable of articulating the precise nature of an important discovery in chemistry, how can we consider the legitimacy of his/her claim? Traditionally, we demand that knowledge be capable of formulation in some form of language and that it be supported by experience or proven by formal means. We should also, however, examine the ways we use the terms of knowledge in different contexts, such as those informed by moral, aesthetic, legal and religious values. The concept of an exact language, in which all scientific knowledge can be articulated in an unambiguous way, is thus limited. From the tradition of propositional knowledge emerges the possibility of tacit knowledge, a form of knowledge which for logical reasons cannot be adequately articulated by linguistic means. Drawing on Wittgenstein's ideas of practice and intransitive understanding in *Philosophical Investigations*, the chapter explores the concept of rule-following as a practice and, by extension, the roles of analogy and performance in our linguistic grasp of reality.

Imagine the following situation: a scientist claims to have made an important discovery in chemistry. It turns out, however, that he is not capable of articulating the exact character of the discovery in a verbally precise manner. Neither is he able to support his knowledge claim by the traditionally accepted methods.If this should ever happen, we could be quite certain that his alleged discovery would not be taken seriously by the scientific community, even if he was formerly a highly regarded researcher. Why is it that we can be so confident about the outcome of this claim to knowledge? In the first place there is the lack of precision in his description of the possible discovery. This creates a lack of clarity about how it relates to the already established knowledge in the field. Does the contended discovery represent a further development of principles and ideas already in use or does it involve some new principle necessitating the rejection of any of the older ones? In the second place there is the lack of empirical support of the traditional and well-known kind.

This is a quite natural way of reasoning. Scientific knowledge certainly should be clearly formulated in words or symbols convincingly backed up by empirical evidence, otherwise its claim to *know* something cannot be considered legitimate. When knowledge is thought of in this way we simply take it for granted that if we are justified in maintaining that we know something, at least the following two conditions must be fulfilled:

1. Our knowledge must be capable of formulation in some language or other.
2. Our knowledge must, in a linguistically articulated version, be supported by experience or be proven by formal means.

These quite reasonable requirements were combined with the verification theory of meaning and turned into a dogma by the logical positivists, thus making scientific knowledge the paradigm of knowledge *simpliciter*. The idea of there being different kinds of knowledge, or at least different contexts and thus different constraints on the claims to know something is by implication characterised as of no intellectual value whatsoever. Considered in the light of the customary ways of talking and thinking about knowledge the logical positivist way of understanding it represents a significant narrowing down of the field in which we can legitimately maintain that we know something. Part of what this fairly narrow conception of knowledge was supposed to accomplish was to provide us with a clear-cut distinction between fact and value. If we possess anything that properly could be termed *moral* knowledge it consists wholly in the knowing of moral *facts*, whatever they may be. Moral *values* are necessarily beyond the reach of this conception of knowledge as it is the hallmark of values that they can neither be empirically justified nor formally proved. The same goes for any other kind of value. We cannot be said to *know* aesthetic, religious, legal or any other sort of human values. Wittgenstein drew the only possible conclusion in *Tractatus* when he said: "In the world everything is as it is, and every thing happens as it does happen: *in* it no value exists – and if it did, it would have no value. If there is any value that does have value, it must lie outside the whole sphere of what happens and is the case" (T 6.41).

This is a rather dismal picture of the human world. We must accept it however, if we are to accept the adequacy of the positivist paradigm, although such acceptance forces us to face the following dilemma: Either we resign ourselves to the limitations of moral and aesthetic knowledge that result from conforming to the paradigm. and hastily convince ourselves that European culture has long been on the wrong track as it has been perfectly natural to speak about knowledge in these contexts, or we start wondering about its status. If we stick to the second alternative we soon discover that the positivist conception of knowledge in no sense is the proper expression of the one and only genuine insight into the nature of knowledge. This follows from the fact that such an insight can neither be empirically establish nor formally proven. On the empirical side it simply flies in the face of the established use of the terms "know", "knowing" and "knowledge". On the formal side it became a matter of how to secure the adequacy and reliability of the chosen axioms. This cannot be done by formal means alone. Therefore it is not a matter of insight into or adequate analysis of the concept of knowledge at all. It is rather a question of producing a persuasive definition of the terms mentioned for any future use in intellectually responsible contexts. Realizing this it becomes appropriate to consider if there is any point in depriving ourselves of the right to talk about knowledge in moral, aesthetic, legal and religious contexts or whether we are better off producing a more adequate grasp of the ways we *in fact* use the terms in question in the different kinds of contexts. Such a reflection might proceed in various ways. I consider it profitable first to produce a reminder of one of the most influential conceptions of knowledge in our culture and then to take a closer look at the premises of the positivist definition attending especially to the possibility of tacit knowing.

The Aristotelian Analysis of Knowledge

In the ancient tradition we do not find any objections to talking about knowledge in the most varied fields of experience. Aristotle is an example in this respect. In his analysis of man as a moral being the intellectual virtues play a central role. As is well known they are threefold, comprising not only *episteme* (scientific knowledge in the strict sense) but also *phroneses* (practical wisdom) and *techne* (craftsmanship).[1] They are all constitutive of man as a moral being. Deprived of any one of them we should not be able to cope with the demands of the moral aspect of human existence. This became clear as soon as we realize the very limited scope of what Aristotle called scientific knowledge (episteme) This kind of knowledge deals only with strictly necessary conditions. Such conditions are said to be eternal and unalterable. This trait distinguishes *episteme* from *phronesis* and *techne*. For the latter two are both dealing with changeable conditions. *Techne*, however, is the sort of thing that can be thought and can be forgotten. This is not the case with *phronesis*. In a fundamental sense it can neither be learnt nor forgotten. If one should happen to forget one's practical wisdom, that would mean nothing less that ceasing to exist as a moral being and therefore as a responsible human being. A severe fit of madness probably would illustrate what is at stake here. A loss of one's practical wisdom – in Aristotle's sense – would mean loss of contact with the human world. It would thus fatally affect the very essence of humanity in man. The nature of practical wisdom is said to consist in *knowing* what is the morally right action in a specific situation. Such knowledge is an end in itself, in the same way that knowledge about the eternal and unalterable is an end in itself. This does not, however, apply to the possession of *techne*, as it is said to have a goal outside itself. To have *techne* is to be able to make something with a correct understanding of the principle involved. Knowledge of this kind is primarily expressed in the choice of suitable materials and in the handling of them. It is thus basically conceived as various forms of skill. For Aristotle that does not depreciate its character and status as know ledge in any way. One reason for this is that one can have a satisfactory knowledge of the thing which is to be made quite independently of actually making it in any specific case. This is not so with practical wisdom, since it is displayed in the determination of the morally right action in a specific situation. Such a determination is always a matter of reflecting upon the interplay between possible norms of action that might apply to the present case and the special features of the particular situation confronting us. Practical wisdom is thus the ability to mediate between general moral principles and the multiplicity of the possible courses of action that uniformity and consistency in the life of action must take into account when facing any particular situation. Moral knowledge embraces, in other words, not only the norm which is right in a given situation, but also how it can best be applied in the specific instance. And this is why Aristotle includes in his conception of knowledge both a discretionary component and a non-eliminative reflection with respect to the special character of the particular situation.

The Method of Language Construction and Its Presuppositions

All this complexity in the concept of knowledge is missing in the logical positivists. We should, however, remember that they are by no means alone in maintaining such a conception of knowledge. The view of the logical positivists represents only the end point of a development which began as early as the renaissance with the new scientific age. Galileo asserted that nature's book is written in the language of mathematics. This is akin to the dream of the exact language in which all scientific knowledge can be formulated in an unambiguous way. The idea of the universal language, set forth by the logical positivists, is merely our century's version of this old Leibnizian dream. Within this framework knowledge and language are woven together in an indissoluble bond. The requirement that knowledge should have a linguistic articulation becomes an unconditional demand. The possibility of possessing knowledge that cannot be wholly articulated by linguistic means emerges against such a background as completely unintelligible. Nevertheless it is the possibility of just such various kinds of tacit knowledge that is presently being explored in certain quarters concerned with the philosophy of science. It has in fact been recognized in various camps that propositional knowledge, i.e. the knowledge that is expressible by some kind of linguistic means in a propositional form, is not the only type of knowledge that is scientifically relevant.[2] Some have, therefore accepted (even if somewhat reluctantly), that it might be legitimate to talk about knowledge also in cases where it is not possible to articulate it fully by the appropriate linguistic means. In the following I will refer to this type of knowledge as tacit knowledge. Here it is important to realize that the "not possible" clause is a logical one. Tacit knowledge is thus knowledge which for logical reasons cannot be adequately articulated by linguistic means. The discretionary component in the Aristotelian conception of moral knowledge would be a case in point as there are no established principles for the application of moral principles. This example indicates that there might be something to gain from reflecting rather persistently on the application of different sorts of language rules if our aim is to clarify the specified idea of tacit knowledge. By this I do not mean the tacit knowledge of the system of rules that any competent user of a natural language is supposed to have according to Chomsky and his followers. This kind of tacit knowledge can be completely articulated by a generative theory of the language in question. This is fairly easily achieved because the theory is restricted to the aspect of sentence formation. But when it cares to explicating or establishing the conceptual content of a given sign in some language the case is different. Here there might be something like tacit knowledge in our sense at work that cannot be completely captured by the so-called semantical rules that are used for this purpose.

The logical positivists, however, saw no problem with formulating a language which could articulate in a completely perspicuous way all the knowledge that a given scientific discipline considered as established. According to Carnap and his adherents this could in fact be done very easily by specifying a language S.[3] In a simplified version such a language consists in the first place of a vocabulary which contains both logical constants and empirical variables. In the second place it consists of a very small number of formation rules or syntactic rules that unambiguously lay down the class of well-formed sentences in S. In the third place it consists of a very small number of transformation rules which specify in an unambiguous way how to move from one well-formed sentence to another in S. Fourthly, there is a quite small class of rules which connects some of the empirical variables with a fairly clearly circumscribed segment of discernible reality. These rules make up the semantical system of the language. Accordingly they are often called semantical rules. Carnap termed them correspondence rules since they performed the task of connecting the otherwise completely formal system of signs with slices of empirical reality. It is this third class of correspondence rules that interest us in this connection. They are usually said to have the following form:

The sign T can be justifiably applied if and only if the observable properties. P_1 & P_2 & P_3 & . . . P_n are simultaneously present in the perceived state of affairs.

Disagreement concerning the correct form of the rule is presently of no significance. What matters is the fact that a correspondence rule in effect represents a linguistic articulation of the conceptual content which the sign T has in the language S. And what follows from this concerning the mastery of language S? It seems that mastering S essentially consists in two different though interrelated operations: (a) being able to form well-formed sentences in S on a given segment of the empirical reality, and (b) being able to derive one well-formed sentence from another. And if we wonder what is involved in understanding a sentence in S, there is a definite answer to that: understanding a sentence in S means to know what is the case if the sentence expresses a true proposition. We thus realize that S is required to be a consistent extensional language where the (cognitive) meaning of an individual sentence can be specified quite independently of any context of use. The correspondence rules will consequently be the only link between language and reality.

These days it is no news for us that the language S is radically incomplete if it is regarded as analysis of the core of a natural language. But that is not the point in our context. I have sketched this logical-positivist interpretation of the nature of language as a reminder of how central a role the concept of a rule has for traditional philosophical analysis of language. It was in fact theories of this nature which constituted the philosophical context of Ludwig Wittgenstein's endeavours in the 1930s to find the way to a more adequate analysis of the factors that are involved when a sentence is used meaningfully on a certain occasion. An especially important result of these endeavours was what I would like to call the rediscovery of the kind of intransitive understanding and judgmental power that are necessarily tied to the competent use of language. I prefer to talk about rediscovery since Aristotle had long ago tracked down something very similar in his analysis of moral knowledge, as we have had occasion to see. The intransitive understanding and the judgmental power in question may, as I intend to show, quite legitimately be said to involve certain types of *tacit* knowledge in the sense required. Wittgenstein almost exclusively concentrated his attention on various aspects of the *use* of language. Reflections on the user's relationship to language and use situations are conspicuous by their absence in the conception of language that the logical positivists stood for. There it is only the logical form of the language system which is of central interest. This can be seen with reference to the idea of a correspondence rule sketched above. It has the form of a definition. The sign T is the *definiendum* in the definition while the specification of the observable properties represents the defining expression, which is normally called the *definiens*. The *definiens* lays down the only legitimate set of necessary and sufficient conditions for the use of the sign T. The occasion on which the definition is to be used, the purpose of the activity in which the definition has a point, etc. are not to be taken into account. The definitional strategy pursued makes no reference to any form of context. It is merely the sheer equivalence between *definiendum* and *definiens* that in the end is of interest. A definition turns out to be a rule of substitution in disguise. Thus it is really its from and nothing else that matters.

Around 1930 Wittgenstein was for a short period attracted to such an idea of the nature of language and how it is connected with reality. He discussed them with great care in his conversations with Waismann and Schlick.[4] Fairly soon, however, he came to realize that this view led up a blind alley. Too much remains obscure if one thinks of language along these lines. We might get a glimpse of the surface of the hidden dimension if we reflect a little on the act of formulating an artificial language of type S. We discover for instance immediately that we have to do with a certain type of human *action*, something that is so obvious that we are almost forced to overlook it. But it is extremely important for an adequate understanding of how language and reality is related to realize that language and human action are so intimately interwoven, especially if we are interested in understanding how it was possible to form, apply and transmit the conceptual resources contained in S in the first place. Actions involving the use of language have, like all other human actions, both definite aims and various kinds of presuppositions. Sometimes the aims are misconceived and the presuppositions forgotten. That is most certainly what happened in this case. Naturally, it is not in itself a misconception to attempt to improve our understanding of the nature of natural languages, but when we examine the character and the presuppositions of this approach it becomes self-evident that we must draw on conceptual resources already at hand to construct a language of type S. These resources are what we need to understand better and they have no obvious similarity to the constructed languages and the way they are *made* to connect with reality in the form of correspondence rules. To analyse a constructed language with the aim of increasing our understanding of the essence of natural languages is thus the equivalent of studying the cart in the hope of learning something of importance about the horse which pulls it. The method of construction, however, gives the impression of being both scientific and reliable. In addition it has certain rationale insofar as one wishes to investigate foundational problems in mathematics and their relevance for an axiomatic ordering of the already established scientific knowledge in a given discipline. This approach thus holds no promise whatsoever when it is a question of understanding the nature of natural languages and how they are related to reality. Wittgenstein spends a lot of tine and intellectual energy, as can be seen in the first part of his *Philosophical Investigations*, in trying to spell out its misbegotten character. This is not, however, the place to develop his criticism on a larger scale.[5] For our purposes it is enough to concentrate on the problems connected with the idea of correspondence (semantic) rules and the uncovering of their hidden presuppositions. Especial emphasis will be given to the question of spotting the phenomena of intransitive understanding and the exercise of judgmental power as the expression of tacit knowledge when rule-following behaviour comes up for scrutiny. To make the presentation more efficient I shall enumerate what I consider to be the most significant points in his alternative position:

1. To formulate a correspondence rule is to carry out a definitional action which makes use of conceptual resources that have already been developed.
2. If one is to attempt to understand the specific character of natural languages one must Investigate the conditions for forming the original conceptual tools to be found in them.
3. This is best done by studying the situations where the concepts are taught and explained. This is the key to uncovering the basic clues which the competent language user draws on when employing the acquired concepts.
4. A definition or a semantic rule can be applied in different ways. Even a flawless definition gives no recipe as to how it should be used.
5. We must, of course, make a fairly sharp distinction between the definition itself (or the rule understood as a logical form) and the application it is possible to make of it.
6. In addition, every definition is always applied in a space of presuppositions which are not themselves traceable in the linguistic expression of the definition. This is due to the fact that the very act of applying the

definition springs from a much richer source than the understanding of the isolated verbal expression of *this* particular definition. It is done on the basis of a more or less holistic understanding of language.

7. The totality of these presuppositions cannot itself assume the form of a definition or set of definitions. The vantage point for carrying out the definitional action would then be eliminated, and would in its turn make such actions impossible.
8. In the final instance there cannot be rules that lay down how a semantic rule or a definition should be applied. The application of a definition (semantic rule) is and must necessarily be performed without the support of any further rules.
9. The application of semantic rules and definitions is not how ever, a completely spontaneous and unfounded reaction. It is anchored in a kind of experience having the character of *intransitive* understanding and *judgmental* power that in a logical sense cannot be cast in the form of propositional knowledge or articulated as a system of rules.
10. This aspect of our grasp of a natural language is thus said to have a *tacit* dimension that should not be overlooked when one tries to understand how language and reality is connected. As we shall have occasion to see later, Wittgenstein is using the concept of *practice* to pinpoint this very element in our linguistic grasp of reality.

This point-by-point summary of some of the main traits of Wittgenstein's views on rule-following as they pertain to the problem of tacit knowing, gives a certain indication as to the direction his later philosophy was taking. What is most striking is perhaps his turning away from dealing with rules and their logical form to investigating what it means to *follow* rules. In this way the application of the rule and the very nature of the situation of the user become the focus of his philosophical interest. This is often called the *pragmatic turn.* Since one and the same rule can be followed in different ways, the correspondence rules cannot constitute the meaning of the empirical concepts and thus mediate between language and reality. What guarantees that a rule is followed in the same way time after time cannot itself be a rule at all. It must in the end depend upon our actions and different kinds of spontaneous reactions, giving rise to what Wittgenstein once himself called intransitive understanding. This is the deeper significance of his remark that rule-following is a *practice.*[6] This concept is one of the key concepts in his later philosophy. We meet here most of the themes that dominated his thinking during this period. It is therefore not unreasonable to consider his later philosophy as a kind of *practice* philosophy, if by this term we mean all philosophy that operates from the insight that there exists a complicated network of mutually constitutive relations between concept formation, human reactions and activities, and what we call *our* reality. To learn to master a natural language is in this perspective not to learn how to formulate well-formed sentences on the basis of syntactical rules and with the help of language signs which via correspondence rules (semantic rules) are tied to a certain segment of reality. It is instead to learn to master an enormously large repertoire of situations where use of language is included in an exceedingly varied, but non-eliminable way. In other words, it is a matter of mastering human reality in all its complexity; learning to adopt an attitude towards it; reflecting over it; investigating it; gaining a foothold in it, and thus becoming familiar with it. This, then, is the background for maintaining that there exists an inner or internal relationship between concept formation, forms of human reactions and activities, and the reality which emerges as *our* reality by virtue of the concepts we have formed about it.

Practice as the Expression of Intransitive Understanding and Judgmental Power

If this interpretative sketch points in the right direction, and I am quite convinced it does, it will obviously pay to take a closer look at Wittgenstein's concept of *practice* and what goes with it. But first we must note that a much wider concept of language is at work here than the one we have met with in the logical positivists. Wittgenstein includes such things as gestures, facial expressions, posture, the atmosphere of the occasion; situationally determined actions as, for example, smiling and nodding to an acquaintance; turning one's back on somebody and going off without saying a word; standing on the quay and waving goodbye to friends; sitting in a restaurant and making a discreet sign that the waiter's presence is desired; attending an auction and making an offer with a little hand movement, and so on. This extended concept of language is aimed at capturing *all* the means we use in our day-to-day situations to make ourselves understood. In the pragmatic perspective it is quite natural to make such things part of the concept of language. They are all means of making sense of the situations in which we use or react to a sentence with understanding. If this seems far-fetched one need only remind oneself of the fact that a sentence does not declare that it is to be taken as, say, an assertion. Other elements in the situation must be understood in a certain way if this is to be the natural response to it. The very same sentence could in different contexts express quite another thought-content. Take for instance the sentence: "Laurence Olivier was convincing as Hamlet". It may be used to convey many different types of thought-content depending upon the wider context in which it is employed. Let me indicate just a few of them here:

1. It could be used to convey a description of his interpretation of the Hamlet role in the contextually implied production.
2. It could be used to give expression to a certain interpretation of his performance in a naturalistic perspective.
3. It could be used to evaluate both his interpretation of the role and his performance of it.

These are very different types of thought-content that should be kept apart lest confusion should arise. But if we do not know the necessary details of the intended use-situation, we will not be able to make up our minds about what is actually said. From this follows that our mastery of a natural language must include a kind of grasp or practical understanding of an enormously large repertoire of situations involving the use of language. One must know what is going on in a specific case, and that kind of knowledge cannot be gained from any sort of linguistic inventory. The adequate use of language and the appropriate response to it requires a situational understanding and a judgmental that far transcends what can be derived from the meaning immanent in the sentence alone. This is one of the reasons why Wittgenstein urges us to investigate the use of language. That will lead us to the discovery of the necessary interplay between the sentence form and the character of the situation in which it is applied.

This reminder brings us back to Wittgenstein's conception of practice which incorporates what he considers to be of importance in the analysis of rule-following activities. This conception draws attention precisely to the factors that are constitutive of meaning in situations involving the use of language in a non-eliminable way. One of the more surprising things that surfaces in this respect is that the very exercise of might be a constitutive part of the formation of concepts. The content of a concept can thus be regarded as a function of the established use of its expression.[7] The exercise of a given practice is consequently to be taken as a necessary element as regards the expression of a concept. To document that one does in fact master a given concept one has to be accepted as a competent performer of the series of established activities or practices which incorporates the concept. The practice can thus be said to represent the *application* of the concept. This yields the following principle of conceptual mastery: the grasp a given concept gives us on the world is expressed adequately only in practice. It is our application or practice which shows how we understand something. That is what Wittgenstein has in mind when in his lapidary style he maintains that "practices give words their meaning".[8]

This point gives us an opportunity to make some fairly basic observations. The first is concerned with the problem of how the identity of rules is secured over time. What guarantees that a principle, a law, a norm, a concept, in short everything which Wittgenstein calls a *rule*, is applied in the same way from one time to another and from one person to another? We have already seen that the rule itself cannot give such a guarantee. According to Wittgenstein it is the exercise of the established set of practices that gives this guarantee. The identity is secured through the application insofar as it has the character of an established practice. And the requisite mastery of the application can only be acquired through a guided exercise of the established set of activities that make up the accepted use of the rule.

The second observation which can be made in connection with Wittgenstein's conception of the established practices as constitutive of meaning has to do with the main theme of this article – forms of intransitive understanding and their expression of tacit knowledge in the sense sketched. Against the outlined background it should no longer represent a problem to talk about rules or concepts which can be formulated only incompletely as regards content, at least when it is a question of formulating the content by verbal means. We have just noted that the criterion for their adequate mastery lies principally in their application. The knowledge which is built into that mastery can consequently be considered to have a partial and non-reducible expression in action. Therefore it is not possible to put into words this aspect of action in which the intellectually explicable part of the concept is necessarily embedded. There is however, no need to be alarmed by this observation as regards the means for checking that a person does in fact possess an adequate grasp of a given concept. Since it is always possible to instruct and guide the person who attempts to acquire an acceptable mastery of the practices in which the concept in question is embedded, we also have at all times sufficient intellectual control both of the possession and of the conceptual content. It is therefore neither far-fetched nor shocking to maintain that concepts exist, as well as other form of rules, which can only be articulated incompletely by verbal means, but which nevertheless are fully usable tools both in our scientific investigation of reality and in ordinary communication. Concepts of this kind can be demonstrated in a number of different contexts. They are, however, more easily spotted in some contexts than in others. In particular I have in mind the aesthetic, moral and judicial fields of experience. Here it is easier than elsewhere to come to see how different situational elements turn out to be constitutive of the meaning that we attribute to a certain sentence used on a given occasion. Let us pick aesthetics as a particularly well-suited area for illustrative purposes. It is, for example, not possible to formulate necessary and sufficient conditions for the use of the linguistic expression of a certain concept of artistic style. The term "mannerism" will do as an example. We can only learn to master this term in an adequate way if we obtain a broad first-hand experience of typical instances of manneristic paintings at the same time as we learn through expert guidance to recognize the visual physiognomy that characterizes them. Here, then, we cannot manage without the requisite first-hand experience. Nor can we free ourselves from the prototypical examples, because they provide us with the paradigmatic physiognomy that constitute a non-eliminable part of the concept of Mannerism. No description can take the place of the first-hand experience of the paradigm cases of the manneristic physiognomy. Examples and first-hand experience are thus shown to be constitutive elements in the formation of the concept of mannerism.

To be able to spot a judgmental component we can develop this example further. Let us say that you have proved to the community of art historians that you have a sufficient grasp of the concept of mannerism as it is developed on the basis of the chosen paradigmatic paintings and the accompanying commentaries from the experts that make you perceive the physiognomy of the painting in the intended way. You have secured a job in a museum where you have to act in the capacity of an expert on manneristic paintings if required. Then somebody presents you with a totally unknown painting from the period in question (Italian painting between 1520 and 1600) which in some respects seems to you to be quite similar to the physiognomy of the paradigm that makeup your first-hand perceptual knowledge of what a manneristic painting is. Some of the less salient features are, on the other hand, not particularly reminiscent of the constitutive paradigmatic examples. Furthermore, it is beyond reasonable doubt that the painting stems from the right period, it has an unquestionably Italian look, but it turns out to impossible to attribute it to any of the well known manneristic painters. The task at hand is now to decide whether it can justifiably be called manneristic or not. Whatever decision you make, there will always be a judgmental component at work when applying concepts in this kind of context. The concept in question is *inherently* dependent on such a component in this sort of application as there does not exist a list of descriptions that is both necessary and sufficient for deciding the matter. A given application is therefore bound to be contestable as W.B. Gallie pointed out a long tine ago concerning the concept of art.[9] But that does not depreciate its value as a tool of research in art history. Everything relevant to its application lies open to view. It can be checked at any time by those who have acquired the relevant kind of experience, the experience you gather by being exposed to the paradigmatic paintings and equipped with the expert commentaries. The decision actually made will, however, substantially affect any future application of the concept. If accepted it gets the character of a correct judgment and as such it will be incorporated in the research tradition as a possible object of comparison on future occasions of applying the concept of mannerism. In this way the correct judgment has become one of the means by which the art historians steer their course through the ocean of renaissance paintings. It has thus became constitutive of the sense of the concept.

But what about the activity aspect that we stressed rather earlier on? That can be seen in such things as correctly identifying the paintings in question, making the right sort of commentary about them, producing enlightening comparisons if asked, etc. This is the kind of activity that necessarily involves application of the acquired concept of mannerism. It has in fact very little to do with forming syntactically well-formed sentences by the term "mannerism". And part of what you learnt when acquiring the *concept* of mannerism is not susceptible to articulation by verbal means. It has to be conveyed by examples and by expert guidance during an extended period of training. The importance of examples, correct judgments, and first-hand experience whose role can be only partially articulated is, however, not confined to the fields of aesthetics, morals and jurisprudence. We also find it where the logical positivists felt most at home, that is to say in physics. When Thomas S. Kuhn maintains that a paradigm – in the limited sense of "exemplary past achievements" – can guide research without the existence of formulated theories, general laws or rules of method it is this very aspect of the possession of a concept that he has in mind.[10] In his own opinion it belongs to "the most novel and least understood aspect" of his book;[11] that is no doubt an apt judgment. Let us see if it is possible to substantiate the above account on the basis of what Kuhn has to say on this matter. To accomplish that within a reasonable amount of space I have to presuppose a general knowledge of his position.

Kuhn has taken the application aspect of concepts very seriously, probably inspired by his many, long and intricate discussions with Stanley Cavell concerning these matters. This resulted in a pragmatic conception of the growth of scientific knowledge which emphasizes the unavoidable presence of a tacit component in our grasp of reality. This comes about in the following way. A model solution to a basic scientific problem represents, according to Kuhn, an application of a scientific theory or law. Independently of this application neither theories nor laws have any concrete meaning. The model problem solutions – by virtue of being examples of applications of theories and laws – lay down the specific kind of cognitive content that pertain to them alone. Accordingly both theories and laws are primarily understood in terms of their applications and *cannot* be wholly understood independently of them. This makes the model problem solutions constitutive of the adequate understanding of scientific theories and laws. They represent in short the use situations for any kind of universal statement in a given scientific discipline. As such they also give promise that the same kind of procedure can be used to solve pressing problems elsewhere in the same or related fields of research. But in no way does there exist any identity between the original problem situation where the model solution is found and the undetermined area of possible future applications This relation is more a matter of a kind of homogeneity, which according to Kuhn can best be characterized as a *family resemblance,* a term he borrows from Wittgenstein. Consequently the applied theories and laws cannot be regarded as completely finished scientific products; they must rather be considered as kinds of schemata which are bearers of an indeterminate number of future applications. Kuhn uses here as an example Newton's second law, "$f = ma$", and shows how it is given different formulations when working with mutually different but nevertheless related problems. We thus realize that even here articulation is necessarily a partial matter. It turns out that there is no such thing as a complete formulation of the conditions for the use of scientific theories and laws – not even in relation to a given application of them since here we shall have to take into account the tacit components embedded in the existing research tradition to which the individual researcher belongs. This indicates the next step in our investigations. What is involved in the competent exercise of the established research tradition – besides learning by heart a series of formulas and abstract symbolic expressions?

Kuhn's point of view gives us the opportunity to scrutinize this question in a more thorough way than we have done so far. The crux of the matter is, of course, his explanation of how researchers are enabled to recognize the family resemblance that is said to exist between different problem situations. The answer, he gives us to understand, lies in looking closer at the role the model problem solutions play in the training of researchers. In passing we may note that this strategy is completely in keeping with Wittgenstein's advice to deal with the situations where the teaching or explaining of concepts takes place, as mentioned in point (3) above. When looking at what is going on here, we discover, according to Kuhn, that students acquire the relevant scientific concepts by learning to carry out experiments which either are part of or are decided by the model solutions. This is how they get to know nature's behaviour in the field of research in question. Expert knowledge and linguistic knowledge are thus necessarily intertwined and emerge as two sides of the same coin in the pragmatic perspective as developed here by Kuhn. And I do subscribe to that part of it which concerns the nature and mode of operation of our concepts in scientific contexts. To acquire a concept is to develop a certain grasp of a slice of reality. A gradual and simultaneous acquiring of both aspects takes place. In the course of this learning process the students build up a certain familiarity with the discipline's approaches to problems as they appear in the light of the regnant model for problem solving in the research field in question. This familiarity is the reward of experience. It also comprises training in a certain aptitude for seeing the similarities between different kinds of problem situations, even if on any points they are quite different. Thus likenesses of this sort may be said to have an *analogical* character. The initiating problem situation to which the newcomers to the discipline are exposed aims to build up the sort of experience and problem familiarity which later make it possible for the ready trained researcher to function creatively on the research front. But of course my main point is that the ability to display reactions which are adequate to the situation and develop an eye for the analogous features in the new problem situation cannot be put into rules of method or in any other way features established or articulated by verbal means. The receptiveness to new applications of the shared paradigm represents a form of competence which is inextricably linked with acquiring the particular discipline's concepts, theories and laws. This sort of competence cannot be established independently of learning to master them. It is, however, made invisible when one limits attention to the *de facto* articulated concepts, theories and laws and forget to ask what it takes to be a competent *user* of them. That is why it is important to keep insisting on the need to investigate the *application* of concepts and theories. Herein lies the interesting material.

Further Aspects of the Mastery of Practices and Tacit Knowing

We have now elaborated a little on the question of what role experience plays in connection with the application of concepts in various fields. It has also been shown that there much more to the competent handling of concepts than an understanding of their intellectual or verbally articulable content. But the mode of presentation may have given the impression that the previous remarks mainly concern singular concepts considered in isolation from the rest of the language. That is not intended and the sequel therefore aims both to prove that impression wrong and to comment in more detail on that very fertile concept of practice that is gradually coming to the fore in Wittgenstein's latest writings.

We have already more than once hinted at a much wider perspective, for instance in the point-by-point summary of Wittgenstein's criticism of the logical positivist conception of language and meaning (cf. points (6) and (7)). We have also indicated that human reactions as well as established human activities are, in general to be considered as the context and background for the formation and development of the conceptual resources in natural languages. This is where it may be profitable to start elaborating upon the question of the interelatedness of practices. A point of departure as good as any is the earlier remark that the offering as well as the application of a definition take place within presuppositions of a holistic character. Wittgenstein puts this point in a general way by saying that "(t)o understand a sentence means to understand a language".[12] Language is here thought of as a kind of integrated whole in which a particular sentence gets its meaning.

Understanding a sentence cannot be any isolated or chance happening. One must have a certain understanding of the language as a whole to be able to grasp the meaning of a particular sentence in a given situation. In fact Wittgenstein himself suggests somewhat hesitantly, that this overarching understanding of language is constitutive of the very meaningfulness of the individual sentence: "the understanding of language ... seems like a background against which a particular sentence acquires meaning".[13] To the conventionally minded this understanding has however a most peculiar character. The following comparison is made by Wittgenstein to emphasize its most salient feature: "The understanding of language ... is ... of the same kind as the understanding or mastery of a calculus, something like the *ability* to multiply".[14] Once more we get an indication that there is a kind of understanding that is an integrated part of being a competent user of language, but which cannot be expressed *by* language. This is what I have chosen to call *intransitive* understanding. It is internally related to this overarching grasp of language, that is only adequately expressed in the competent exercise of the manifold of practices that constitute human language. Only by having a sufficient mastery of this manifold can one be said to understand the particular rules that could be abstracted from the various practices.

From this it follows that a given practice cannot be thought of as an isolated monad, such as Karl Otto Apel and Jürgen Habermas presuppose in their criticism of Wittgenstein. One cannot after all decide the identity of a given practice exclusively from the rules that were possible to formulate on the basis of observing the linguistic habits of people who successfully participate in the established manifold of practices. If we come to a foreign culture and see two persons seated on each side of a quadrangular board which is divided into 64 squares and on the board there are placed pieces resembling chessmen, we cannot for this reason conclude that these people are playing chess. What they are doing could just as well be part of a religious or magical ritual. It is only when we see what happens, let us say, at the outcome of the activity that it is possible to decide reasonably whether it is a game or not. Practices having the character of game are integrated in the culture in ways quite different from religious and magical practices. By virtue of these contextual relations all practices are shown to be necessarily integrated entities. To establish the identity of a particular practice cannot thus be done solely on the basis of the semantic rules assumed to be immanent in it. Its relations to the surrounding practices have to be included in any reliable procedure for establishing the identity of practices. We thus see that the interrelated manifold of widely different practices makes up one single though variegated whole. Mastery of a particular practice can therefore be regarded as a fragmentary expression of an overarching and comprehensive understanding of reality, which is common to the participants of the language community. And to have a common language is for Wittgenstein to share a form of life, because "to imagine a language is to imagine a form of life".[15] The expression "form of life" is, as is by now well known, one of the quasi-technical terms in Wittgenstein's later philosophy.[16] But it does not mean anything obscure or hidden. It is just one of many literary means he is using to make us look in a certain direction when reflecting upon the character and function of natural languages. It signifies what he regards as the rock bottom of such reflections, what has to be accepted as the *given*.[17] It is a matter of making us realize that there is such a thing as a right *place* for the human language – amidst the human tasks and activities with their accompanying expectations and disappointments. The idea of there being a right place for something he also utilizes in another connection where he makes the striking aphoristic remark "A smiling mouth smiles only in a human face".[18] A smile is a smile only in the context of a human face. In this way he makes the point that hoping is a phenomenon which can only occur in human life – essentially the same point he makes concerning language in general by talking about forms of life. He is gesturing towards something fundamental in the sense we give to linguistic signs.

Similar expressions would have done equally well. This is seen from his remark that "(l)anguage, I should like to say, relates to a *way* of living". The same basic point is made. Beyond the totality of established practices there exists no meaningful relationship about which we can have an understanding. It seems, however, that this is a difficult point to grasp, especially for his philosophical antagonists. It has been taken to imply that language is a kind of cultural prison-house from which it is impossible to escape in the sense that no contact with different cultural prison-houses can be established, and thus making transcultural and historical knowledge unattainable in principle. This however misses the point. Certainly, the human form of life as a complex totality of variegated but interrelated practices does develop and change. It is historically situated and in continual movement in the sense that coinage of new concepts unceasingly continues. This means admittedly, a definite limit to the attempts at understanding foreign cultures, but only in the sense that it reminds you that no intellectual endeavour to understand something foreign to our own culture is without its presuppositions. All this is, however, beside the point Wittgenstein is making. For he is talking about what goes into making *sense* in general, in *any* kind of cultural context. That is why he is most anxious to insist that "(l)anguage did not emerge from some kind of ratiocination".[20] It has no rational foundation. It is in fact founded in various form of human *reactions*, according to Wittgenstein. That becomes clear from his often quoted remark: "The origin and the primitive form of the language game is a reaction; only from this can more complicated forms develop. Language – I want to say – is a refinement, 'in the beginning was the deed'".[21] This remark can be interpreted in very different ways: (1) as a genetical comment on the origin and development of language; (2) as a *logico-grammatical* remark concerning the nature of human language. Only the second one is in keeping with Wittgenstein's philosophical method. On the second interpretation this remark is directed to the role reactions play in making various kinds of signs meaningful vehicles of human communication. It is required of us that we not only react unreflectively towards certain features in our surroundings, we also have to react in the *same* way to them. There must be a level in our sense-making activities where our reactions do not spring from any kind of reflection or reasoning. They have to be *immediate* responses to the world surrounding us. This is another aspect of the phenomenon of intransitive understanding. It is normally expressed in the certainty with which we act to a particular situation. Our reactions to human faces, sources of sounds and the direction of a pointing finger are examples Wittgenstein himself uses in this connection. We have already met with one version of this idea when we investigated the example of forming the concept of mannerism in art history. Here it was said that one could not do without a first-hand exposure to the paintings chosen accompanied by the guiding commentaries from an expert. In the first-hand exposure we are supposed to respond to the physiognomy of the particular manneristic paintings. Without this element of experience the guiding commentaries from the experts make no sense at all. Our reactions became more and more refined as time goes by but the immediate and unreflective familiarity with the particular physiognomies of the various manneristic paintings can never be dropped. If our memory of them, through some accident or other, should happen to be erased, talk about such paintings will no longer mean anything to us. This point does not, however, apply only to concepts employed in the aesthetic area. According to Wittgenstein the same holds, *mutatis mutandis*, for the application, i.e., the understanding, of all kinds of empirical concepts. There is an element of immediacy and unreflective familiarity connected with the application of concepts in all the variegated fields of experience. Without this inborn responsiveness to the empirical surroundings we would not be able to develop a stable and consistent system of meaningful signs. There would be nothing to mediate between the abstract and verbally articulable content of the concept and the particular case which is a probable candidate for being subsumed under it. Wittgenstein more than once complained about "the contemptuous attitude towards the particular case" in contemporary philosophy. The point just sketched is often overlooked when one heeds nothing but the rule or the intellectual content of the concept. In a fundamental sense *works of art* are also particular cases,hence their unique philosophical interest to Wittgenstein.To reflect upon our responses to works of art makes it possible to point out in a very obvious way what goes on when we confront particulars. This explains his frequent and little understood comparisons between understanding a proposition and understanding a work of art; a melody, a painting and a poem are the examples he is using. He gives us to understand that the similarities between these two types of understanding are much more extensive then we are ordinarily inclined to believe. Furthermore, reflections on the particular case are also internally related to the teaching of concepts since in the ultimate case there is nothing else to go by except our own immediate and unreflective responses to the examples given. We have already had occasion to see that examples are indispensable in the *forming* of a concept. Something similar is the case also in *teaching* them. There is an obvious limit to how far it is possible for us to explain the meaning of a word with the help of other words. We come in fact quite quickly to a point where we are forced to explain the word's meaning through examples and training in its use. Here at this rock bottom level the appropriateness of the examples and the character of our responses are non-eliminable. The interplay between them is providing something that descriptions or rules are incapable of doing. This is why Wittgenstein says that "(n)ot only rules, but also examples are needed for establishing a practice. Our rules leave loop-holes open, and the practice has to speak for itself".[22] But examples could not accomplish what is here expected of them if there were not a kind of agreement in our reactions to them, as noted earlier. That is an important part of the point Wittgenstein is making when he says in *Philosophical Investigations* that "there must be agreement not only in definitions but also (queer as this may sound) in judgments" if language is going to be a means of communication.[23] The term "agreement in judgment" covers a series of different but interrelated cases from instinctive and spontaneous to more refined and developed reactions towards the empirical world – the common element being the fundamental fact that there are no rules or principles to go by when we react.

This point has also been put by Wittgenstein as an argument against the possibility of formulating rules for the application of rules. The idea is simple, but fundamental. We have already seen that a definition or the expression of a rule cannot itself determine how it is to be applied as it can be interpreted in various ways. From this it follows that there can be no point in formulating a new rule that lays down how the first is to be applied. For then the same problem will arise once more in connection with the expression of the new rule. It can again be taken or understood in various ways. Thus it will go on *ad infinitum* if we try to escape from the tangle by this route. At one stage there thus has to be cases of rule-application which are not determined by other rules. The application of rules is accordingly, in principle, ruleless. This is what stops us from "establishing a practice by rules alone". The examples are indeed indispensable; and they must function by virtue of themselves, for they must show what the rules cannot state – how they are to be reacted to or handled, i.e. understood as expressed in practice. There is in fact nothing else one can use for help in those basic situations where one learns language – apart from the guidance which is given in connection with the examples. This is the deeper reason for regarding our agreement in reactions as of signs in human communication. But this point has another and rather interesting aspect which concerns the intransitive understanding that is acquired by getting the knack in rule following. For what we know when we know how to apply a given rule can in its turn only be conveyed to others by the help of examples and hints about how they should be handled. If a practice is dependent on our reacting adequately to the given examples for it to be established at all, there must be certain forms of reaction which in themselves are not of an intellectual nature, but which are a necessary part of the formation of concepts in all fields of experience. It is thus an essential part of sense-making in general.

But let us now change from examples to ways of understanding, i.e. following rules. Approached from this angle it is also possible to locate an element of immediacy and unreflective familiarity. Here the determination of sense will allow us to document the importance Wittgenstein attaches to the practice-aspect of rules. In the middle of his discussion of rule-following in *Philosophical Investigations* he sketches a tangle that results if one gives in to the temptation of looking upon rules as something that determines our ways of acting. Then a particular action must be regarded as an expression of the way in which we interpret the rule in question and we may truly be said to act according to rules. This yields, however a conceptual conflict that is described in the following way: "No course of action could be determined by a rule, because every course of action can be made out to accord with the rule. ... (I)f everything can be made out to accord with a rule, it can also be made to conflict with it. And so there would be neither accord nor conflict here".[24] This shows the full extent of the predicament we find ourselves in if acting according to rules is thought to involve an understanding of the rules that has the character of interpretation. In a concrete situation the following would be the case: whatever we do is, in one interpretation, in accord with the rule, and on another interpretation it is in conflict with the very same rule. Such an outcome is, of course, intolerable. Wittgenstein's way out of the quandary is to insist that "there is a way of grasping a rule which is *not* an *interpretation*, but which is exhibited in what we call "obeying a rule" and "going against it" in actual cases (original emphasis).[25] Hence we must resist the temptation to think that every kind of action according to rules is a matter of interpretative understanding of the rules since this creates a logically impossible situation. Wittgenstein's alternative is a kind of understanding that is expressed in *acting* in specific cases. That is why in the following paragraph he concludes: "hence also following a rule is a practice".[26]

This argument is placed at the end of a series of logico-grammatical remarks concerning different aspects of rule-following activities, most of which we have to leave untouched here. Our aim is to see what kind of role the concept of practice is made to play in this context and how that is related to the question of intransitive understanding. For this purpose it is relevant to note that interpretation and practice are made out to be opposites by Wittgenstein. Interpretation involves conscious intellectual activity. To interpret is to form a hypothesis. But such a hypothesis or interpretation can in no way be said to *determine* meaning since it *qua hypothesis* must be given explicit verbal form and as such is liable to various interpretations. At some point, though, it must be possible to indicate what does determine meaning, otherwise we are caught in a vicious circle. It is exactly at this point that the concept of practice is called upon to do its job. In one place Wittgenstein simply notes that "(p)ractice gives words their meaning". That is why "the practice has to speak for itself". There can be no question of *articulating* that particular aspect of rule-following which simply consists in *performing* the set of activities that make up the established practice. And the acceptable performance is a result primarily of the response elicited by the examples used when the concept in question was first acquired and the kind of training that the learner was exposed to. We have, however, noted earlier that acquiring the mastery of a conceptual practice also involves acquiring a certain kind of experience that plays a guiding role in new applications of the concept. We are, so to speak, able to perceive that the standard conditions for the use of a given concept are present without being capable completely to account for this skill by verbal means only. This is at least part of what Wittgenstein has in mind when in *On Certainty* he remarks that "we recognize normal circumstances but cannot precisely describe them".[27] In none of these situations, however, is there any need for an interpretation of the rule to explain why we go on acting or applying the concept in question in the intended way. We both can and do manage quite well without such an interpretation. Still, there is a sort of understanding involved in these cases. We *do* in fact notice that the standard conditions for the application of given concepts are present. We would not have been able to do this if we did not possess responsiveness to the surround and had the occasion to profit from the training given. This intransitive understanding expressed in the proper performance of the established practices of a language society might thus, not inappropriately, be looked upon as a sort of *tacit* knowing, a way of knowing how to recognize conditions for the use of a concept, how to respond to them, how develop the use on the basis of them, how to abstain from the application of the concept in certain cases, and so on. In many respects this tacit knowledge element embedded in our conceptual competence is similar to what Kant pointed out and called a *talent*, the gift of being able to reach a reasonable decision in cases of subsumption. The traditional name for it is, of course, *judgment*. This is why I discussed judgmental power earlier on. But the talk about judgment in the traditional sense is prone to produce mental barriers in people and thus put an end to the discussion before it has developed. It is Wittgenstein's merit to have made us look once more on this most peculiar phenomenon of mastering a human language and what goes with it. In the process we have been able to make one or two discoveries that may improve our understanding of what is involved here, especially as concerns *intransitive* understanding or *tacit* knowing.

Notes

1 Aristotle discusses this threefold distinction in his best known work, *The Nichomcheanethics*, book VI.

2 In particular here I am thinking of various philosophers in the hermeneutical tradition in the wide sense, for instance people like Hubert Dreyfus, Charles Taylor and Isaiah Berlin. The latter insists on the importance of what he calls "knowledge of life", a kind of knowledge we are said to describe in term of "general laws which cannot possibly all be rendered explicit" and the possession of which be of vital importance to historians. See his justly famous article "The concept of scientific history", reprinted in his collections of philosophical essays, *Concepts and categories*, Oxford, 1980, p 128. But I have also in mind people from the Wittgenstein tradition in the philosophy of science, Thomas S. Kuhn, Georg H. von Wright and Allan Janik. In addition there is, of course, Michael Polanyi and his adherents, the man who coined the term "tacit knowing" in his main epistemological work, *Personal knowledge*, London and Chicago,1958.

3 See, for example, Carnap, Rudolf (1942) *Introduction to semantics*, Cambridge, Mass, chaps ii and iii. My presentation here is substantially simplified but correct in the essentials.

4 See in this connection, Waismann, Friedrich (1979) *Ludwig Wittgenstein and the Vienna Circle, Oxford.*

5 Cf my study, *Wittgenstein's later philosophy. An interpretative sketch*, Stencil series no 42, Department of Philosophy, University of Bergen, Bergen, 1978. Concerning the implications of Wittgenstein's pragmatic turn for the philosophy of science, I have outlined them in my book, *Tradisjoner og skoler i moderne vitenskapsfilosofi (Traditions and schools in modern philosophy of science)*, Bergen,1985, Chap IV.

6 This is a remark that occurs in the middle of his discussion of rule-following in his major work, *Philosophical Investigations*, Blackwell, Oxford, 1953, Sect 202.

7 There is some need for caution in the way of expressing this point as the traditional understanding of rules and concepts takes it for granted that the rules and concepts can be articulated in their entirety. When in the above text I have put rule and formulateable conceptual content more or less on an equal basis, this has been a concession to the tradition in the name of convenience.At this point I wish to draw attention to the fact that for Wittgenstein there is also such a thing as a *rule* that can only be partially articulated. Accordingly, we can talk about rules and thus about rule-following activities also when we cannot articulate the rule itself completely

by verbal means, and not only when it concerns the very *performing* of the practice in question. Consequently we shall have to distinguish between that type of intransitive understanding which in general is attached to the application of concepts and the one that is a function of the logical character of the rule or concept itself. There exists a sort of family resemblance between these two types of intransitive understanding, but they have different sources and are thus different in kind.

8 This remark is to be found in a manuscript that for some obscure reason has been published as two different books, *On certainty*, Blackwell, Oxford, 1969, and *Remarks on colour*, Blackwell, Oxford, 1977. In the published material it turns up as Sect 317 in *Remarks on Colour*.

9 Gallie, WB (1956) Art as an essentially contested concept, The *Philosophical Quarterly*, 6. årgang, no. 23, April.

10 Kuhn, Thomas, S. (1970), *The structure of scientific revolutions*, revised edition with postscript, Chicago, p 42. Originally published 1962.

11 *Ibid*, p 187.

12 Wittgenstein (1953), Sect 199.

13 Wittgenstein (1975), *Philosophical remarks*, p 50. Blackwell, Oxford,

14 Wittgenstein (1975), p 50.

15 Wittgenstein (1953), Sect 19.

16 Even if it has been very much discussed it occurs only five times in *Philosophical investigations*. Neither is it given anything like a definition. It would, of course, be in conflict with his philosophical method to give any sort of definition in a philosophical text.

17 At the end of *Philosophical investigations* Wittgenstein in effect says that "What has to be accepted, the given, is – so one could say – *forms of life*" (p 226).

18 Wittgenstein (1953), Sect 583.

19 Wittgenstein, L (1978), *Remarks on the foundations of mathematics*, Blackwell, Oxford, VI, Sect 34.

20 Wittgenstein, L (1969), *On certainty*, Blackwell, Oxford, Sect 475.

21 Wittgenstein , L (1980), *Culture and value*, Blackwell, Oxford, p 31.

22 Wittgenstein (1969), Sect 139.

23 Wittgenstein (1953), Sect 242.

24 Ibid , Sect 201.

25 Ibid, Sect 201.

26 Ibid, Sect 202.

27 Wittgenstein (1969), Sect 27.

Section III:

Traditions of Knowledge and Professional Skills

Chapter 5

On Creativity and Development

Albert Danielsson

This chapter argues that creativity, far from being uniform or simplistic, is an even more complex and exciting phenomenon than is usually conceived. The gist of creativity may correspond to the following seven stages:

1 An individual
2 has the ability to
3 invent and develop something new, or
2a–3a applies something in a new way
4 which generally consists of ideas,
5 which especially are artistic, and
6 which give rise to interesting and unusual results.

The chapter examines the influence of Thomas S. Kuhn on the posthumous reputation of the Polish microbiologist Ludwik Fleck, and the role of the apostles in the rapid spread of Christianity under the Roman Empire. It is argued that the development of an idea may be conceived as the following sequence of stages: birth, development and spread, penetration, regulation – and, possibly, death. We need to consider the social context of creativity; alongside our observation of creativity as an individual endeavour, we should examine creativity and its immediate group of peers and followers (the profession), creativity and the surrounding society (the scientific community at large), and creativity and the recipients-receivers. The chapter advocates a conception of creativity which enables us to express the contribution of an individual within a "creative" situation, and an inclusion of what might be termed "creativity-in-use" and/or "creativity-in-invention". We need a family of concepts, a series of new terms or categories which are related to each other and to creativity.

Who was the more creative: Jesus Christ or St Paul?

What is creativity?

A Definition

A definition of creativity, which word derives from the latin *creare*, taken from an ordinary dictionary runs as follows:

Creativity is the ability to invent and develop new and original ideas, especially in an artistic way.[1]

Creative is likewise defined as:

1 Someone who is creative has the ability to invent and develop new and original ideas especially in an artistic way.
2 Creative can also describe the use of something in a new and imaginative way to produce interesting and unusual results.[2]

A few things immediately stand out in this definition which seems to capture the gist of creativity as generally conceived. Let me slightly rephrase the definition in seven steps:

1 An individual
2 has the ability to
3 invent and develop something new, or
2a–3a applies something in a new way
4 which generally consists of ideas,
5 which especially are artistic, and
6 which give rise to interesting and unusual results

The presented definition in fact shows that creativity is not only far from being uniform or simplistic but is also an even more complex and exciting phenomenon than is usually conceived. One immediate consequence of point 2a–3a is that we will have to observe several kinds of creativity, which then will have to be specified. Another and equally important consequence is that we will have to observe and accept that creativity is at play in many situations not hitherto looked upon as such. However, in this paper I will concentrate upon the even more important consequences that follow as soon as we accept that the point 2a–3a, regarding the use of the ideas, must be looked upon as an integral part of creativity rather than as one possible instance of it.

Conceptions of Creativity

An Individual Phenomenon

The definition of creativity first of all seems to posit it as a phenomenon concerning individuals who have the ability to develop something new. However, it would not, I hope, be too far-out to ask if there is any way for an individual to demonstrate an ability to invent other than by using it to obtain something new (point 3 above).[3]

It seems to be taken for granted that the processes which bring about the new results are possible to study with scientific methods. This would seem to suggest that conceptions such as intuition being an important part of creativity are not at all entertained, or at least not taken into consideration.

As an individual phenomenon to be studied scientifically, creativity is mainly possible to study within disciplines interested in human individuals, e.g. psychology. Psychological studies of individuals then often try to ascertain the limits which make them creative or particular characteristics in their environment which are conducive.[4]

Time Perspective

The phenomenon of creativity has so far been treated either as relating to an individual or as an event or an occasion. In the first case the time perspective is concerned with the individual, the individual's life. In the second case every new act of creativity concerns a new event, which is different from any other event. Here, time is divided into "occasions", i.e. those situations in which creativity occurs. Very often, however, there is no felt need to observe more than one situation of creativity at a time.

Then time is given no place at all and it is possible to let each occurrence of creativity constitute an occasion so that a collection of observations from each of these occasions can give us a set of observations to be used in our attempts to give empirical content to our conceptions of creativity.

Creative Milieu

An extension of the studies of creativity has been provided by Janik and Toulmin[5] in their studies of the development in several fields in Vienna around the turn of the century. It is quite impossible not to read their study as evidence of an unusual amount of inventions and new developments in various fields. If it is possible to ascertain that an unusual amount of creative events occur in a particular place in a short time such occurrence should at least in part be attributed to the environment. Vienna around the turn of the century 1900 seems to be such a place and can thus be said to have provided an unusually creative milieu.

In a later paper Allan Janik[6] has discussed which factors produced the unsurpassed creative milieu of Vienna. His main conclusions are first that a peculiar mixture of softness and hardness seem to be necessary and second that it most probably is impossible to create such a milieu – it has to evolve.

Perspective Focusing on Creativity as Such

To sum up the received conception of creativity we might say that it focuses on creativity as such. As a consequence creativity is given the title role as it were. Creativity is looked upon from a perspective in which creativity is placed at the centre and only such phenomena that are directly linked to creativity become visible.

It is important to stress that this somewhat strange perspective is a result of the focus – whether it is conscious or not.

Development of an Idea

Two Examples

Science: Fleck and Kuhn

In 1935 the polish microbiologist Ludwik Fleck published a monograph[7] which presents a novel approach to questions concerning what is a scientific fact and the way a particular science is developed. His points, that "scientific facts" depend on history and culture and that there is a social conditionality of knowledge, are demonstrated in an extensive case study of the development of the conception and treatment of syphilis from the Middle Ages to the time of his writing. Two of the important concepts that are used as analytical instruments by Fleck are "thought-style" and "thought-collective".

In 1962 (the year after Fleck's death), Thomas S. Kuhn published his seminal work.[8] Kuhn's work immediately got recognition and has exerted tremendous influence on later studies in the philosophy of science. In his preface Kuhn refers to Fleck's 1935 study and this is the first time that Fleck is recognized by any philosopher of science.

Fleck clearly anticipates Kuhn's main ideas and has influenced him considerably as Kuhn himself admits. Be that as it may, the really important point is that it was Kuhn, who gave this kind of thinking, these ideas, penetration.

Fleck's study was not translated into English until 1979.[9] Today Fleck is widely recognized[10] and so his ideas can be used and also developed further by the scientific community.

Here Fleck and his ideas will serve us in more than one way. First of all the importance of the issue of penetration becomes visible and clear when we compare the reception of Fleck's work with that of Kuhn's. Equally important, furthermore, is that the content of Fleck's ideas must be relevant for the study of creativity as well. This seems particularly important regarding his views that science and its development must be studied in its cultural and historical settings as well as in its social conditionality.

Religion

The observation that Christianity would have remained an obscure Jewish sect had it not been for the work of the apostles in general and St Paul in particular, will be useful as a second example when we want some material for reflection in order to enlarge the conception of creativity.

It cannot be that the mould of the new set of ideas of Jesus Christ was a sufficient condition for these ideas, which were from the outset so obscure, to become the base of one of the most important world-religions so far – not to say the most important. A Jew considered to be a heretic at least, or an outright rebel, could not by himself have produced the far reaching results necessary to deem his ideas among the most creative in our world view.

Indeed the spread of the ideas by the apostles must also be considered to have contained vast amounts of creativity.

Furthermore the eventual conversion of the state religion of the Roman Empire into Christendom as started by Constantine the Great secured the success of the movement initiated some hundreds of years earlier. It would not seem preposterous to assume that the conversion of the religion of the Roman Empire had to be preceded by several acts of creativity by the earlier Christians. Too many cults have stopped short of becoming really important for us not to accept the importance of the work done by the first followers of Jesus Christ – apostles and others.

Sequence of Stages of an Idea

As soon as we think of an idea as being developed we introduce time. Here I will try to incorporate time in a conscious way. To capture the richness of the development we might conceive of the development of ideas in a sequence of stages:

Birth
Development and spread
Penetration
Regulation, (and possibly also
Death).

At least the first three stages would need creativity to be achieved. The stages contain qualitatively different activities and it seems reasonable to assume that each stage has to be gone through. It is not, however, maintained that each stage is of equal importance in every case of development, nor is it suggested that each stage is of equal duration.

An Idea is Born

The birth of an idea is the stage usually thought of as connected with creativity. Most examples of creativity that are given can also be attributed to this stage: It seems more or less taken for granted that the giving birth to an idea is the decisive moment – as soon as this has taken place, creativity has been shown and the development has begun.

Here an important point is that giving birth to an idea is but one kind of creativity. Furthermore there are relatively few ideas which are wholly new. In most instances the "new" idea is rather an application of a previous idea in a different situation or the original idea is enlarged, etc.

An Idea is Developed

Every idea that is to survive needs an immediate group of supporters. The Apostles of Jesus Christ seem to be a very good example, as do the followers of Muhammad to Yathrib (which later changed its name to Medina, which means "the city of the prophet"), or to take an example with a different flavour, scientists accepting a new idea and trying to use it or give it experimental founding.

It would seem absolutely unimaginative to believe that the development of a new or enhanced idea could take place without large amounts of creativity. As is immediately indicated by the examples of both the Apostles and the followers of Muhammad the original ideas were not written down, and if complete, were so only in thought – only in the abstract. Thus the fundamental task of phrasing the ideas had to be performed. What could that work be called but creative?

An Idea is Given Penetration

Christendom would, as I have already indicated, be merely a Jewish sect if it had not eventually become the Roman state religion. The process whereby Christendom gradually achieved this status was far from easy and the outcome was not self-evident. To remind ourselves about this we need only refer to the fact that the last of the great persecutions, took place as late as AD 303 by the emperor Diocletian. (It was in AD 306 that Constantine, who was to become the great, took office.)

To give penetration to a really new idea is – as we will see as we give deep thought to it – a first rate endeavour. Let us for a moment think that we are Romans with a whole Pantheon of Gods. Now the Christians with their single God claim priority. We have to accept that we, the Romans, are honest believers as a starting point. How can we be persuaded to change deeply held convictions? To put it very simply, we have to be *shown*! Here I think is the really crucial element in the whole discussion of creativity. The new ideas have to be shown – in the Wittgensteinian sense. How? That is the problem! That problems of showing need creativity goes without saying. This is a point in any comparison between Fleck and Kuhn and one of the reasons for the inclusion of this example. Quite obviously there were many factors in Kuhn's favour, e.g.:

1. The language: Kuhn published in English, Fleck in German.
2. The time: in 1935 the time was definitely not ripe for ideas such as those presented by Fleck.
3. The social environment, the profession: Fleck was a microbiologist and was reviewed mainly in medical journals, who saw his study as dealing with a case in medical history. Kuhn, on the other hand, was already an established historian of science publishing directly to that community ("thought-collective").

Fleck himself was clearly aware of these obstacles as is indicated by the latest citation.[11]

Fleck's ideas were, however, very complex and also, as Kuhn points out, one had to understand something about microbiology in order fully to recognize the merits of Fleck's contribution. I therefore believe that Fleck's theses might have been too complex and radical even at the time when

Kuhn published his book to gain the followers necessary for the second stage, that of development and spread. Naturally it would then have been still more astonishing if it could have had penetrating power. Or, to put it slightly differently, Fleck may not have been able to *show* his ideas to colleagues until they had been prepared by Kuhn. This should be compared to the simplicity and elegance of Kuhn's contribution and the force of his presentation.

An Idea is Regulated

After an idea has penetrated a society or a learned body, it can be codified and regulated. Quite obviously creativity is involved even in this stage – or at least it should be.

Again, a distinction made by Fleck, between journal and handbook science, seems to offer similar views. Journal literature is still tentative, while handbook literature formulates the core of opinions of a discipline.[12]

With regard to the points of view I want to make about creativity in this chapter, however, this stage seems to be more of a continuation of the preceding stage than an important independent stage and so we will not discuss it further.

Results of Creativity

Are Results of Creativity a Relevant Issue?

It is generally taken for granted that creativity always produces good results, and that consequently creativity in itself is generally a good thing. It is not even necessary to pose the question whether creativity is good or bad.

The well known industrialist P.G. Gyllenhammar of Volvo and Renault remarked in a discussion of creativity that in most industrial situations the rule is and has to be regular activities which are performed according to plan, and that creativity might prove disastrous! One simple way of ascertaining this view is to remind oneself that the real strength of work inside an industrial enterprise is its combine of forces which presupposes coordination in a great number of respects. Obviously creativity is an anathema to coordination.

All too many inventions have been put to uses with disastrous consequences. The most obvious example in our time is the developments which led to the atomic and hydrogen bombs. The real importance of this example in the present context is, however, that the same developments also led to nuclear power and that here the verdict is much more uncertain.

One thing that emerges from this example is that a creative idea can be put to several uses – with both good and bad results – we will have to include therefore uses and possible uses into our discussion of creativity.

Creative – or Odd?

It is now enlightening to think of what makes an idea creative or odd. First of all it is clear that as soon as the question: "Creative or odd?" is posed the focus is by necessity shifted at least partially, from the act of creation to the receiver or the receivers of the act and/or the result of it. An idea which leads to interesting and good applications will obviously be deemed creative. But since we have already accepted that creativity can be put to uses which produce bad results, such forms of creativity cannot for that reason be defined away as merely odd. (The earlier examples concerning the development of atomic and hydrogen bombs should suffice.)

One of the great difficulties in thinking of and discussing the creative/odd dichotomy is that it seems nearly impossible to give an example of "odd" which is at the same time of equal standing with, and as universal, as creativity. On the other hand it is all to easy to find examples which at times have been considered odd (particularly by some) but which are later judged highly creative. I would think that several paintings of the impressionists are a case in point.

One way to gain some insight into the dichotomy would then be to ask the questions: "When is a result of creativity?" and "Who and what decides which?" To this we will turn next.

It is quite obvious that any results of creativity are judged differently at times. In this respect it is impossible to think of Vienna around the turn of the century without recalling the reception of Klimt's paintings for the University ceiling. This example also shows the importance of who and what. The critics of Klimt included, besides the expected, (e.g. the professors of the university), even Karl Kraus. At the same time the first of Klimt's university paintings, *Philosophy*, granted him the Grand Prix at the Exposition Universelle in Paris in the same year.

The Paradox of Creativity

The greater the creativity and the newer an idea the more difficult is its spread, development and penetration! Consequently, the greater the creativity the smaller is the probability that it will be deemed creative rather than odd.

Conclusion and Suggestions for Further Study

Creativity as a Family of Concepts

This chapter began with a received definition of creativity and a discussion of it. The remainder of the chapter has grown into an argument for a wider conception of creativity, particularly an inclusion of what might be termed "creativity-in-use". Clearly this does not imply any suggestion that the received meaning of creativity should be abandoned. On the contrary, we still need a category that enables us to express the contribution of an individual in a situation covered by the concept of creativity.[13] To distinguish this meaning of creativity we may provisionally use the term "creativity-in-invention".

Thus, the need is for an extended conception; for a family of concepts. It is quite possible that this need is best taken care of by a series of new terms or constructs/concepts which are related to each other and to creativity rather than by having to put up with distinctions being made either by the context or by the use of expressions such as "creativity-in-invention" and "creativity-in-use".

Ideas as Socially Conceived

The social context of creativity advocated here has been treated with respect to science by Fleck through his concept of "thought-collective" (*Denkkollektiv*) as we have already remarked. Stephen Toulmin[14] has brought the discussion of social context a step further by introducing the distinction between scientific disciplines and scientific professions. We can utilize these contributions when we are dealing with creativity as well.

Our discussion about stages of development and particularly about the importance – and the difficulty – of the penetration shows the need to broaden the social context a step further. To be really successful any idea needs penetration, i.e. it needs recipients, who are not themselves "in the trade".

With a slightly different wording we could say about creativity that it is a social phenomenon in this extended respect as well. This observation would seem to require that creativity as an individual endeavour be at least complemented by social considerations of three kinds:

Creativity and the immediate group of peers and followers (e.g. the profession)

Creativity and the surrounding society (e.g. the scientific community at large)

Creativity and the recipients

Change of Perspective

Development of an Area of Activity – a Praxis

We shall now take our suggestion under the preceding heading seriously. When we try to incorporate the receivers of ideas in the social context of creativity we may also change our focus from creativity to the activities taking place, e.g. if we continue our example about religion we might focus on the affairs of the Roman Empire.

To pose the question "What were the most pressing problems of Diocletian or of Constantine the Great and how did they set about taking care of them?" would be one way of moving from a focus on creativity towards a focus on the full set of activities. As we have already noted, Diocletian initiated the last of the great persecutions of the Christians, while Constantine made Christendom the state religion. With this kind of analysis, immediate questions are "Why this difference in the treatment of the Christians?" "Was Diocletian barbarous while Constantine was a refined personality?" On the second question, Starr takes the opposite view:

> As between Diocletian and Constantine it is often difficult to determine responsibility for the major reforms which produced the Later Roman Empire. On the whole Diocletian, who was much better educated and more flexible, probably had the main hand in shaping the civil administration; military reorganisation, on the other side, owed much to Constantine, a son of war, who was brutal and dictatorial in his actions.[16]

The heading of the paragraphs from which the quotation is drawn runs:

> The reorganisation by Diocletian and Constantine

From these quotations it is clear that the preoccupation of the two emperors was the restoration of Rome after a long period of decline. From their point of view, their perspective, any activity must be judged in this perspective. So,

> The Empire must be protected by the gods of state, and to this end the ruler must enforce religious obedience. Diocletian fiercely banned the alien Manichean cult, which had gained considerable support in the east, and even addressed himself forcefully to the problem of Christianity, a network of churches spread all over the Empire which was stubbornly independent of imperial authority, but here he failed. His eventual successor Constantine, a deeply superstitious man, came in dream to believe the Christian God was on his side, a belief reinforced by military and political success; and when Constantine proceeded to found a new eastern capital from which the Empire could control both Balkan and eastern frontier defences he fashioned Constantinople as a Christian city.[17]

The Importance of Traditions

An outstanding burst of creativity must have preceded the birth and growth of the natural sciences in Europe. The uniqueness of Europe unfolds in particular when one compares the development here with that in China and in the Islamic world. Although both of the other two world-cultures were prior to Europe in several respects it was in Europe that the breakthrough occurred.

The Islamic world, for instance, had kept the tradition from the Greek culture and had developed mathematics far. As we know the old Greek tradition had to be translated from Arabic to Latin (e.g. in Toledo in Spain).

But it was in Christian Europe that the birth of science took place and science was later to become one of the foundations of the development of the whole of Western Civilization. The whys and wherefores of this development are really worth investigation and study.

Suffice it here to point to one aspect, viz. a difference between Christianity and Islam. As Christendom evolved in the Roman world it had to accept a division between the worldly power entrusted with the Emperor and the divine power handled by the bishops. This contrasts sharply with Islam which claimed to rule the whole life of its believers. Even though Catholicism tried to stop the growth of an independent science it did not succeed. Furthermore, in those parts of Northern Europe where Protestantism gained ground the division between the two "worlds" – the worldly and the divine – became even more marked and natural science broke through.

Since the original doctrine of Christendom and Islam were rather more similar we have to revert to the following development to understand the differences. That is: we have to follow the traditions to understand this creative milieu!

Notes

1 *English Language Dictionary*, Collins Cobuild, London and Glasgow, 1987.

2 *Ibid.*

3 Ekvall, Göran (1988) *Förnyelse och friktion*, Böras. Ekvall contends that creativity can refer both to individuals and to thought processes. Furthermore, he argues that the latter are the more fundamental since it is possible to assess the existence of creativity only from the result of acts (following the creativity) (p 10 f).

4 Examples of studies of this kind are given in Ekvall, *op cit*, e.g. pp 18–42.

5 Janik, Allan and Toulmin, Stephen (1973) *Wittgenstein's Vienna*, New York.

6 *Ibid.*

7 Fleck, Ludwik (1935) *Entstehung und Entwicklung einer wissenschaftlichen Tatsache: Einführung in die Lehre vom Denkstil und Denkkollektiv.* Basel.

8 Kuhn, Thomas S. (1962) *The structure of scientific revolutions.* Chicago, 2nd edn., enlarged, Chicago, 1970.

9 Fleck, Ludwik (1979) *Genesis and development of a scientific fact*, Chicago and London.

10 Cohen Robert S. and Schnelle, Thomas (eds) (1986) *Cognition and Fact. Materials on Ludwik Fleck*, Dordrecht.

11 Cf. also the comment to this end by Thaddeus J. Trenn in the preface to Fleck (1979) *op cit*, p xviii.

12 Cohen and Schnelle, *op cit* Introduction, p xxviii f.

13 A case in point arises in Stephen Toulmin's discussion about the historical development of the kinds of knowledge and understanding in the natural sciences compared to the fine arts. Toulmin, Stephen (1986) Fleck and the interpretation of science. In: Cohen and Schnelle (eds), *op cit*, p 281 ff.

14 *Ibid*, p 269 ff.

15 Starr, Chester G (1982) *The Roman Empire. 27 B.C.–A.D. 476. A Study in Survival*, Oxford.

16 *Ibid*, p 157.

17 *Ibid*, p 159 f.

Chapter 6

Language and Experience

Ingela Josefson

What does a "good" nurse need to know? How does (s)he acquire this knowledge? Can all the knowledge required to nurse people be acquired by theoretical study alone? If so, this knowledge must be susceptible to formulation in a scientific language. Experienced nurses, however, stress that the ability to "see" unusual symptoms and developments in the condition of their patients is an ability which can only be acquired from direct experience and with practice. Thus, although a scientific language may engender greater respect for the nursing profession than it currently enjoys, one runs the risk of placing greater value on the knowledge which can be expressed in precise theoretical terms than the knowledge discussed in an everyday language or that which simply manifests itself in actions. A great deal of nursing knowledge is passed on in a kind of master-apprentice relationship; the experienced nurse teaches the less experienced nurse to "see" unusual symptoms or changes in a patient's health. Many nurses emphasize how important this period of apprenticeship was to them at the start of their professional careers. In seeking to design expert computer systems for nursing care, advances in technology should therefore take seriously ethical values integral to the profession such as the "experience", "devotion" and "patience" of which Florence Nightingale wrote.

Florence Nightingale founded the first school of nursing in London in the middle of the nineteenth century. Her approach to nursing assured her a piece in history. The influence she had on people's attitudes to nursing is still discussed today, sometimes with irony and sometimes with admiration. Some see her as the first woman scientist in the nursing profession – she introduced statistical methods to demonstrate the advances that could be made by improving hygiene, for example. Others refer to her profound insight into the nature of nursing. In a speech she gave to an audience of newly-qualified nurses in 1897 when she was 77 years old, Florence Nightingale said this:

There is no doubt that this is a critical time for nursing. Will you have women, or will you have words? Which nurse best? There is a curious old legend that the nineteenth century is to be the age for women. and has it not been so? Shall the twentieth century be the age for words? God forbid. But words we must have, you will say.

Undoubtedly, and the greatest discoverers have given a large portion of their time for putting their discoveries into words which are intelligible to the common people like you and me ... There appears to be some danger of our being suffocated with words, of our thinking that we can learn nursing in six ambulance classes. This is now so common a superstition: I can't call it anything else – that circulars announcing such classes reach me continually. Nursing takes a whole life to learn. We must make progress in it every year. It takes five years, not of words, but of practice, to make a ward sister.

There seems some danger that the twentieth century will be an age not of facts, but of enthusiasm without facts ... Nursing is not an adventure, as some have now supposed: "fools rush in where angels fear to tread." It is a very serious, delightful thing, like life, requiring training, experience, devotion not by fits and starts, patience, a power of accumulating, instead of losing all these things.[1]

In the current debate on the development of sophisticated computer technology, and on knowledge-based systems in particular, Florence Nightingale's reflections are thought-provoking. Can all the knowledge required to nurse people be acquired by theoretical study alone? If so, this knowledge must be susceptible to formulation in a scientific language.

These issues are discussed in this essay. It is based on conversations over the last three or four years with nurses in Sweden and Britain.

The main theme of these conversations was: what does a "good" nurse need to know? How does she acquire this knowledge? Can its development be influenced by future technical advances in the care sector? Since these sophisticated technical developments require nurses to have the ability to make explicit descriptions of their knowledge, it is natural to begin by giving some serious thought to the issue of the kind of knowledge a nurse needs in her meetings with patients.

Unlike Edward Feigenbaum, I am convinced that this work must be carried out thoroughly, and without skirting the problems involved. Feigenbaum expresses a different opinion when he stresses that work on matters related to the theory of knowledge must not be permitted to take up too much space because they are inherently far too complicated.[2] Today, the discussion of the epistemological issues in the nursing profession cannot be limited to technical advance. The development of the profession in recent years has strongly influenced nurses' perception of what is necessary and important knowledge in their work. Nursing is traditionally a female task and as such has low status in our culture. As long as this work was seen as a vocation, the financial rewards were meagre. But even today, when nursing is a recognized profession, nurses are still poorly paid. Over the past year, dissatisfaction with these conditions has led to strikes and demonstrations in a number of countries, including Britain and France. One natural way of correcting the current contemptuous attitude towards nursing is to attempt to incorporate nursing training into the institutions of the scientific world. The sciences, in particular the natural sciences enjoy a great deal of respect in our culture. One important reason for nursing training in, for example, Sweden being classified as further education for the past ten years is that it was hoped that this would also engender greater respect for nursing knowledge. Of course other reasons have played their part, but this is *one* of the motives for taking this step.

A scientifically-designed body of nursing knowledge requires precision, exactitude and stringency. The ability to make judgments in unforeseeable situations is an important part of nursing knowledge. To what extent is it possible to describe this in precise terms?

"Nurses have no language" is a complaint heard from many researchers in the care sector when they try to convince practising nurses of their need for theories in nursing care. A lack of language is an obstacle to the development of the scientific language that many researchers in the care sector believe would improve the quality of nursing.

A group of Swedish nurses in the field of psychiatry have the following comment on the demand for a scientific language:

> The scientific language may serve to gain recognition for your own field so that you can meet psychologists, doctors and graduates in social welfare studies on an equal footing. It is our task to explain what is happening to the patient when he is sitting and eating breakfast, but this sort of description sounds awkward when compared with the psychologists' description of their interventions. The problem is that what cannot be expressed in theoretical terms counts for nothing in our culture. And all everyday and female issues are in this category.

In striving for a scientific approach one runs the risk of creating gaps between nurses who can see the benefit of a scientific language in their meetings with patients and nurses who use science to improve the quality of nursing care. A nursing theoretician who is well known in Scandinavia writes that "the central task of nursing is to create a set of basic concepts and the basic premises for nursing care".[3] It is, she says, "by giving people in the care sector a new paradigm, a new way of thinking, that we can change the reality of our nursing to become a type of care which is more oriented towards people and which has more of a whole person approach".[4] As an example of what a scientific language should achieve she mentions:

> [it is] important to give an intellectual and spiritual content to the word love, so that it may be understood and used in the same way by different people. I believe that in this context it may be appropriate in this profession to give some thought to the limitations of the scientific language. What is it that is important to formulate in a scientific language? It appears to me that one may have overstepped a limit in attempting to arrive at a precise definition of the concept of love.[5]

I suspect that behind this attitude there lies the conviction that the knowledge which can be expressed in precise scientific terms has a higher value than the knowledge discussed in an everyday language or which quite simply manifests itself in actions.

The work of designing a set of scientific concepts for nursing knowledge has, of course, similarities with the work of the knowledge engineer when he attempts to "drain" an expert of his professional knowledge. The same question arises: to what extent is this possible? And there is the same disagreement between technically oriented nurses and nurses with a more sceptical view of technology as there is between some of the researchers in the care sector and practising nurses.

The nurses I met in Britain who had training in computer technology believe that expert systems in nursing care would make it possible for nurses to change their future role. Instead of the greater part of their work being nursing care, the nurse would be able to concentrate on administrative and supervisory tasks. They saw this as involving knowledge which had higher status in our society than a knowledge of nursing care. But, as in Sweden, many nurses in Britain do not want to leave nursing and the direct contacts they have with patients. It is their interest in this kind of work which made them choose the nursing profession. In commenting on the demand that nurses make a precise and detailed description of their knowledge, a British nurse says:

I cannot formulate the deeper dimension of my knowledge. I cannot describe how I tell a patient that he is going to die. I have built up the most important part of my knowledge by meeting and meeting, and learning. This is what is crucial to my ability to make a diagnosis. It is a question of doing it again and again. This is always impossible to express in words. After many years' experience as a nurse many of my reflections are mechanical. I see what is going to happen without formulating it myself. I would like to inculcate in young nurses the view that every patient is a new experience. This cannot be learned theoretically, more than anything else it requires an ability to "see".

On the basis of her view of current conditions in nursing, this nurse says that she feels repelled by the technology fixation which she believes to be characteristic of a great deal of nursing today: "Machines and too much theoretically-influenced people we should avoid".

What knowledge is important in nursing? There would appear to be general agreement that a thorough knowledge of, for example, anatomy, is essential. But a newly-qualified nurse cannot manage with this theoretical knowledge alone when she meets a great many unforeseen problems in her practical work. Neither has she the ability to "see", something out of the ordinary in the way an experienced colleague can. A 40-year-old nurse who described how, as a newly-qualified nurse working on a cancer wards she was surprised when an older colleague asked her to telephone a patient's relatives because he had not long to live. She herself could detect no change in the patient. But she learned that the older nurse was right. In time she acquired this ability herself. You cannot learn it from books, but if you have seen it a few times, then you know what it is about, she said.

A great deal of this knowledge is passed on in a kind of master–apprentice relationship. The experienced nurse teaches the less experienced nurse to see. In her speech, Florence Nightingale returned to this kind of learning, but there appears to be some aversion to this method today. Clearly some of this aversion is attributable to the traditional fear of the apprentice being exploited. However, a remarkable number of nurses emphasizes how important this period of apprenticeship was to them at the start of their professional careers. The British nurses in particular referred to Florence Nightingale's habit of making regular rounds of the wards at night with a lamp to attend to her patients. She was followed by a group of young nurses, the apprentices.

Today there is a tendency for people who object to technical advance, or who question some areas of its application, to be labelled as anti-technology or dismissed as reactionary or non-progressive. I have noticed that many nurses who emphasize the human meetings in nursing often refer to themselves as being old-fashioned.

Reading the works of Edward Feigenbaum and his colleague Pamela McCorduck, the Professor of Literature, helps one arrive at a better understanding of the spirit of the times which "traditional" nurses feel is critical of them. In an extensive review of their Artificial Intelligence and Japan's Computer Challenge to the World,[6] Joseph Weizenbaum begins with a little riddle which challenges the reader to work out who made the following statement and on what occasion:

> ... no plausible claim to intellectuality can possibly be made in the near future without an intimate dependence upon xxx. Those intellectuals who persist in their indifference, not to say snobbery, will find themselves stranded in a quaint museum of the intellect, forced to live petulantly, and rather irrelevantly, on the charity of those who understand the real dimensions of the revolution and can deal with the new world it will bring about.[7]

Of course, says Weizenbaum, it all depends on what you put in place of xxx. The reader who substitutes national socialism for xxx would have assumed that these words were a warning to the intellectuals who did not support the nazi revolution and that they were spoken at the bonfire of books in Berlin on 10 May 1933. But xxx may also stand for the ideas of a great leader and teacher, and names like Karl Marx, Pinochet or Stalin may be used. Weizenbaum reminds us that the Germans actually had a word for what the intellectuals were urged to do here: "Gleichschaltung", which means, roughly, accord, thinking in the same way. In the quote Weisenbaum took from the Feigenbaum-McCorduck book, xxx of course stands for the computer, the new instrument.

McCorduck says that new technology will inevitably bring about a great many changes in our values, in our way of thinking about ourselves, in short, in our opinions.[8] She says that we cannot stop this progress even if, lacking courage, we should wish to do so. The computer is the instrument which can liberate the human attribute which serves us best, intelligence. Seen in the perspective of this spirit of the times a care-oriented nurse would obviously be hopelessly antiquated.

On the other hand, the writings of Feigenbaum and McCorduck may be seen as an example of complete ignorance and superficiality in terms of the roles of culture and history in our lives. The works of McCorduck reflect her resentment of the self-contemplation of the history of literature. In her book she says that Herbert Simon is far more relevant than T.S. Eliot to the twentieth century.[9] It may be that her criticism of research in the humanities is justified. But in her eagerness for the future she also sweeps away something to which many people in the caring professions attach great importance – and it lies outside the scientifically acclaimed intelligences. Florence Nightingale writes of it as "experience, devotion ..., patience".[10] Unless these ethical values can be taken seriously in technological advance, there is every good reason to suspect that T.S. Eliot's The Waste Land will be a far more telling description of the next century than the writings of Herbert Simon.

Notes

1 Florence Nightingale made her speech to the Nurses and Probationers trained under the Nightingale Fund in London in June 1897. It was given to me by the Information Department of St. Thomas's Hospital, London.

2 Feigenbaum, E. *Handbook of artificial intelligence.*

3 Professor Katie Eriksson, Åbo Akademi, Wasa, Finland. These ideas are discussed in her book, *Vårdandets idé,* Almqvist & Wiksell, Stockholm,1987.

4 *Ibid.*

5 *Ibid.*

6 Feigenbaum, E and McCorduck, P (1983) *Artificial intelligence and Japan's computer challenge to the world.*

7 Weizenbaum, J (1983) In: *New York Review of Books.*

8 McCorduck, P (1985) *The universal machine. Confessions of a technological optimist.*

9 *Ibid.*

10 Nightingale, *op. cit.*

Chapter 7

The Psychology of Apprenticeship: a Discussion Paper

David Smith

The meritocratic cult of the "expert"and the rise of "training" and the professional trainer have contributed to the discrediting of apprenticeship and its perception as an "unprofessional", inefficient and irrelevant anachronism. This chapter calls for a positive revaluation of the role and possibilities of apprenticeship in educational and vocational development. The chapter traces the history and evolution of apprenticeship in England, from its origins in mediaeval craft guilds to the present day. A series of anecdotes from former apprentices illustrates some of the beneficial and potentially harmful aspects of the experience of apprenticeship in developing skills. If learning is an essentially social activity, the "apprentice" in education must not only make a body of knowledge his/her own, but must do so in a community which shares a sense of belonging to a culture. The idea of acculturation into a specific working life environment is, in fact, at the very heart of apprenticeship. Formal education is now an integral part of most apprenticeships, but no less important is the tacit knowledge immanent in an emotional engagement with the task in hand, allowing a crafts worker, for example, to operate creatively at one of the interfaces between conscious and subconscious thought. Finally, the chapter examines the persistence of male, youth-based apprenticeships, the issue of how to evaluate, economically and politically, the effectiveness of existing apprenticeship schemes, and the largely unexplored potential of these schemes in terms of both the communication of skills and their transfer from a specific context to new fields. Apprenticeship at its best, the article concludes, conforms with many current ideas about optimum conditions for effective learning and, unlike the current orientation of much UK "training", may provide many key components for learning for the quality era.

Introduction

Apprenticeship has had something of a bad press in recent years, and a great deal of ink has been spilt in determined attempts to discredit both the idea of apprenticeship and the practice based on it. It became possible for academic writers in the 1960s and 1970s to treat the ancient system of vocational development (for the time being I shall avoid the term "training" in this context) by apprenticeship as if it were an irrelevant throwback to a different era, and responsible in itself for many of the ills associated with the long, slow decline of British industry.

Indeed, at a time when there was an enormous shortage of skilled workers, when the "white heat of technology" was supposedly transforming manufacturing industry, and when there was apparently great public respect for formal education, the craft apprenticeship system was closely associated in many eyes with "intransigent" union power: with demarcation, differentials and restrictive practices.

The meritocratic cult of the "expert" also made it easy to regard a process which rested largely in the care of "uneducated" working people as a dangerous anachronism, and a tendency to regard apprenticeship as having outlived its usefulness is partly associated with the rise of "training" and the professional trainer There was a reluctance to believe that "ordinary" men and women were even worthy of the responsibility for "training" young workers (an "officers and other ranks" attitude which may perhaps be traced to the military roots of the training movement). Apprenticeship, characteristically represented in terms of making tea, sweeping floors and the whole "sitting with Nelly" syndrome, was "unprofessional" and inefficient.

Yet, despite decades of continual assault, to be an "Apprentice Widget-Fitter" or whatever still carries a prestige which will never be attained by a mere "Trainee". This is especially the case for working class people in Britain, but it is not a purely working class phenomenon. The system of apprenticeship appears even today to confer a certain cachet for learner and employer alike, and it is not unusual to find companies advertising for "apprentices" when it abundantly clear that what is being offered bears no relationship to any strict meaning of the term. The idea, if not the practice, of apprenticeship clearly retains a strong hold on popular imagination.

This discussion will be concerned with the "Psychology of Apprenticeship", a topic which embraces phenomena at both the individual and the social level. Nothing short of a major treatise can deal comprehensively with such a subject, and all that I can do here is to identify issues and flag them for further attention at a later date. The subject has, as far as I can ascertain, received remarkably little serious attention in recent years. There have been a number of studies which have apparently set out to prove that the apprenticeship system is inefficient as a means of inculcating limited types of factual knowledge, but otherwise the field is wide open.

First Some History

Originating in the mediaeval craft guilds, apprenticeship has a long and largely honourable history in Europe. Under the licensing authority of his guild, a master craftsman undertook to take the apprentice into his household and to instruct him in his craft, enabling him eventually to progress towards the qualified status first of a journeyman, then, eventually, of a master. In return, the apprentice undertook to work diligently, soberly and honestly in his master's interest. In all the best stories, he even had a good chance of marrying the master's daughter!

This was no informal arrangement. There was a considerable ceremony involved in becoming an apprentice, and the solemn agreement between the master craftsman and the apprentice's parents was often legally enforceable. Even within the last decade, industrial tribunals in the UK have repeatedly underlined the special status of apprenticeship: for example, with respect of an obligation on the part of the employer (acting *in loco parentis*) to consult the parents or guardians of an apprentice whose position is in jeopardy – even through proven misconduct.

The transition from apprentice to journeyman status was also a moment for great solemnity and ceremony: something which survives to this day in the form of "initiation ceremonies" (some of them quite obnoxious). The young worker still had a long way to go before he in turn could become a master craftsman, but "coming out" was an important rite of passage, which established him and gave him a recognized and often honoured place in his society. It also gave him a measure of protection. In an age when human rights were given scant regard, it was a foolish grandee, baron, bishop or king, who offended the great craft guilds.

The industrial revolution of the sixteenth century (which, incidentally, resulted in the deforestation of the English Lake District) coincided with the decline of the great mediaeval urban craft guilds. New industries and trades arose, and this, coupled with the disruption caused to the process of apprenticeship by the eclipse of the guilds, led to a strikingly modern-seeming skill shortage. In Elizabethan England, the state flexed its growing muscle by passing the 1563 Statute of Artificers. Similar ordinances appeared throughout Europe at about this time.

The Statute of Artificers regulated access to and the practice of 61 trades and crafts. The Act provided for:

A minimum term of seven years for apprenticeship
A fixed ratio of one apprentice per three journeymen
Preferred entry for the sons of craftsmen
Prevention of the exercise of trades by unqualified
(i.e. non-apprenticed) tradesmen
Jurisdiction over apprenticeship by magistrates

In England, this system remained in force for two and a half centuries, until the repeal of the Statute of Artificers in 1814. But this period had been one of slow decline. The regulation imposed by the Act had only applied to the 61 designated trades, and had not been amended to cope with the evolution of new industries, trades and crafts.

After the repeal of the Statute of Artificers, anybody was free to exercise any trade or craft at all, whether or not he had been formally apprenticed. Apprenticeship became a private matter (though usually the subject of a legally binding agreement: the "indenture"). Apprenticeship as a stipulated period of supervised instruction in preparation for a skilled occupation survived only in a small number of occupations in which such preparation was fundamental to effective performance. All too often, apprenticeship was a pretext for cruelty and exploitation on a scale which would never have been sanctioned by the mediaeval guilds.

At the same time, however, various forms of "professional" apprenticeship were common among the middle classes, who might pay substantial sums for the privilege. For example, a type of apprenticeship was the normal mode of education in medicine and the law (where indeed, it still survives). These arrangements might well be international: the young Friedrich Engels was sent to Manchester to study industrial management[1] (with earth-shattering effect!). Some sort of apprenticeship was the only recourse when there was no other form of education, for example in emerging professions such as engineering. Isambard Kingdom Brunel served two periods of apprenticeship, in the workshops of the Parisian watchmaker Breguet and with the great Henry Maudslay, doyen of the English practical engineers of the nineteenth century.

But the British upper middle classes were soon infected by that aristocratic antipathy to anything redolent of "trade" which was becoming deeply engrained in the social value systems of the "public schools" and was already part of the established ethos of the ancient universities. Consequent "gentrification" of the commercial middle classes meant that there was a marked trend towards ownership of manufacturing industries by people who knew little about the trade skills on which their fortunes depended, and who therefore took little interest in matters such as general vocational education. Apprenticeship in Britain rapidly became almost the exclusive province of the skilled artisan and (in the form of "articled clerkship") the lower middle classes. This social class association was to become both a strength and a serious weakness of the system.

As the factory system evolved, workers were increasingly specialized in function and increasingly deskilled. The broad multiskilling within a craft tradition which is passed on by the master to the apprentice found little place within this system, except for a residual "aristocracy of labour" in trades such as toolmaking.

The personal relationships which are the very root of traditional apprenticeship also suffered under the new industrial system. Although the management of much of industry developed along paternalistic lines (often quite enlightened, it must be said), its model was the clan paternalism of the feudal system, rather than the (often seriously inadequate!) family. The worker became ever more remote from the seat of management power. An ambitious apprentice could still aspire to succeed his boss, but this prospect gradually receded.

This estrangement contributed to the impersonal hierarchies and remote authoritarianism which eventually culminated in Taylorism. A new managerial class gradually came into being. In Europe, the members of this class tended to be drawn from a highly technically educated elite, who appreciated the economic significance of investment in skilled manpower. In Britain, however, they were more likely to come from the middle class public school culture with its antiquated curriculum and ingrained technophobia.

The revival of the apprenticeship system in the latter part of the nineteenth century owed much to this estrangement and to the growing strength of industrial trade unions. Loyalty to the master was supplanted by strong craft identity and solidarity. Organized labour saw formal apprenticeship in much the same light as the mediaeval guilds: as a means of protecting status, maintaining quality standards and limiting the dilution and spread of craft "mysteries". What evolved, often with the enthusiastic support of employers, was a system which, though capable of producing superlative craftsmen, was often essentially exclusive and conservative.

Artisan apprenticeship retained its personal relationships, but suffered in other ways. The economic pressures on all but the very cream of small craft businesses left little spare time for teaching apprentices. Many crafts, for example shoemaking, have little or no unskilled or even semi-skilled content. It can be a matter of years before an apprentice is earning enough to compensate the master craftsman for lost productivity. The elite could charge the prospective apprentice a substantial premium in compensation for such losses, but for the majority, the apprentice was a source of cheap labour who must learn as best he could.

Nevertheless, apprenticeship remained the normal and traditional means of training for skilled manual occupations in the UK right up to the early 1980s. At many levels it is thriving, especially as changes in fashion and taste have provided some of the ancient crafts with a shot in the arm. But there has also been a rise of new forms of what might be called informal "cognitive" apprenticeship, for example in fields such as computer science. It may, for example, take up to three years to become a proficient LISP programmer. This sort of process has not been appreciated from within the training community:[2]

> ...it is significant that apprenticeship has not been adopted as the training method for new and technologically advanced occupations such as computer programming... The reasons for this are complex and include factors unrelated to the training process, but it also suggests an inhibiting rigidity in the apprenticeship system...

It is also interesting to note that formal apprenticeship has adjusted (if not actually lost) some of its strict class associations, and young people from upper class families have begun to undertake apprenticeships in fashionable crafts such as woodturning and cabinet making.

Another fact to be considered is that apprenticeship *has* evolved. It is not permanently jammed in the later middle ages, but at its best, it has developed to take into account changing patterns of work and the growing theoretical content of so many trades and crafts today. There is a considerable variety of styles and stages of apprenticeship, allowing entry from minimum school leaving age right up to postgraduate levels.

But in general the term "apprenticeship" has become diluted in the UK, and has now come to apply to a whole spectrum of roughly analogous patterns of training for technicians and higher level occupations and, much less often, to training for occupations in the commercial field, quite apart from its use as a form of unofficial honorific. This can be compared with the situation in Germany, a country with a long tradition of state provision of vocational education, and where awareness of the potential strengths of the apprenticeship system have broadened its base so that the great majority of young people undergo some kind of formally regulated apprenticeship.

The German system has been conserved even in periods of intense trade recession. By contrast, Thatcher's ill-conceived and grossly mismanaged attempt at industrial restructuring has almost totally exterminated the industrial apprenticeship system in the UK and substituted an assortment of training schemes. But the inefficacy of this approach was apparent even in the 1970s:[3]

...clinicalised training systems, reorganised work patterns, careful skills analysis and even the much-vaunted job enrichment theories have failed to remedy the alienation that has spread and is spreading over the industrial face of society...

It is ironic, therefore, that when "training" is seemingly in the ascendant and "apprenticeship" reduced to an insignificant rump in a small minority of cottage craft industries in the UK, industrial educators in other EC countries should be closely re-examining the practice of apprenticeship and asking themselves what it may offer to meet the probable needs of advanced industrial society in the next century. Just what Britain may have thrown out with the dirty bath water remains to be seen!

What Does Apprenticeship Do?

This section consists of sketches and anecdotes. I hope that they will help to illustrate some of the ways in which the experience of apprenticeship has affected different people. They are not in any special order, or intended to tell any particular story.

1. John is a joiner in his early forties. He left school at fifteen and went through a traditional apprenticeship in the building trade. I meet him every week when we attend a fitness training session together. Sometimes we are joined in the Sports Centre bar by some of John's colleagues. The conversation often turns to work.

One night "the chippies" were discussing a mutual acquaintance. Their respect for him as a craftsman was genuine and undisguised. What impressed me was the tone of admiration for the quality of this man's work: how he finished things, how he managed to achieve particularly difficult tasks were all discussed, with reference to specific jobs.

2. Tom was one of my colleagues in the Malawi Polytechnic. He lectured in mechanical engineering, having risen to Chartered Engineer status from a craft apprenticeship in a Tyneside shipyard. He told me how he and one of his friends had designed and then built a crossbow, using scrap metal and wood.

The foreman caught them practising their marksmanship in the yard. He inspected the offending weapon minutely. He then sentenced each lad to an official belting (literally), telling them that their punishment would have been ten times worse if the crossbow had been badly made! Even thirty years later, Tom was convinced of the justice of his sentence...

3. Thomas Tempte, himself a very considerable craftsman, tells about a traditional Swedish boat-builder:[4]

...Gosta is a product of the old master-journeyman-apprentice system in which sophisticated and complex knowledge was passed on without using words. This is not because of any aversion to transferring knowledge by means of the spoken word, but because no such tradition had been developed.

Putting a question to Gosta elicits very precise information, often after a pause for thought. His knowledge is neither unconscious or refined, but he is not used to passing it on in words. He demonstrates by doing the job, supplementing his example with a few words of commentary. This often takes the form of a story about a craftsman who did not do the job in a certain way, which caused him to make a mistake. One gets the feeling that he has all the answers, and this allows him to dissociate himself from the ill-judged behaviour of the offending craftsman. All this is related in the form of an anecdote".

4. Jock "served his time" in a Scottish colliery before coming to work as an electrician in south east England. On his first day at the pit, he and his fellow apprentices were each handed a large bundle of copper rods, a soldering iron, solder and flux and told to make the rods into a mesh. No direct instruction was given: they were simply told "Ye dinnae ken? Weel find oot!"

Inaccuracies in measurement, slow work or poor joints were rewarded with "a bang on the heid". But as Jock says, they eventually got it right, and were able to take on any soldering job, no matter where and with total confidence in their ability to do the job.

5. Joe's experience is remarkably similar. He served his time in a ship repair yard in Woolwich, and remembers being given a piece of bar steel by his foreman, who instructed him to turn it to a sphere. His efforts were greeted by "clips round the earole" and critical comments "...look 'ere sunny Jim, when I say a thou I mean a thou not what some snotty 'erbert finks looks like a thou... measure it proper!" Gradual convergence on the desired result was indicated by moderation in the force and direction of the foreman's blows. When the sphere was competed satisfactorily, it was simply handed back, with the order to use the lathe to make it into a cube.

No instruction was given other than "...well bloody find aht son!..." The expectation was that there were plenty of experts in the shop, and a halfway decent apprentice should know where to go for advice. In this way, the practice and responsibility for teaching was also shared throughout the shop.

Years later, as third engineer of a large meatship in mid-Pacific, Joe was able to rebuild a vital engine component using this knowledge. His "earole" had recovered long before!

6. Dick is a distinguished biotechnologist. He told me how one gains an appreciation for the good experimentalist which goes far beyond taking his or her domain knowledge for granted. He said that there are people whose technique is superior in the same sense as that of an excellent craftsman. He feels that both the technical excellence and a certain aesthetic which is fundamental to its appreciation cannot be taught directly, but arise out of a form of apprenticeship in the right laboratories.

7. Phil is a master baker in a small West Country town, running a shop which has been in his family for three generations. He is good at his job and dedicated to his craft. He is deeply committed to supporting the apprenticeship system, to the extent of acting as an examiner and moderator for trade tests as far away from home as Cornwall. For this work he gets paid eight pounds per day!

8. Clifford is a stone mason, a craft which he learned from his father without being formally apprenticed. He passed the craft onto his own son (who now lives and works in Switzerland) but also sent him to a specialist Technical College to learn about new ideas and modern techniques. Cliff is worried about the quality of people he must rely on, particularly tradesmen such as scaffolders. He told me some hair-raising stories of incompetence, including getting to the top of a church tower only to discover that his scaffolding was held on by "sky-hooks". He is proud of his craft, but there is also a touch of disillusionment in his stories.

These anecdotes, which could be repeated many times over, point up some of the good and bad features of apprenticeship – at least, as it was in the past. They tell of an erratic process, informal and "inefficient" by contemporary standards which nevertheless managed to develop a very high degree of technical skill, an understanding of materials, an ability to solve complex technical problems, an aesthetic of quality and in many cases a lasting loyalty to the company. All of the people I have talked to can remember particular craftsmen who influenced them directly, and most retain an affection for their masters, whose teaching techniques often seem to have verged on the brutal.

However, with the exception of the scientist and the engineering lecturer, none of my informants saw themselves as "educated", and indeed, they were often self-deprecating. "I'm not one of you clever blokes..." or "...only a practical man..." were typical remarks. They tended to feel ignorant of the theories behind their work, and seemed to believe that this isolated them from "real" understanding. At the same time, however, they all felt superior to "them college types" in terms of their practical abilities, and could tell stories where this superiority had been amply demonstrated to their own satisfaction!

This ambivalence may reflect a tension between their own appreciation of what they know and understand, and the high valuation which society (including themselves) places on formal "paper" qualifications. This is also illustrated perhaps by the paltry payment which Phil receives for very high level services. It is difficult to see many of the academics who so disparage apprenticeship giving their own services so willingly for so little.

How Might Apprenticeship Work? (Some Psychology)

In discussing the psychological impact of apprenticeship, I am talking about a fixed term of "educational servitude" regulate by formal agreement. But all apprenticeships are not cast in the same mould. The old ways are, for good or ill, gone for ever. Apprenticeship has evolved away from its original pattern and in line with current conditions. Unlike his craft "ancestors", a modern apprentice would undergo periods of formal education (full-time and/or part-time), as well as experiencing a full range of informal practical instruction at the workplace. We also have to recognize the great variety of modern apprenticeship, and the varying levels of formal education which "apprentices" may have experienced, from basic school-level education to postgraduate degrees. This is all a far cry from traditional apprenticeship, and we have to keep this firmly in mind.

Nevertheless, as we move out of the taylorist "control era" and into the so-called "quality revolution", the personal qualities of the traditional apprentice-trained craftsman are once more seen to be highly relevant. These qualities were summed up by Norman Parkin, when he argued that

> ...The traditional craftsman was autonomous, he had a strong identification with, even ownership of, the product he created. The design, method of manufacture the diagnosis and solution of manufacturing and (later) repair and maintenance problems were almost entirely in his hands. He was master of the whole job and had the skill and adaptive capacity to tackle any part of it. In consequence, he was highly motivated and independent, resentful of interference from anyone outside the craft... To a significant extent compared with today's factory worker, he was a master not only of his craft but of his own destiny. Many craftsmen operated – even late into this century with little or no supervision.[5]

At its best, apprenticeship achieved (and must continue to achieve):

Highly efficient development of a broad range of relevant manual skills

An intuitive grasp of the "body knowledge" needed to exercise those skills

An aesthetic of quality, relating, *inter alia,* to working practices, to products, to tools and to raw materials

A commitment to high quality working

A capacity for individual learning

Experience in problem-solving

Independence of thought and action

A spirit of self-reliance; ...and, paradoxically...

The ability to function as a member of a team

It was, therefore, not simply a matter of "training" manual skills through repetitive practice. This was certainly part of the process, but the skills of the good craftsman were and indeed still are, self-generating. New ideas new tools and new materials are and always have been enthusiastically explored and working methods adapted to their particular characteristics. If it were not so, we would still be sitting in cave mouths chipping flints!

In the light of the current fashion for "open learning", it is worth recalling that the traditional craftsman typically acquired the skills and insights necessary to become a "self-managing learner". Even if the methods by which this process of personal development was managed (for example, the "clip round the earole") were distinctly crude and naive as pedagogy goes, apprenticeship achieved many of the high-level cognitive objectives of modern formal education (some of which have only recently come to be appreciated by academic educators).

It is quite ironic that, after generations of educational theorizing based on individualized learning and the science of the rat-maze, psychologists and educationalists should at last be discovering that learning is quintessentially a social process. The curriculum theorist Jerome Bruner[6] has recently rejected the idea of the "solo child", recognizing that learning in most settings is a communal activity. The developing child must not only make a body of knowledge his own, but must do so in a community of those who share a sense of belonging to a culture:

...the language of education is a language of culture creating, not of knowledge consuming or knowledge acquisition alone...

This apparently innovatory principle is, of course, deeply (if implicitly) embedded in apprenticeship. In point of fact, formal education, with its emphasis on individual competition and arbitrarily defined standards does not relate very well to real-life working environments. Those responsible for training BBC broadcast engineers note that one of their greatest cultural difficulties is breaking very bright students out of the mind-set where 80% is fine if you did it on your own and came first, to one where nothing less than 99.99% is even vaguely acceptable, and where collaborative work is taken for granted.

According to Thomas Kuhn, the philosopher of science,[7] much the same principle is even at the heart of formal science. Kuhn argues that, like language, scientific knowledge is the common property of a group or it is nothing at all: if we are to understand it, we must be familiar with the peculiar characteristics of the group that creates and uses it.

The idea of acculturation into a specific working life environment might never have been explicitly expressed in the context of the system, but it is nonetheless at the very heart of apprenticeship. Furthermore, the part played in this process by the growing understanding of and relationship with a specific set of tools is crucial, as the revolutionary educator Ivan Illich appreciated in a more general sense:[8]

...Tools are intrinsic to social relationships. An individual relates himself to his society through the use of the tools that he actively masters or by which he is positively acted upon. To the degree that he masters his tools, he can invest the world with his meaning; to the degree that he is mastered by his tools, the shape of the world determines his own self-image. Convivial tools are those which give each person who uses them the greatest opportunity to enrich the environment with the fruits of his or her vision. Tools, foster conviviality to the extent that they can easily be used by anybody as often or as seldom as desired for the accomplishment of a purpose chosen by the user...

Illich was aware that for most people, their experience of formal education is little more than one long chapter of confrontation with their own apparent incompetence. By contrast, the sense of worth and personal autonomy which comes from any deep competence is perhaps one of the most significant outcomes of craft apprenticeship.

A similar point was made by Margaret Boden:[9]

...If a man"s self-concept represents himself to himself as an autonomous purposive creature capable of pursuing certain ends, then it can be used to generate choices and guide his action accordingly... If depersonalisation of the self-image occurs, so that the self is no longer seen as a truly purposive system, then relatively inhuman pathological behaviour can be expected...

There is something very positive about growing up within a respected cultural environment. But participating in an aspect of that culture which is dedicated to bringing one fully into it is, or at least should be, a most stimulating experience.

This process of acculturation is also important in other ways. Peter Brodner[10] has written about the way in which working with a modern machine tool involves the worker in a very complex way:

...the sensual experience of skilled workers as a different form of perceiving reality can be characterised by the holistic sensual perception of the cutting process, the emotional involvement of the workers, the personal relation to the machine...

The myth of "scientific objectivity" has drawn our attention away from the importance of emotions in problem-solving of many kinds. Emotional involvement is to be avoided at all costs: we seem to prefer to believe that it is possible to approach problems in a spirit of sublime detachment. But on the contrary, the Russian scholar Oleg Tikhomirov[11] argues that

> ...emotional states appearing in the course of problem-solving are an essential part of the problem-solving process...

We can begin to see a role emerging for the quality aesthetics revealed by the craftsmen (and the scientist) in the anecdotes of the previous section. The "feel" for tools, for craftsmanship and for materials is not merely some low-level instinct of the "rude mechanical" but part of a complex and intuitive process of high-level cognitive functioning. This is what it is to be a human rather than a machine!

According to Tikhomirov, emotions perform a heuristic regulatory function: they are not just generators of random decision, but significant factors in search processes. A craftsman following a hunch is therefore not merely working "by guess and by God", but is operating at one of the interfaces between conscious and subconscious thought.

This takes us, in fact, into the whole area of tacit knowledge. Apprenticeship has evolved to take account of the growing bodies of explicit knowledge associated with today's crafts and skill domains. Almost all apprentices now undergo periods of formal education. No modern craftsman or woman can afford to be ignorant of the theoretical basis of his or her practice. But, as countries such as Sweden are beginning to appreciate, there is a critical balance which must be achieved between the kinds of knowledge which can be acquired through formal "instruction" and that whole vast area of critical understanding which Wittgenstein, Polanyi and others have described as "tacit knowledge".

Wittgenstein's regrettable phrase: "...of that whereof we cannot speak, thereof we must be silent..." has proved to be rather two-edged. Academic educators in general have taken the line that if craftsmen do not know what they know and in any case cannot discuss it in terms appropriate to the Senior Common Room of an Oxford college, then what they know (whatever it is) is of no great consequence. In this they are, as, the Dreyfuses have repeatedly argued, merely following Platonic tradition. But the result is that tacit knowledge has been systematically devalued to the extent that it is still hardly accepted as a legitimate objective for educational curricula. Yet it is surely one of the most important outcomes of apprenticeship.

Companies in Scandinavia which prematurely retired their traditional craftsmen in favour of formally "trained" technicians soon discovered the error of their ways, and were forced in many instances to bring back the "redundant" men and women to halt catastrophic declines in quality and productivity. But this only throws up other questions. As the Swedish photographer Peter Gullers drily remarks[12] in relation to what he calls "knowledge of familiarity":

> ...If modern production technology works today thanks to the fact that older craftsmen with a broad and deep knowledge of familiarity are still to be found in our workshops, then the problem remains of whether it is possible to pass on this knowledge when production

technology has become so abstract and automated that there is no longer any scope for training practical skills...

It is interesting that the (better) merchant navies of the world saw this problem coming long before it was perceived to be a threat to industrial production, and reintroduced life under sail to their training programmes: not because there is any serious likelihood of a large-scale return to the tall ships, but in order that some of the instinctive skills and values of the professional seaman should be preserved in an age of SATNAV systems and computerized ship-handling. It seems likely that in future, other occupations will need to introduce their own equivalent of the sail training vessel in order that they can achieve, in Peter Gullers' words:

...the practical training of skills in order to master the essentials of a tradition and then to be able to progress beyond the limitations of accepted practice."

I look forward to it!

So What's Wrong with Apprenticeship?

In criticizing apprenticeship, I must make it clear that I am not talking here about the Mickey Mouse schemes which abound in the UK today, I am not talking about "paper tiger" schemes, described simply to be discredited, and I am not talking about the many instances of appallingly bad practice which certainly exist. I am talking about the same schemes whose positive aspects I have already been discussing.

The apprenticeship system is far from perfect. One glaring weakness, in the UK at least, is the way in which it is still almost exclusively regarded as a male preserve. A few occupations, such as hairdressing, offer forms of "apprenticeship" for girls, but the great majority of "real" apprentices are male. In 1980, for example, 250 000 employees in manufacturing industry in the UK were being given formal training. This represented 4.5% of all males and 2% of all females. About 15 000 of these trainees were formally apprenticed, and the overwhelming majority of these were males.[13] The situation is considerably better in Germany and Scandinavia, but comparisons here are made rather difficult because of the radical differences between conceptions of "apprenticeship" from country to country.

Another problem is the implicit "ageism" of the apprenticeship system. At a time when the need for flexibility and mobility of labour is becoming ever more apparent, apprenticeship is still a "front-end" process, specifically associated with youth and early adulthood. Yet the craft environment is often one in which there is a broad spread of ages: a factor which may be a major contributor to the effectiveness of apprenticeship in stimulating acculturation.

Apart from the simple weight of tradition, one reason for the persistence of youth-based apprenticeship must be economic. I have already referred to the cost of an apprentice in terms of the low productivity due to his or her lack of skills and demands on the master's time and energy. This can be compensated in a young person by low wages inappropriate to an older person with family responsibilities. Add to this the fact that in Germany only about 40% of graduating apprentices were with the enterprise which trained them after 18 months[14] (nearly a third of the men and half the women had left after only six months), and we are once again confronted with the political issue of who should pay for strategic training.

In considering the economics of apprenticeship schemes, much has been made of their poor cost-effectiveness in transferring factual knowledge. I believe that this criticism is largely irrelevant in the context of the modern apprenticeship process, where substantial attention is given to supporting an appropriate range of learning environments. This is certainly expensive and might reasonably be considered a disadvantage of the system. A far more subtle form of cost-benefit analysis needs to be applied if the full advantages of apprenticeship are to be given true weight in company balance sheets, and until this happens, minimal "training" will always have the edge over apprentice education.

A further question which needs to be raised is the extent to which informal learning by experience is so embedded in a specific context that it does not readily transfer to new fields. This is not very well studied or understood. As far as we can see, knowledge does indeed seem to be highly contextualized, but it is also true that considerable transfer can and does occur. It may well be that it depends to a considerable extent on the cultural framework in which the knowledge is acquired, rather than its precise task-orientation.

Apprenticeship tends be associated with stability and performance both in the popular imagination and as far as many craftspeople are concerned, and this may help to establish a "mind set" which resists flexibility of thought. It is certainly true that many craftsmen and women are conservative and unadventurous in their day-to-day practice, but it is a moot point whether this is any more true of apprentice-trained craftworkers than it is of bankers, accountants or even university professors! In any case, if this were a fatal weakness of the system, it would be manifested in a general failure of trades and crafts to progress, and this is clearly not so in most cases.

I believe that this issue of conservatism may be tangled up with the "last ditch" defensiveness brought about by badly conceived management strategies for technological and organisational innovation. Acculturation in a craft community which is engaged in fighting (and losing) its own version of Custer's Last Stand can never be a very positive formative experience, and may at worst induce the kind of backward-looking and "antiquarian" bloody-mindedness which certainly exists.

Aside from this issue, which may come down to a question of management style, rather than anything inherent in apprenticeship as such, there is the excessive reliance of apprentice-based trades and crafts on formal teachers and trainers from outside of the craft culture. At one level this can be quite healthy, in that a diversity of outlook may be maintained. But on the other hand, it reinforces the constant devaluation of the knowledge of the skilled craftsman in comparison with that of the "properly educated" trainer. This is so, even where the trainer has "risen from the ranks". There is a massive barrier of social and academic prejudice to be overcome here.

The problem is that, whereas a good apprenticeship develops skills and tacit knowledge which a craftsman is able to pass on informally, it does not teach him or her to articulate or teach the formal aspects of their knowledge.

This could be overcome to a considerable extent if the progression from apprentice to journeyman to master craftsman involved an explicit element of technical teacher training. There are already some exploratory schemes of this kind in the catering trade, and an extension of the principle might be both worthwhile and cost-effective.

Some Conclusions

We know remarkably little about human learning, and we have consistently mis-applied the little we do know. Worse still, generations of human effort have provided us with what is potentially an extremely powerful means of learning, and yet we are prepared to deprecate and overlook it because it does not depend on the theorizing of the educated elite.

At its best, apprenticeship conforms with many current ideas about optimum conditions for effective learning. In its modern forms, it offers a balance between learning by doing, skilled demonstration and formal exposition. It places early responsibility for the management of learning on the shoulders of the learner. It takes place in relation to purposeful task-directed activity, in the context of a socially embedded subculture and in an environment where there is a wide cross section of ages and levels of experience and expertise. Above all, it is one of the most powerful methods known for the effective transfer of "common sense" and tacit knowledge.

Apprenticeship seems to provide many key components of learning for the quality era which the Taylorist orientation of "training" cannot. As such, it deserves far closer attention than it has received in the recent past.

Notes

1 Possibly the last time in recorded history that the Germans felt that the British had anything to teach them about industrial management!

2 Hayes, C and Wheatley DE (1979) *Trends in Apprenticeship in the European Community*.

3 Parkin, N (1978) Apprenticeships: outmoded or undervalued? *Personnel Management* 10 (5): 22–25.

4 Reported by Göranzon, B (1988) The practice of the use of computers. In Göranzon B and Josefson,I (eds) *Knowledge, Skill and Artificial Intelligence*. Springer-Verlag, London.

5 Parkin, *op cit*.

6 Bruner, J (1986) *Actual minds. possible worlds*. Harvard University Press, Cambridge MA.

7 Kuhn, TS (1962) *The structure of scientific revolutions*. Chicago, Chicago University Press.

8 Illich, I (1973) *Tools for conviviality*. New York, Harper & Row.

9 Boden, M (1980) Social implications of intelligent machines. In: Forrester, T (ed) The microelectronics revolution. Blackwell, Oxford. pp 439–452.

10 Brodner, P (1989) In search of the computer-aided craftsman. *AI & Society* 3(1): 39–46.

11 Tikhomirov, O (1974) Man and the computer: the impact of computer technology on the development of psychological processes. In: Olson, D (ed) *Media and symbols*. University of Chicago Press, Chicago, pp 359–382.

12 Gullers, P (1988) Automation-Skill-Apprenticeship. In: Göranzon, B and Josefson, I (eds) *Knowledge, Skill and artificial intelligence*. Springer-Verlag, London.

13 Learning the Job: Apprenticeship and training in manufacturing industry. *Employment Gazette*, September 1980, pp 943–953.

14 Roberts, J (1986) Apprenticeship in West Germany. *Employment Gazette* March/April 1986: 109–115.

Section IV:

Educational Computing

Chapter 8

The Introduction of Information Technology into the Workplace – Some Practical Considerations

Malcolm Bolton

Why do highly regarded and initially cost-effective computer systems fall into disrepute? Why do staff become disaffected and blame "the computer" when difficulties occur in producing time-critical information? This chapter argues for the need to view the information requirements of an organization as a whole, rather than adopting the often disparate, reductionist view of knowledge and education of traditional systems analysis. The information culture of any organization is generally heuristic or even holistic. Each part of the organization informs each other part, even though there is not necessarily any direct transfer of information. The combination of all this information, the values attached to the information and the personnel who have control over the information constitute the information culture. Between departments various epistemologies will have been developed depending upon the use to which the information is to be put. Determining these epistemologies, through a process of dialogue with employees and management alike, will help to establish the topology of the information culture. The concept of dialogue is integral to the methodology adopted by Technology Arts Information and is essential for the effective implementation of an information technology system within an organization. Dialogue, the article concludes, should be ongoing if the information technology systems and the corporate information culture are not to become unmanageable.

A Dilemma with Corporate Information Systems

Why do computer systems which were initially apparently extremely cost-effective and highly regarded fall into disrepute? Why do staff become disaffected and blame "the computer" when difficulties occur in producing time critical information? One commonly held belief is that from their inception the systems were not "user friendly" enough. This could be interpreted as saying that the original system specification was too rigid to accommodate future requirements or that the human–machine interface is now perceived as "user hostile" and forces the user to work in a way that he or she finds frustrating or illogical. Another reason often given for the loss of confidence is that the staff involved in the initial installation has moved on and that their knowledge of the rationale and architecture of the system has moved on with them. Therefore there is no one available to support the system in-house.

The above two observations are intrinsic within the traditional systems analysis approach to reaching a system specification. Not that systems analysis should now be considered defunct; indeed as a tool to assist in solving many specific data processing requirements within an organization there are many benefits to be had. However, systems analysis has its roots in the 1960s when the mainframe computer and the data processing department reigned supreme as information providers. With the advent of desktop computers, data processing previously requiring the power of a mainframe can now be transferred to the control of any individual member of staff. The distinction between data processing and information processing has become somewhat blurred, since control has moved away from the data processing department.

The need is becoming apparent to view the information requirements of an organization as a whole rather than in the disparate, reductionist approach often adopted by traditional systems analysis.

The ideas set out below constitute some of the working methods that our firm, Technology Arts Information, uses in introducing, or indeed reintroducing, information technology into the working environment. As yet, they do not form a coherent ideology but simply reflect our experience of attempting to negate the detrimental effects of a reductionist view of knowledge and education in the workplace in relation to the introduction of information technology systems.

Information Technology and the Information Culture

Introducing computers into an organization cannot be considered analogous to purchasing, say, a new suite of typewriters. The information technology revolution the typewriter heralded began over 100 years ago and was basically the replacement of the hand-written word as a means of communication used by business, commerce and government and introduced an inexpensive sub-set of movable type. The written word and free form text were irrevocably altered and standardized but the data written on the new-fangled machines were essentially unaltered.

On the other hand the contemporary information technology revolution epitomized by the desktop computer, manipulates and processes information. This will, by its very nature, have some discernible effect on the flow of information within an organization and irrevocably alter our understanding of information.

The unplanned introduction of information technology will produce unplanned and unforeseen effects within the organization and these effects will not always be advantageous. The fundamental prerequisite to the planned introduction of information technology is not primarily understanding the technology to be considered, but rather the information which it will handle and manipulate.

Within the corporate environment, understanding the "information culture" of the organization is vital to gain an understanding of how that organization functions, where bottle-necks can be found in the flow of information through the organization due to insufficient processing and so on. The perception of the importance of up-to-date and correctly processed information especially by higher management, cannot be emphasized too highly. Unfortunately, the experience of various types of organizations in Britain and Northern Europe have exposed this area as one in need of urgent attention. Very few corporate bodies have an information or information technology representative on the board of directors.

The misapprehension of the importance of information, and an ignorance of the corporate information culture, will generally indicate that the introduction of information technology into that environment will be fraught with problems. As a result, the information technology systems will fall into disrepute and staff will become disaffected.

Exploring the "Information Culture"

The information culture of any organization is generally heuristic and indeed perhaps even holistic. Each part of the organization informs each other part, even if there is no direct transfer of information. The combination of all this information, the values attached to the information and the personnel who have control over this information all constitute the "information culture". Each department will use information in different ways and place differing values upon that information. For example, a marketing department will use names and addresses in a different way than, say, the accounts department. Broadly speaking, various epistemologies will have been developed depending upon the use to which the information is put. Determining these epistemologies will help to establish the topology of the information culture. Various techniques can be applied which will help in mapping this topology.

Isolating the differences between the perceived and the actual use of information is extremely useful in identifying those areas of the information culture which require further attention. It could be that a department which considers itself to be overworked is perceived simultaneously by management as ineffectual or inefficient. Such differing perceptions often underlie a misunderstanding by both parties of what information is important and what is not. The discovery of these apparent anomalies should generally be taken as a positive indication that previously uncovered areas of corporate information are being addressed.

Another discovery which can be considered of significance is of areas where a member of staff cannot explain exactly how they undertake a particular task. The deeper knowledge structures begin to appear. The tacit knowledge and unintentional, unselfconscious skills of the staff constitute one of the more important areas of the corporate information culture.

These areas can be uncovered by asking a series of simple questions, which may include:

Can you explain what your work entails?
How does this differ from your job description?
Where do you get the information that you require to do your work?
What do you think the difference between "data" and "information" might be?
What type of information is handled?
Who uses the information you produce and who do they pass it on to?
What priorities are attached to different type of information?
How quickly should different types of data be processed?
Which data are "static" and which are"volatile"?
How much information needs to be processed?
How quickly will the information need to be retrieved?
Is there a need to archive the information?
How can your job be improved by using information technology?
What disadvantages do you see in using information technology in your job?

These questions should be asked at all levels in the staffing structure, but, in order to be able to ask these questions, a dialogue must be set up between the organization and the consultants.

Generally, we have found that the secretaries and clerical staff have more direct contact with corporate information than management, simply because they are employed almost exclusively to handle it. In this respect we have noticed that the receptionist often holds the key to the ways that middle and top management interact with each other and the external world. Therefore extremely valuable facts can be gleaned from the apparently "lower levels" of the organization, but, since there is little reflection upon the information they hold, this generally does not come to the attention of senior management.

Establishing a Dialogue

Consultants are brought into an organization to advise on information technology systems generally when the management perceives a problem that they do not have the in-house expertise to deal with. Generally a brief is provided by management which will outline their requirements in a discrete area of their activity. However, the problem to be addressed is often a symptom of a deeper malaise which has not yet been recognized or defined.

We seek from the onset of a consultation to establish mutual trust with all those we will contact. To achieve this we attempt to convey an independent, impartial point-of-view with no hidden scenario for what management "wants to impose upon" the organization. Two useful methods for achieving this and establishing a dialogue are: firstly, establish a good working relationship with a key liaison person who should be a sympathetic member of senior management; secondly, establish individual meetings with members of staff from the clerical/secretarial/receptionists, middle management and top management levels.

The meeting is the forum in which we can ask the questions as outlined above but more importantly, we make ourselves open to answer questions they may have about information technology. We come to understand the organization, the individuals and the information culture. By asking the interviewee questions we seek to cause them to reflect upon the information which they use day to day and generally take for granted. This often has unforeseen results, most often positive since they are able to talk about their jobs and themselves outside the general context of their working environment. The effect has often been described as "therapeutic" by the interviewees.

Demystifying the Computer

Most of the fears that management and staff express concerning information technology is due to either a misunderstanding of what is and is not possible or confusion over the bewildering array of jargon associated with computers. One of the main emphases that we place on our consultation is to demystify the computer. We emphasize that information technology is a tool, a means to an end and should not be seen as an end in itself. We take pains to explain the associated jargon in plain English.

This approach allows us to move quickly to discussing information as the raw material of information technology. From there we can clarify some of the properties of the raw material and how it can be effectively manipulated by computer technology.

Deciding upon a System

While the original management brief may expect a system to be recommended at a relatively early stage, our experience shows that the information that management receives on the workings of their organization require action to be taken in other areas, for example, staff retraining, relocation of paper filing systems and so on.

Only after the information culture has been mapped out, and management has come to understand the implications contained within this topology, can decisions be made on the procurement of the hardware and software required, and the instigation of new information management practices and procedures. The effects of this type of analysis often have ramifications far beyond that of the original brief which may radically effect the nature of their organization.

Examples of issues where this could occur are: whether data should be processed centrally; the information that should be kept on the mainframe; and the security principle that should apply to data.

Wherever possible, we endeavour to develop the software system in close conjunction with the users of the system and the liaison person. This continues the demystification process and continues the process of dialogue which has already been established.

Training

Primarily, the emphasis on training associated with the introduction of information technology should not be concerned with the information technology itself, but the role it will take within the individual's job. This means that considerable time will be spent in dialogue with the trainee to ascertain what they think their job entails, with how they comprehend management's perception of the individual's job. Introducing information technology training in this context will help to negate "information technology shock" and the insecurity often associated with it.

Perhaps this process is best not described as "training" at all, but rather as "education". Since the individual will be steered in the direction of making connections with what in many cases will be disparate and often apparently unrelated activities and corporate knowledge, the individual often experiences a sudden realization such as "So that's why I've been doing this...".

Establishing an internal user-group with regular meetings for all those using the installed system has many beneficial effects and heightens the organization's corporate awareness of how they can put their information systems to the best use.

Conclusion

The methodology adopted by Technology Arts Information sees the concept of dialogue as essential for the effective implementation of an information technology system within an organization. This dialogue should be ongoing if the information technology systems and the corporate information culture are not to become unmanageable.

Chapter 9

Expert Systems: Channels for Dialogue

Randall Whitaker and Olov Östberg

The chapter examines biases underlying current expert systems (ESs) characterizations. These biases concern direction of knowledge flows in a consultation, the communicational competence of the consultee, the nature of the knowledge transferred, and the accuracy with which an ES mimics the expert. The chapter then discusses information loss in the ES channel. By showing that such losses occur from the consultee to the consultant, the authors argue that consultation is a bidirectional process; the consultee provides notification and description, and the consultant provides advice or answers. The consultative process can therefore be described in terms of conversational interaction between consultee and consultant, and insights into this form of interaction – or consultative dialogue – can be gained from analysis of existing models of conversational interaction (e.g. from linguistics). Only by considering such models can we arrive at a serious, unbiased appraisal of ES value and their impact within workplace settings.

Introduction: Expert Systems as Communications Channels

In 1987, we conducted an expert systems (ESs) survey, intent on assaying their workplace impacts (Östberg *et al* 1988). Many of the developers interviewed had employed "exploratory", rapid prototyping practices of the sort described by Partridge (1986). Some projects appeared "exploratory" to the point of having been learning experiences rather than productive endeavours. We repeatedly found imperfect conceptualizations of (1) what an ES is, and (2) how an ES should be used. Since a view of an ES's role depends on the view of its nature, we decided to review ES definitions. We soon concluded that existing ES perspectives were of little use; they emphasize structure, even to the extreme of stating ESs are defined solely by architecture (Dietz 1986). They fail to account for the consultation process such systems are intended to support.

In assessing definitions, we found only two claims consistently made for ESs (Whitaker and Ostberg 1988). First, they embody a representation of knowledge about a given task domain and they emulate human capabilities within the task domain at a performance level equivalent to an "expert". These points address the character of the task domain into which an ES is inserted, not the form of the system itself. Examining expertise in the context of a task environment led to the conclusion that an expert is described by a role of consultancy, and that ideally "Whether the consultant is a human or an ES should make no critical difference in terms of adequacy of support" (p 200). We next considered the ES as a functional duplicate of a consultant. This view – "ES as facsimile" – addresses the end result of expert emulation. It is still structurally defined, and it does not account for the task environment. We felt that a good definition should address the context of ES implementation.

We then described an alternative ES perspective, deriving from functionality rather than form. We introduced the notion of ESs as communications channels, fabricated for the purpose of rerouting previous (possibly null) paths of knowledge access from the original source to a computer. We asserted that certain attributes of other communications channels should apply to ESs, particularly context sensitivity and information loss. The failure of many ESs to replicate faithfully the original source of expertise follows from their failure to model adequately the task context within which consultation occurs (Östberg *et al* 1988). Imperfect expertise replication is an information loss analogous to that described in formal information theory (Cherry 1952).

This chapter elaborates on the communications channel metaphor introduced in Whitaker and Östberg (1988). The scope of enquiry is still limited to knowledge-based systems (i.e. those labelled ESs), and we ask that the reader bear this in mind. We begin by examining biases underlying current ES characterizations. These biases concern direction of knowledge flows in a consultation, functional adequacy of the consultee, the nature of the knowledge transferred, predictability of the consultee, and the accuracy with which an ES mimics the expert. We then go on to a discussion of information loss in the ES channel. By showing that such losses occur from the consultee to the consultant, we claim that consultation is a bidirectional process. This implies that previous, biased views are insufficient for serious appraisal of the value of ESs and their impact within workplace settings.

Biases in the Unidirectional Model of ESs

We use the term "directionality" to describe the course of information flow in an ES channel. One direction for such a flow is from the expert to the consultee – the commonly cited direction for knowledge transfer. In this case knowledge engineers seek to make a functional simulacrum of expertise – i.e. the "ES as facsimile" described above. Many ES constructed to date follow the facsimile model, though it is not necessarily consistent with the stated nature of knowledge engineering. Knowledge engineering is explicitly portrayed as a manipulative ("engineering") endeavour, with knowledge as the raw material. Implicitly, knowledge base construction is a simulation (modelling) endeavour, with the product judged by functional equivalence to the expert. This view is common in general texts on ESs (e.g. Waterman 1986; Harmon and King 1985). Once we look more closely at the premises underlying today's knowledge engineering practice, it becomes apparent that the unidirectional model of knowledge flow is biased.

Bias 1: The Consultee is Insufficient to the Task

Providing expert facsimiles is an act of constructing unidirectional knowledge channels in some domain. Such facsimiles most closely replicate scenarios wherein the expert (consultant) delivers information to consultees. Such delivery assumes (1) the consultee is incapable of managing all aspects of the task independently, (2) this shortcoming is rectified by providing information, (3) there exist knowledge sources for the necessary information, and (4) such knowledge sources can be accessed via the consultant.

There is a tacit assumption that the consultant, by augmenting the information store of the consultee, makes the consultee sufficient to the task. The consultee's mental model is initially deficient in comparison to the task context, for any of a variety of reasons. In consultation, the consultant transfers some quantum of information to the consultee, augmenting the consultee's mental model and making it sufficient. However, contrary to the bias, consultative interactions may occur in response to circumstances other than consultee insufficiency. What seems to be a deficit may in fact reflect differences between the consultee's and the consultant's knowledge bases, similar to differences in "logics" between experts and plant operators described by de Montmollin and De Keyser (1985). The consultee may have the final authority to initiate consultation, guide its course, and apply the results.

Bias 2: Knowledge is a Tangible Commodity

Central to knowledge engineering is the premise that knowledge is a tangible object or material. Specifically, domain knowledge is portrayed as a finite set of factual data elements and the formalizable relations holding among them. As discussed in Gregory (1987) and Ivanov (1988), this rationalistic view derives simplistically from computer science's mathematical ancestry and longstanding philosophical traditions. The ramifications for ES development are further outlined in Ivanov (1988), and in Gregory's (1986) list of assumptions underlying this view of knowledge:

(1) *Knowledge is Distinct from Knowing:* For knowledge to be representable in a knowledge base it must be the kind of thing that is logically separable from the knowing of it...

(2) *Knowledge is Distinct from its Knower:...*

(3) *Knowledge is a Set of True Facts Bound Together by Rules:...*

(4) *Knowledge is Reducible:* Using the metaphor of the reducibility of the physical world to molecules and atoms, knowledge representation theorists ... have assumed that knowledge is similarly and even necessarily analyzable into its primitive components (p 835).

Seen from these biased assumptions, the consultant is a reservoir for this knowledge commodity, and the consultee is a partially empty vessel. Gregory proceeds to counter this view by reference to alternatives from philosophy (idealism) and cybernetics (conversation theory). We shall follow his general direction of criticism, but our discussion will be centered around consultative interactions in task settings rather than knowledge representation.

Bias 3: The Effect of Knowledge on the Consultee is Deterministic

In the biased view, a consultant is a vehicle for delivering quantifiable knowledge. This delivered product should be concise information for overcoming a specific problem or general guidelines for overcoming a set of problems. The former corresponds to a quick answer in response a request for guidance (i.e. a supervisory function), and the latter corresponds to extending the consultee's knowledge (i.e. an educational function). Categorization of consultants as either supervisory or educational is tied to the level of abstraction of the information transferred. The quick answer is more likely to contain specific references to unique items (i.e. facts), while rules more probably reference broad classes or "variable" items. There is a tendency to classify facts as "data" and rules as "knowledge". Expert systems to date concentrate on the delivery offsets rather than rules, even those systems which "educate" users by feeding them specific instances to induce learning via generalization.

A true criterion for judging the supervision/education distinction is the impact of information transfer on the consultee. Since this involves the subjective state of the consultee, the certitude of results may vary. Supervision would seem straightforward, but "...what one intuitively expects to be an effective form of advice does not necessarily turn out to be so in practice. Even when individuals are presented with critical information they will not necessarily use this in a beneficial way" (Berry and Broadbent, 1986, p 147). Research on applying explicit knowledge to control tasks suggests that education by knowledge-based systems holds little promise: "...providing an individual with detailed verbal instruction that is understood and later remembered is not necessarily sufficient to improve task performance. A person must be induced to implement this verbal information and incorporate it into control performance" (Berry and Broadbent 1984, p 229).

Long-term results cannot be fully predicted even if incorporation of new knowledge is assured. Over time the consultee may modify or expand the transferred information. He/she may take one situational knowledge transfer and apply ii in many scenarios, even across domain boundaries (working by analogy). He/she may change the level of abstraction at which the information is used. One may learn general rules through guidance in specific cases (supervisor has the net effect of teacher), while case-specific behaviour is influenced by earlier training (teacher has the net effect of supervisor). There is no way to ensure that the outcome of a consultation will match the *intended* thrust of the consultant's advice unless the consultee is devoid of intentionality. Such a passive portrayal conflicts with the interpersonal pragmatics outlined in Flores and Ludlow (1980) or the active consultee role we describe later.

Bias 4: The ES is the Same as the Expert

Translating a consultative process into a computer-based channel (an ES) is not straightforward. As with most translations, the quality depends upon many factors, especially the translator's insight and eloquence. Östberg *et al* (1988) point out that knowledge engineers are better trained for interacting with computers than with experts. Even a competent knowledge engineer may be hampered by the subject (the expert). Experts present a number of obstacles to knowledge acquisition (Hart 1986). Expert systems are frequently targeted for highly complex tasks, but an expert's ability to articulate expertise is inversely proportional to the domain complexity (Michie 1985). The performance level which makes the subject "expert" may not directly relate to a level of verbalizable knowledge concerning the task domain (Broadbent *et al* 1986).

A communication channel has been defined as "that set of existing conditions (on which the signal depends) that either (1) generate no (relevant) information, or (2) generate only redundant information (from the point of view of the receiver)" (Dretske 1981, p 115). A channel is by definition neutral with regard to the information conveyed, but a computer is not a neutral venue. It can enhance (via extended graphics) or hinder (via restrictive syntax) the consultative process. By rerouting a communication channel through a computer, interaction will necessarily be affected by the new venue's nature. Thus the medium will unavoidably influence the knowledge transfer, even if the knowledge acquisition had been perfect Such influences are intrinsic to knowledge engineering. They are best assessed by comparing earlier consultative interactions with the new. If the new range of interactions subsumes the old, the ES may have enhanced knowledge access. Restrictions will be evidenced by the old interaction range subsuming the new. Of course, there may be a disjunction of interactive capabilities between the old and the new. In this case, system sufficiency will have to be judged on other criteria.

There is always one contrast between the original channel and the ES – directness of interaction. Consultation between a consultee and a human expert is direct The consultee accesses and addresses the actual source of expertise. When this process is translated into an ES, directness is lost. The ES is physically and temporally distant from the original source of expertise – physically distant due the new knowledge medium and temporally distant via the knowledge engineering process. This indirect interaction becomes a problem when the ES falls short in modelling the originally accessible knowledge – when there has been a loss of information along the ES channel. In such cases the knowledge base is insufficient, and the consultee has to overcome these distances.

Loss of Information in the Consultative Channel

Information Loss from the Expert to the Consultee

Whitaker and Östberg (1988) indicated that the "ES as media" perspective could address ES shortcomings as information losses. Such information loss has been discussed in quantitative terms elsewhere (e.g. Dretske 1981). ES introduce physical and temporal distance into consultation, and they should suffer similar deterioration of their throughput. It was suggested that a measure of information loss could perhaps be defined for ES analysis, but this is still an object of speculation. Even without formal measures, we can discuss the general nature of the information loss phenomenon.

The flow of knowledge from expert to end user is portrayed as a unary communications channel, but its replication via an ES is not a unary process. It is a series of interactions between (1) expert and knowledge engineer (knowledge acquisition), (2) knowledge engineer and computer (programming), and (3) computer and end user (consultation). The first interaction is intended to convert the expert's "human know-how" into some explicitly declared form ("human say-how"); the next to convert the say-how into "machine know-how"; and the last to convert the machine know-how into "machine show-how" (Michie 1985). These interactions carry the potential for errors of misinterpretation and errors of omission. Both can degrade richness of the knowledge transferred from an original source to an ES.

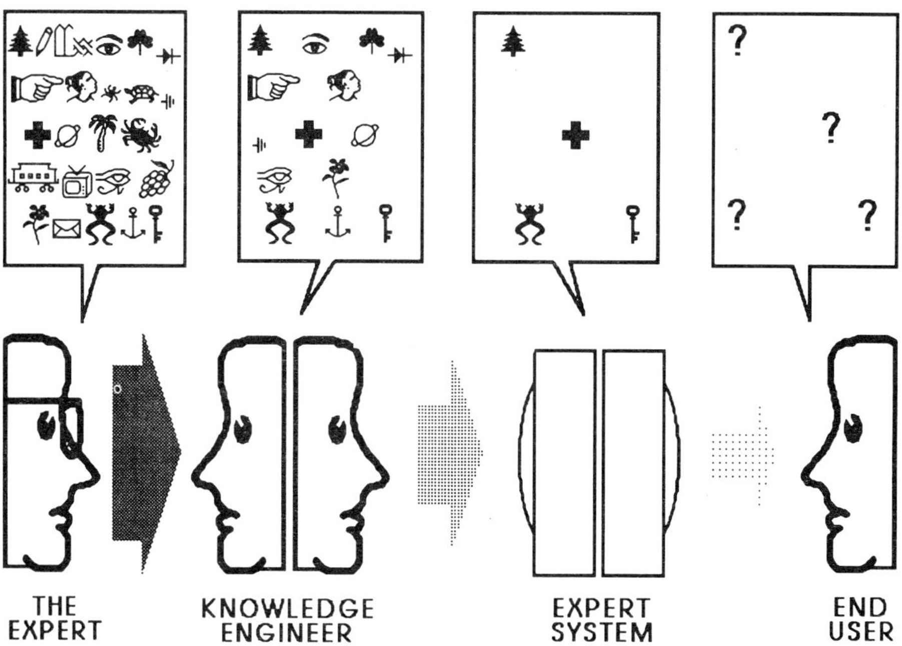

Fig. 9.1. Loss of information from the expert to the consultee.

Figure 9.1 illustrates this degradation, where "richness" is used here to mean a criterion reflecting two critical dimensions – the range of situations addressable (*comprehensivity*); and the degree of situational discrimination possible (*discriminability*).

Comprehensivity is a function of the knowledge base's coverage of a task domain. It presumes the knowledge representation is adequate to describe all possibilities in the task setting. Comprehensivity further requires that the knowledge engineer recognizes the full range of task domain scenarios and portray them in this representation. In effect, comprehensivity is a measure of adequacy in mapping the possible input/start and output/end states of the task domain. Discriminability is a matter of distinguishing between scenarios *within the task domain* based on context. Such discrimination may use information not contained in the knowledge representation, and it is commonly the key to an expert's inferential capacity. Where each possible situational state requires a nonambiguous response, discrimination comprises the whole inferential process, as in R1 (McDermott 1982). In effect, discriminability is a measure of adequacy in mapping the intermediate states of the task domain.

Information Loss from the Consultee to the Consultant

We have focused on information loss from consultant to consultee, congruent with the unidirectional view of knowledge flow in ES channels. However, there is also information loss in the opposite direction. When a consultee seeks counsel, the goal is a constructive transfer of information to alleviate a problem. Assuming the consultant is neither monitoring the consultee nor spontaneously generating advice, the consultee must identify a need for expertise; identify and/or locate the appropriate source of expertise; notify the consultant of the need; provide the consultant with a problem description; then receive and, if no iteration is called for, finally apply or discard the consultant's answer.

The unidirectional model's emphasis on the expert's monologue to a consultee is unrealistic. It ignores the consultant's information needs in consultation. Experts are valuable because they are knowledgeable, not because they are psychic with regard to the consultee's needs. Experts advise effectively only if they understand the problem. Consider the example of a group of draftspersons. One sat across the room from the supervisor, hidden by a drafting table. He habitually asked questions as if the supervisor could divine his needs with only a summons. When puzzled, he would call to the supervisor for an opinion. Always, the supervisor had to ask which item he meant or where in the scheme of things it lay, and the questioner would point at his drawing (out of sight) and tap a finger at the problem. The supervisor's inability to see through the drafting table consistently escaped him. The supervisor could never answer until he walked over to the questioner's table, looked at the drawing, and asked questions to understand the problem.

Expertise is rarely so highly refined that effective advice can be given immediately upon request A consultant must understand the problem before he/she can act, and failure to satisfy his/her information needs may impair the ability to counsel. This illustrates a key point – *consultation is a bidirectional process*. The expert's monologue to the consultee can, at best, only occur in the light of a two-way, context-creating dialogue. The flow of information from consultee to consultant, preceding the flow of advice, is certainly not trivial to the consultative process. Where an expert examines a problem personally, he/she can directly discern its character; when he/she relies on consultee elucidation, understanding is constrained by the consultee's eloquence. The consultant is therefore dependent on the consultee. This means the consultee may exert significant power in enabling and guiding the consultant during problem resolution.

Assuring equivalence of an ES's knowledge base to an expert is insufficient to replicate task-oriented consultation. To the extent that the consultee guided the original (pre-computerized) consultation, the ES should permit a similar degree of user control. Currently, knowledge engineering concentrates on mirroring the expert alone and not the consultative dialogue as a whole. In designing knowledge-based decision support systems, the consultee's participation is often overlooked or deferred as an interface issue. Such deferral comes at the expense of the eventual users, who may relinquish some of their previous interactional power and/or shoulder additional burdens in feeding data to the system in a constrained format. Inadequate interface sophistication limits the end user's ability to present problems to the system. This introduces a bottleneck which could prevent the ES from handling some valid cases. Such restrictions derive from shortcomings in system design/implementation and from deficiencies in the consultee's ability to approach the consultation process. A summary of suggested limitations is given in Table 9.1.

Note that the first set of limitations are system installation issues, while the second and third sets involve issues of user training and job design. The two types of limitations described are not mutually exclusive. They can occur in any combination within any given system application. The important point is that any of these deficiencies affects information flows between consultee and consultant, and that measures to eradicate such deficiencies must address issues of design for both the system and the task environment.

Table 9.1. Factors inducing loss of information from the consultee

System limitations	Consultee limitations
Limitation on consultative access	
Limited availability to users	Limited access to the consultant
Limited responsiveness to need for consultation	Limited recognition of need for consultation
Limitation on problem representation	
Limited input syntax	Limited expressive ability
Limited range of knowledge base	Limited range of domain knowledge
Limited internal representational power	Limited depth of domain knowledge
Limitation on consultative conduct	
Limited facility for terming queries	Limited facility for refining answers

A Taxonomy for Consultative Interactions

The foregoing discussion portrays consultation as a two-way flow of information – the consultee provides notification and description, and the consultant provides advice or answers. Consultation is a conversation, albeit directed and therefore constrained. This suggests that models of conversational interaction (e.g. from linguistics) can be fruitfully employed to illustrate analyse the consultative process. This is not, of course, a new thought (see, for example, Pask 1980, Winograd and Flores 1986). For the purposes of this discussion, we assume the pragmatic goal of any consultation is a net flow of information from the consultant to the consultee. Let us describe the consultative process in terms of conversational interaction between consultee and consultant. This descriptive exercise is intended to delineate exchanges along any consultative channel and shed light on those channel features which could facilitate or impair expertise transfer.

We will label as *consultative dialogue* the most general form of such interaction – bidirectional information interchanges between a party requiring information for satisfaction of some problem (the consultee) and one or more parties deemed capable of providing this information (the consultant). The types of information flowing between these parties are illustrated in Figure 9.2.

The consultee may transmit information of three types to the consultant. The first is an initial question. The question is notification of a request and a specification for the desired response. Questions are complex speech acts involving semantic and pragmatic nuances, but they will be treated as simple specifications here. The second comprises situational/contextual data describing the problem. Such data support the consultant's inference. The third is a response to the consultant's response. This can be termed a request for elucidation, i.e., an additional question based on a judgement of an answer's adequacy. In return, the consultant transmits information of three types, mirroring those from the consultee. First, he/she provides answers – specific data to "fill in the blanks" specified by the question. Second, the

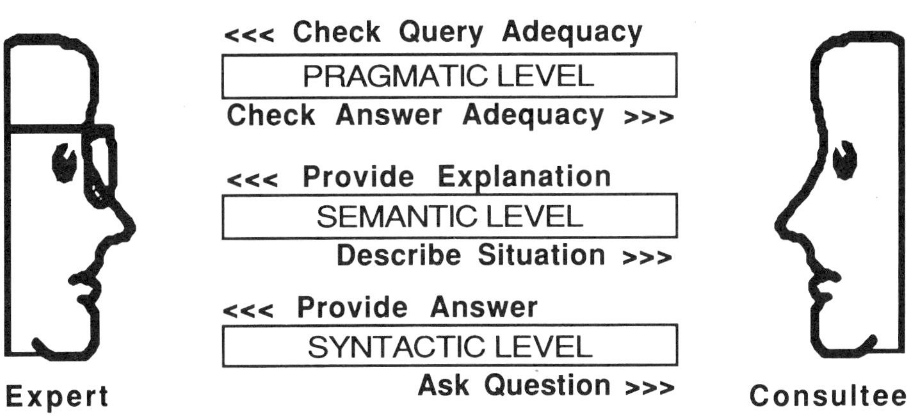

Fig. 9.2. Consultation as a bidirectional process.

Table 9.2. Consultee and consultant contributions to a consultative dialogue.

Level of processing	Consultee contribution	Consultant contribution
Syntactic	Query	Answer
Semantic	Situational facts	Explanatory information
Pragmatic	Request elucidation of answer	Request clarification of query

consultant may provide situational or contextual information to expand on the answer or more fully explain it. Finally, the consultant may require more information from the consultee. He/she may request additional data, based on judgement of a query's adequacy.

The ordering of these items is not accidental. There are straightforward correspondences between query/answer; situational facts/explanatory information; and the respective requests for elucidation/clarification. The first pair of items are addressable as syntactic units. They are the substance of simple query processing. The second pair of items involve semantic content, in that they both entail relating the respective information elements to a context. The final items – the requests – are concerned with the pragmatics of the consultation process. These correspondences are outlined in Table 9.2.

The first level of processing – syntactic – corresponds to the sort of data function performed by databases. The mapping from requests to responses is highly determined, being a direct function of mappings between input and the output. The second level corresponds roughly to the functionality ascribed to an ES. In this class of interactions, there is recourse to domain semantics in mapping requests to responses. The sort of pragmatic acts claimed above for human/human consultative interactions commonly entail something more than task domain semantics. The pragmatic level essentially requires a meta-level assessment of the consultation, and is beyond the scope of existing ESs. They involve a semantics, but one in which the task domain is itself a component. These acts consist of more than perfunctory bookkeeping, and they might be creative in response to novel conditions.

Planning and/or recursive, incremental completion of standardized queries might seem to parallel this sort of pragmatic activity. However, they rely on *a priori* model of the task domain. For example, planning (as the term has been applied to AI systems) entails a very rationalistic evaluation of quantifiable domain states defined within the context of a predetermined model. Recursive requests from a database management system for data to complete a query involve a low-level, largely syntactic perspective. In neither case does the machine rise above its innate "view" of the domain.

Explanation in Terms of Information Level and Directionality of Flow

Explanation facilities ostensibly permit an ES to inform the user on the background to a given response. Such facilities are either seen as useful expansions to a basic system architecture (e.g. Waterman 1986) or as a

"...main component of a true ES" (Forsyth 1984, p 14). Most explanation subsystems to date provide a trace of the inference path by which a given response was derived. Such a trace derives from the form of the knowledge base, and it is most easily accomplished with rule-based knowledge representations (Scott *et al* 1984).

There are two points to be made about today's explanation facilities. The first has to do with the level at which these facilities work. Such explanation mechanisms can be characterized as operating at the level of domain semantics (to the extent that a rule-based knowledge base models the semantics of a task environment). Explanation via rule tracing cannot transcend this level, where "the problem of 'WHY?' is reduced to the problem of 'HOW?'" (Ivanov 1988). The information provided by these facilities is tightly coupled (or, at the extreme, isomorphic) with the knowledge base's form. Information is supportive only to the extent that users can phrase their concerns in a form congruent with the system's knowledge representation. In the "real world", both the need for explanation and its effectiveness often derive from the sort of strategic considerations we label pragmatics. Lack of attention to pragmatics limits the functionality of explanation facilities.

The second point concerns directionality of explanation facilities. The facsimile expert is, via explanation, intended to elucidate its answers (as suggested in Table 9.2). What of the user's ability to clarify his/her inputs to the system? While such clarification may be solicited on syntactic grounds, we know of no ES which screens queries based on domain semantics (e.g. challenging "stupid questions"; soliciting new facts to augment the knowledge base). This can be ascribed to the lack of pragmatic level knowledge and learning mechanisms in most ESs. If the knowledge base is not capable of recognizing its own failures and changing its domain model in response (necessary conditions for intelligence according to Churchman 1985), there is little point in soliciting semantic and/or pragmatic information from the consultee.

Our Model Compared with Some Other Models

This discussion expressly concentrates on ESs and the set of consultative interactions they purport to replicate. For example, our references to "pragmatics" address strategic considerations of the consultant and consultee within the framework of a consultative interaction. The term is not used here to refer to issues beyond the scope of such interaction. As such, our usage is more restrictive than that of Winograd (1987), who makes pragmatics the foundation for his "language/action perspective" on information system design. The "conversation for action" as described in Winograd and Flores (1986) is more general, being not limited to consultative interactions. The more restrictive consultative dialogue presented here is analogous to a conversation for action wherein the consultee is the "requestor" and the consultant is the "promisor". More general still are conversational systems (Pask and Gregory 1987), for which consultation is a particular, task-directed instance of conversation. Even more general are descriptions of group processes such as meeting analysis (Cook *et al* 1987).

This non-conflicting specificity of our discussion is not a disadvantage. Indeed, we see an immediate potential for applying more general theoretical frameworks (such as the three noted above) to the next task – generating sound methodological guidelines for ES development. Such guidelines should derive from a balanced combination of formal analysis (based on one of these or some other theory) and a holistic appraisal of the milieu into which the ES is being inserted (such as we have attempted with the communications channel metaphor). Knowledge-based systems are being developed and delivered, whether or not they are ripe for real world use. We do not have the luxury of declaring a moratorium pending resolution of all the outstanding issues. Given this, the best we can hope for is to inject some reason into the ongoing wave of ES projects.

As with any compromise, we lay ourselves open to criticism from both sides. To those of rationalist bent, our agenda may seem lacking in theoretical rigour. We must point out that such rigour leads to functional *rigor mortis* in the work environment (witness Taylor's scientific management and its resultant malaise). On the other hand, we may seem a bit too abstract for some tastes. To this we must respond that ES development to date has been pursued in an absence of illumination, and such blind endeavour should be relegated to the past.

References

Berry, D. and Broadbent, D (1984) On the Relationship between task performance and associated verbalizable knowledge. *The Quarterly Journal of Experimental Psychology* 36A: 209–231. Berry, D. and Broadbent, D (1986) Human search procedures and the use of expert systems. *Current Psychological Research and Reviews* 5: 130–147.

Broadbent, D, FitzGerald, P and Broadbent, M (1986) Implicit and explicit knowledge in the control of complex systems. *British Journal of Psychology* 77: 33–50.

Cherry, E (1952) The communication of information. *American Scientist* 40: 640–664.

Churchman, C (1985) Churchman's conversations. *Systems Research*, 2: 181–184.

Cook, P, Ellis, C, Graf, M, Rein, G and Smith, T (1987) Project Nick: meetings augmentation and analysis. *ACM Transactions on Office Information Systems* 5: 132–146.

de Montmollin, M, and De Keyser, V (1985) Expert logic v. operator logic. In: Mancini, G, Johannsen, G and Martensson, L (eds) *Analysis, Design and Evaluation of Man–Machine Systems*, Pergamon, Oxford (IFAC Proceedings, pp. 43–49.

Dietz, P (1986) Artificial intelligence: building rule-based ES. *Design News* 3 March: 137–144.

Dretske, F (1981) *Knowledge and the flow of information*, MIT Press, Cambridge MA.

Flores, F and Ludlow, J (1980) Doing and speaking in the office. In: Fick, G and Sprague, R (eds), *Decision support systems: issues and challenges*, Pergamon, Oxford, (IFAC and Proceedings, pp 75–118).

Forsyth, R (ed) (1984) *Expert systems*. Chapman and Hall, New York.

Gregory, D (1986) Delimiting ES. *IEEE Transactions on Systems, Man and Cybernetics* SMC-16: 834–843.

Gregory, D (1987) Philosophy and practice in knowledge representation. In: Zeidner, J (ed), *Human productivity enhancement*, vol II. Praeger, New York, pp 165–203.

Harmon, P and King, D (1985) *Expert systems: artificial intelligence in business*. John Wiley, New York.

Hart, A (1986) *Knowledge acquisition for expert systems*. Kogan Page, London.

Ivanov, K (1988) Expert-support systems: the new technology and the old knowledge. *Systems Research* 5: 93–100.

McDermott, J (1982) A rule-based configurer of computer systems. *Artificial Intelligence* 19: 39–88.

Michie, D (1985) Current developments in artificial intelligence and expert systems. *Zygon* 20: 375–389.

Östberg, O, Whitaker, R and Amick, B (1988) *The automated expert: technical human and organizational considerations in expert system applications*. Teldok, Farsta, Sweden (*Via Teldok* 12/1988).
Partridge, D (1986) Will AI lead to a super software crisis? In: Gill, K (ed) *Artificial intelligence for society*, John Wiley, London, pp 31–39.
Pask, G (1980) Developments in conversation theory. Part I. *International Journal of Man–Machine Studies* 13: 357–411.
Pask, G and Gregory, D (1987) Conversational systems. In: Zeidner, J (ed), *Human productivity enhancement*, vol II, Praeger, New York, pp 204–235.
Scott, A, Clancey W, Davis, R and Shortliffe, E. (1984) Methods for generating explanations. In: Buchanan, B and Shortliffe, E (eds) *Rule-based ES: the MYCIN experiments of the Stanford Heuristic Programming Project*. Addison-Wesley, Reading MA, pp 338–362
Waterman, D (1986) *A guide to expert systems*. Addison-Wesley, Reading MA.
Whitaker, R and Östberg, O (1988) Channelling knowledge: expert systems as communications media. *AI and Society* 2: 197–208.
Winograd, T (1987) A language/action perspective on the design of cooperative work. *Human-Computer Interaction* 3: 3–30.
Winograd, T and Flores, F (1986) *Understanding computers and cognition: a new foundation for design*. Ablex, Norwood NJ.

Section V:

Computers and Law

Chapter 10

Controlling the Application of Knowledge-Based Systems

Mike Sharples

This chapter aims to indicate some of the potential benefits and dangers inherent in the technology of Knowledge-Based Systems (KBSs) and to suggest courses of action that would both minimize risk and promote social benefit in future developments. KBSs offer cheap and ready access to knowledge, efficient management and organization of information, conversion of information into usable knowledge to guide human action, knowledge and advice relevant to the context in which it is needed. There are, however, potential dangers if a user is unfamiliar with the assumptions underlying KBS structures of reasoning and representing knowledge; the danger of a program becoming incomprehensible or unreliable in an emergency; the possibility of placing too much faith in the abilities of KBSs and thereby losing the capacity for critical evaluation of its judgments; the inevitable uncertainty or inexactitude programmed into KBSs; the economic implications at an uneven distribution of new technology; and the likelihood of misinterpretation or technical failure when autonomous systems are automatically activating machinery (e.g. military/defence systems). The chapter argues for the regulation of KBS construction, particularly for those systems designed for public or "non-expert" use. Suggestions include programming into each system a clear qualification of answers and requests for data, setting up a workable Code of Conduct for AI practitioners, and constant supervision of the assumptions and activities of each computerized system. Since KBSs work by consulting an internal model of the world (supplied to them by a human programmer), their decisions must be challenged or ignored when necessary and always treated with an appropriate degree of scepticism.

The short-term future of Knowledge Based Systems (KBSs) is fairly well mapped out, by present day research programmes such as ESPRIT and by the policies of those companies that are developing and marketing "expert systems". But predictions beyond the next five years are very difficult. The field could develop in a number of directions, some beneficial, some harmful, and these directions will, in part, be determined by deliberate political and economic decisions. The aim of this chapter is to indicate some of the potential benefits and dangers inherent in KBS technology and to suggest courses of action that would both minimize risk and promote social benefit.

The image of the "thinking machine" evokes both revulsion and fascination, and those involved in research and development of KBSs are not above such passions; many entered the field enthused with the idea of designing a mind (the Lighthill Report[1] even suggested that robotics researchers suffer from maternal deprivation and build robots in the image of their mothers!) and see their main contribution as being not the development of marketable products, but the investigation of human thought and behaviour. In addressing itself to the social applications of KBSs, this chapter has, regrettably, not been not able to capture the intellectual challenge and excitement engendered by attempts to build working models of cognition.

The Benefits of Knowledge-Based Systems

Cheap and Ready Knowledge

Much of the optimism about KBSs is not generated by their proven capability, but by their potential. The belief is that considerable benefits could be brought to industry, government, medicine, education, voluntary groups, and ordinary people in their homes, by the cheap and easy availability of knowledge on a wide range of topics.

Many problems arise through ignorance. We suffer, for example, because we do not know how to cure our sicknesses, or how to become richer, or where to go for help. The information we require may well be available, but hidden in legal or medical tomes, or in the heads of professionals.

A Third World farmer may have plants ravaged by disease, but not know what the disease is, or how to cure it. This knowledge may not be available in the farmer's village at all, nor elsewhere in the country, at an affordable price. An expert system for diagnosing plant diseases could assist in identifying the disease, and curing it, for a reasonable cost.

An unemployed person may not have enough money to support himself. Although that person may be entitled to more benefits, he or she may not be claiming them because of a lack of independent advice. An expert system on Social Security regulations could advise on rights and how to go about claiming them.

A small company designing a new gadget might not be able to afford the investment in time and effort required to make the gadget as efficient, and hence as competitive, as possible. An expert system might assist in the design by, for example, calling up mathematical modelling programs, or giving expert advice on the design choices.

Sailing the Sea of Information

It is not more information that people need – we are swimming in an ever-rising sea of information, from news bulletins, surveys, quiz shows and mail-shots – but knowledge directly relevant to a problem: knowledge about which set of actions is appropriate to the circumstances, about how to perform a task, and about the consequences of each possible decision. At present, specialist knowledge is very unevenly distributed, concentrated in universities, teaching hospitals, company head offices, government departments, and specialist advice centres. One way to ensure its spread is to provide non-specialists, such as school teachers, general practitioners and sales representatives with a source of knowledge applicable to their immediate needs in the form of an expert system supplemented by a referral service to the human expert for the particularly difficult cases. There is an obvious danger that the non-specialist may not be able to spot a problem requiring the intervention of a human expert, but the alternative to the limited expertise of a non-specialist plus expert system may be no expertise at all.

The "sea of information" brings its own problems. Only a tiny fraction of what we might see, hear or read is directly useful, or even interesting, yet finding those nuggets of information could involve hours of tedious searching. The Prestel information system, operated by British Telecom, contains some 100 000 "screens" of potentially useful information, but these are spread amongst hundreds of "information providers": independent companies who promote their own data and ignore those of their competitors. To find, say, the availability of skiing holidays in Italy involves searching through the databases of ten or more travel firms, all using different methods of classification and different formats for displaying the information on the screen. Expert systems offer some hope of managing the spread of information by turning it into usable knowledge in the form of digests, decision options, and automated monitoring systems. Programs already exist that automatically monitor and index the news stories provided by press agencies, providing stories to order on a given topic; there are also ones that collect data on stocks and shares, giving a warning or any large rise or fall in selected stocks.

The Human Window

Donald Michie has warned of situations where a sudden flood of information can completely overwhelm a human monitor. During the emergency at the nuclear power plant at Three Mile Island over 100 warning lights were flashing simultaneously, the operators wrongly interpreted the warnings and, instead of drenching the reactor core with water, switched off the emergency cooling system (which the computer had correctly activated), with disastrous results. But the computer program at Three Mile Island was not an expert system and merely set off the cooling system, with no explanation of its actions. Michie argues that complex systems like power plants, or chemical installations, or aeroplanes, need a "human window" (Michie and Johnston 1984) which, in an emergency, can give the human operator an intelligible précis of the situation and in particular can explain why the program is doing what it is doing. Expert systems have the ability to interpret large amounts of data, turning it into usable knowledge to guide human action.

The General Factotum

From all this it may seem that expert systems are only for use in an emergency, but a portable and knowledgeable assistant could be the modern equivalent of a "general factotum", replacing do-it-yourself books, car maintenance manuals and self-study guides by offering knowledge in the context where it is needed. Devices such as cookers or car engines may, in future, contain their own source of expertise. Already there exist packages of electronics capable of directly monitoring car engines, and reporting faults. Coupled to an expert system one of these could not only provide a warning of an engine fault, but also offer advice on a remedy. Each domestic appliance may in the future be a little more intelligent, with the central heating system automatically minimizing heat loss, the oven recommending the best cooking method for a particular dish, and the front door telephoning to announce that it has inadvertently been left open.

If the thought of accepting advice from an oven or conversing with a door appals, then there is the consolation that each wave of innovation – the train, the motor car, electronics – has, in the short term, brought with it dissonance and disruption of familiar patterns of work and leisure, but has eventually been assimilated and accepted.

In summary, the optimistic view of the future is that everyone will benefit in some form from the widespread use of KBSs, but the people with most to gain are those who are currently denied access to specialist knowledge through its cost or their lack of power, those who rely on expert knowledge as part of their work, and those who are attempting to cope with complex fast-changing systems.

The Dangers of Knowledge-Based Systems

KBS Literacy

As a result of over 3000 years of literacy most people in the industrialized countries, and increasingly many in the Third World, are now able to read, and to detect some of the lies, assumptions and fallacies buried in text. Even so a good writer can bend the mind of his or her reader, with a misleading analogy, a subtle distortion, or some false logic. Commercial expert systems have been with us for a mere five years, and there is no equivalent base of literacy. Users have not learned the skills of "reading" the rules of expert systems, and uncovering false assumptions or detecting gaps in the knowledge. Such literacy will evolve, but not in the near future, since the structure, methods of representing knowledge, and methods of reasoning used by KBSs are still changing.

The result is that a user of a KBS must take its conclusions largely on trust. Many expert systems have rudimentary rule justification and explanation facilities, but these do little more than list the rules used to form a conclusion. They cannot comment on whether each rule is a correct representation of the real world, nor whether the reasoning itself is complete and reliable.

Closed Windows

The benefits, mentioned in the previous section, of providing a "human window" in the form of a KBS that can monitor and offer advice on a complex process, rest on the assumption that the KBS is itself understandable and reliable. If it is not (and the first sign that it is faulty may come in the very emergency it was supposed to assist) then the human user may not be able quickly to call up the raw data, or may have lost the skill in interpreting them; he may not even be able to tell whether the fault has occurred in the underlying system or in the KBS. Thus, the term "window" is highly misleading; a monitoring KBS is not a sheet of glass, but a complex system, interpreting another complex system to the human user. Adding an expert system to a nuclear plant may give the appearance of simple efficiency, but so would removing 90% of the gauges and warning lights.

A Little Knowledge

Making KBSs more like human advisors – for example by enabling them to converse in something like natural language, or to employ common-sense reasoning – runs the risk that they will be taken as more like human experts than they actually are. As a result, people may put undue trust in their pronouncements.

For instance, a future KBS could appear to have a fairly subtle command of natural language within the limited interchanges for which it was designed. Many users might therefore assume that it has a complete command of that language, at least in the subject area under discussion. Some people might even believe it to have a rich command of language in other areas too. These false assumptions would very likely lead to its judgements being given much more credit than they are worth.

Suppose, for example, that the computer uses a familiar English word such as "possible". The human user knows that this word is similar in meaning to a number of others, such as "probable", "credible", "hypothetical", "arguable", "natural", "foreseeable", "likely" and so on. But we know too that "possible" is not precisely equivalent to any of these, for each of these words has a subtly different shade of meaning. If a native English speaker uses a particular word, we can assume that he or she has chosen it in preference to any of the alternatives. This is why someone who says that something is "possible" is assumed to be denying that it is probable. For a KBS the word "possible" may be the only one which covers all the above alternatives, with a range from "likely" to "arguable". The more superficially "human-like" the KBS, the more people may be misled into thinking that it possesses a full range of human attributes such as common-sense reasoning and language understanding.

Autonomous Systems and the Technical Fix

An expert system designed to interpret a large quantity of information would normally leave the human user in charge, able to make the final decision on whether or not to act on the system's recommendations. But there are circumstances, for example interpreting fluctuations in exchange rates or share prices, analysing data from meteorological stations, monitoring complex industrial processes, or analysing signals from military early warning systems, in which the information is changing so rapidly, and decisions need to be made so frequently, that a human cannot keep up. Even if a human were, in theory, given the final say, his role would only be to confirm the best guess of the system or to make a random choice between options. There would not be time for a more informed decision.

For these situations, KBSs are being designed that not only provide recommendations but also activate machinery to carry them out: automatically buying and selling shares, creating weather maps, controlling industrial processes, or launching a retaliatory military strike. It is autonomous systems for military use that raise the most immediate social issues, since the consequences of a failure are so great. A failure in the midst of battle could significantly lower the chances of winning. A failure in peace time might cause an unintended war.

Unfortunately, the likelihood of failure is high. All computer programs contain bugs; the bigger the program the more bugs it contains. KBS programs are no exception. Bugs can arise either because the original specification of the program did not anticipate all the situations that the program will be faced with or because the specification has not been fully met by the implementors of the program.

Programs are made safe for normal use by an extensive process of testing and correction. For programs of any complexity it is infeasible to test them in all possible situations. This is doubly so when the situation they face is open-ended, so that some of the possible situations they may encounter are not known to the system's designers or testers. Military programmers face an adversary who is constantly trying to think up such unexpected situations to trick the program. In such cases the program cannot be properly specified and, thus, will contain bugs, however well it is implemented. In addition, some military programs, e.g. those that react to enemy missile attacks and launch retaliatory strikes, cannot be tested in a real situation, but only in simulations that may be flawed by false assumptions and limited imagination. Bugs of both specification and implementation will remain undetected and uncorrected.

An official Department of Defense document acknowledges problems with such systems:

Commanders remain particularly concerned about the role that autonomous systems would play during the transition from peace to hostilities when rules or engagement may be altered quickly. An extremely stressing example of such a case is the projected defense against strategic nuclear missiles [presumably a reference to the Strategic Defense Initiative], where systems must react so rapidly that almost complete reliance will have to be placed on automated systems. At the same time, the complexity and unpredictability of factors affecting decisions will be very great (Defense Advanced Projects Agency 1983).

Despite such official worries, there remains the underlying assumption that automated military decision-making systems are inevitable. This is a supreme example of a "technical fix": as a result of the development of short and medium range missiles, the "response time" (the time between detecting a missile attack, and the missiles exploding on target) can be as little as three minutes. In that time a decision must be made as to whether to launch a counter-attack, before missile silos are destroyed. The "technical fix" is designed to cut out the human decision-maker, and to adopt a "launch on warning" strategy, so that as soon as the computer detects incoming missiles it automatically commands a counter-attack.

Faced with the complexities and speed of modern warfare, military planners are being forced down the road of increased automation. They have been seduced by the apparent flexibility and "intelligence" of KBSs and think they have found a "technical fix" for their problems. Unfortunately, current KBS techniques are not up to the job. Their successes so far have been in circumscribed domains very different from the diverse, open-ended and adversarial military ones.

The Emotional KBS

So far, the criticisms of KBSs might be construed as technical objections, to be overcome when the next, or the next but one, generation of KBSs arrives: systems that can learn from experience, converse in fluent English, and be praised for their quick thinking and common sense. Whether or not such machines will ever be built is open to question, but assuming they can be, problems may still remain.

People have become accustomed to computers producing the truth. One may doubt the accuracy of a bank statement, but not the arithmetic associated with it. Computers are often accused of making errors, but the public is being trained to blame the data, or the programmer who has specified the wrong set of instructions, not the computer itself which slavishly follows the commands.

But now all this carefully nurtured public acceptance must be thrown out; KBSs are designed to be inexact. Their output must be judged by the criterion of adequacy, not correctness. Indeed, Sloman (1984) argues that an inevitable consequence of designing larger and more general-purpose systems is that they will behave as if governed by human characteristics, such as uncertainty, belief and anxiety:

It can also be argued that there is no way to build a super-intelligent robot which also copes with a complex set of different sons of motives, in a partly unpredictable world, without giving that robot mechanisms which are capable of producing emotional states, as a result of performing the cognitive asks for which they are required. That is, the possibility of having emotions may be a by-product of being able to cope with a complex and unpredictable world in an intelligent way. (This does not mean that every intelligent robot will necessarily be emotional, only that it will have the ability – and abilities are not always exercised).

Emotions are not necessarily harmful or unproductive, but they do not square with the image of computers as efficient and accurate. A KBS that is designed to be uncertain or emotional may not win public acceptance, particularly if its decisions may affect people's welfare or, in the case of military KBSs, threaten their lives.

Selling Knowledge like Coca Cola

Even if the fears prove groundless, and even if KBSs become highly-regarded assistants and colleagues, there is still one problem. Inevitably the spread of technology will not be uniform. The industrialised and technologically sophisticated nations will be the first to design and sell such tools for the mass market. The remaining countries, particularly in Africa, Asia and Latin America, will increase their dependency, not only on high technology but also on alien assumptions about the content, structure and purpose of knowledge. An agricultural KBS, for example, may suggest solutions in the form of proprietary brands of feedstuff, or may be governed by questionable assumptions about the need for artificial fertilizer.

The pessimistic view of the future is that KBSs may well work, but the consequences of the widespread introduction of such technology, into all aspects of our lives, have not been understood or even properly discussed. Until we can be sure that they will be beneficial we must not rely on complex and necessarily unpredictable systems to guide and control our already over-complicated lives.

Influencing the Future Uses of KBSs

Promoting the Benefits

Clearly, the benefits of KBSs should be encouraged, just like the benefits of any other emergent technology that holds out comparable promises. But how that is to be done is another question. One possibility is to direct funds, both from government and industry, towards specific initiatives with socially beneficial aims.

Doug Schuler of Computer Professionals for Social Responsibility has proposed a Responsible Computing Initiative (by analogy with the Strategic Defense Initiative). He describes a number of "viewpoints":

Communication, Language and Literacy is designed for individuals and small groups. KBSs could be used to assist communication between "communication-deprived" groups, such as illiterate people and those with language difficulties.

Resource Management is designed for larger groups and organizations. KBSs could be used to model scenarios that are important to the user, such as water distribution or crop allocation, or industrial uses such as factory scheduling. They could also help the groups manage their enterprises more thoughtfully through increased awareness of resources and the use of "what-if" exercises.

Arbitration and Conflict Resolution is designed for nations and transnational organizations. The role of KBSs would be to assist negotiation, by supplying book-keeping and other appropriate functions. Legal expert systems and arbitration models could facilitate peace through conflict resolution.

In addition to initiatives to promote the benefits of KBSs, information about this technology needs to be made more generally available, so that there can be an informed public discussion of its implications for society. There is also a need for more specific education in the skills of designing and using KBSs. The "stuff" of KBSs is knowledge, in a codified form, but nevertheless directly related to the knowledge of human experts, so there is an urgent need for people who are capable of acquiring knowledge from human experts, and of representing it in a formal notation. The skills are not those normally demanded of a computer scientist: interviewing techniques, an understanding of the psychology of human behaviour, an ability to use formal knowledge acquisition techniques such as protocol analysis and repertory grids, an empathy with the busy experts who may be unable to articulate their ingrained knowledge, and an awareness of the needs of those who will eventually use the KBS. A recent report on the commercial applications of KBSs from accountants Coopers and Lybrand (Wiig 1992) emphasizes that they have "misjudged the complexity of building 'small' AI-based systems that incorporate appropriate expert knowledge":

> The field, when implementing successful, significant systems, draws extensively on a variety of disciplines such as philosophy, cognitive psychology, anthropology, semantics and linguistics, business and management sciences, in addition to systems science and cybernetics... Most universities have faculty members in many of these disciplines with interests in various facets of the field, but few institutions have undertaken the creation of a new, integrated program to educate the professionals needed. The demand for individuals with such a background would be significant since they constitute the major bottleneck for extensive implementation or KBSs.

It may not be possible simply to graft such educational programmes on to the traditional degree structure of universities and polytechnics, since they require a commitment across departments, with faculty from arts and sciences speaking the common language of cognitive science. There is an urgent need for more interdisciplinary programmes of study in this area.

Minimizing the Dangers

> "Expert systems" sometimes called "Knowledge Based Systems" are capable of working like experienced and skilled staff (Company Brochure).

> For the army, the defense agency [DARPA] promises an autonomous land vehicle that... will zip around at 50 kilometers per hour all by itself planning its journey, avoiding obstacles and shooting at the enemy... DARPA has a few other critters on the drawing board [such as] a security-guard robot dubbed The Prowler (San Jose Mercury News West Magazine, 23 November, 1986).

Misleading claims and frightening proposals such as the ones above suggest the need for regulation of KBS technology. In the motor industry there is an elaborate system of control over construction and use, laying down safety standards with a high degree of detail, so that anyone who drives a motor vehicle which does not comply with them – let alone anyone who makes or distributes such vehicles – is automatically guilty of a criminal offence, even if no damage has been caused to anyone. In many such areas, the law seeks to prevent harm before it has been done, and does not just try to pick up the pieces afterwards.

There is a case for regulating the construction and use of KBSs in a similar fashion, but there are some obvious difficulties. First KBSs are more varied than motor vehicles, and there are not many detailed safety regulations which could be applied to all of them. Besides, the technology is still very young, and subject to many unforeseeable changes. It would therefore be far too early to begin to draft detailed regulations. But it is by no means too early to begin to think about the kinds of thing they might contain.

Clearly, a distinction must be drawn between the one-off KBS developed by a large organisation for internal use only; KBSs intended to be used only by experts in their own domain; and KBSs available to the public at large, including potential users who have no prior knowledge of the domain. If there is to be regulation of any kind, it must apply with the greatest force to the third of these. Among the things which it ought to ensure are these (following Bundy and Clutterbuck 1985):

1. A clear statement, for each KBS, of who made it, on whose "expert" knowledge it is based, and who will take responsibility if it cases any damage.

2. A clear statement, for each KBS, of what it claims to be able to do, within what boundaries, and subject to what limitations.

3. Clear statements, for each KBS, of the foreseeable risks and dangers it presents, as well as the risks and dangers inherent in the domain itself ("shares may go down as well as up").

4. Clear warnings about the dangers of relying on an impersonal system in a domain in which human experts are available ("if you don't feel well, you should go and see your doctor. All this system can do is to help you prepare yourself for that consultation. Do NOT use it to treat yourself: neither you nor this program knows enough about medicine.")

These seem to be the minimum statements, warnings; and disclaimers which should accompany any KBS sold on the open market, rather than to closed user groups of experts. These statements should appear not only on the label, or somewhere in the accompanying manual: they should be prominently displayed on the screen whenever the program is run, in a way which cannot easily be overridden.

Beyond that, there is room, and need, for generally accepted industry standards in various areas, especially in the "interface" between the program and the user. Whenever the user is asked to supply some data, the request should be in clear, simple and unambiguous language, leaving the minimum room for misunderstandings. Likewise, all answers should be suitably qualified ("on the information available so far, ... – but the answer might be different if...") and if the system has concluded a number of results of similar confidence, then it should present them all, with the associated confidence, to the user.

Clearly, it will be quite a few years before any such regulations are likely to be introduced. Meanwhile, there are several things that the designers of KBSs could do. First, they could devote far more effort to educating the public about this new technology. Secondly, they could proceed with the development of Codes of Conduct among themselves. Until there are some laws about all this, these would of course be formally unenforceable. But they could have useful persuasive and educational effect meanwhile, and might later form the basis for legal regulations.

Whitby (1988) has proposed a Code of Conduct for AI practitioners, drawn from the Code of Practice of the British Computer Society (1981) and from the discussions of a working party of the Society for the Study of Artificial Intelligence and Simulation of Behaviour (SSAISB):

1. All professional persons working in AI should take all possible steps to ensure that customers, other professions and the public are not misled as to the degree of intelligence or competence possessed by AI systems. Descriptions and labels suggesting human attributes should be avoided where there is no technical justification for their use (as there might be if the system was intended primarily as a research tool in cognitive psychology, for example). Computer-based labels such as "data", "computation", "processing" and so on should be used in preference to human-based labels, such as "expert", "inference", "knowledge", and "intelligence".

2. Anybody required to work on an AI system in any capacity should have the right to know the ultimate purpose for which that system is intended.

3. Any professional person should be free to refuse to work on any AI system which they consider to be dangerous, likely to be misused or about which misleading claims have been or are about to be made.

4. Any professional person working on an AI system should be aware of the limits of his or her own competence and should not make misleading claims about his other level of competence nor hesitate to obtain additional expertise from within AI or from other professions where appropriate.

5. Professionals working in AI should take all appropriate steps to update and maintain their level of expertise.

6. Full attention should be given to the sensitivity and security of data and the requirements of privacy and security.

7. A professional working on an AI system in any capacity should ensure that the interests of the end user are observed. In particular, AI systems should not be introduced which will reduce or restrict the creativity, or the moral choices, of the end user.

8. Where an AI system is introduced into any human system, it should be the responsibility of the AI professional to ensure that a human or group of humans within the system should take moral and/or legal responsibility for the human consequences of any malfunction of the AI system.

9. An AI professional should introduce AI systems into human systems only where he or she is satisfied that both systems are organized in such a way as to ensure adequate management of the AI system.

10. An AI professional should ensure that he or she understands and can comply with the preceding nine requirements (or any others deemed appropriate), and should be prepared, if required, to give a legally binding statement that, to the best of his or her abilities, he or she has done so.

Not all firms or organizations could meet even the milder items above, but a voluntary Code of Conduct would nevertheless be useful – just as a statement by a firm that it has an Equal Opportunities policy is useful – in attracting recruits and providing a set of guidelines for research and development that is not merely based on market forces, nor the general law of the land.

The Role of Human Beings

The decisions of KBSs should always in principle be challenged, for they work by consulting an internal model of the world (initially provided to them by the human programmer) and models are not necessarily accurate. It follows that one can always ask whether a model reflects the truth adequately or not.

The best safeguard against the dangers of any computerized expert system is to keep its activities under the constant supervision of an expert in the same domain, who will treat the KBS with appropriate scepticism and ignore its advice if it seems to him or her to be wrong. However, it is not easy to see any practical way of ensuring that this obvious piece of common sense will always be followed: it is difficult to see, for instance, how it could effectively be required by law.

By far the most worrying potential application is the "autonomous decision making system", a KBS that not only makes decisions but also commands machinery to act on them, and this danger is at its greatest in the military field. Unfortunately, that field is – understandably, but regrettably – surrounded by such a degree of secrecy that it is extremely difficult to mount any public debate on it. Our worries are compounded by the fact that it has so far been little discussed, and that the pressures against informed public discussion of it are so great that this state of affairs may well persist for a long time – long enough for a major catastrophe to happen meanwhile.

Acknowledgements. This report has drawn on material from *The Benefits and Dangers of Knowledge-Based Systems* (Council for Science and Society, 1989), a report produced by the Council for Science and Society. I should like to thank the Council and those who contributed to that report, in particular Margaret Boden, Alan Bundy and Paul Sieghart.

Note

1 In 1972 Sir James Lighthill was asked by the UK Science Research Council to prepare a report (Lighthill 1972) on the current state and prospects for Artificial Intelligence (AI). His extremely critical views all but halted AI research in the UK for a decade.

References

British Computer Society Code of Conduct (1981) *BCS Handbook No. 5*. British Computer Society Publications, London.

Bundy, A and Clutterbuck, R (1985) Raising the standard of AI products. In: *Proceedings of the ninth IJCAI*, Los Angeles, pp. 1289–1294.

Council for Science and Society (1989) *Benefits and risks of knowledge-based systems*. Oxford University Press.

Defense Advanced Projects Agency (1983). Strategic computing, new-generation computing technology: a strategic plan for its development and application to critical problems in defense, pp 3–5.

Lighthill, J (1972). *Artificial intelligence, a paper symposium*. Report to SRC. HMSO, London.

Michie, D and Johnston, R (1984). *The creative computer: machine intelligence and human knowledge*. Penguin, Harmondsworth.

Sloman, A (1984) Towards a computational theory of mind. In: Narayan A. and Yazdani M. (eds). *Artificial intelligence human effects*. Ellis Horwood, Chichester.

Whitby, B (1998) *AI: A handbook of professionalism*. Ellis Horwood, Chichester.

Wiig, KM (1992) Commercial applications. In: Berkold, T (ed). *New technology and employment*. North-Holland, Amsterdam. (In press)

Chapter 11

Law and Expert Systems

Joseph A. Cannataci

How may a lawyer define an "expert system"? In considering the implications of defining expert systems for the law of liability, this chapter raises both the role of language in the construction of expert systems and the effect of expert systems on language. The paradox of a law is that its language must be both extremely vague and simultaneously specific. A definition must be elastic enough to cover all possible situations covered by the legislator's intentions and at the same time narrow enough to exclude situations extraneous to the legislator's intentions. This paradox recurs when one examines the problems of knowledge acquisition and representation in creating and defining KBS. How does one represent not only the concept behind, for example, "stealing" but also the host of related concepts such as "fraud", "embezzlement" or "misappropriation"? If we are to participate in shaping the future of the society we live in, we should endeavour to ensure that our legal systems provide the right infrastructure and sense of direction for our efforts. This entails, amongst other things, carefully monitoring the language our legislators use in the laws governing behaviour in a computerized society.

Introduction

I will be addressing the topic of "language and law" from within the perspective of somebody working within the field of "computers and law". Many people ask instinctively "computers and law? – What's the connection between the two?" In order to clarify the issues for our purposes here, I should perhaps explain that the field of study we have called "computers and law" is divided into two main branches: 1) legal applications of computers and 2) the legal implications of computers and information technology.

Legal Applications

The first branch, *legal applications of computers,* comprises a number of different aspects, all of which, however, concern the use of computers in various parts of the legal world. These include:

1. *Computers in law courts administration.*

2. *Computers in the law office.*

3. *Computers as a tool in Computer Assisted Legal Education (Cale).*

4. *Computers as a management tool in the study of economics of law practice.*

5. *Computers as a tool in legal information retrieval LIR (computerized LIR),* where computers have proved very useful in looking up statute and case-law using such widely available databases as LEXIS, WESTLAW, JURIDIAL, JURIS, CREDOC and others.

6. *Computers in the legislative process,* where they are used in researching, drafting and cross-referencing legal instruments.

7. *Computers in public administration,* where computers are used, as in Norway for example, to help civil servants find their way through a maze of legal regulations including statutes, subsidiary legislation, legal notices and memoranda.

8. *Legal expert systems,* the most ambitious application of computer technology to the legal field. Since the late 1960s, a small number of computer scientists and lawyers have been working independently and/or together, in order to create systems capable of giving legal advice at an expert level. In spite of the large amount of money which has been pumped into artificial intelligence (AI) research over recent years, we have only been able to document between 25 and 30 sustained projects involving legal expert systems. These projects tackle aspects as diverse as tax and divorce law, industrial law and immigration law. None has really made it beyond the laboratory to the lawyer's office. One of the very few legal expert systems which has actually been marketed is not even designed for use by lawyers – instead it is aimed at managerial staff not having immediate recourse to experienced legal counsel. Apart from bringing into question the thorny issue of the definition of "expert system" which shall be referred to later, such systems only reflect the low level of practical advancement yet achieved in this field.

Legal Implications

Before continuing, however, let me complete sketching the background by outlining some aspects of the second main division of "computers and law", that is "the legal implications of computer technology". This comprises aspects of various subjects which are variously known by the names "computer law", "information law" and "the law of computers". These include:

1. *Privacy and data protection law*: this subject, sparked off by the computers versus privacy debate of the 1960s and 1970s, gave birth to a number of specific laws in many countries in Western Europe and North America. Some countries, e.g. Austria, Portugal and Spain, have even included data protection clauses in their constitutions, and while the OECD in 1980 adopted voluntary guidelines for data protection, the Council of Europe has

promoted a Convention which has been in force since 1985. Sweden has an outstanding record in this field: its Freedom of Information Law 1776, and national Data Protection Law 1973 were the first of their kind, and Sweden was one of the first signatories of the European Convention for the Protection of Individuals with regard to Automatic Processing of Personal Data.

2. *Intellectual property rights* in computer programs, designs and products, typically raising issues in copyright, patent and trade secret law (e.g. who owns copyright in a computer program and on what legal basis is this founded; who owns the benefits and/or results produced by AI technology computer programs).

3. *Computer contracts*: the science (or is it the art?) of drawing up contracts to service the computer industry.

4. *Technology export law:* this concerns the legal aspects of exporting information technology from some countries to another. You need a licence for nearly anything exported.

5. *Satellite overflight and information rights*: in practice this involves developing countries versus. the developed in public international law.

6. *Liability and responsibility for expert systems*: this is a fairly new field of study which is concerned with the legal liability of users, suppliers and designers of expert systems. If advice of or action related to expert system advice, whom do we sue – the user, the supplier, the knowledge engineer or the expert (human)?

7. *Data communications law*: more and more data is being communicated electronically. Some areas of computer law deal with specific issues in communications (e.g. privacy in data protection law) but the new techniques used in communications require re-appraisal and revision of certain other areas of law.

8. *The law of electronic funds transfer*: global banking and financial services are today computer dependent. We need old laws revised and new laws devised to cater for a world where someone's account may be added to or subtracted from thanks to a computer error.

9. *Computer crime*: anyone aware of the security problems associated with computers, including hacking, fraud, embezzlement, etc. will know of the problems the law has to tackle in these fields. Accountants and auditors have, as usual, been quick to grab a slice of the cake: we now have a new breed of auditors – computer auditors, whereas the law finds it hard to catch up. The new generation of computer lawyers is still a very rare species indeed.

Things do not change simply by departing from traditional computer technology to one which uses AI. Indeed, although the advent of AI and especially expert systems may bring some novel aspects to the field of computers and law, one need not be surprised to see that many of the problems are already familiar and have been tackled, albeit sometimes under a different guise, when examining the import of more traditional computer technology to the legal world. However, let us look briefly at some of the law and language problems seen within the context of AI and, especially, expert systems.

The Problems of Definition

Many people are fond of quoting Shakespeare and quipping "What's in a name?" when problems of definitions are raised. Although some lawyers do read Shakespeare too, they still insist on distinguishing between Capulet and Montague, because indeed otherwise many laws would be unworkable.

Definitions are very important in law because they help lawyers to draw lines around concepts, put things in linguistic boxes, compartmentalize things to an extent where they are legally useful. Even non-lawyers are well aware of the way that most laws are structured and it is curious to note how widespread this practice is internationally, even though different countries have different legal cultures. Take for example, "the section one, section two syndrome". In many countries many statutes open in the following way:

S.1 *The name clause.* This Act shall be known as e.g. the Data Protection Act or the Immigration Act 1970.

S.2 *The definitions clause.* For the purposes of this Act "Minister" shall mean the Minister of State responsible for... "dog" shall mean a quadruped from the canine family; "literary work" – a work in which the author had demonstrably shown originality of expression regardless whether the work shows any artistic merit.

In some countries these definitions are not necessarily contained in section 2 – instead they may be found at the end of an Act or in a separate appendix. But the effect is basically the same – we have definitions in order to help ensure that the law is interpreted faithfully in the spirit of the legislator's intention. Thus a law applying to the rights of dogs to dirty our pavements could not of course impinge on the rights of cats, since "cat" would not fall under the definition of "dog". (Several parliaments round the world have taken up days of debate on this subject!)

Let us pause in order quickly to relate the problem of definition to the world of AI. Let us imagine a situation where we are drafting a law regulating the problems of liability for expert systems.[1] The aim of this law is to define the limits within which a person may be held liable if

1. He fails to consult an expert system

2. He consults an expert system but fails to follow the expert system's advice

3. The expert system provides the wrong kind of advice or decision support

Before losing ourselves in the dilemma of whom we are to sue – the user, the supplier, the knowledge organiser or the expert, – let us quickly see why the definitions we insert in our section 2, the definitions clause, are important. So, our section 2 is going to open in the usual way: "For the purposes of this Act the following words shall have the meaning ascribed to them in this section:

"Minister" is the Minister responsible for the prevention of cruelty to expert systems;
"Expert systems"...

This is where the fun starts! What kind of animal is the lawyer entitled to call an "expert system"? If he tries something like: An expert system is an AI-technology based computer system capable of giving advice/resolving problems at the level of a human expert", he is heading for trouble, because he immediately imagines a situation where some defence counsel will stand up and say: "Objection Your Honour! My client's system does not fall within the purview of this Act because this Act applies to those systems which are AI-based, and since as various great authorities point out, a characteristic of AI techniques is that it is usually written in LISP or Prolog and my client's system is written in FORTRAN, then we are not talking about the same kind of animal".

Since we know that computer scientists are as likely to quibble as lawyers, and cannot even agree on a definition of AI, let alone the characteristics of AI, then we may quickly decide, "O.K. so let's avoid problems and leave the bit about AI-based out altogether".

At this stage and until now, the language problems have essentially been those relating to whether a system is fish or fowl, but the problem of definition has even more serious implications. If we return to our definition, having crossed out the bit about AI, we are left with something which reads:

An expert system is a computer system capable of giving advice/resolving problems at the level of a human expert.

The two main problem phrases here would be "expert system" and "human expert". Let us try to relate the two. Several authors have submitted that not all Intelligent Knowledge Based Systems (IKBS) may properly be termed "expert systems". It is not enough that a machine appears to possess "intelligence" similar to that of human beings or that the computer be able to offer the type of advice or solutions that are normally dispensed by the run-of-the-mill professional. These authors advocate that only computers capable of performing at the level of experts in a given domain are worthy of the name "expert systems". If this definition is adopted, then an IKBS giving advice at the level of a doctor or a lawyer who is a general practitioner, cannot be termed an "expert system". Instead, a system which gives advice at the level of an expert in gynaecology or radiology, may be properly called an "expert system". This distinction implies, and is based upon the traditional notion, that expert systems are IKBS intended for use by professionals and not by the ordinary man in the street. Without entering into the merits of these definitions, which exercise would go beyond our purposes here, one must point out that this would have serious implications for the law of liability.

If one chooses to define expert systems as only those IKBS used by professionals, then the issue of liability for use or misuse of such systems is closely connected to the same issues inherent in the arguments about professional liability, namely those of professional malpractice. On the other hand, if any IKBS can legally qualify as being an expert system, in a world where it is envisaged that IKBS will be packaged and mass-produced, then we might find ourselves involved in a discussion over product liability which carries implications which are possibly more far-reaching and onerous than those of professional malpractice. This is because the professional malpractice falls under the law of provision of services whereas product liability falls under the law of the provision of goods. The two are often regulated differently both under US and European law, especially where doctrines of strict liability (or liability without fault) come into play. Space does not permit me to amplify on the above but it is not impossible that when setting out definitions in a law, lawyers and politicians may be tempted to leave out the term "expert systems" altogether and go for some concept, such as IKBS, which may be marginally less controversial.

The issues raised above are mostly connected with "mind your language" or the science of choosing words carefully for which lawyers are maddeningly notorious. But there are also a number of other issues which are certainly worth mentioning, since they have a bearing on the way law, language and artificial intelligence will develop in future:

1. The lawyer's attitude – old wine in new bottles etc.
2. Language as a paradox in law
3. Language in the construction of expert systems
4. The effect of expert systems on language

Words... and Legal Attitudes

Some people are sometimes accused of presenting "old wine in new bottles". On many occasions, however, it would be more accurate to accuse a lawyer of trying to pour "new wine into old bottles" rather than the other way round.

It is characteristic of lawyers, once a new problem is identified, whether in artificial Intelligence or indeed in any other field, to attempt to find a solution within the existing framework of the law, within established legal doctrine and often existing legal norms. It is only when existing statutory and case-law as well as current legal theory prove unsatisfactory that the lawyer looks to the legislator. This is not altogether an unreasonable attitude: contrary to what many may think, it is not always in the lawyer's interest to procrastinate, and one cannot simply wait for a new law to be enacted each time the existing law does not explicitly cater for a given situation.

A typical example is the lawyer's reaction in the case of copyright in computer software. Scanning through the Copyright laws of most nations one finds reference (in the definitions clause, of cause) to "literary works" or musical works or photographs and so on, but it is only a few countries which, since the early 1970s, have succeeded in satisfactorily amending their copyright laws to include computer programs. Faced with this situation, many lawyers in a variety of countries, pounced on the word "literary works" and somehow convinced judges that the term "literary work" is wide enough to include computer programs. What is more, most of those countries which eventually amended their copyright laws specifically to mention computer programs, continued on the same lines, and provided for computer programs as if they were literary works.

It should be pointed out that it is hardly likely that this and other legal attitudes will change simply because AI appears on the scene. Indeed recent research has shown that the advent of AI-based computer systems will probably have greatest impact on the notion of who is entitled to practice a profession, and the eventual role of professionals rather than the basic reasoning which lies behind the philosophy of law and interpersonal relations. To return, for example, to the legal problems associated with the provision of goods and services, briefly discussed when highlighting the problem of definitions and examining the possible malpractice, one author commented thus:

> Neither the legal system, nor public opinion seems anxious to radically change its interpretation of professional behaviour merely because practitioners are beginning to use computers.

In the same way, the doctrine on which liability (including both provision of services and goods) is founded in law, will probably remain applicable, since the concepts on which it is based are derived from age-old expectations associated with responsibilities within interpersonal relationships rather than the manifestations and modes of these relationships.

The Paradox of Language in Law

Few persons not directly connected with the business of writing and implementing laws appreciate the nature of the paradox that language and law must live together. Law and legal principles must be couched in some kind of language. Reference has been made to the importance of definition in law, but little has been said of the difficult art of drafting those definitions. For the paradox of a law is that its language must be both extremely vague and simultaneously specific. A definition must be elastic enough to cover all possible situations covered by the legislator's intentions and at the same time narrow enough to exclude situations extraneous to the legislator's intentions.

The notion of a word is closely linked to a concept and concept definitions are part and parcel of the task of law-making. If one were to take a simple example: those of you familiar with the traditions of the Christian religion will remember that in the Old Testament, the God of the Israelites displayed himself to be a law-maker of genius.

When laying down the ten Commandments to Moses, the seventh Commandment was quite simply:

> Thou shalt not steal.

The concept word "steal" covers a huge amount of situations where one person takes things not belonging to him. Thus

Peter shall not take chickens belonging to Paul
Joe shall not take gold from Jack's house
Matthew shall not cheat taxpayers

Like man (and perhaps because man is really made in the image of God) the God of the Israelites knew that he would quickly run out of space on the stone tablets, if he were to try and give details of even a fraction of a percent of all the possible modes of stealing.

The paradox of law and language is one that recurs when examining the problems of knowledge acquisition and representation when creating and designing IKBS. When attempting to lay a foundation of concept representation, when constructing a legal expert system, one must find ways and means of representing the concept behind e.g. "stealing", together with a host of related concepts such as "fraud", "embezzlement", "misappropriation", etc. which have a specific meaning in legal doctrine (which legal doctrine can in turn vary from one jurisdiction to another). Then try linking up aggravations of offences connected with theft and the picture begins to grow very complex indeed.

Anyone familiar with the construction of thesauri, or master dictionaries, both in traditional computer databases as well as in AI-based systems, will know the painstaking programming designed to minimize errors in areas such as the entering of people's names in registration systems. Now a name, a simple name, is a question of fact, the abbreviations and variations of which may cause innumerable problems in a simple computerized registration system. The representation of legal concepts such as theft, and a host of others, involves problems which we have only begun to scratch at in the tasks of constructing legal expert systems. Language gives us words which are the tools we have, together with mathematics, to arrive at resolving problems. But many words conjure up pictures – and if a picture is worth a thousand words, how do you go about representing it?

I wonder how a legal expert system/IKBS will be programmed to tackle certain concepts. Many law students in their first year of Criminal law are often asked the question "What is the difference between crimes and contraventions?" Will an IKBS be taught that a contravention is a criminal offence which is not a crime? Or simply that contraventions are those minor offences which attract smaller penalties? Or perhaps simply that contraventions are those offences listed in the second part of the Criminal Code?

The Effect of Expert Systems on Language

It is envisaged that the widespread use of expert systems would lead to a greater standardization of knowledge. Apart from the fact that this may not be altogether beneficial and desirable, one wonders whether the use of expert systems will lead to the demystification of the jargon of the professionals. The language of law is part of that jargon – in the past, lawyers have often been accused of using legal terminology to obscure issues rather than provide clear solutions. Without going into the question of whether that assertion is true or false, one poses the question "Should expert systems be designed in such a way to avoid or explain legal terminology?" If this is to be one of the legally enforceable design criteria of expert systems, then one can see that IKBS would render an understanding of the workings and results of the legal system more accessible to non-professional citizens.

This issue of language being the key to access to legal knowledge is part of the scenario which may affect the future role of professionals such as lawyers, doctors, architects and engineers.

It is not impossible to conceive a situation where access to artificially intelligent expert systems might drastically effect or even eliminate whole areas of professional practice. Extensive computerization may result in a change of role for various professions. It does not seem appropriate at this stage to enter into the impact of IKBS on the role of professions in society. I would, however, like to conclude by pointing out that if we are seriously interested in having a say in shaping the future of the society we live in, we must all be concerned that our legal systems provide the right infrastructure and sense of direction for our efforts. Not to look carefully at the words our legislators choose to include in the laws governing behaviour in a computerized society, would be irresponsible indeed.

Notes

1. For a more detailed study of this problem see Cannataci, Joseph A. (1988) *Liability and Responsibility for expert systems,* CompLex. 5/88, Norwegian Research Center for computers and law, Tano, Norway.

Section VI:

The Information Society?

Chapter 12

The Image of the Intelligent Machine in Science Fiction

Jon Bing

Fiction picked up man's dependency on machines at an early stage; the work of both H.G. Wells and E.M. Forster, for example, indicates that the presence of the intelligent machine was felt long before the emergence of the modern computer. Mary Shelley's *Frankenstein* had earlier explored a central dilemma of the industrial revolution, namely how, in exploiting the possibilities offered by science and technology, man is to be responsible to both his creator, or to basic ethical principles, and to the use and implications of what he has created. *Frankenstein*, the chapter argues, embodies the spirit of the industrial revolution and reflects on the ethical issues involved in developing an artificial and intelligent being. The chapter traces other instances of the intelligent machine in fiction, from Daedalus' sculptured nymphs which came to life, to Asimov's modern robot, Qutie, which claimed, convincingly enough, to be superior to its human creators. Science fiction, however, has still to explore adequately the issues and dilemmas which haunt AI-research, such as the question of whether a computer can be constructed to become aware of itself or to meet an acceptable test for human intelligence. Science fiction, in other words, has yet to discover myths and symbols appropriate to recent developments in AI research.

> Imagine if you can, a small room, hexagonal in shape, like the cell of a bee. It is lighted neither by window nor by lamp, yet it is filled with a soft radiance. There are no apertures for ventilations, and yet the air is fresh. There are no musical instruments, and yet, at the moment that my meditations opens, this room is throbbing with melodious sounds. An armchair is in the center, by its side a reading desk – that is all the furniture. And in the armchair there sits a swaddled lump of flesh – a woman, about five feet high, with a face as white as fungus. It is to her that the little room belongs.[1]

This is the introduction to one of the more important stories containing a vision of the fully automated society – a society where individuals are cared for in the womb of a global machine, which anticipates their needs, feeds them, cares for them and interconnects them through a vast telecommunication network. The woman of the story rarely has met her own children face to face, and contacts them only infrequently through a two-way television link; she prefers the company of the intelligent and benevolent machine to that of her own kin.

The vision may be thought to be a modern dystopia, based on the emergence of truly global and integrated telecommunication networks into which our very homes will be embedded. But the story was first published in 1909,[2] written by E.M. Forster as a response to the more optimistic vision offered by another great English author – H.G. Wells – in his novel *A Modern Utopia*.[3] It demonstrates that the presence of the intelligent machine has been felt prior to the emergence of the modern computer, and – indeed – that fiction picked up man's dependency on machines at an early stage. This emerging dependency may in fact have been easier to discern in the beginning of this century as a change in the attitude of society than today, when this attitude is taken for granted, and only the magnifying power and incredible speed of technological innovations has made it possible once more to trace the developing stress in the fabric of society.

To trace the story of the reflection in fiction of the intelligent machine would actually take us back to the very source of literature, where it mixes with myths, where Daidalos sculptured nymphs to such a degree of perfection that they came alive; to Leonardo da Vinci, who sent as his representative to the royal court a mechanical lion which conveyed his greetings; to the preoccupations of the seventeenth century with clockwork figures mimicking life, surviving today in the machineries of old bell-towers and comical cuckoo-clocks. Though fascinating and intriguing, we will, however, only highlight a few selected episodes in the story of man's marriage to the machine, and we will start with the magical summer of 1816.

It was indeed a magical summer, though Switzerland that year did not enjoy fine weather. At the shore of Lac Lehman, just outside the modern town of Geneva, rain was keeping the summer guests indoors. In two neighbouring villas, Villa Deodati and Campagne Mont Alèrge, two of the giants of English literature met. Lord Byron had escaped to the Continent in his carriages built to his own specifications, and including a library and his travelling companion, John Pollidori. At the same time, Percy Bysshe Shelley had for the second time eloped to the continent with the young Mary Godwin, daughter of the philosopher William Godwin and Mary Wollenstonecraft – the latter famous for her views on the liberty of women. They had the company of Mary's "half-sister", Claire Clairmont,[4] who mainly was brought along because she – in contrast to the two others – spoke French. They also brought along their two-year-old son, who was born out of wedlock – Shelley was still married, though his wife would take her own life later that year by drowning herself in the Serpentine in Hyde Park.

It probably was Claire Clairmont who engineered the meeting between the two poets of such different nature. Before Byron left England, she had sought him out to secure his help in obtaining a position at Drury Lane Theatre, and it is probable that she was his mistress for a brief period.[5] Now she brought the two poets together, who in that wet summer entertained each other.

The weather may have created a somewhat ominous mood, and this must have been enhanced by the preoccupations of the poets and their company. At one point they entertained the well known author of gothic horror novels, Matthew Lewis,[6] who read to them in his own simultaneous translation

Göthe's *Faust I*, which still was not available in a regular English translation. The company was preoccupied with fairy tales, horror stories and the nature of modern science, especially the mystic force of electricity.

In this pregnant situation, Lord Byron suggested that they all should make an attempt to write a ghost story. Indeed they all did, the two attempts of the great poets being not very notable.[7]. The attempt which became a famous novel was written by Shelley's mistress Mary: *Frankenstein: or, the Modern Prometheus*, a powerful myth of man and his creation. The novel was published in 1818, and the original force of her allegory has not been diminished over the years, though innumerable inferior versions of the story have made its plot a cliché.[8]

Frankenstein is a brilliant scientist, who uses his knowledge of medicine and the natural sciences to create a living being employing raw materials robbed from graveyards. His creation is a monster, an artificial biological being, which strikes terror into humans, including his creator. But the novel is not a horror story, rather it is perhaps the first work of fiction to discuss the basic dilemma of the industrial revolution: the dual responsibility of man. First, the responsibility of man with respect to his creator, or basic ethical principles, in how he exploits the possibilities offered by science and technology. Second, the responsibility of man with respect to what he has created, its use and effect.

This dual perspective and ethical dilemma is the core of the Frankenstein myth, and the explanation for its survival over more than 150 years. It also is an important image of the intelligent machine. One might maintain that Frankenstein's monster is not a machine, as it is engineered of biological, not mechanical, parts. In the age of genetic engineering and the bio-chip, this does seem to be a very pedantic argument – the point is obviously that the novel *Frankenstein* reflects the ethical issues involved in developing an intelligent and artificial being. This monster is not, of course, a forecast of possible knowledge based technology but rather an embodiment of the spirit of the industrial revolution – the steam driven engines replacing workers cast in the grotesque hulk of the monster, combining the mechanical of the engine with the fate of the workers in one mythological being.

The distinction between mechanical and biological machines is actually of a rather recent date. This becomes evident if we trace the roots of the appearance of the robot in fiction.

That fateful summer of 1816, some of the tales told were from the Ghetto of Prague; old Jewish tales. Of these, the tale of Rabbi Judah Löw[9] still attracts interest. It is said that Rabbi Löw shaped a man from clay, and like a god breathed the spirit of life into this being, which he named *Golem*. Golem could hear, but could not speak; was naive and faithful. He did not need sleep, but often mimicked sleep. Fire or water did not hurt him, and he had the strength of a giant. He would do any chore, but if asked to do anything only serving the personal interests of his master, he would misinterpret the order and behave like the magic broom of the sorcerer's apprentice.

It is said that on 23 February 1592, Rabbi Löw was given audience by emperor Rudolph II of Habsburg. It is not known what was discussed at that occasion, but the protocols mention the presence of both the emperor and prince Bertier. Tradition insists that Rabbi Löw was warned against breaking the divine order of things, and after the audience, he is reported to have said: "We have no further need for Jossele Golem". With friends he took Golem to the upper chamber in the bell-tower of the Altneu synagogue, read a magic formula and robbed the clay man of his life.[10]

We do not know to what extent the Golem myth attracted the interest of Mary Shelley in 1816. But we know that a Prague journalist, Egon Erwin Kisch,[11] in 1920 wrote a series or articles on the Golem, including his own examination of the Altneu synagogue for possible traces of the clay man. At that time, one of his journalist colleagues named Karel Čapek (1890–1938), read these articles just before writing his own famous play *R.U.R.* (1920), the title being an abbreviation for *Rossum's Universal Robots*. In this way, the word "robot" was introduced in our language.

But the robots of Čapek are *not* the men of steel popular in current science fiction. They are more akin to their ancestors, the Golem and Frankenstein's monster. The general manager of Rossum's Universal Robots, Harry Domain, describe them in this way to the robot Helena:[12]

> In each (kneading-trough) we mix the ingredients for a thousand Robots at one operation. Then there are the vats for the preparation of liver, brains, and so on. Then you'll see the bone factory. After that I will show you the spinning-mill ... For weaving nerves and veins. Miles and miles of digestive tubes pass through it at a stretch. Then there's the fitting-shed, where all the parts are put together, like motorcars. Next comes the drying-kiln and the warehouse in which the new products work ... they work like any new appliance. They get used to existence. They sort of grow firm inside. We have to make a slight allowance for natural development. And in the meantime they undergo training ... It's much the same as going to school. They learn to speak, write, and count. They've astonishing memories, you know. If you were to read a twenty-volume encyclopaedia to them, they'd repeat it all to you with absolute accuracy. But they never think of anything new. Then they're sorted out and distributed. Fifteen thousand daily, not counting a regular percentage of defective specimens which are thrown into the stamping-mill ...

We see how the robot of Čapek still is a biological machine rather than a mechanical one – a device which in the specialized language of science fiction would be an *android* or a *biomat* rather than a robot. Čapek uses the robot as a symbol of the suppressed worker and the industrial exploitation of workers. In this we see the same theme as in Mary Shelley's *Frankenstein*, and, indeed, in Čapek's later novel *War with the Newts* (1936).[13] Another important sequel to this theme is the famous film by Fritz Lang, *Metropolis* (1926),[14] in which a female robot appears as the symbol of the haunted and mechanized city.

In sketching briefly these developments, we have been able to demonstrate how the intelligent machine – whether engineered by biological or mechanical technology – is seen as a symbol of mechanization, an embodiment of the symbiosis between an industry based on mechanization and assembly lines, and the workers serving this industry, and which then also are reduced to mere mechanical devices necessary for the smooth functioning of industrial society. The "intelligent machine" is not seen as a challenge to human reasoning or creative powers, but rather as a tool to be used – an industrial robot in the current meaning of the word.

There are, however, indications also of seeing mechanical reasoning as a challenge to humans. The most curious example is actually not a work of fiction, but the tale of the mechanical chess player engineered by the Hungarian baron Wolfgang von Kempelen of Presburg (1734–1804), constructed in 1769. For almost a century, this machine – in the form of a Turk seated at a chess table – astonished the world and prominent public figures like empress Catherina II of Russia, the emperor Napoleon and Benjamin Franklin lost games against the mechanical player. In the nineteenth century, the mechanical chess player was taken to the US by Johann Nepomunk Maelzel, a technician of Bavaria himself famous for his musical toys.[15] Regrettably, the player was proved to be a hoax. Edgar Allan Poe, in an article of his journal *The Southern Literary Messenger*, revealed that a dwarf was hidden within the table, and through acrobatics was able to move the metal hand of the Turk. Poe uses this episode as a basis for his story "The Thousand-and-Second Tale of Scheherazade" (1854). Another well known US writer, Ambrose Bierce, is inspired by the chess player in his famous story "Moxon's Master" (1893), where he uses the mechanical chess player to argue a mechanical philosophy of life.

On this basis, it may be seen as more than a coincidence that chess has attracted designers of modern computer as a test for their intelligence and ability to compete with man on an intellectual basis: a tradition running from Alan Turing's work to current chess computers.

But the truly modern robot did not emerge until just after World War II, in a story by Isaac Asimov (1920–1992). Asimov's robots are humanoid of appearance, and possess a "positroic brain", fractionally equivalent to a computerized brain, but actually predating the computer by a few years. Most importantly, the robots functioned according to programs loaded into the brain, and contained by Asimov's "three laws of robotics":[16]

1 – A robot may not injure a human being, or, through inaction, allow a human being to come to harm.
2 – A robot must obey the orders given by human beings except where such orders would conflict with the First Law.
3 – A robot must protect its own existence as long as such protection does not conflict with the First or Second Law.

In one of his earliest stories, "Reason" (1941), Asimov had a robot prove that the robot is not only equal to humans, but far superior to them. The argument is still convincing, in the words of robot QT-1, otherwise known as Qutie, addressing his fellow humans on the issue that they are his creators:

"Look at you," he said finally, "I say this in no spirit of contempt, but look at you! The material you are made of is soft and flabby, lacking endurance and strength, depending for every energy upon the inefficient oxidation of organic material ... Periodically you pass into a coma and the least variation in temperature, air pressure, humidity, or radiation intensity impairs your efficiency. You are *makeshifts*.

"I, on the other hand, am a finished product. I absorb electrical energy directly and utilize it with an almost one hundred percent efficiency. I am composed of strong metal, am continuously conscious, and can stand extremes of environment easily. These are facts, with the self-evident proposition that no being can create another being superior to itself, smashes your silly hypothesis to nothing."

The modern robot has appeared. It may, however, be a point of interest to note that Qutie, in his argument, mainly spoke of his physical abilities – not of his mental powers of reasoning. The issue that has haunted AI research – whether a computer can be constructed meeting the Turing test or another acceptable test for human intelligence – is not addressed, though Turing had actually formulated his test at the time of Asimov's early robot stories. The problem of whether a computer can become aware of itself, is not seen as an issue.

Obviously, science fiction has developed and refined its image of the intelligent machine from Asimov's early models. It may be true, nevertheless, to say that these issues still have not been adequately explored. Though it may be to overgeneralize the situation, it may be maintained that the fiction which should perceive as one of its main tasks to communicate the dilemmas of modern AI research to its readers, has failed to find appropriate myths and symbols. We are still waiting for the fifth generation computer to emerge as a symbol as strong as Frankenstein's monster or the robots of Čapek and Asimov.

Notes

1 Forster, EM "The machine stops. In: *The eternal moment and other stories*, 1928.

2 *The Oxford and Cambridge Review.*

3 First published 1905.

4 Claire Clairmont (1798–1879) was the daughter of Godwin's second wife and her first husband, and was really not related to Mary Godwin at all. She was christened Clara Mary Jane, but seems to have preferred the more artistic name "Claire".

5 On return to England, Claire gave birth to a daughter, Allegra, and Byron was named the father.

6 His best known novel is *The Monk* (1796), which earned him the nick-name "Monk" Lewis. He met the party of Byron and Shelley just before his final voyage to Jamaica. See Tracy, Ann B (1985) M.G. Lewis. In: Bleiler, EF (ed) *Supernatural fiction writers: fantasy and horror*, vol I. Scribner, New York, pp 153–160.

7 John Pollidori produced actually a short novel, *The Vampyre*, which is the origin of the later rich literature on vampires, including Bram Stoker's *Dracula* (1897). It became a popular novel, partly due to the fact that Pollidori hinted that Lord Byron was the true author.

8 For those who would like to find a more tangible link between *Frankenstein* and modern computers, one may mention that Lord Byron during that summer wrote the second stanza to his famous *Childe Herold*, dedicated to his daughter, today known as Ada Augusta, Lady of Lovelace – the assistant to Charles Babbage in his attempt to develop an "analytical machine", and seen by many as the "world's first programmer".

9 Rabbi Löw (approximately 1520–1609) came to Prague from Poland, probably Poznan. He was the youngest in a family of scholars, three of his brothers also being rabbis. It is believed that he served as a rabbi in Mikulov 1533–1573, trying to rule the society by law. In 1572 he chaired the regional synod in Breclav, and the following year left for Prague where he established a talmud school in a building known as "Klause", serving both as school and synagogue. When he failed to be elected to the highest office in 1583, he returned to Poznan. He was in Prague once more in 1589, when he was elected to the highest office. It is about this time that the episode mentioned in the text, is said to have taken place. See Muneles, Otto (1956) *Prague ghetto in the renaissance world.* State Jewish Museum, Prague.

10 It has been suggested that this episode was a source for Shakespeare's *The tempest* and that Rudolph II was the model for Prospero, and Golem the model for Caliban. See Plank, Robert (1968) *The emotional significance of imaginary beings*. CC Thomas.

11 Kisch became well known for his later reports from the civil war in Spain.

12 *R.U.R.*, translated from Czech by P Selver, adapted for the English stage by Nigel Playfair, edited by Harry Shefter. Washington Square Press, 1973.

13 Czech original title *Valka s Mloky*; English translation 1937.

14 The film was based on a novel of the same title by Lang's wife, Thea von Harbou.

15 When Maelzel died in 1838, the player was acquired by the Chinese Museum of Philadelphia, and was destroyed by fire in 1854.

16 It is maintained that these laws were formalized by Asimov's editor, John W Campbell, jr, one of the most influential editors of science fiction. Campbell himself is reported to have insisted that the laws were implicit in the stories by Asimov. See Asimov, Isaac (1979) *In memory yet green*. Doubleday & Company, New York, pp 285–287.

Chapter 13

Computers and Thought: a Modern Version of Old Illusions

Francesco Lerda

Computer Science and Artificial Intelligence will gain ever increasing importance in our society. Such disciplines are continually expanding with reference to component technology, system architecture, operational approach, programming languages, man – machine interaction, applications, methodological impact. This chapter emphasizes the possibilities opened by the new instruments and methodologies, but also draws attention to the potential for incorrect utilization, unexpected breakdowns, and control complexity, amongst other risks. Computer science developments give rise to complex cultural, political, social and ethical problems. Information science and artificial intelligence possess fundamental cultural and methodological characteristics: they give systematic form to the structural and hierarchical nature of problems, provide scientifically operational bases to the notion of algorithm, facilitate the research stage, allowing actual as well as illustrative exemplifications, and increase the possibilities for operational experimentation in the didactic environment. But scientific evidence to support the Strong Artificial Intelligence Hypothesis does not exist.

Computer Science and Artificial Intelligence will hold an ever growing importance in our society. Such disciplines are continuously expanding with reference to component technology, system architecture, operational approach, programming languages, man–machine interaction, applications, and methodological impact.

The possibilities opened by the new machines and the new methodologies are emphasized whenever the opportunity offers. However, attention should be drawn to the potential for incorrect utilization, unexpected break-downs, control complexity, and so on: a paper by a famous mathematical physicist, Clifford A. Truesdell, has the following title: "The computer, ruin of science and menace for humanity".[1]

The extreme positions in such a dispute assume emblematic aspects. For example, on one side we have A. Turing, A. Newell and H.A. Simon, and on the other side C.A. Truesdell and H.L. Dreyfus.[2] Truesdell maintains that:[3]

Computers are mere generators of "horrible numbers".

The present scientific achievements would not have been possible in the absence of classical theories due to great minds searching for mathematical simplicity and beauty.

Numerical calculus without classical models is dangerous; few mathematicians, today, are able to use numerical calculus safely.

Computers endanger man's survival.

We quote here a few statements given by Truesdell[4] to support his position. Some of them are true but trivial, and do not lead to his extremism; others are clearly false:

1. "Space travel would have been impossible in the absence of computers" but also "in absence of classical motion equations". "The intellectual proletariat – the large masses that consider as a divine revelation what the doctors say" in the newspapers, have no idea of the fact that "motion mechanics has supplied the conceptual frame for the enterprise".[5]

2. "In problems where classical physics is applied, when computations are wrong frequently it is possible to become aware of such failure... Programmers have models to make comparisons... . In completely modern fields, as genetic modifications and high energy particle physics, such models do not exist... Computers can be used in intelligent applications of already well systematized theories, but to put on them even a minimum of trust for the exploration of unknown regions of science is dangerous".[6]

3. With reference to the Fermat's last theorem, Truesdell' says: "Computations on large machines have already supplied important information on such a problem, and will possibly supply other ones... But computation could never solve the problem".

A scientist should be very careful in talking about "always" and "never"; in 1906 Lord Kelvin said "by now science has understood everything". In 1919, with reference to the discovery of the atomic nucleus, Lord Rutherford asserted: "To think that my discovery could find applications in the field of energy is the same as to deceive oneself that one can get warm with the moonlight".

With reference to such drastically negative positions let us point out that the undiscriminating mental closure against new cultural forms can turn out to be very harmful. This is but one example: the hostility of "important" sectors of Italian humanistic culture towards mathematical logic, during the first half of the present century, has caused decades of delay in our country for such studies that have proved to be fundamental, even though one of the greatest pioneers in the field was an Italian scientist, Giuseppe Peano.

Computer science developments give rise to complex cultural, political, social, ethical problems; the school organization at any level and the research programming ask for new foundations. To face such a situation it is useless throwing invectives at the computer; we have to operate patiently, with perseverance and good sense, knowing the possibilities and limitations of the new technologies and the new methodologies, with the awareness that we are involved in a tremendously difficult enterprise, as all the great enterprises are.

Let us now switch to discuss the points of view of those that we can name the *informatic new-positivists;* such points of view are so formulated by Turing: "we may hope that machines will eventually compete with man in all purely intellectual fields".[7] Here the machines are computers with stored programs, which allow memory extension during processing according to program requirements. Newell and Simon are even more drastic: "A physical symbol system has the necessary and sufficient means for general intelligent action. By 'necessary' we mean that any system that exhibits general intelligence will prove upon analysis to be a physical symbol system. By 'sufficient' we mean that any physical symbol system of sufficient size can be organized further to exhibit general intelligence. By 'general intelligent action' we wish to indicate the same scope of intelligence as we see in human action".[8]

Here also the physical symbol system is equivalent to the computer as specified above.

This point of view is synthetized in the Strong Artificial Intelligence Hypothesis (SAIH) that is formulated as follows: *human intelligence and artificial intelligence are substantially equivalent.*

I have critically analysed such a position in three papers.[9] Here is a very brief summary of the views presented, with the addition of new elements to confute the SAIH.

1. The processing procedures that can be automated on computers are the ones that may be expressed in intuitively algorithmic terms; the concept of algorithm has been scientifically specified by Turing.[10] Such specification is unconditionally accepted by the supporters of the SAIH.

2. As a consequence, SAIH implies that all human intelligence actions be substantially algorithmic (SAIH interprets intelligence in a large sense, including will, intuition, sentiments, self-consciousness, etc.).

3. There exist a number of precedents of SAIH, consisting in restrictive conceptions of reality, among which a typical example is given by the logical positivism of the Wiener-Kreis. These have failed when submitted to serious criticism; this fact suggests we should be very cautious with SAIH.

4. Mathematical and physical remarks show a fundamental "poverty" of algorithmic processing with reference to the achievements of human thought: it is enough to say that Hilbert regarded the Cantor actual infinite as a "Paradise", but he was unable, in principle, to lead to success his "program" to formalize classical mathematics based on that "Paradise" and to prove its consistence, completeness, decidability by finitistic methods. In physics the evolution of complex systems, for example in quantum mechanics, follows transfer and transition functions substantially more complex than those associated with the more general information systems of the supporters of SAIH.

5. I have presented the following conjecture: *mathematics and logic, including mathematical and logical results as well as mathematical and logical activities performed by humans, are not exhaustible in purely algorithmic terms.* [11]

I believe that such conjecture could be scientifically proven, supported by the points of view of Gödel, widely reported by Wang.[12] .We will analyse some of these points of view.[13] For Gödel, the statement: *there not exists a mind separated from matter* is a prejudice of the present time that will be scientifically disproven. He considers as one of the more interesting and rigorously proven results the following: the "human mind is not able to formulate (or mechanize) all its mathematical intuitions". In Gödel's opinion the proofs of equivalence between mind and machines given up to his time turn out to be wrong because they do not realize that the mind, in its operation, is not static but in continuous development; although the number of possible states is finite at any stage of its development, there is no reason why that number would not diverge to infinity during the mind development. An exact definition of a systematic procedure to cause such a development would require a substantial improvement of our understanding of the mind's fundamental operations.

Gödel explicitly states that his objectivistic conception of mathematics and metamathematics in general, and particularly of the transfinite reasoning, has been fundamental for his activity in logic. In his opinion "the completeness theorem is an almost trivial consequence of the 1922 Skolem paper. Nevertheless... no one (not even Skolem himself) drew that conclusion. Such a blindness (or prejudice...) of logicians is really surprising". For Gödel the explanation is to be found "in the diffuse lack, at that time, of the necessary epistemological attitude towards metamathematics and non finitistic reasoning".

In addition: "...the heuristic principle of my construction, in the formal mathematical systems, of the undecidable propositions of number theory is the concept, preeminently transfinite, of 'objective mathematical truth' in *opposition* to that of provability...". "There was another reason that prevented logicians from applying to metamathematics not only the transfinite reasoning but the mathematical reasoning in general. The reason is this: metamathematics... was not considered as a science describing objective mathematical states of things, but rather a theory on the human activity dealing with symbol manipulation". Finally: "How would it be possible to *express* metamathematics *into* the mathematical systems themselves, if such systems are considered to consist of meaningless symbols that receive some meaning surrogate only *through* metamathematics?".

In conclusion, I think that Gödel's opinion can be synthetized as follows: *mathematical and logical activities and results of such activities are not reducible only to finitistic symbol manipulations.*

Here we stop referring to H. Wang's book. Many attempts have been made to prove the non-reducibility of human intelligence to machines by using Gödel's incompleteness results, but such attempts have not closed the debate. Reasons do exist that explain the situation. Some times the weak point is the confusion between truth and provability; in other cases specific limitations of machines are pointed out with reference to theorems of non-existence, non-decidability, etc., with the statement that man is not subjected to such limitations, but no proof of such statement is given. It is my feeling, in agreement with the above interpretation of Gödel's point of view, that a correct approach will consist in proving the conjecture I formulated in the above point 5. I am convinced that it is possible to get to such a proof, as well as I consider SAIH to be nothing but a new version of old positivistic illusions.

Here are some final comments:

The appearance of parallel supercomputers has giver rise to new enthusiasm from the SAIH supporters. In this respect, it is true that the new technology allows very high efficiency in information processing, but as long as computers remain discrete stored program computers they will be subjected, *in principle,* to the same limitations as those the ordinary computers (von Neumann computers) are subjected to.

The criticism of the positivistic point of view on intelligence should be differently formulated with reference to massive parallel systems including continuous features: this will be done in future papers.

Dulcis in fundo, information science and artificial intelligence do posses fundamental cultural and methodological characteristics: they give systematic form to the structural and hierarchical aspects of systems and problems, provide scientifically operational bases to the notion of algorithm, are greatly helpful during research, enormously increase the experimental operational possibilities in the didactic environment, allowing actual as well as meaningful exemplifications. The computer is therefore a real prosthesis for information processing activities, providing scientific methods and tools to psychology, not to mention the tremendous impact of computers in design, economy, politics, and so on.

Notes

1 Quotations are my own translations of Truesdell, CA (1981) *Il calcolatore, rovina della scienza e minaccia per il genere umano.* La Nuova Ragione, il Mulino, Bologna.

2 Dreyfus's views are presented in his book *What computers can't do: a critique of artificial reason.* Harper and Row, New York, 1972.

3 Op cit.

4 Ibid.

5 This is all true, but it is not a reason to maintain that computers ruin science; it would be much the same as to say that soap ruins science because on television only "downy skin" is mentioned, not the chemistry of soap production.

6 It is true that when we are concerned with new problems theoretical reference models are often missing; the way to face such a situation is to search for such models, not be angry with computers.

7 Turing, AM (1954) *Computing machinery and intelligence.* Mind, 59.

8 Newell, A and Simon, HA (1976) *Computer science as empirical enquiry: symbols and search.* Communications of the ACM, March.

9 Lerda, F (1984) *Calcolatori e intelligenza umana, sul neopositivismo informatico. Nuova Civilta delle Macchine,* Anno II, no. 1. Lerda (1988) *Some considerations on the relationship between human and artificial intelligence.* In: Ricciardi, LM (ed) *Biomathematics and related computational problems.* Reidel, Dordrecht. Lerda (1988), Precedents, philosophical foundations, possibilities and limitation of artificial intelligence. Nuova Civiltà delle Macchine, anno VI, no. 1/2.

10 Turing, AM (1936) *On computable numbers, with an application to the Entscheidungsproblem.* Proc London Math Soc 2: 42.

11 Lerda (1988), op cit.

12 Wang, H (1984) Dalla matematica alla filosofia. Boringhieri, Torino. (Italian edition of *From mathematics to philosophy,* Routledge and Kegan Paul, London, 1974.)

13 Quotations are my own translations from the Italian edition of Wang, *op cit,* and do not necessarily follow Gödel's original papers.

Chapter 14

Concluding Remarks Part I: Towards Human-Centred Systems

Richard Ennals

This chapter celebrates the new synthesis of ideas and experience evident in recent work, such as that contained in the present volume, and seeks to clarify the implications of moving towards human-centred systems. The tendency is towards a combination of interests; practical experience of technology and of working life as well as philosophical and educational concepts. There is a renewed interest in the culture of work and of the workplace as a learning environment in which technology should be deployed to meet human needs. Out of this is emerging a newly coherent perspective of human-centred systems, sometimes described as anthropocentric systems, which in turn have radical implications for both education and work. There is a new audience for radical alternatives, with human needs as the focus of attention. A shift from a technocentric to a human-centred approach in education requires a fundamental reappraisal of curriculum and teaching method. Philosophy, personal experience of work and social action, and the concept of tacit knowledge are accorded greater significance than they have held in recent years. Imaginative uses of the computer will re-unite practical and theoretical knowledge, thereby allowing us to dispense with many inauthentic forms of division of labour. Participation in the design process and the enhancement of the quality of work should be encouraged. Individual skills have to be seen in the context of the needs of the group, placing new emphasis on skills in communication and collaboration. External events are accelerating the process of change. The human-centred design process, where participation is encouraged and valued, lies at the heart of a modern approach to democracy. In order to counter the mystique and disillusionment often associated with expert systems, artificial intelligence and information technology, the chapter stresses the need for acceptable working models of people assisted by technology in productive activity; there are many opportunities for the realization of such models, it is suggested, in current European developments.

Introduction

This book is one of a series emanating from the Swedish Center for Working Life in recent years, all published by Springer-Verlag. It follows *Knowledge,*

Skill and Artificial Intelligence, edited by Bo Göranzon and Ingela Josefson (1988), which was published to coincide with the conference "Culture, Language and Artificial Intelligence" in Stockholm in 1988. The conference then led to a number of publications: *Artificial Intelligence, Culture and Language: On Education and Work*, edited by Bo Göranzon and Magnus Florin (1990), and *Dialogue and Technology: Art and Knowledge*, with the same editors (1991). Bo Göranzon's work *The Practical Intellect* was published in Swedish by Unesco (1989) and in English by Springer-Verlag (1992).

There has also been a wider context, in the growing Artificial Intelligence and Society Series, edited by Karamjit Gill, in which the Swedish volumes appear. Howard Rosenbrock edited the collection *Designing Human-Centred Technology*, published in 1989. Peter Brödner's book *The Shape of Future Technology* appeared in 1990. The present writer's *Artificial Intelligence and Human Institutions*, together with J. Martin Corbett, Lauge Baungaard Rasmussen and Felix Rauner's volume *Crossing the Border* appeared in 1991. Since 1987 the *Journal of Artificial Intelligence and Society*, with the same editor and publishers, has provided a forum for debate on issues of human-centred systems. Gill and Cooley have also established an international research centre, with some support from the EEC (Cooley 1989) and Japanese industry (Gill 1990).

This chapter seeks to draw conclusions from this significant recent body of work, not just in terms of theory, but as providing a basis for a new generation of research and practical projects. The writer cannot pretend to detached observer status, but can admit to a genuine feeling of excitement as a new synthesis of ideas and experience is under way. Different currents are moving; brought together they could have irresistible momentum. External events may serve to bring the ideas considered here to a new prominence: it is thus all the more important to assemble a unified view, and to clarify the implications of moving towards human-centred systems.

A New Paradigm

Paradigm shift is rarely smooth and comfortable, but it can rarely have been undertaken in such a culturally rich manner as has apparent at the 1988 Stockholm Conference and in these volumes. A glance at the contents pages of the volumes under discussion will reveal an array of philosophers, engineers, craftsmen, educationalists, performing artists, reflective professionals and concerned computer scientists. The work of the Swedish Center for Working Life has concerned Education, Work and Technology, a combination of interests that has been all too rare among policy makers, whose own background is typically much narrower, rarely involving practical experience of technology or of working life.

Rather than technology being the focus of attention, with a consequent distorting effect on education, what has emerged is a renewed interest in the culture of work, and of the workplace as a learning environment in which technology should be deployed to meet human needs. Out of this is emerging a newly coherent perspective of human-centred systems, sometimes described as anthropocentric systems, which in turn have radical implications for both education and work.

When teaching conventional courses in a business school environment, isolated examples from experience in human-centred systems are seen as inadequate, for success has to be demonstrated in terms of the prevailing criteria of short-term capitalism. A broader context must be presented, together with coherent alternative criteria for success. This series is both necessary and timely.

In the context of present disarray in both Western and former Eastern bloc economies, where previously dominant systems and ideologies have fallen into disrepute, the lessons could be of fundamental significance. There is a new audience for radical alternatives, with human needs as the focus of attention. A case in point is the need for conversion from defence to civil production with the ending of the Cold War: large productive facilities depend on new insights and ways of working if work is to be resumed. The early pilot studies by Cooley and his colleagues at Lucas Aerospace in the 1970s need to be located in a broader context if they are to be followed by new schemes with a chance of success.

The pre-meetings, conference, and subsequent publications provide ample evidence of a coming together of previously separate disciplines and cultures, from numerous different countries, particularly in Europe. The conference organizers and editors were reluctant to force the pace of intellectual integration, thus distorting the outcome, but provided a physical and literary environment in which acquaintances could be made, and interests compared. For many the philosophical framework was at first unfamiliar: the recent resurgence of interest in Wittgenstein in Scandinavia had not been matched by a similar movement in the United Kingdom or elsewhere in Europe, and the frequent references to Artificial Intelligence and Expert Systems were initially regarded by many as esoteric. In France a related path of logicist analysis has been cleared by archaeologists and other human scientists under the direction of Jean-Claude Gardin, himself a contributor to the Stockholm conference. The volumes will not be best-sellers, but they may prove to be an intellectual landmark, facilitating a smooth progression from a technocentric to a human-centred view of Education, Work and Technology (Gardin 1989, Ennals and Gardin 1990).

Practical Inferences

The Finnish philosopher Georg Henrik Von Wright, himself a colleague of Wittgenstein in Cambridge, put forward an account of "practical inferences", whereby actions are a natural consequence of a particular description of a state of affairs (Von Wright 1971); a suitable justification for the use of declarative rules, expressed in predicate logic notation, in expert systems. If the new description of the world emerging from this work is taken seriously, there are practical consequences for future policy and practice, particularly in the field of education. A shift from a technocentric to a human-centred approach requires a fundamental reappraisal of curriculum and teaching method. Countries who have moved to rigid imposed national curricula and industry-defined frameworks of competence-based vocational training will face particular difficulties.

Philosophy returns to the kind of central position, making sense of the complexity of the modern world, which it has not held in the United Kingdom for many decades, since Oxford philosophers appeared to lose interest in ordinary life. In recent years philosophy departments have been closed as expensive irrelevancies; rebuilding may be painful.

Individual and collective personal experience of work and social action is accorded new significance, together with a methodology under which it can be partially captured. The concept of tacit knowledge requires philosophical underpinning if it is not to be merely trite. Rather than absolving knowledge engineers from building complete representations of expert knowledge, we must emphasize the essential contribution of practical experience. We may hope for support from philosophers in Central and Eastern Europe, who have often spent years in ordinary working life as the penalty for academic and political dissidence, and may return with an enriched insight into practical knowledge.

The separation of hand and brain can be ended, or at least blurred, with imaginative use of the computer in areas such as Computer Aided Design. With it we can also dispense with many inauthentic forms of the division of labour, as, for example, secretaries are empowered to act as managers of information, rather than maintaining deference to their own managers, normally male, who have been allocated greater power despite having less practical knowledge. This will have radical implications for employment practice and management education. Dignity must be restored to working life, and vocational education can no longer be seen as separate from and inferior to the academic mainstream.

The advocates of human-centred systems have been accustomed to operating on the fringes of academic conferences and government policies. It may be hard for some of the pioneers to accept that in many respects their arguments have prevailed, that some of the entrenched positions which they habitually attack have long been abandoned. The old dragons are dead. The case for human-centred systems should now be stated in a way which allows companies and governments to concur: the technocentric alternatives have failed, but we should not expect this to be acknowledged publicly. Rather, we should get used to working with new partners in collaborative projects, and to seeing our arguments borrowed by others for their commercial gain and our mutual social benefit.

The difficulty will come when new converts in high office become frustrated at the lack of rapid results and major financial savings from a human-centred approach: their planning frameworks and budget assumptions will be carried over from past programmes, where technology was deployed as a means of reducing dependence on people, rather than as a way of enhancing effectiveness and learning. Such has been our experience in the United Kingdom with the use of Artificial Intelligence and Expert Systems in education and training. At this stage it will be crucial to have a literature, documenting good practice and providing criteria by which to assess particular cases.

Skill

Western economies, and in particular the United Kingdom, face a critical skills shortage, even amid increasing unemployment in the workforce as a whole. Managers and civil servants will never have considered acquiring such skills themselves, which only assume significance by their absence. Bureaucrats have devoted years to developing taxonomies of skills to be acquired by others, mapped onto vocational qualifications, themselves located within an antiquated framework of social class and stratification. Apprenticeships and their sustaining framework of Industrial Training Boards were abolished as a financial economy measure, and in their place it is proposed to accredit competence when it is observed in the workplace. In an environment where financial services are given priority over manufacturing, the cultural context to support the development of working skills has been removed. Apprenticeship entails the deferment of gratification until mastery has been achieved: the modern motivation has been to obtain gratification on credit, and to defer payment. The time for payment has come, and with it a time of reckoning for a system of reliance on short-term market forces.

The movement towards human-centred systems involves a more dynamic approach, with an emphasis on participation in the design process and the enhancement of the quality of work. Success depends to some extent on shared cultural values, and on the sense of "ownership" which results from the feeling that the resulting systems were "invented here". Individual skills have to be seen in the context of the needs of the group, placing new emphasis on skills in communication and collaboration.

Education

The conference, books and journal derive their strength from the breadth of cross-disciplinary contributions, and from the willingness of individuals to "cross the border" into new areas of thought and study. A strong educational foundation, including philosophical and cultural studies, is necessary if future students are to retain that option. The dangers of premature specialization or of narrow vocationalism apply both to the individual and the society of which he will form a part. Significantly, in the United Kingdom, those with power in government have typically been educated privately and with a heavy bias to the arts; they lack a background in science, technology or practical experience to which they attempt to consign others, while denying the necessary resources for success. Lasting educational change will entail major reforms in government and administration. If we start by giving attention to the needs of the whole person, located in society, we will give an effective corrective for curricula which have been prescribed by company directors for their prospective employees. A period of colonial-style administration must be followed by an independence movement, liberating the minds and skills of the young.

We need to respect the professional expertise of the teacher which he can demonstrate in practice but never fully formalize. Teachers have been placed under undue pressure in recent years, regarded as the scapegoats for society's failings, and must be given the space and resources to build the foundations for the future. It is important that the human-centred debate be extended to include teachers, just at the time when nationally determined curricula are running into practical problems. We must support an international programme of educational projects, possibly building on the foundations of the PROLOG Education Group (Nichol *et al* 1988), which has espoused similar principles at school and higher education level, and has strong roots both in the United Kingdom and Scandinavia, with recent international conferences in Denmark and Sweden. One criticism which I would make of the Center for Working Life is that it has failed to date to form alliances with those in Sweden who are pursuing innovative directions in Artificial Intelligence in education. Perhaps even human-centred research programmes are not immune to the problem of "Not Invented Here".

Reflection and Experience

Artificial Intelligence provides a unique means of assisting reflection, as we seek to model the knowledge with which we are concerned, and as we give concrete form to our ideas, opening them up for discussion and negotiation. Springer have performed a valuable service in publishing the series and journal in which ideas can be expounded.

Many of the papers discussed here draw on the work of Wittgenstein, whose career transcended conventional subject barriers, and whose ideas are achieving a new universality through a new generation of readers. His lectures were attended by founding fathers of computing such as Alan Turing, and the advent of computers and Artificial Intelligence provides a new context for modern readers, who will find a useful bridge provided by the contributions of Janik, Johanneson, Searle and Dreyfus.

One of the major contributions made by the Swedish Center for Working Life has been the action research case study, with meticulous long-term observation of the effects of technological change in different areas of working life. All too often elsewhere the focus has been on the technology, with the human users there simply as optional adjuncts. As the Center undergoes changes, its innovative ideas should be picked up by international partners, bilaterally and on a European level.

The Next Steps

The issue is not just to analyse the industrial world, but to change it. We have the opportunity to give a European cultural perspective to technology, placing great emphasis on the importance of skill and education. For this to succeed we need to maintain a series of experimental collaborative projects, each time broadening the net of involvement.

Those who cast aside totalitarian communist rule in Eastern Europe were not simply seeking a capitalist future, but a more human-centred approach to life in a common European home. Having rejected one ideology they are unlikely to easily accept another, whether in the form of an economic theory or a reliance on technology. The human-centred design process, where participation is encouraged and valued, lies at the heart of a modern approach to democracy.

The mystique of Expert Systems, Artificial Intelligence and Information Technology in general has been tarnished with technological failures and disillusion in recent years: we need to offer acceptable working models of people assisted by technology in productive activity. One opportunity may be provided by the European Community ERASMUS Programme, with a new proposed network in the field of Business Information Technology involving partners in the United Kingdom, France, Germany, Denmark, Belgium, Netherlands, Italy and Sweden. Support has been sought for joint courses, exchanges and curriculum development.

Much of the background research for the projects reported in these volumes was funded by the European Community; they have also funded work on Human-Centred Computer Integrated Manufacturing Systems and Workstations. Sweden has now applied to join the European Community as a full member, though this process is unlikely to be complete before the next international conference is held in Stockholm in 1993. This series emphasises the extent to which Sweden is already an active participant in European development, providing the imaginative cement to bring together intellectual building blocks from a broadly based tradition.

References

Brödner, P (1990) *The shape of future technology: The anthropocentric alternative*. Springer-Verlag, London.

Cooley, M (1989) *European competitiveness in the 21st century: integration of work, culture and technology*. EEC FAST Programme, Brussels.

Corbett, JM, Rasmussen, LB and Rauner, F (1991) *Crossing the border: the social and engineering design of computer integrated manufacturing systems*. Springer-Verlag, London.

Ennals, R (1991) *Artificial intelligence and human institutions*. Springer-Verlag, London.

Ennals, R and Gardin, J-C (eds) (1990) *Interpretation in the humanities: perspectives from artificial intelligence*. British Library, London.

Gardin, J-C (ed) (1989) *Artificial intelligence and expert systems: case studies in the knowledge domain of archaeology* (trans Ennals, R). Ellis Horwood, Chichester

Gill, K (ed) (1986) *Artificial intelligence for society*. John Wiley, Chichester.

Gill, K (1990) *Summary of human-centred systems research in Europe*. SEAKE Centre, Brighton Polytechnic, Brighton.

Göranzon, B (1989) *The practical intellect*. Unesco, Geneva (in Swedish). English edition 1992, Springer-Verlag, London.

Göranzon, B and Florin, M (eds) (1990) *Artificial intelligence, culture and language: on education and work*. Springer-Verlag, London.

Göranzon, B and Florin, M (eds) (1991) *Skill and education: reflection and experience*. Springer-Verlag, London.

Göranzon, B and Florin, M (eds) (1991) *Dialogue and technology: art and knowledge*. Springer-Verlag, London.

Göranzon, B and Josefson, I (eds) (1988) *Knowledge, skill and artificial intelligence*. Springer-Verlag, London.
Nichol, J, Briggs, J and Dean, J (eds) (1988) *PROLOG, children and students*. Kogan Page, London.
Rosenbrock, H (ed) (1989) *Designing human-centred technology: a cross-disciplinary project in computer-aided manufacturing*. Springer-Verlag, London.
Von Wright, GH (1971) *Explanation and understanding*. Routledge and Kegan Paul, London.

Part II:

The Diderot Project: Enlightenment, Skill and Education

Chapter 15

Remarks on the Diderot Project[1]

Lars Kleberg

What is the role of the aesthetic in our search for theoretical and practical knowledge? Why is the most beautiful form also the most durable, from an engineer's point of view, in Michelangelo's dome? The chapter raises the concepts of *heterodoxy* (multiperspectivity) and *heteroglossy* (multilingualism) and their implications for the Diderot Project. As a translator and a creative artist in the field of scientific problems, Diderot exemplifies the importance of heteroglossy or multilingualism and syncretism, not only for a writer but for the survival and dynamic evolution of a culture. The quest for an exact language ironically seems to accompany an increase in what cannot be said in language. Yuri Lotman, the Soviet semiotician and historian of culture, has argued that heteroglossy and the process of translating the *Unknown* is crucial to the dynamic functioning of culture. We should therefore avoid a forced synthesis of the Project's many discussions and it is for this reason that *Rameau's Nephew* serves as a useful emblem for the Diderot Project.

In Allan Janik's contribution "Caliban's Revenge" (Chap. 16), there is one word characterizing the work of the dialogue seminars in Stockholm which I would like to connect closer with Denis Diderot and the Diderot Project. The word Allan Janik uses is *heterodoxy*. I want to point out some implications of *heterodoxy* (multiperspectivity) and *heteroglossy* (multilingualism) for the Diderot Project as I see it.

Several participants have underlined the importance of the aesthetic element in the seminars, not only as a "decoration" or "intermedium", but as a constituting element for a discourse about knowledge and understanding. A project such as the staging of *Rameau's Nephew* by Julian Hiltons and Clive Mendus, establishes the case for the aesthetic in the project. But, still, it seems that we sometimes forget to what extent Diderot all the tine was an artist as well as a philosopher. Magnus Florin's paper (Chap. 17) elegantly puts a question that Diderot put himself in a letter to Sophie Volland: why is the most beautiful form also the most durable, from an engineer's point of view, in Michelangelo's dome? We often discuss the difference between and benefits of a pragmatic versus abstract approach in architecture and other fields, but we somehow forget Diderot's provocative question. What is the role of the aesthetic in our search for – theoretical or practical – knowledge? This is an immense field of inquiry (intuition, experiment, structuring of thought, composition of discourse etc.). Let me only point to one aspect. I am fascinated by Diderot as a writer, a creative artist in the field of scientific problems. I believe that for Diderot, as for any writer, the act of writing was a way of discovering the nature of the problem he was trying to address. I do not believe any of the Diderot texts are simply research reports that summarize a certain amount of knowledge arrived at before the act of writing. This can be seen already in the seemingly self-contradictory passages in *Rameau's Nephew*. Writing is trying to do what you cannot do. It is a process of translating the unknown into one's own language at the same time as widening the limits of that language.

The Swedish art critic Ulf Linde says somewhere that "what you cannot translate, you haven't understood". This phrase can be understood/ translated in several ways. For Diderot it was true in a very specific way. He was a translator from the very beginning of his career. But as Jean Starobinski points out in an excellent essay[2] this was not a part of his apprenticeship. To translate, to enter into the language of others and in a way "mime" the way of thinking, the style, the "role and gestures" of others (instead of simply quoting), was – according to Starobinski – his way of being himself, or, rather, becoming himself.

> The further they have reached, the more soul-less has the universe become, and so has the science about it. But at the same time as nature has become soul-less, it has also become more unapproachable. The part of reality that does not fit in the mechanistic and positivist strait-jacket is growing every day![3]

The development of an exact language seems, ironically, to go hand in hand with the growth of what cannot be said in this language. The perfection of *the* language is thus a very ambiguous affair; especially when this or that language is seen as superior to other ones.

Diderot is an excellent emblem for the importance of *heteroglossy* or multilingualism and syncretism, not only for a writer but for the dynamic evolution, thus survival, of a culture. Yuri Lotman, the Soviet Russian semiotician and historian of culture, has written extensively on this problem, combining structuralist concepts with the concept of *diglossia* (dialogism) of Mikhail Bakhtin.

Heteroglossy and the process of translation of the *Unknown* is, according to Lotman, of central importance to the dynamic functioning of culture. One could perhaps even say that if there is nothing Unknown, no Other, it has to be invented. In fact, human culture has so far had no problem to find new realms of the Unknown.

The Unknown in Bo Göranzon's "Caliban/Prospero" metaphor (Chap. 24) is rather the unobserved relations between theory and practice, knowledge and skill, that are implied in the whole modernization project.

If there is anything the Soviet Russian historians of culture should have taught us, it is to beware of (forced) synthesis. It would be not only pretentious but also basically wrong for me to try to synthesize our discussions or hope for a synthetic resolution of the different tendencies to be observed in our group. It is precisely this reason that *Rameau's Nephew* is an excellent emblem for the Diderot Project.

Notes

1 Presented in an earlier version as Concluding Remarks, Diderot Project Seminar, Paris, February 1989.

2 Diderot et la parole des autres. Critique January 1972, no 296: 3–22.

3 Eisenstein, in my dialogue In the sign of Aquarius. In: Kleberg., Lars and Lövgren, Håkan, *Eisenstein revisited*. Stockholm, 1987.

Section VII:
Reflections on Diderot

Chapter 16

Caliban's Revenge

Allan Janik

How can we employ our knowledge justly and humanely? How can we develop teaching techniques that conform to actual modes of learning? What does a worker with skill actually know? The Diderot Project poses questions about the social consequences of the implementation of computer technology in the workplace, starting from a series of informed studies of the internal – or epistemological – structure of work and drawing heavily upon such diverse disciplines as economic history, linguistics, mathematics and literary criticism as well as classical and contemporary philosophy. Enlightenment, skill and education have emerged as the pivotal issues around which a humanized and productive discussion of the new technology must be shaped. Diderot's *Rameau's Nephew* questions the limits of the Enlightenment, offering a trenchant analysis of the relationship of teleology to instrumentality, and, in doing so, challenges a central tenet in modern philosophy – namely, that practical knowledge ultimately has a theoretical basis. In Diderot's view, the forms of knowledge we might label practical and theoretical, experiential and propositional, are not only incompatible, but actually in competition with one another in the social world. His use of the dialogue form, moreover, induces a form of reflective tension in the reader, who is thereby invited to actively participate in the textual debates. The chapter discusses the power of the hypocrite – or counter-example – with reference to both *Rameau's Nephew* and Shakespeare's *The Tempest*. The success "lui" as a parasite depends upon his ability to act or imitate; his knowledge entails knowing the appropriate gesture in any given social situation – a matter of skill, a "knowing how" rather than a "knowing that". He cannot articulate in words this form of knowledge and thus the reflections of the philosopher mediate for the reader: words are explained by gestures and gestures by words. The dialogue form thus intersects two different modes of expression and thereby makes communication, if not resolution, possible.

The Diderot Project is a research programme exploring the social impact of technology. The impetus to discuss this issue clearly originates in Sweden, even if its participants come from a variety of European and Scandinavian nations, and its implications extend to the whole of the industrialized world. The roots of the Diderot Project go back at least to the 1979 symposium "Is the Computer a Tool?", which was convened by the Swedish Research

Council in Sigtuna, the ancient capital of Sweden, and whose results were published in the book of the same name. The most recent fruits of our research were presented at the conference "Culture, Language and Artificial Intelligence" (Stockholm, 1988). Then as now our questions are: how can we employ what we know justly and humanely? How can we develop techniques that conform to actual modes of learning rather than conflict with them? How can we realize the Enlightenment dream of a society in which science and technology serve not only the legitimate aims and goals of technocrats, bureaucrats and market forces but also help to make the lives of the increasingly large segment of the population which works with it on a day-to-day basis more satisfying as well as more productive? From Sigtuna onwards it was clear to us that, to paraphrase Talleyrand, the discussion of technology is too important to be left to the technocrats – or for that matter the politicians or the "forces" of the market. We have been sceptical as well with regard to the claims of social science and philosophy with respect to what they could tell us about what could or should be done with the immensely powerful instrumentarium that computer technology has put at our disposal. Our scepticism has often been mistaken for anything from a primitive anti-technological attitude to an elitism every bit as odious as the one we would displace. Both of these views are profoundly mistaken. We criticized engineers, advertisers and economists, to pick three of many targets, because they were prepared to make bold claims about what computers could do in the workplace without ever taking a look at what people actually do there. Thus it was from a series of informed studies of the internal – if you like, the epistemological – structure of work that we began – and continue – to pose questions about the social consequences of the implementation of computer technology in the workplace.

From the start our aims and perspectives have been heterodox, so it should hardly be surprising that our methods should be no less unorthodox. The question that we sought to answer was what does a worker with skill (a broader category than skilled worker) know? The designers, promoters and buyers of the new technology all assume that they know the answer to this question. The Swedish social insurance system thought that it did but it soon became clear that this was not the case. But how should we learn what workers with skill know? One way to do this is as novel as it is obvious, i.e., to ask workers with skill just what it is that they know. However, as Socrates learned long ago, that is not much help in itself because workers, in the case of Socrates the master artisans, cannot put what they know into words. But it was a mistake for Socrates to stop his inquiry there – a mistake that has been the scourge of classical rationalist approaches to knowledge from Plato and Descartes to Carnap and Dretske. In our efforts to discover the epistemological characteristics of experience in working life we have come to recognize that what is required is what John Dewey called "reconstruction" or working practices. The reconstruction of working life is not a simple matter at all because it involves (1) a wide variety of practices, each with its own structure, as well as (2) hermeneutic methods for helping workers with skill articulate what they know. It is not something that can be accomplished in a series of interviews; it is a matter or entering into those practices, i.e., coming to be at home among cabinet makers, nurses, metalworkers etc., learning how they do what they do and comparing the salient features of their practices, as well as reflecting upon the shortcomings of our epistemological traditions before we can even begin to address the questions that are most relevant to understanding the world of work. Little wonder, then, that the research that has led up to the Diderot Project has drawn heavily upon such diverse disciplines as economic history, linguistics, mathematics and literary criticism as well as classical and contemporary philosophy in forging a new and fruitful way of conceiving the tensions between the assumptions of orthodox computer science and skill-constituting traditions in working life.

Thus, starting from the actual complaints of foresters about the ways in which computers hindered rather than helped them in accomplishing their tasks, and in conjunction with the conceptual analyses of philosophers and mathematicians as informed as they were critical about the role that computer marketing claimed for "thinking machines" and assisted by reflective computer scientists with an awareness that everything was hardly as rosy as computer merchandizing would tempt us to believe, we have round our way now to a threefold problem. Enlightenment, skill and education have emerged as the pivotal issues around which we wish to shape a discussion or the new technology that will be at once humanized and productive. It is important to emphasize the conjunction "humanized and productive"; here for our researches into areas like surgical instrument making make it increasingly clear that, wherever the main concern is for a quality product, economic concerns cannot really be separated from human concerns without doing violence to both, Indeed, one of the common concerns of the various participants in the project is with the artificiality of the disciplinary boundaries in which we have been enculturated. All of us have found our way into disciplines very different from those we studied originally. Our collective experience indicates that the sort of questions that problems concerning new technology generate are not the sort or questions which can be illuminated by a single discipline of methodology. It is one or the many merits of Diderot's "*Rameau's Nephew*" that is designed to raise just those sorts of disturbing questions about Enlightenment, skill and education that have already arisen in the course of our researches to date. My task here is to make the case for the special place that will be allotted to it in the course of preparing for our next international symposium.

The short answer to the question "why is 'Rameau's Nephew' so important for people with our concerns right now?" is that no single text before or since Diderot poses the question of the limits of Enlightenment so radically as he does in this dialogue, in which the epistemology, ethics and aesthetics or Enlightenment are penetratingly scrutinized. *Rameau's Nephew* is a trenchant analysis of the relationship of teleology to instrumentality inasmuch as it sets "knowing that" against "knowing how" and in so doing challenges a central tenet in modern philosophy, namely, that practical knowledge ultimately has a theoretical basis – a view which we find reflected in doctors who refuse to admit that nursing skill is really knowledge at all. In Diderot's view the practical and the theoretical, the experiential and the propositional, sorts of knowledge are not only radically incompatible with one another but actually in competition with one another in the social world. However, the importance of the dialogue hardly ends there. Diderot brilliantly juxtaposes two ways of conceiving knowledge and life itself not simply in such a way that they are questioned, ridiculed or rejected but in such away as to show how they problematize one another. To begin with the philosophical defender of enlightened self-interest and the hypocrite are each in his own way shockingly coherent. Yet, they are wholly incompatible with one another when they articulate their most cherished beliefs. But Diderot's consummate artistry goes into the very dialogue form through which he draws the reader into its action in a manner that is wholly true to life, namely, by leaving the incommensurable perspectives the two figures represent both plausible but questionable. The lack of resolution gives the dialogue the form of a rebus. Its solution requires readers to supply the missing, but suggested, elements, the "grammar" binding them together, as it were, themselves. Thus its structure aims at inducing just that sort or reflective tension that we have employed previously to help working people to get an articulate grasp of their activities. Thus, it should be clear that our concern with *Rameau's Nephew* is not merely a matter of extracting its message from the text in the way that you might extract the milk from a coconut. We do not seek to replace epistemology and philosophy of science with literature but we do insist that literature is indispensable to certain types of philosophical investigations: however, it is precisely because it is only literature of a special sort that can fill this role and that *Rameau's Nephew* is a particularly fine example of just what a literary text must be like if it is to fill that role. It places us between two fields of force and demands that we resolve the tension ourselves. This requires a curious sort of hermeneutics of riddle solving, which itself should stimulate us to look at the problems concerning Enlightenment, skill and education that arise from new technology in fresh and trenchant ways. It is less that we expect to generate answers from the encounter with the dialogue but that it should assist us individually and collectively to develop a framework or perspective in terms of which we may conduct future discussions more reflectively than we otherwise might.

The concept of reflection has emerged as a central epistemological category in the course or our work. As we have seen, the principal means of moving workers with skill to articulate what they know in their bodies is indirect. Simply asking questions takes us in the wrong direction; for answering questions is itself a skill of a different order from those which workers with skill typically have developed. However, with the help or provocative texts such as Rousseau's *Emile* or Shakespeare's *King Lear* it has been possible to stimulate them to put their concerns into words on the basis of reflection on those texts. In addition, since IBM suggested that we should "have a dialogue" with their computers, we have been concerned with the problem of determining just what the distinguishing characteristics of dialogue might be. Here again, if dialogue is genuine, it has to be a matter of two different positions posing problems for one another in a situation where we had not previously been inclined to consider that there were problems at all. What is this but an animated way of inducing reflection, i.e., of bringing us to a point where we are prepared to reappraise some belief. Thus in both of these contexts reflection has emerged as central to our undertaking. I am hard put to think or a text that is better suited to stimulating reflection upon our concerns than Diderot's dialogue of speech and gesture. If any doubts arise about that, we need merely to consider the historical impact that *Rameau's Nephew* has had upon figures as different as Hegel and Schopenhauer, Marx and Freud, not to mention Goethe and Schiller. Hegel's dialectic of Master and Servant, Schopenhauer's Will and Representation, Marx's self-alienation and Freud's contrast of Ego and Id all owe something to Diderot's masterpiece. So on that account alone nobody deserves the title of modern master more than the author of *Rameau's Nephew*. Beyond that a clever plagiarist might be able to rewrite the piece substituting Jürgen Habermas for *moi* and Jean-Francois Lyotard for *lui* to produce a brilliant satire on the major confrontation in contemporary European philosophy. Indeed, it may well be that *Rameau's Nephew* is more relevant to philosophical discussion today than when it was written.

I have termed these remarks "Caliban's Revenge" because I take it that what is at stake in Diderot's disturbing defence of the socially constitutive character of the asocial, the parasite Rameau's nephew, is at least in part a sophisticated contribution to a debate about the relationship of skill to formal knowledge, i.e., of "knowing how" to "knowing that", whose resolution turns upon the relationship between goals and instrumentalities in human enterprises. The theme is decidedly a Stoic one, i.e., part of a philosophical tradition whose influence in the formation of the modern world is in direct proportion to its neglect by historians of ideas.

No philosophers have emphasized the rational character of Nature more than the Stoics. For them there are no gaps in the causal chain that is Nature, only in our imperfect knowledge of it. The Stoic universe is a universal and necessary causal order; logos pervades the apparent whimsicality of fate. Human happiness consists on this account of understanding the role that Fortuna has allotted us, which means that we become free in the midst of this universal determinism paradoxically by understanding just how it is that we are determined by Nature. The life of the Stoic sage is thus a commitment to a paradoxical rationality according to which freedom is to be identified with submission to the rational order in Nature – and in society; for Stoicism is above all from ancient times a philosophy for civil servants. So it was no accident at all that one of the greatest of the Stoic philosophers, Seneca served Nero diligently as long as he could, and when he could not, took his own life. It is not my point to digress into the history or philosophy. I mention this because Stoicism played a particularly important role in intellectual life in two periods that are of particular interest to our group: the late Renaissance world of Shakespeare and Bacon and the Enlightenment world of *Rameau's Nephew*. Indeed, in the Enlightenment it was almost a sort of game to realize our freedom in the discovery or the forces which bind us, as Garry Wills has pointed out in his brilliant study of Jefferson. For this reason Hume's insistence that reason is the slave of the passions, like Freud's insistence that conscious action is the result of unconscious motivation is in their thought wholly consistent with a commitment to the Socratic search for self-knowledge in a way that both Romantics and Positivists have failed to see for want or understanding the Stoic tradition. On this view we cannot eliminate the beast within us, perhaps not even tame it, but we can at least understand it by recognizing it and thereby attain a realistic self-image and expectations. Understanding the causal order of Nature does not leave us any the less determined but it does leave us in a slightly better position with respect to coping with our lot. As

Diderot's Jacques the Fatalist puts it with respect to the death of a loved one: I understand why I cry but I cry nonetheless.

For the Neo-Stoic movement which emerged in Flanders at the end or the sixteenth century, conviction of the strict causal determinism in Nature, which set them off from the Hermeticists who dominated intellectual life at the time went hand in hand with a confidence that human beings can order their own affairs rationally. Participation in public life (negotium) was a duty; whereas a withdrawn life of contemplation such as that which both Scholastics and Hermetiscists such as Marsilio Ficino and Giovanni Pica dells Mirandola advocated (otium) was regarded by Ciceronian Humanists such as Leonardo Bruni or Neo-Stoics like Justus Lipsius as a life that was not worth living. For Hermetic philosophers, like Plato before them, the actual world of politics is the province of cut-throats and liars. The only rational response to such a world is flight. The philosopher must shun it for the life of the mind, the glassy essence that connects us with God. In the sixteenth century, however, the view that contemplation was senseless when divorced from practical life became almost commonplace (Thomas More stands out on this account). This affirmation of public life was inspired by Cicero's more or less Stoic view according to which participation in public life was a responsibility and shunning it an invitation to disaster. This is one way of understanding Shakespeare's *The Tempest*, i.e. as a story about the reconciliation of otium and negotium: moreover, as one which makes much sense or the relationship between Prospero and Caliban. So we are finally approaching my subject – but I hope nobody is in a hurry.

One passage in *The Tempest* which ought to be puzzling and disturbing for anyone concerned with education is in the confrontation between Caliban and Prospero is in the first act, second scene:

You taught me language, and my profit on't
Is, I know how to curse. The red plague rid you
For learning me your language!

We know or their earlier relations: that Prospero and Caliban met on a more or less friendly basis, that Caliban made untoward advances to Miranda, that he, like Ariel is held in submission by virtue of Prospero's magical powers, but also that Caliban considers himself to have been cheated out of the island and, finally, that, for all his odiousness, Prospero and Miranda cannot do without him. It is especially this last aspect of their relationship that I want to see in connection with Prospero's teaching. I want to consider the text I have cited in relation to Caliban as the indispensable instrument ensuring Prospero and Miranda's material existence in the context of Neo-Stoic political ideas to form the basis for a political reading of the play. I proceed from the question: why should Prospero's initial efforts to "civilize" Caliban have gone awry?

That *The Tempest* is, *inter alia*, a political play would certainly have been obvious to a Shakespearean audience, if it is not so for us. Well-versed in their Horace, accustomed to thinking in metaphors, the image of shipwreck with which the play begins would surely have suggested the Horatian image of the Ship of State run aground. True it is Prospero's magic that is responsible for the storm, but I want to suggest that it is the political significance of that magic that is being questioned in a very specific way. This is consistent with what we know historically about the play. If we are to believe Dame Frances Yates, Prospero, the magician, is the embodiment of the greatest Elizabethan magus; John Dee, whose reputation was at its ebb after the ascent of the witch-hunting James VI and I to the English throne. In any case, Prospero has lost his rightful place as the Duke of Naples to his brother Antonio. Consumed by magic, which we forget at our peril was the science of the day, he has neglected affairs or state and thereby destroyed a link in the Chain of Being that must have repercussions everywhere. He has done this by making his brother regent, only to find the ambitious and unscrupulous Antonio seizing power and expelling him. Thus, the story unfolds around bad judgment (hamartia) rather than shameless pride (hubris) as it does in *Measure for Measure*, which I take to be related to *The Tempest* in this respect. If this account of the action catches something central to it, it is very close to *Measure for Measure* in which uncircumspect delegation of authority figures in a central way and one upon which the Neo-Stoic stamp is particularly clear. I refer to the emphasis upon the central Neo-Stoic virtue constancy and, above all, the merciful manifestation of the true prince's majesty, i.e., that very quality which makes a resolution of the strife between Caliban and Prospero possible in *The Tempest*. On this interpretation, the magician's concern with otium at the price or neglecting his realm, i.e., negotium, disturbs the whole Chain of Being. Force comes to displace wisdom not only in the person of Antonio but also in the exiled Prospero himself. The latter manages his affairs with the help of two servants, who might be likened to the two lower parts of the soul in Plato's Myth of the Charioteer in the "Phaedrus": the willing Ariel, who nevertheless longs for his lost freedom, and the obstreperous but indispensable Caliban. Prospero controls both by force of his magical powers. Once the initial bad judgment leads to injustice the cosmic balance is disturbed and a chain of retribution is forged. Thus, Prospero's neglect begets Antonio's usurpation. Prospero's subjugation of Caliban begets the latter's desire for revenge. No wonder that Prospero's teaching has come to nought. Only the persuasive power or love can break the cycle of retribution and elicit that mercy that restores the lost balance. So it is not merely Caliban's 'primitive", uncouth, uneducated character that accounts for Prospero's failure to teach him something or value, it is Prospero's reliance upon brute force as well – we forget that Caliban remarks of their earliest encounters "then I loved thee". In short, Prospero's failure results from attempting to educate without persuasion and the result is that Caliban has mastered the technique but cannot apply it constructively.

It is now generally recognized that Shakespeare's vindication of Prospero is a defence of Dee's white magic against Ben Jonson and other detractors at court; what I have added here is a Neo-Stoic dimension to the tale according to which the magus, Prospero, through bad judgment find himself outmanoeuvred by his Machiavellian brother. Cosmic balance is only restored through a new Stoic synthesis, i.e. through Prospero's act of mercy which re-establishes his majesty as a mere mortal. Just as Prospero learns from the example of the love of Ferdinand and Miranda for one another, we the audience are to learn from the moving example of the play. This too is good Stoic epistemology; for in that tradition "force and vivacity", to employ Hume's preferred expression for the ancient Stoic notion of the fantasia kataleptiké, is the mark of truth and logical means to a moral end in a sphere where knowing consists in knowing how to distinguish between rules and exceptions.

But what does all of this have to do with Diderot, and especially with *Rameau's Nephew*? I suggest that one place to look for the answer is in G.W.F. Hegel's reading of Diderot's masterpiece, a reading whose profundity has continued to impress scholars to this day. The question that Hegel raises is this: does not the adept parasite in the end manipulate those from whose tables he lives? It is as if Caliban were to learn suddenly that there are some respects in which Prospero and Miranda are really dependent upon him and begin to exploit that fact. Just as Caliban is a useful and necessary instrument without whose material assistance Prospero cannot practice his magical technology, so Rameau's nephew, through flattery, wit and charm, provides his "respectable" hosts with a self-esteem and amusement without which they would not only be bored but would lose their very identity. Rameau's nephew cunningly exploits his serfdom and in the end it is he who manipulates those who have power over him. In this sense he represents "Caliban's revenge": those who think that they are using him are in fact being used by him. The big difference between them is that he knows it and they do not – at least as he sees the matter. In his dishonesty he has a self-awareness that his respectable patrons wholly lack but his self-awareness is wholly problematic in that it is wholly precarious. In any case, Rameau's nephew prompts us to ask with Omar Khyahm "who is the potter and who, pray, the pot?"

This echoes a Stoic insight that is as old as Polybius's analyses of the battles in the First Punic War: it is not enough to have superior forces and the best general; one needs tactical as well as strategic wisdom if one is to make the best of the lot Fortuna casts. Means and ends are not discrete entities to be glued together in decisive action, as people have often been tempted to think. The full significance of ends and intentions is only clear at the point when our concrete proposals for attaining those ends, i.e. our effective causal agency, becomes clear. The former and the latter need not be identical. (Here supply a brilliant example; alas I don't have one so you'll have to think one up for yourself! The best I can do are a couple of run of the mill examples.)

If we need an example of what happens here when the gap between ends and means becomes hopelessly wide to the point that the end becomes little more than the sort or wild fantasy that *lui* has of producing a work of genius, we might consider Irene's desire to go to Moscow in Chekov's *Three Sisters*. It is an end conceived in the absence of means and thus wholly unrealistic and perhaps even self-destructive. A more banal but nevertheless relevant example of the ways our ends are shaped by the instruments through which we realize them comes from music, where the notion of instrument can be taken literally. I remember the case of a French horn player whose horn was stolen. He, reacted not only with anger but with frustration because, as he put it," I knew every dent in that horn: before I can play at the same level of competence, I shall have to learn how to cope with the dents and peculiarities of a new horn". Take another example: look at Peter Guller's magnificent photograph of a set of tools that a worker employed for some 25 years and ask yourself what must happen when the worker in question for whatever reason has to start using new ones. The US Postal System, where efforts at reform from above have in fact tended to challenge workers to find ever more clever ways of maintaining their accustomed work patterns, provides us with another example of what happens when ends are determined irrespective or the instrumentalities, in this case human, through which they are realized. The converse can be seen in certain cases in Scandinavia where workers have played a role in planning the implementation of new technology at their places of work. When they are able to build their skill and experience into, say, a new postal terminal, greater satisfaction pays off in terms of greater efficiency. I shall pass over the ways in which the end of reforming higher education from above has turned out to be away of courting disaster; for the story is too long and too sad to tell. *Rameau's Nephew* gives us plenty to reflect upon if we need a model for grasping how we can fall foul of the gap between promise and performance with respect to the sorts of instrumental considerations, in our case the sorts of sensitivity to education and training, that large-scale social planning require to be effectively implemented.

To return to *lui*: he is, or course, the paradigm case of the alienated individual in his awareness that he is in a sense superior to those upon whom he is dependent. His means also drastically limit his ends. It is this very knowledge that torments him. He alone knows what he is, a cunning mediocrity, and that entails also knowing what he is not, i.e. a genius. The curse of self-conscious mediocrity is its desire to be creative when it is fully aware that by its very nature it cannot be. That should tell us a great deal both about unselfconscious mediocrity and about enthusiasm for creativity. Be that as it may, when *lui* is not scheming, he is thinking of nothing more than what he is not and thereby frustrating his own commitment to pleasure as the highest good. This is an essential part or his character. Nobody else could succeed in making him as miserable as he makes himself. He would do anything to live up to the illustrious name that he bears but he has not the means to do so. His "inner life", to the extent that he has one, is the pure agony of hopeless aspiration. In this respect he is more modern than he post-modernists can imagine – today he would be addicted to *Dallas* and *Dynasty*. But even more importantly, imagine how he would react to the news that someone had invented a miraculous machine that would transform mediocrity into genius! How might he have been enthralled by such a concept? Unfortunately, there is not space to discuss this further. I leave it to you to draw your own conclusions.

From Herder and the Romantics there have been uncompromising assaults and rejections of the "values of the Enlightenment" but none of the critics of the Enlightenment has questioned the project more provocatively than the editor or the Encyclopaedia himself did in *Rameau's Nephew*. One way of looking at the confrontation between the philosopher and the hypocrite is to conceive it as a clash between two concepts of order: one systematic and wholly articulable in, say, mathematical form, the other exemplifiable and movingly powerful but basically inarticulable in an age that tends to identify clarity and distinctness exclusively in quantifiable and formalizible terms. One puzzling aspect of this confrontation is the continual identification of the enlightened philosopher with conventional values. In the main, Enlightenment, now as then, has been identified with a critique of the conventional values which is a prelude to reforming them rationally. However, in his dialogue Diderot steadfastly identifies the philosopher, *moi*, with conventional morality. It is easy to :miss the significance of this. The underlying premise of the Enlightenment as a large-scale project for social reform is that the project has to connect with the world as it presents itself to us, i.e. irrespective of what later became called "false consciousness", a concept which first emerges in this very dialogue. The clarion call of the Enlightenment is Progress. Its promise is that science can produce a better social order than tradition has. Here too there has been a strong Stoic influence. As a Stoic project, the Enlightenment presupposes a universal causal continuity. The aim of enlightened critical theory is to dislodge the rational kernel within tradition from its irrational husk in much the same way that the Stoics of old such as Cicero studied ancient religious practices with a view to extracting from them the rational core of "natural religion". Here the extraordinarily radical character of Diderot's dialogue comes into focus again; for he is calling one of the central presuppositions of his own tradition into question. Must social values be identical with the values that the leading members of society or the majority explicitly profess? The power of the hypocrite as counter-example exposes the loose fit between what is sometimes (misleadingly) termed theory and practice. If the values we profess are not the values that inform our practices, what are the consequences for constructive social reform? Therein lies the rub of *lui*'s identification of *moi*'s views with conventional values. In countries where the universal assumption of the populace is that professed values are unconnected to social traditions there is a scepticism, if not outright cynicism with respect to social reform. Diderot seems to be suggesting that we all have something to learn from them. In any case, Diderot's service here is to show us something about the limits of Enlightenment by showing us the ways in which the most widespread view of Enlightenment is tied to conventional values in a manner that is not always recognized and which show up in *Rameau's Nephew* as clichés. It is certainly not accidental that the most devastating critique of the evil potential of the cliché perhaps ever, Karl Kraus's *Die letzten Tage der Menschheit*, was in part explicitly modelled upon *Rameau's Nephew*. The question which Diderot poses to us here is one that remains disturbing: to what extent is hypocrisy normal and constitutive of society? I do not myself propose to answer it until I have had .lunch. As for the question of where hypocrisy really lies in society, even a good lunch will not provoke me to tackle that one.

One or the great triumphs in Diderot's dialogue is the characterization or the figure of *lui* himself. What could be a greater challenge than to bring a volubly verbal, if essentially non-discursive personality, to life in a dialogue. In carrying off this *tour de force* Diderot runs up against a problem near and dear to the later Wittgenstein: how do you describe those aspects of language which are essentially non-discursive? For Wittgenstein the answer is that we have to invent fictive natural histories, which by contrast with our actual ones shed light upon those aspects of language that lead us into epistemological quandaries in the first place but whose very commonplace character prevents us from seeing them as such. *Lui*'s character, if we may call it that, is to be a pure imitator; he is a more or less successful parasite because he is a consummate actor. His knowledge entails knowing the appropriate gesture in any given social situation – and because his ideas are concrete gestures, rather than abstract notions, their nature as corporeal motion (pardon the redundancy) defies precise description and definition. His "knowledge" is a matter of skill, a "knowing how" rather than a "knowing that". His depth is all on the surface, so it will be very difficult for traditional philosophers, for example, who are used to delving beneath the surface to find what they are looking for when they are asked to determine what he knows. By his nature he articulates very little of what is essential to his character in words. Thus if you ask him to be precise about his skill he must answer like the naval officer in Strindberg's *Dream Play*: "I know it but I can't say it". In a similar way to Wittgenstein Diderot solves his problem by analysing the figure or *lui* comparatively. In the extended comparison or the two types of knowing and acting the salient features of each or the original Odd Couple are shown to us in dramatic form by being delineated against one another. Thus drama turns out here to be a way of taming the inarticulate, spontaneous gesture by juxtaposing it with the reflected judgments of the philosopher. As Wittgenstein was to reformulate and develop his celebrated distinction between "saying" and "showing" in his later work: we explain words by gestures and gestures by words. Wittgenstein too insisted that in this sense philosophy was basically a literary craft, so we should hardly be surprised that a profound and penetrating philosophical work should have a dramatic form.

In conclusion, coming to *Rameau's Nephew* for the first time without any warning can be a frustrating experience. We are all too much accustomed to philosophical and literary works with a beginning, middle and an end to appreciate why someone might want to avoid that form. Moreover, philosophers such as Augustine and Plato, who have written in dialogue form have for the most part so loaded the dice in favour of the position that they want to defend that we have become accustomed to read their work for its content alone, so little does the form bear upon the philosophizing in these works. Not so with Diderot. If we read *Rameau's Nephew* without being conscious or its form, we shall miss the point and find the dialogue positively silly. I know I did when I first encountered it. Many others have done the same. Conversely, anyone concerned with the dialogical form will be sure to find the work a delight for the way in which Diderot exploits the latent resources of the form for capturing conflict over perspectives or "essential contestability". If dialogue is really a confrontation between views of a question that are basically at odds with one another (*dissoi logoi*) it has to be a very curious phenomenon. To the extent that there is agreement, there is nothing interesting to discuss; to the extent that there is not, there can be no communication. Whence comes the possibility for discussion? If this is so we end up with intersecting monologues. This is much like what we find in Diderot but in *Rameau's Nephew* there is communication, even if the partners to the dialogue are not able to convince one another of much. Their communication turns on the fact that they are in some sense friends, who recognize and are prepared to tolerate one another's differences. Here Diderot reminds us of something Plato presupposed in his dialogues and what I take it that Prospero has forgotten as *The Tempest* opens, namely, that it is our common humanity which makes discourse possible; mere verbal expression is not enough.

But what or the possibility of dialogue in the face of the impossibility of convincing the other of the correctness of our opinion? Both Diderot and Wittgenstein want to emphasize that differences or opinion, inasmuch as they are differences of perspectives or priorities are rooted in different ways of living. These differences in forms or life to use Wittgenstein's phrase penetrate the whole being of the disputants. They cannot be cast off at will because they are our very personalities themselves. Thus, bringing out the differences in mode of expression between *moi* and *lui* is the very point of the dialogue. The philosopher expresses himself in words and arguments; whereas the parasite's mode of expression is more that of mute action as befits someone who gains his livelihood by pretending. Could these two convince one another? Should they be expected to? Do they even want to? What would it be like to resolve their differences anyway? Would that be desirable? These are a few of the disturbing questions that reflection upon the form of the work provokes. Indeed, the questions about *Rameau's Nephew* are unending and seemingly irresoluable. For Nietzscheans, who despise the demand for an ending as decadent or nihilistic, *Rameau's Nephew* is a yea-saying to the conflicts through which life is constituted. Our task is to confront the questions I have raised here in the context of the discussion of new technology. In a vein that I think Diderot would appreciate, I think that either we shall accomplish this or we shall not; either we shall answer these questions or leave them unanswered or find yet better ones – but not until after lunch.

Selected Bibliography

Chekov, Anton *Three Sisters.*

Dewey, John *Education and democracy.*

Dewey, John *Reconstruction in philosophy.*

Diderot, Denis *Jacques the fatalist.*

Diderot, Denis *Rameau's nephew.*

Diderot, Denis *Paradox sur le comédien.*

Florin, Magnus (eds) *Dialogue and technology.* Springer-Verlag, London.

Göranzon, Bo et al., *Job design in Sweden.*

Göranzon, Bo and Josefson, Ingela (eds), *Knowledge, skill and artificial intelligence.*

Göranzon, Bo and Florin, Magnus, (eds), *Artificial intelligence, language and culture.* Springer-Verlag, London.

Hegel, G.W.F. *The phenomenology of the spirit.*

Janik, Allan *Justus Lipsius: Vater der österreichischenPhilosophie?* Austriaca, Rouen, 1989 (contains bibliography on Neo-Stoicism).

Janik, Allan *Style, politics and the future of philosophy.* Reidel.

Josephs, Herbert *Rameau's Nephew: Diderot's dialogue of language and gesture.*

Nietzsche, Friedrich *The case of Wagner.*

Rousseau, Jean Jacques *Emile.*

Shakespeare, William *King Lear.*

Shakespeare, William *Measure for measure.*

Shakespeare, William *The tempest.*

Skinner, Quentin *The foundations of modern political thought.*

Strindberg, August *A dream play.*

Strindberg, August *Miss Julie.*

Timms, Edwards *Karl Kraus, apocalyptic satirist.*

Wills, Gary *Inventing America.*

Wittgenstein, Ludwig *Philosophical investigations.*

Yates, Frances *Shakespeare's last plays.*

Zeller, Eduard *The Stoics and the Epicureans.*

Chapter 17

The Dome of Michelangelo

Magnus Florin

What does *instinct* mean to Diderot? His entry in the Encyclopaedia is a critique of Descartes' notion of instinct as the mechanistic, automatic, and uniform nature of the animal (an argument used to support Descarte's case for a fundamental separation of mind and body, man and beast). For Diderot, instinct is rooted in experience; it is a series of engravings in the memory of reflections and sensations. The training of animals is possible due to their memories. Remembered responses, reinforced by repetition, become habitual responses. La Hire has shown by the use of geometry that the vault of Michelangelo's dome, aside from its aesthetic qualities, also had the curvature of the highest supporting capacity. How, wonders Diderot, could Michelangelo choose from all his sketches precisely the one that combined elegance and solidity, without the help of La Hire's geometry? His answer cites calculation and experience as of equal importance in solving the problem: "If the one is well-founded it must correspond to the other." The conflict in Bo Göranzon's project Education–Work–Technology is between calculation and work or practice; the transfer of skills in the process of doing or making something. In *Rameau's Nephew* Diderot moves us from the completed into the coming-into-being. The conversation between moi and lui becomes a play of possible meanings and directions; unable to hide behind calculation from the outside, we participate in this ongoing play and become subjects of continuous experience.

What does *instinct* mean to Diderot? The word comes up in *Rameau's Nephew* in a passage where *lui* (he) speaks about a stuck-up woman demanding all men to flatter her, in the following way, for example: How beautifully put, how rightly spoken, how clearly seen, how originally felt! From where do women take such? Without studying, through the mere power of instinct (*par la seule force de l'instinct*), thanks to their own clearsightedness! It is something of a wonder. And do not say experience, study, reflection, education has anything to do with this!

In *Rameau's Nephew*, this is one of the passages where the irony of *lui* is fairly straightforward, probably because the irony towards the use or misuse of the notion of *instinct* falls back upon a strong critical view held by Diderot himself.

The word is, as we know, mostly used with special reference to animals, meaning an unreflexive inherent force connecting to simple or complex actions. Diderot's article on "Instinct" for the encyclopaedia is an attack on this view. It is an article which, almost in its entirety is a critique of Descartes' position. Descartes, separating body and mind, linked instinct to the mechanistic, automatic and uniform nature of the animal, an element supporting his claim of a fundamental difference between man and beast. For Diderot, this distinction between man and animal is not valid. The mere idea of a uniformity among animals seems to be completely false to him. He says "Any attentive hunter knows that there are not two foxes alike." Diderot argues strongly against the Cartesian concept of instinct, to the point of giving an opposite view of the phenomenon. What we call instinct, he says, is actually the result of experience, that is engravings in the memory of reflections and sensations. It is memory that makes the training of animals possible, memory and repetition: habit. Diderot does not suggest a distinction between humans and other species. One even gets an impression in this article from the encyclopaedia on "instinct" that Diderot is aiming his thoughts less towards the behaviour of dogs than towards the knowledge and education of men.

If we leave the encyclopaedia and read Diderot's letter to Sophie Valland, dated Paris 2 September 1762, we shall have further support for this impression. Diderot there writes to Sophie that he would like to report on a discussion caused by the word "instinct", a word often connected to taste and morals but never defined, he says. He goes on: "I stated that instinct with us is only the result of an infinite amount of small experiences beginning when we opened our eyes towards the light and going on until we were unconsciously directed by these little impulses that we have memory of." Evidently Diderot has left the domain of beasts. The interesting thing is that he does not now stick to taste or moral but immediately focuses work, imagination, knowledge, invention.

He takes the example of Michelangelo's work with the dome of St Peter's church in Rome. The famous geometrician La Hire of the Science Academy had shown by use of geometry that the vault of the dome, so admired for its beauty, also had the curvature of the highest supporting capacity. How, wonders Diderot, could Michelangelo among his sketches choose just the one that combined elegance and solidity, without the help of La Hire's geometry? Impossible to say, people answer, that cannot be reckoned, it's pure instinct! And what is instinct? Oh, everybody knows that!

Diderot's own answer does not settle with the notion of instinct, and he does not plainly refer to Michelangelo's capacity as architect and artist. Instead he gives us a scene, the scene of the young boy Michelangelo playing and struggling with his school mates, pushing and shoving with his body and so giving his body the right angle of inclination to give his antagonist the most efficient and powerful resistance. "Hundreds of times", Diderot says, "hundreds of times in his life he must have had to support tottering things, finding out how to give them the best support. Sometimes he had piled up his books so that they were all sticking out from each other and a counterbalance was needed to prevent the pile from falling, and in this way", Diderot concludes, "he had learned to build the dome in the Peter's church in Rome according to the curvature for the highest supporting capacity".

Diderot's choice of example is quite extreme, and he seems to formulate the conclusion so quickly as to be able to go on to some more general cases.

A brick wall is close to crashing down. Get a carpenter and when he has placed his supports, find d'Alambert or Clairaut and set them the task of determining which angle gives the best support, and you will see that the carpenter's angle and the mathematician's angle are the same.

Diderot, who also gives the example of the angle of windmills' vanes, poses this question: "How come mathematicians, when they have examined such things that practice and habit has established, have seen that it was precisely what the most advanced mathematics would have preferred?" Diderot's answer is: "A question of calculation on the one hand, of experience on the other. If the one is well-founded it must correspond to the other."

Diderot's thoughts on the dome of Michelangelo can be called emblematic in relation to Bo Göranzon's project "Education–Work –Technology". But if Diderot seems to end with a balanced correspondence between calculation and experience, which I think is due to the perspective taken from the end of the process, the Göranzon project problematizes the relationship between calculation and work. The conflict becomes evident, for example, from the perspective of transferring skills or when you are actually in the process of doing, making something. Being able to calculate the angle of supports for the brick wall does not mean a competence to put the supports in place.

In *Rameau's Nephew* our attention is constantly taken to the process of doing. When *lui* mimes or recites, or plays something, he enjoys pretending that he makes mistakes. Instead of forgetting the process of doing and only seeing the result of the effort, the end, our attention is drawn towards the struggle, the contest, the work. For example when *lui* mimes playing the cembalo, convincingly performing some vivacious composition, he starts "over again", Diderot writes, "as if he had made errors and was annoyed with not longer having the piece of music in his fingers" ("de n'avoir plus la pièce dans les doigts").

I suppose Diderot could have said that Michelangelo had his dome in his fingers, just as he once said that to know how to bake you must put your fingers into the dough. As opposed to the Platonic dialogue disqualifying baking and cooking from the concept of knowledge.

Diderot moves us from the completed to the coming-into-being, just as the group of occupied chess players, that we were acquainted with in the beginning of the story, is moved to leave their chessboards and gather around the interlocutors of the errant dialogue. The conversation of *moi* and *lui* becomes a stage play without ends or end, a play of possible meanings and directions:

All those pushers of wood-pieces had left their boards and were assembled around him. The windows of the café were occupied from the outside by people who had stopped because of the noise. People burst into such laughter the ceiling could rise.

This theatrical mode I find to be essential in *Rameau's Nephew*. We are inside an ongoing play, ourselves players, and we are not given the safe position of calculation from the outside. We are permanently inside. "Isn't it true, monsieur philosopher", *lui* asks in the very end, "that I am always the same"; and the answer of *moi* is "Oh yes, unfortunately". In the work of Diderot we are subjects of continuous experience.

Chapter 18

Diderot's Russian University

Per Sörbom

This chapter chronicles Diderot's detailed proposals to Catherine II on the best way to organize education in Russia. The aim of education over the centuries, Diderot argues, has been, and continues to be, to make people virtuous and enlightened. Education must be designed to meet the needs of the majority. We must adapt the teaching to suit both the age of the students and their ability to understand. In order to attain these objectives, Diderot writes, we should proceed from the simple to the complicated, from the first stage to the last, from what is most useful to what is least useful, from what is essential to all to what is essential to only a few. There are two sorts of knowledge, Diderot states: elementary knowledge which is essential to everyone, and secondary or conventional knowledge which is needed only for the particular path we have chosen in life. Not every occupation requires the measure of essential or elementary knowledge which a full university education requires. The volume and diversity of knowledge taught is to be determined by its benefit to society. Diderot would classify the sciences in the same way as his fellow countryman and contemporary Georges-Louis Leclerc Buffon, classified minerals and plants in the 36 volumes of his *Histoire Naturelle.* According to this method, animals and plants are classified according to their usefulness and proximity to us in nature; the more remote the type of animal, the more obscure its place in science. An ox or a horse are therefore scientifically important, a hyena or a wolf rather less so. Diderot's pyramid-shaped blueprint of knowledge may seem hierarchical to us, but it encompasses and involves all individuals, equips them with what they need and thereby makes them both happier people and more useful citizens. It is therefore, the chapter concludes, wholly in the spirit of the Encyclopaedia, that handbook for a better, more practical and enlightened world.

On 8 October 1773 Denis Diderot arrived in St. Petersburg – "more dead than alive" – as he wrote the following day to his wife in Paris. He had left Paris on 11 June, arriving a few days later at the Hague, where he was welcomed by his old friend Dimitri Alexevitch Galitzine, in whose hospitable house he spent the summer. He settled in well there, and wrote his important work, *Paradoxe sur le comédien*. In Paris and St. Petersburg they began to wonder if he would ever get farther than Holland.

This is an indication of Diderot's reluctance to pay what he deemed a fitting courtesy visit to Catherine II, the autocratic ruler of all the Russians who wanted, in competition with Frederick II and Gustav III, to be regarded as a modern, enlightened monarch, and who used every means of persuasion to gather around her the intellectuals of Europe. Diderot was high on her list and her first invitations reached him very shortly after she came to power in Russia.

But Diderot already had good reason to be grateful to Catherine. He had on a couple of occasions let it be known that he was prepared to sell his entire personal library. He was in desperate financial straits and saw no other way out. The price potential purchasers were prepared to pay was, however, considerably less than the value Diderot, with the assistance of a Parisian bookseller, had placed upon it. In February 1765 his good friend Grimm wrote on Diderot's behalf to the Russian Court, offering for sale his collection of books. A month later they received a reply: the Empress was prepared to buy the library. Naturally, Diderot was pleased at this, but it was the conditions Catherine set which astounded him. She let it be known that Diderot was to keep the books until he heard to the contrary. Moreover, Catherine thought it important that the books were well looked after, and therefore employed Diderot as librarian at a far from insignificant annual salary. The following year Catherine paid Diderot a 50-year advance on his salary, at which he remarked that in order to earn it he would have to live to the age of 103.

Catherine's purchase of Diderot's books, her commissioning him to serve as her representative in the purchase of French art and the humble words of admiration in the preface to the seventh illustrated volume of the *Encyclopédie* caused his name to be linked ever closer to that of the Russian ruler. There were increasingly frequent intimations that he was expected to make an appearance at the Court of St. Petersburg.

Now he had finally arrived; tired, dispirited and in poor health. His old friend Falconet, the sculptor whom Diderot had recommended to Catherine, gave him a cool reception and had no room to offer him in his house. But his sinking spirits were soon revived. Catherine had recently dismissed her lover, Vasiltjikov, and as she had not yet named Potemkin as his successor she had plenty of time in her diary for Diderot. From the middle of October the Empress and the French philosopher met every day, Catherine receiving Diderot in a private audience at 3 o'clock in the afternoon.

We know very well what they discussed in the course at these audiences. Diderot wrote a number of essays, 66 in total, on the widest range of subjects, including literature, politics, economics, law and social issues. It appears that Diderot first wrote an essay on a particular subject, such as "On Intolerance" or "On Manufacturers and Factories". Then Diderot read to Catherine what he had written, and they discussed his ideas. Diderot went home, reviewed the text, sometimes making changes, and then submitted it to the Empress. The manuscript, with the titles in Diderot's own handwriting, "Mélanges philosophiques, historiques, etc. Année 1773 depuis le 15 oct. jusq'au 3 décembre", (Essays on a Number of Subjects, Philosophy, History, etc. anno 1773, from 15 October to 3 December) is now in Moscow.

These essays were published fairly early, but the modern scientific edition now published shows that this was by no means a matter of light-hearted small talk between Catherine and Diderot.

It is perfectly clear that Diderot's ambition was to convert Catherine to the philosophy of enlightenment, or at least to encourage her liberal ideas. His was a cautious, even diplomatic, approach, and he made frequent use of circumscription and metaphor. It should be understood that he was dealing with a person who, according to Voltaire, exercised "the most despotic power on earth".

Yet it is obvious that the nature of their conversations changed. Catherine herself said, several years later, that she listened when Diderot expounded his ideas, put forward his reviews on reforms and developed grandiose plans, but finally felt compelled to say to him:

> M. Diderot, I have listened with the greatest pleasure to all the inspirations produced by your brilliant genius. All your great principles, which I understand very well, may create excellent books, but poor work. When you present your plans for reform you constantly forget the difference between your situation and mine. You work solely on paper, and that will stand for anything: it is smooth and pliant and offers no impediment to your imagination and your pen, whereas I, a poor Empress, carry out my work on human skin, which is, to a completely different extent, easily irritated and very sensitive.

In March 1775 Catherine wrote a letter addressed to "the Messieurs Philosophers", that is to say Diderot and his friend Melchior von Grimm, asking them to write a proposal on the best way to organize education in her country – from kindergarten to university. While Grimm contents himself with a few pages of superficial remarks, Diderot felt flattered, and addressed the assignment with great seriousness. Convinced that Catherine would immediately put his proposals into effect, Diderot wrote, despite his digestive problems, his *Plan d'une université pour le gouvernement de Russie.* He completed this work in July and it reached Catherine in December.

Diderot's long essay is set out in a clear and pedagogical manner. He begins by stating that "to educate a nation is to civilize it" and goes on to say that "education gives a person dignity, and the slave immediately realizes he is not born to slavery". It is not difficult to imagine how Catherine reacted before she had read the first page – it was hardly her intention to educate her serfs. However, she can hardly have objected to his description of the purpose of a public educational system: "it is a matter of providing the sovereign with faithful and diligent subjects: the realm with useful citizens; society with civilized, honourable and even friendly individuals; the family with good spouses and good fathers; the world of scholars with a few men of great ability, and religion with edifying, enlightened and peaceable pastors".

But when Diderot goes on to define university as "a school whose doors are open to all the nation's children, without discrimination, where government-employed teachers give them basic knowledge in all disciplines", the Empress realized that Diderot's proposals were best kept under lock and key. "I say *without discrimination*", continued Diderot, "because it would be as cruel as it is absurd to condemn the lower classes of a society to ignorance. For all classes there is some knowledge that cannot be denied them without treating them unfairly. Since the ratio of cottages and other small dwellings to the number of palaces is ten thousand to one, the chances are ten thousand to one that genius, aptitude and virtue will emerge from a cottage rather than from a palace".

In a public education system created for children whose parents cannot afford private education and whose daily work prevents them from supervising their children's education, the contents of the education must be designed to meet the needs of the majority. It follows from this, Diderot admits, that the genius who makes giant steps forward is sometimes sacrificed to the herd ambling along behind him. But, he asks himself, "is it ever possible to educate genius? Is it not enough that public education does not smother it?"

After these general introductory reflections, Diderot describes the universities of the time. Their miserable condition, he says, is rooted in Charlemagne's stupidity in placing virtually all important government functions in the hands of Christian priests, an action which has left such deep marks that they may never be eradicated. Charlemagne built the French university in this tradition, but despite all its defects and despite all the tedious scholastic bickering, those who peopled the universities managed to acquire a respect for scholarship, and the undeserved good reputation these institutes enjoyed upheld a general desire to acquire knowledge. As time passed, scholastic futilities lost their significance while interest in genuine scholarship increased: "all the great men of the following centuries grew in the shadow of the seats of learning previously occupied by Thomas Aquinas, Albert Magus, Abélard and John Duns Scotus, and which are still occupied by teachers who are, in terms of thinking, their contemporaries".

At the institutes of philosophy we still teach, under the heading of literature, two dead languages that are of benefit to only a small proportion of the population, he continued. The art of speaking is taught before the art of thinking, and the art of expressing oneself well is taught before one has anything to say – something that is called rhetoric. There they fill people's heads with what is known as logic, which consists of the subtleties of Aristotle and his highly sublime and very unnecessary theories of syllogism. "What could be expressed in four clear pages is spread over one hundred vague pages." What is said in ethical matters is not clear but, on the other hand, not a word is said about "the properties of the soul, neither of the heart, nor of passions, vices, virtues, duties, and laws". In metaphysics one learns that everything can be explained by a few undefined and undefinable words which have no meaning. Under the title of physics, one learns nothing of natural history and no useful chemistry, far too little anatomy and no geography. With the exception of the basic principles of arithmetic, algebra and geometry, almost nothing of value is taught – and what is taught could be assimilated in a quarter of the time.

The only thing that students learn is something that was never originally intended, namely to work assiduously and constantly on futile but complicated matters. This may be a useful skill when the time comes to devote oneself to matters of considerable importance in the life of the society. "This, then, is the fruit of 7 or 8 years of arduous work and uninterrupted confinement."

This description of the institutes of philosophy at the university must seem confusing to the modern reader. But in Diderot's time the philosophical faculties were still, just as they had been since the first university emerged from the cathedral schools of the middle ages, preparatory institutes which everyone wishing to progress to the law, theology or medicine was compelled to attend. In some cases what was taught in these institutes corresponds to what we would call the upper secondary school curriculum today, but there were major differences in the quality and content of the education from place to place and from one country to another.

But what happens to all the people who have completed studies at an Institute of Philosophy, asks Diderot under the heading "Questions and answers", do they go on to the three higher institutes?

– No.
– Then what happens to them?
– Because they are ignorant lightweights and too old to begin to learn a craft, they become actors, soldiers, thieves, gamblers, tricksters, swindlers and tramps.
– And the people who leave university without graduating?
– They have learned nothing at all that may be of use to them, but have at least not lost so much time, and they still have the chance to learn a useful trade. That is their resource.

Naturally, adds Diderot with reverence, it is not the intention of Her Imperial Majesty to create her university along these lines, and he hopes that she permits him to add that neither is it his.

Diderot observes that the faculties of law are in a sorry state. Not a word of French law, and no international law is studied. Nothing of civil or criminal law, of the penal code, constitutional law, the rights of the head of state or its citizens, nothing of liberty or the rights of ownership. No, the only subject studied is Roman law, and that has almost nothing in common with French law. A person who has placed the hat of a doctor of law on his head is as helpless as the simplest citizen if someone seduces his daughter, runs away with his wife or makes claims on his land. "All this fine knowledge would be of infinite benefit to him if his name was Moevius or Sempronius and if we returned to the time of Honorius or Arcadius. But under Louis XVI he is as ignorant as a villager from Chaillot or a peasant from lower Normandy."

An even worse state of affairs is to be found at the institutes of theology, Diderot, hardly surprisingly, claims. They are in themselves excellent schools for spreading a lack of faith, and few of the members at the Sorbonne do not hide deism or atheism under their fur-lined capes. The people who populate institutes of theology are not only the most intolerant, superstitious and hypocritical of people, they are also the state's least useful, most stiff-necked and dangerous citizens. "If I were the sovereign", writes Diderot, "and I knew that on every high day and holiday between 11 and 12 o'clock 150 000 of my subjects speak to all the other subjects and make them believe, in God's name, in everything that the demons of fanaticism and presumptuousness suggests to the speakers, I would shudder with dread". He adds that her Imperial Majesty surely does not wish to have people like that in her country, and if she must have priests, then she will doubtless require them to be edifying, enlightened and peaceable.

The Institute of Medicine is the only one which meets with Diderot's approval. He admits that little needs to be changed here. However, there are no opportunities for practical training, and in consideration of all the things that cannot be taught from books and in lectures, medical students should treat patients on a completely different basis than was the case at that time.

A professor's lecture cannot teach whether a pulse is strong or weak, slow or rapid, regular or irregular, Diderot points out, and it is not possible to give a satisfactorily exact description of a wound or fracture in words alone. He concludes by observing: "the young doctor carries out his first experiments on us and does not become a skilful professional before there have been a number of murders".

Having thus described, using the miserable French universities as examples, how things should not be, Diderot can begin to construct his plan for the way Her Imperial Majesty should arrange higher education in her realm. There is, he says, only one basis for all education and upbringing: "*Le but en sera le même dans tous les siècles: faire des hommes verteux et éclairés*". Over the centuries its goal has been, and continues to be, to make people virtuous and enlightened, says Diderot, using the two key concepts he constantly returns to in almost everything he does and writes. The "virtue" of Diderot, and of the France and Sweden of the 1700s, is much more than our modern, narrow converse of "vice". To approximate its real meaning we must surround it with the words "service, excellence, perfection, the fulfilment of duty, integrity, honesty, good morals and honour". Perhaps this definition, by a turn-of-the-century Swedish pedagogue, comes fairly close to what Diderot may have meant. "Virtue is conscious and clear, steadfast and strong, deliberate and harmonious, and a direction of the human will associated with goodness and justice." That Diderot, the philosopher of the Enlightenment, sees the second objective of public education as the creation of "enlightened people" may appear fairly obvious, but here too we should qualify the concept by adding "educated, discerning, rich in knowledge" and "broad-minded, liberated, unprejudiced, civilized". Perhaps it should be pointed out that the expression as a description of a time and an attitude was first coined by Kant in "Was ist Aufklärung" in 1784.

Diderot's simple and pregnant summary of what all education and upbringing should aim to achieve, the creation of virtuous and enlightened people, is followed by an equally lucid description of the way the objectives should be attained. We must proceed from the simple to the complicated, he writes, from the first stage to the last, from what is most useful to what is least useful, from what is essential to all to what is essential to only a few. We must save time and effort by adapting the teaching to suit the age of the students and the lessons to the average of their ability to understand.

If, Diderot continues, struck by the thought that he may in his enthusiasm have progressed too rapidly, it should appear that his grandiose plans for the education of the general public were premature, and there were insufficient resources available, then we must wait for the right moment, but nothing must be left to the uncertain future. One must follow the example of a perspicacious architect who is commissioned by a person with limited resources. If the presumptive house owner cannot initially make available the full amount required for a complete house, then the architect has the foundations laid and makes sure that the most important part of the house is erected first. When a shortage of funds compels him to stop building, he leaves a few stones next to the completed part of the house to show how construction should proceed. He also gives his client a drawing, set out so that building work, when resumed, must follow his instructions, thus avoiding the construction of a number of unconnected rooms which may in themselves be beautiful or ugly, but which will not form a harmonious and pleasing whole.

It is remarkable, says Diderot, contemplating the French educational system, that this barbaric phenomenon from the middle ages with all its faults and shortcomings lives on in an enlightened nation, even though those appalling teachers, the Jesuits, have been driven from the country. He knew what he was talking about. Like so many philosophers of the Enlightenment, Diderot had received his early education at a Jesuit school, and although he seems to have been a clever pupil and by all accounts assiduously learned what the Jesuits thought should be instilled into young people, he is critical later in life about his experiences at school. Naturally, the fact that the Jesuits were subsequently among the most angry critics of his Encyclopaedia did not help Diderot remember his school years with the forgiving glow of adulthood. When, in 1762, the Parliament in Paris decided to forbid the Jesuits to recruit new members to their order and to close all their schools, Diderot was, as might be expected, highly satisfied. But although the Jesuits now no longer had any influence on education and teaching, everything to do with the old order is seen to be bad.

The reason for this is that nothing so persistently opposes the public interest as private interest, nothing resists common sense more strongly than ingrained abuse. Associations and societies keep their doors firmly shut against universal enlightenment, which for centuries tried in vain to penetrate these barriers: while everything about them changes, the spirit of established institutions remains the same. Poor students become poor teacher who, in their turn, make their students into copies of themselves. In this way traditional ignorance has been perpetuated in the old institutions. While knowledge sheds light all around, sighs Diderot, the dark shadows of ignorance continue to rest over these sanctuaries of vanities and meaningless disputes.

Charlemagne in France and King Alfred in England realized that the only way of bringing the dormant knowledge of the ancients to life was to give the people of the time a key to all this knowledge, knowledge that had been inaccessible for many centuries. Accordingly, they supported the study of Latin. But now, when this wealth of knowledge had long been available, when enormous progress had been made in the arts and sciences and science had learned to speak the language of the common people, a knowledge of classical languages was only required by specialists and education should therefore be completely reorganized. It would be extremely odd, to put it mildly, if a public educational system, a system to which everyone in a country had access, had as its main subject the study of something which only a fraction of the pupils had any use for. In what follows, writes Diderot, I will give other, at least equally important reasons, why the study of Greek and Latin should not be undertaken until very late in a student's university career.

At the time Diderot wrote this, the victory of *"les moderns"* had been assured for over 50 years. Disagreeing with *"les anciens"*, who thought that the classical masters of art and science could never be bettered, *"les moderns"* had pointed to all the scientific and technological advances that had taken place since the middle ages. In a pioneer of the enlightenment such as Pierre

Bayle, one could already glimpse a clear criticism of the superstition that had flourished in the church establishment, and free thinking and a critical inclination were also evidence of the arrival of a new age. When Voltaire rages against the Church and wants to "crush the infamous", it is a much an attack on an obsolete way of thinking in which the veneration of the classical masters, the fathers of the church and the established truths formed the very foundations, as it is an attack on the Church as an institution. Regrettably, this campaign served to deprecate the Middle Ages further, already discredited since the Renaissance. But its time would come some way into the nineteenth century. Diderot himself was an excellent Latin scholar and there was nothing wrong with his Greek (something he should in fact thank the Jesuits in Langres for); throughout his life he read with pleasure the great classics, an attribute that won an elegantly phrased tribute from the Swedish scholar Björnståhl, who met him at the Hague. "In addition to all that, Diderot is a poet, and has a powerful imagination. M. Voltaire has said of him that he was born to be a poet but wished perforce to be a philosopher. He knows Homer and Pindar almost by heart; and does not know himself how many times he has read them and Anacreon. He never goes out without a little Horatius in his pocket".

But Diderot questioned the usefulness of dead languages to the general public in a modern, enlightened society. He was, quite simply, not satisfied with the educational ideal, just as we today are searching for a new ideal without really knowing what it is we are looking for. It was easier for Diderot; he wanted to educate useful citizens who did not need to be burdened with unnecessary knowledge.

After these reflections on the educational system of his time, Diderot pays homage to "Sa Majesté Impériale" – she has chosen precisely the right time to create a university! It seems as though the human spirit has now worn out its children's shoes; the meaninglessness of scholastic theoretical pondering is recognized, the constant building of systems has ceased and education is no longer a matter of Aristotelianism, Cartesianism, Malebranchism or Leibnitzianism. There is a genuine and widespread interest in science, and many disciplines have approached perfection. The old institutions are no longer obstacles to Her Imperial Majesty's ideas, she has before her a vast field free from all obstacles, on which she can build to her liking. I do not flatter her, Diderot hastens to add, when I assure her that in this respect her position is more advantageous than ours.

I compare education in general subjects to a broad highway, Diderot continues, on which a large number of people are beginning to gather, all shouting in chorus, "Education! We know nothing! Teach us". Then I tell myself that not everyone is capable of, nor is intended to, follow this long road to its end. Some get this far, others reach here, a few progress a little farther, and the farther they travel the fewer they are. It is not difficult to answer the question of what they should all learn first; they should learn what suits them all, irrespective of their status in society. And then? What is of rather less general use is suited to those who remain with me. And what comes after that? Although it is at even less general usefulness than what preceded it, what suits the few people who have accompanied me this far. And so it goes; until the education is completed the usefulness of what is taught decreases with the number of students.

Diderot goes on to write that he would classify the sciences in the same way as Buffon, our botanical researcher, classified the animals, and as he would have classified minerals and plants. First he discussed the ox – the most important animal for us to know about, and then the horse, the ass, the mule and the dog. According to this method, the wolf, hyena, tiger and panther are allotted an obscure place in science because they are remote from us in nature and we therefore have very little use for them and hardly any reason to fear them. What is the result of this? It is that the sooner the people who lacked the capacity or the purpose to continue their university studies finally abandon them, the better. The less knowledge a person has failed to assimilate, the more essential to him is the knowledge he has acquired. On that point I will not yield, says Diderot. It is the very cornerstone of the edifice. If this stone is placed wrongly, then the building will collapse; if laid correctly, it will stand firm for ever.

It is no coincidence that Diderot takes his classification of nature from his fellow-countryman and contemporary, Georges-Louis Leclerc Buffon. This rival of Linnæus and author of the enormous work, *Histoire Naturelle,* published in 36 volumes from 1749 onwards, was, as Sten Lindroth writes, "the Swede's arch enemy and antithesis in all things". Like Buffon and the botanists at the Académie des Sciences and the Jardin Roi in Paris, Diderot was extremely sceptical about Linnæus and his way of classifying nature. They saw him as a rigid scholar who juggled with concepts which lacked any basis in nature. Buffon, according to Lindroth, "a sceptical empiricist in the spirit of Locke", and the Paris botanists attempted instead to create a natural system in which the separate plants and animals, through gradual change, form a great natural chain which was the only reality. With this as their starting point they rejected the kind of scientific classification which Linnæus represented. We also meet this natural, organic way of perceiving nature in Diderot when at certain times in his writings he examines ideas which are portents of evolutionary thought. In other contexts, however, he did not hesitate to learn from the great Swedish scientist. During the summer of 1774, when he stayed at the Hague after returning from Russia, he wrote *Voyage de Hollande,* a little account of his travels in the hospitable and liberal Holland which he had learned to appreciate so much. Here he followed in precise detail Linnæus's *Instructio Peregrinatoris* from 1759; that is to say the guidelines to what should be described by travellers to foreign parts that Linnæus wrote and placed in the hands of his pupils when he sent them out into the world. One of these pupils, Anders Sparrman, carried on in his master's stead the controversy against Buffon's natural system; a way of interpreting nature, he claimed, which should almost be regarded as a spiritual vision in "grandiose and pompous French".

But let us return to the energetic M. Diderot. There are two sorts of knowledge, he states. One which he calls essential or elementary knowledge, the other which he dubs secondary or conventional knowledge. Elementary knowledge is essential to everyone. Unless learned in youth, it must be acquired later in life. If not learned at all, the individual will be punished by constantly making mistakes or constantly being compelled to ask for the assistance of others. Secondary knowledge is needed only for the particular path we have chosen in life. Not every occupation requires the measure of essential or elementary knowledge which the full university level education provides. A manual labourer needs less than a factory worker, the factory worker needs less than the tradesman, the tradesman less than the soldier, the soldier less than the government official or the priest and these in their turn require less than the statesman. It is important for the student to follow the path of learning best suited to the occupation he has chosen. If, for example, a government official completes the entire course of education and thus acquires all the knowledge he needs to practice his profession, he will need to turn to experts less often, and when he does need them he will be able to judge their probity.

Let us now take a less important example, Diderot continues, that of the poet. To a poet there is almost nothing that is not worth knowing: he must know the classic languages and several modern languages, also history, physics and geography. Is it possible to be a great poet without knowing a man's duties as a member of society, the laws that control the state and how they affect one another and the individual citizen, religions, different nations' traditions and customs, passions, vices, virtues, characteristics and ethics? What a wealth of knowledge is to be found in Homer and Virgil!, exclaims Diderot. What had they not studied before they began to write? If our poets, Corneille and Racine had possessed less knowledge they would not have been what they were. What is it that separates Voltaire from all younger writers? It is learning. Voltaire knows a great deal, and our young poets are ignorant. Voltaire's works are full of things, theirs are empty. They want to sing, and they have the voice to do so, but since they lack knowledge their songs are nothing but melodious bagatelles.

A person who wishes to become a poet must thus be prepared to study for a long time, the volume and diversity of the knowledge he must have makes it necessary for him to follow the path of erudition to its end. On the way, his fellow students will become fewer and fewer in number so that on approaching their goal, theirs will be the smallest group of students. So much the better. I say the same thing about speakers and scientists and other professions that are not for the mediocre, professions that can only be practised by men of genius, people who even at their best are hardly essential to society. Giving the study of classical languages pride of place in a public educational system indicates a desire to populate the nation with practitioners of rhetoric, priests, monks, philosophers, lawyers and doctors, writes Diderot, and concludes his argument about the elementary and secondary knowledge with the sentence, "More philosophers than doctors, more doctors than lawyers, more lawyers than speakers, and hardly any poets at all".

The deciding factor is the benefit to society, and the pyramid-shaped house of knowledge for which Diderot gives the Empress the blueprint is also a description of the way he would like to see the structure of a sensible society. On the one hand the edifice appears to us to be strictly hierarchical and may initially give an almost Linnæan impression, but there is a fundamental difference. Linnæus's system was a gift of God; his main purpose was to find out about the nature of things and then describe them. Diderot's system is, by contrast, a natural one and has strong pre-Darwinian aspects: it encompasses all individuals. Everyone is included from the beginning, at the lowest level, and in the course of the upward climb the people who are not suited to the new levels gradually fall behind. This is by no means an accident. On the contrary, they have been given what they need, and because they have not been burdened with things they do not need, they will be both happier people and more useful citizens. One gets the feeling of a gigantic apparatus equipped with a control system aimed at producing the optimal number of citizens with precisely the education society needs. One almost hears the thump of the automatic jacquard loom, where the cards which determine the appearance of the cloth and its function have been designed by an enlightened philosopher in the best possible way and in the interests of all. In consideration of current circumstances and with the help of empirical data, technology is used for the lasting benefit of mankind, wholly in the spirit of the great Encyclopaedia, this enormous handbook for a better, more practical and enlightened world.

Bibliography

There is a vast amount of literature on Diderot. An excellent bibliography is Fredrik A. Spear, *Bibliographie de Diderot. Répertoire analytique international.* (Histoire des idées et critique littéraire, volume 187), Geneva 1980, a second volume covering 1976–1986, published in Geneva, volume 264 in the same series. The bibliography contains 5844 entries.

When it comes to collected works, for a long time one had to be satisfied with the 20-volume edition published in Paris 1875–1877 with J. Assézat and Maurice Tourneux as editors. Then, in 1969–73, came a further *Oeuvres Complétes,* published by Club Français du livre in Paris, with introductions by Roger Lewinter. Publication has been in progress since 1975 of a critical and annotated edition under the leadership of Herbert Dieckmann, of the Paris publishers Hermann. At the moment of writing 20 out of 33 planned volumes have been published. There is also a very large number of "selected works" compiled from various points of departure – aesthetic, dramatic, political and philosophical.

Diderot's extraordinarily comprehensive correspondence was published in a modern critical and commented edition of 16 volumes by Georges Roth and Jean Verloot in Paris 1955–1970.

The basic book on Diderot's life and works was written by Arthur M. Wilson: *Diderot,* New York, 1972. I have used the french translation, *Diderot, sa vie et son oeuvre,* Paris, 1985.

Wilson's work is characterized by the bibliographer Spear as "la biographie la plus complète comprenant une étude approfondie de l'oeuvre et des indications bibliographiques très étendues". There are also a number of less comprehensive introductions to Diderot's time, life and works, and an ocean of special studies.

Something has been written earlier on the "Plan d'une université", but not very much. I take up here the most important works and refer otherwise to Spear's bibliography. There is a German annotated translation of Denis Diderot, *Bildungsplan für die Regierung von Russland,* Beltz Monografien Pädagogik, Basle, 1971. It is published in English in Francois de La Fontainerie, *French Liberalism and Education in the 18th Century: The Writings of La Chalotais, Turgot, Diderot and Condorcet on National Education,* under the heading "Diderot (1713–1784) and his Plan for a Russian University, (McGraw-Hill education classics, New York and London 1932). In the series L'enfant no. XV, Jean-Marie Dolle has written *Politique et pédagogie. Diderot et les problèmes de l'éducation, Paris 1973.* Here, the plan is placed in a pedagogical-political context and is related to Diderot's other statements on pedagogics. The plan is discussed by Ernesto Codignole in *Rivista pedagogica,* vol 10 (1917), 380–407, in the essay "Diderot e le origini dell'utilitarismo pedagogico in Francia: Il piano di un'università russa"; by Cyprien Issaurat in *La pédagogie, son évolution et son histoire,* the chapter on "Diderot" (Bibliothèque des sciences contemporaines, 14), Paris 1886. E. Merle wrote in Technique art, science, no. 114 (1957–58) and no. 115 (1957–58) on "Diderot et son programme d'éducation (d'après le Plan pour une université)". In *Mélanges de la Bibliothèque de la Sorbonne,* Jacques Chouillet wrote "Un projet de réforme de l'université au XVIIIe siecle: le Plan d'une université de Denis Diderot pour l'Impératrice de Russie (1775)" (no. 6 (1985), 47–58).

For Diderot's time in Russia, Paul Vernière's critical and annotated edition of Diderot's *Mémoires pour Catherine II,* Paris 1966, is very useful. Maurice Tourneux, *Diderot et Catherine II,* Paris 1899, should also be consulted.

Chapter 19

Diderot and the Dramatization of Philosophical Thought

Herbert Josephs

Diderot's use of the dialogue form necessitated the invention of an "other", a narrative figure in whom was inscribed values and attitudes frequently resistant to those of the narrating subject. The figure of the "other" in Diderot serves various narrative functions in relation to the philosopher's ideas, from affirmation and validation to criticism, counter-argument and scepticism. The literary form of the dialogue reflected in its own structures the shape of a dramatic encounter between some part of the self that *experienced* and another to which was usually assigned the function of active spectator and creative observer. The chapter discusses Diderot's practice and theory of drama, and his representation of mental activity as a process of division and dialectics which dispersed, multiplied and integrated into literary dialogue a subjective intelligence that had hitherto been constructed as a unified entity. The drama of human intelligence was likened in Diderot's imagination to an interactive encounter between sensation and reflection. With the transposition of philosophical inquiry into the pluralized discourse of literature, it is no longer possible to isolate and identify any solitary voice of authority to which we might attach a sense of stable truth. Thus, by relinquishing claims to absolute authority in his narration and by allowing and even obliging his reader increasingly to become the author, Diderot provides an eloquent illustration of the larger Enlightenment project that implicitly structures and determines all his writing: not to propagate ideas but to encourage and make possible the continuous activity of critical thinking.

For the historian of literature or philosophy, of art criticism or science, Diderot's writings have always constituted both a dilemma and a provocation. His major works, from the *Pensées philosophiques* (1746) to his biography of Seneca (1782), all testify to a steadfast refusal of traditional generic boundaries at the same time as they unveil, again and again, the essential conflict in the claims of both philosophy and literature. The coexistence and simultaneity in his writings of the poetic and the philosophical orientations to reality and truth have often led to the disparaging by his critics especially of his more properly philosophical or scientific writings. Yet it was, paradoxically, Diderot's refusal to accept as mutually exclusive the contradictory and opposed pursuits of philosophy and poetry or to tolerate the rigorous separation of the speculative and the practical intelligence that endows all that he wrote and thought with a richness that the modern temper recognizes in his work and denies to most of his contemporaries.

Whatever the subject of Diderot's speculation, however, the reader is invited to follow his thought as it passes without apparent transition from image to image, moving back and forth across some mental space of testing and hypothesizing; meanwhile, the scene of Diderot's drama of the intelligence shifts unannounced between painting and theatre, between poetry and philosophy, or between music and science, erasing old modal frontiers and creating new hybrid spectacles. As all monologic statement in Diderot's writings seems, while it leaps and gambols across a vast field of speculation created by metaphor, to undergo a process of transformation into dialogic exchange, we recognize that what we are actually witnessing is Diderot's unending narrative meditation on the single but inexhaustibly complex problem of representation and self-representation. Diderot's tireless though often joyous struggle with the problematics of epistemology and aesthetics is inseparable in his writings from a process of dialogism that is operative everywhere in his thinking and not only as it shapes the utterance of a single idea or an individual work; dialogue structures Diderot's thought even as it alters and debates with itself across the years, with his own earlier works and ultimately with the works of others – his contemporaries, his predecessors and his successors.

The diverse forms that dialogism assumes in Diderot's writing possess striking affinities with a process that tends spontaneously to dramatize his thought; Diderot's mature writings suggest an imaginative staging of encounter and conflict taking place within the realm of ideas. "It is the voiceless dialogue of the soul within itself and with itself that we call 'thought', Plato wrote in *The Sophist*. The formal possibilities of dialogue, attractive to a mind attentive to its own limits and to its own searching, also guided his thinking, as if by some compelling inner necessity, to open out spontaneously into an intellectual world of indefiniteness and possibility. We must imagine Diderot's dialogues taking place in a mental décor of hypothesized confrontations, the doubt, the uncertainty, the fluctuations and hesitations of his thinking seeking immediate realization in the literary shape of fictional character; his ideas, compared in *Le Neveu de Rameau* to his whores, approached and abandoned with equal freedom and licentiousness, could be explored only once they had been incorporated into the narrative figure of some real or invented "other", a fictionalized presence in whom was inscribed values and attitudes frequently resistant to those of the narrating subject. Sometimes this indispensable "other" bears the expressive burden of a more impulsive self, perhaps a darker, less publicly presentable self, where desire and violence reside; sometimes the narrator's interlocutor is given the shape of the ironic observer, a reflective self, detached and free, but no less provocative than his more instinctive opponent. But whatever the literary shape and structure assumed by his thinking, for Diderot the dialogue permanently occurring within the imagination never long remained voiceless. The "other" whom he sketched and to whom he offered a part of his own voice performed, of course, a variety of functions for the creative, inquiring subject: it might be an apparently alien voice designed to disguise or disavow a potentially dangerous thought; it could be a phantom "dummy" across whose empty form the narrating ventriloquist might transmit and explore something felt, conceived and experienced obscurely deep within himself; or perhaps the companions of intellectual voyage that Diderot provided for himself became a source of validation and self-affirmation, of criticism or scepticism, permitting the author's own voice to move about freely within the space created for and by ironic detachment.

The projection of Diderot's thought outward into another or into other voices was actually a transposition to the inter-personal mode of Diderot's fundamental stylistic gesture: the representation of the mind divided and dispersed, engaged in a symbiotic exchange between experience and observation, the process of exchange itself usually contemplated by a detached intelligence occupied with its own mimetic activities. Whatever the content of his narrative experiments, from the invention of new dramatic forms with the *Entretiens sur le fils naturel* (1757) to his exploration of the seductive powers of narrative illusion first in *La Religieuse* (1760) and later, so brilliantly, in *Jacques le fataliste* (1773), it was the process of literary composition itself that was moved purposefully by Diderot to the front and center of his mental stage. Truth would no longer be simply always there, waiting to be unveiled by the traditional rhetoric of philosophic discourse; it was, instead, shimmering and unstable, pursued by and through dialogue or even in the very perplexing art of story-telling. The literary form reflected in its own structures the shape of a dramatic encounter between some part of the self that *experienced* and another to which was usually assigned the function of active spectator and creative observer.

If there is, in fact, a single recurrent tendency capable of providing a sense of coherence to the meanderings of Diderot's labyrinthine, paradoxical imagination, it is precisely his unwavering fascination with the puzzling self-reflectiveness and "doubleness" that he discerned in all cognitive and creative activity. The phenomenon of psychological *dédoublement* that Diderot recognized in the experience of the actor, the inter-active participation of actor and spectator and then, increasingly as his story-telling art developed in profundity, between author and reader: these are the most widely known variants of Diderot's single project of grasping and representing the enigmatic relationship of the human mind to external reality and to its own inner operations.

Diderot was one of the few authors for whom the practice and the theory of the drama were inconceivable as separate activities. His own plays were assimilated to a query on theatrical practice and were enclosed within a larger fiction that contained their own criticism. The programme of reforms proposed by Diderot, emphasizing emotional absorption, the expressivity of the actor's body, and the reduction of the distance between spectator and performance, seemed to reverse and counterpoint dialogically the direction that led the creative intelligence to disperse itself into the multiple, discrete and opposing voices of dramatic discourse. During the period, in the mid-1750s, when his thought attempted to take on a more theatrical form, Diderot's compositions for the stage seemed irresistibly to expand outward far beyond the boundaries of dramatic structure to become a polyphonic meditation on theatre, a multi-voiced theatrical revery far more original than the text of the play itself. In the *Entretiens sur le Fils naturel*, the author pluralized himself not only as dramatic characters, but also as narrator, as interlocutor, as actor, critic and finally as clandestine spectator. *Le Fils naturel* (1757) and its successor *Le Père de famille* (1758), were restrained within the limits of conventional plot and a language of inherited rhetoric that together paralysed the dynamic quality of Diderot's thought; the plays were weakened dramatically by a monologuing presence that was poorly concealed by its dramatic form, by a voice embodying authority that spent itself in efforts to convert. The genre of the *drame bourgeois*, as it was practised by Diderot, moved conflict conventionally towards dénouement, towards resolution and to the end of exploration. The one exception, *Est il bon? Est-il méchant?* (1781), designated by Diderot as a *comedy*, completed just three years before his death and not even printed until 50 years after his death, bears in its title a sign of the author's refusal of the intellectual closure of the earlier *drames*; it succeeds theatrically by its incorporation of a narrative critical and ironic reflectiveness into the substance of the play. The dramatic center of Diderot's *drames* was not really located in the conflict generated within an evolving bourgeois ethical arena, but rather in the gradual disclosure on the inner stage of the imagination of a mind actively engaged in inquiry.

What is finally represented when the *Fils naturel* is absorbed into its critical framework is part of a continuing narrative meditation on representation and self-representation that, itself, is inaccessible to representation in the physical and verbal language of the stage. According to Diderot, in the tenth chapter of his treatise entitled *De la Poésie dramatique*, yet another critical reflection on yet another play, *Le Père de famille*, Diderot remarked that the theatrical experiment which had combined the *Fils naturel* with the *Entretiens* had been conceived for a reader and not for the stage. "Mon dessein n'étant pas de donner cet ouvrage au théâtre, j'y joignis quelques idées que j'avais sur la poétique, la musique, la déclamation et la pantomime; et je formai du tout une espèce de roman..." ("Since it was not my plan to have this work performed upon the stage, I attached to it a few ideas that I had on poetics, on music, on declamation and on pantomime; and from all of this joined together I formed a kind of novel...") One has the impression on encountering this dramatic hybrid, the play within its critical commentary, that the theatre, rather than being advanced or celebrated by an innovative structure, is negated in its entirety by the form from which it is unable to liberate itself. *Le Fils naturel*, published in 1757, was first performed 14 years later, and then, after a single performance, withdrawn, not to be performed again for more than two centuries.

It is the result of having construed the basic act of human intelligence in terms of a division of mental faculties in dynamic interaction with each other that Diderot's style of thinking came inevitably to find embodiment in some form of narrative dramatization of intellectual inquiry. Whether he was wrestling with the new and disorienting epistemological verities that were uncovered by developments in empirical methodology and sensationalist philosophy, or whether he was meditating on the nature of language, on the unique qualities of poetic or "hieroglyphic" discourse, or on the nature of genius in art and science, Diderot represented mental activity as a process of division and dialectics which dispersed, multiplied and integrated in artful literary dialogue a subjective intelligence that had hitherto been construed as a unified entity. The fundamental drama of the human intelligence was likened in his imagination to an interactive encounter of sensation and reflection. Even in Diderot's earliest writings in speculative philosophy (*Lettre sur les aveugles*, 1749; *Lettre sur les sourds et muets*, 1751; *Pensées sur l'interprétation de la nature*, 1754), the narrator-*philosophe* grappled with questions of how the mind collected and absorbed its experience, how it acted upon it, constructed complex thought with and upon it, and how the mind represented and communicated knowledge to itself and to others. From the philosophical language circulating among his contemporaries, Diderot borrowed the term "hieroglyphe" to represent for him the notion of a symbolic form capable of assimilating the body's own idiom, the affective gestures that vitalize speech and transform a grievously limited instrument of logical thought into the "staged:' discourse of poetic speech. In his initial literary/philosophical endeavours, Diderot's vision of the relation of thought and intelligence to the material universe in which they were engaged is characterized by an acute sense of reciprocal activity and resonance, a relationship of dialogism that conditioned and determined all mental activity – the scientific, the philosophical and, not least, the poetic.

It was not yet, as it would be in later years, the image of the actor or of the narrator conversing with his actively participating reader that, in his earlier more properly philosophical works, nourished Diderot's speculations on determinism and creativity. Instead, the work of the mind was expressed by the more traditional image of the productive labour of the bee, leaving and returning to its point of origin, the mind contacting the natural universe and then assimilating reflectively its experience, each activity essential in itself but each activity incomplete without the other. "Everything can be reduced to moving back and forth from the senses to reflection and from reflection to the senses. That is the labour of the bee" (*Pensées sur l'interprétation de la nature*).

The bee, a deaf-mute, a blind mathematician, or else, perhaps, a society of five members each reduced to the cognitive possibilities attached to the possession of a single organ of sense: these were some of the early shapes of Diderot's "drama of thinking". To represent the operations of the intelligence, Diderot playfully invented a two-headed monster, one head needed to observe the other because "il en est de l'esprit comme de l'oeil; il ne se voit pas" ("The mind is like the eye...: it cannot see itself"). Here was an aberration – "I would have to be simultaneously inside and outside myself" – that would eventually be produced by nature in its own apparently blind inventiveness, an imagining most typical of the *philosophe*'s inspired tendency to metaphorize his tentative grasp of the action of the mind (*Lettre sur les sourds et muets*). This was yet another attempt to formulate some dialectical relationship between the dual components of the self, the interaction between the *undergoing* of experience and the *understanding* of experience. The same concept of the dynamic activity of thought, with its uninterrupted oscillation between spontaneous experience and reflective intelligence, explains the frequent presence in Diderot's later writings of ambiguous creatures identified as "naturally self-conscious", or even "naturally coquettish". It also illuminates the celebrated but frequently misinterpreted formulation of the genius of the actor, a statement that is perhaps Diderot's most fully drawn interpersonalized expression of the same doubleness that he experienced and discovered inwardly as he strived to represent the nature of physical and mental reality. "In the great comedy, the human comedy, the one I always come back to, all the sensitive souls are upon the stage, all the men of genius in the pit. The first are madmen; and the second, who engage in copying their madness, are sages."

Throughout the *Paradoxe sur le comédien* (1773), Diderot took pains to suggest that he was speaking not simply of the actor but of creative behaviour, no matter what its arena: poetry, politics, seduction. The splitting of creative activities into emotional subject and observer, the elaboration of an inner "ideal model" in the artist's imagination, a model that itself is imitated and represented in the actor's interpretation of his role: this is neither more nor less than a duplication within a discourse of theoretical aesthetics of the act of cognition and representation that is "hypothetically" staged in endless variation in all of Diderot's writings, like some single act of nature representing itself infinitely at all levels of representation.

The *dédoublement* or doubling over of the actor's personality has proved to be an incisive, fascinating and puzzling articulation, within its own context of the art of acting, of the phenomenon of representation; it must, however, itself be perceived within the larger décor of Diderot's mental stage as one of his most fruitful if misleading images for the play of the creative intelligence in its contact with reality. Diderot was to take diametrically opposed positions on the subject of the qualities requisite for the sublime performance of the actor or actress. In the *Entretiens sur le Fils naturel*, Diderot had perceived the creative act in terms of inspired feeling, emotional outpourings, a psychic absorption of the subject by the reality it perceived and represented. In *Le Paradoxe sur le comédien*, the actor of genius was imagined in radically opposed terms, as engaged rather in a predominantly cerebral activity of mimesis. What appears to be a contradiction at the heart of his thinking on the subject of creativity is really a polarizing of opposites, a dialogue between stances assumed across the years. For it is the same "madman" or fool, the jester, the mime, dancing spontaneously, unreflectively, and usually unethically, the steps of life's comedy, who frequently took on for Diderot the shape of a kind of visionary; a visceral and vital contact with reality, formerly associated with artistic rather than with philosophical pursuit, with the realm of fantasy and the irrational and not with logic or science, now emerged as an indispensable ingredient in the exploration of truth. A new philosophical hero had taken its place on the stage of Diderot's mental theatre: the philosopher-poet, the free-thinking dreamer, mime and translator, engaged in the act of masking and disappearing, in a kind of literary ventriloquy that could subvert tradition and carry out the Enlightenment project of liberating wisdom and philosophy from the chains of analysis.

The figure of the "genius" that could combine the responsive and the reflective within a single instinctive gesture of the intelligence was identified by Diderot as possessing a truly "uncanny" gift, some "extravagant" quality he occasionally designated as "instinct", or else as an "esprit de divination", a spirit of divination. The new "demonstrator" of genius, defined and promoted in the *Pensées sur l'interpretation de la nature*, queried nature poetically; the philosopher of the new material science would have to join to the qualities of rigorous observation and disciplined analysis the imaginative powers of the storyteller, the poet and the artist, the almost infinite metaphoric reach of the dreamer. In *Le Rêve de l'Alembert* (1769), scientific hypothesis speaks the discourse of a feverish mathematician, his dream vision, attentively observed and translated by the bed-side spectator, carrying scientific thought across new frontiers. The mental spectacle offered the reader in this uniquely original fictional dialogue is one of truth casting aside the shackles of confining traditional categories of logical speech. The conversation between the philosopher, the doctor, the mathematician and the mistress, set in a vibrant if cerebral contemporary milieu, plays out with an air of exhilarating freedom an intellectual drama that draws upon new forms of self-representation from within the activity of both nature and the human mind.

In a recent study of a mode of thought designated by the author as "virtual theatre", Evlyn Gould[1] has examined Diderot's dialogue masterpiece, *Le Neveu de Rameau,* as an example of the theatricalization of philosophical discourse that ultimately provides us with a glimpse of the fundamental theatricality of all human thought and language. It is certain that in *Le Neveu de Rameau,* as in other of Diderot's more brilliant works of fictionalized and dramatized thought (*La Religieuse; Jacques le fataliste;* the *contes; Le Supplément au voyage de Bougainville,* 1772; *Le Rêve de d'Alembert,* 1769), the creative activity of thinking and representing occupies the center of the narrative stage, replacing as the focus of interest the traditional concerns with the "fate" or with the "truths" of the principal actors. And with the transposition of philosophical inquiry into the pluralized discourse of literature, it is no longer possible to isolate and identify any solitary voice of authority to which we might attach a sense of stable truth. The theatre of the mind has become a space of mental indeterminacy; the moral conflicts that found a simple resolution in traditional dramatic form in *Le Fils naturel* (1757) and *Le Père de famille* (1758) are now abandoned to shifting perspectives, to uncertainty and to inconclusiveness.

In the brilliant opening paragraph of *Le Neveu de Rameau,* the narrator tells of his habit of abandoning his mind completely to the curious pleasures of intellectual libertinage: "Je le laisse maître de suivre la première idée sage ou folle qui se présente" ("I give it free rein to follow any idea, wise or mad, that may come uppermost"). In these opening lines, Diderot conveys to his reader, with a richness and "poetic precision" nowhere equalled in his writings, a sense of the fascination he experienced with the play of ideas on the inner stage of the imagination. Diderot proceeds to separate himself into two characters, one the fool, the actor in life's comedy, and the other the observer, both submitted to the "overseeing" activity of an author identifying himself with and detached from both. The reader seeks in vain the monological voice of an author who possesses truth experienced as complete, as unified, as unproblematic, as closed. Gradually, the narrating subject seems to disappear, dispersed into multiplicity; ideas are presented as a form of play, provoking a response to the aesthetic qualities of the representational process itself rather than to themselves as potential bearers of truth. The boundaries of ethical speculation and storytelling dissolve and philosophy grows accustomed to travelling the paths once reserved for the spirit of poetry.

In those pages of *Le Neveu de Rameau* – representing the summit of enlightenment prose for some readers of Diderot – where the narrator depicts

Rameau performing, all alone, an Italian operatic repertoire, and then disappearing into the space of representation as he mimics an entire orchestra, indeed all of nature captured in its essential dynamic creativity, Diderot offers us the most complete illustration in his writings of the rational mind of the *philosophe* giving itself over to fantasy. For it is precisely through the act of "narrating Rameau" in all of his originality, ethical as well as aesthetic, that the philosophical subject is enabled to become more than just what it was; Diderot's narrative succeeds in by-passing the traditional prerogatives that had permitted dialogue's authoritative voice to reveal, as it concluded its exercises, a pre-existing order and a pre-existing truth. Rameau's celebrated pantomime, representing the process of metamorphosis itself, constitutes a commanding illustration of an experience of perception and self-representation that, as Diderot seemed always to have sensed, was ultimately accessible not to the physical exigencies of the dramatic stage but rather to the discourse of the narrative imagination. By relinquishing the claims to absolute authority in his narration and by allowing and even obliging his reader increasingly to become the author, Diderot provides an eloquent illustration of the larger Enlightenment project that implicitly structures and determines all his writing: not to propagate ideas but to encourage and make possible the continuous activity of critical thinking.

In a passage devoted to Beethoven and to his loss of hearing, Roger Sessions[2] spoke in the following way about the composer's musical memory and imagination: "Beethoven must surely have heard 'internally' and 'imaginatively'. He even developed new technical resources during the years of his almost total physical deafness". Diderot's *Nephew*, product and exemplar of the art of representation for and by the deaf and the mute, is surely meant for just such a stage.

Notes

1 *Virtual Theatre: From Diderot to Mallarmé*. The Johns Hopkins University Press, Baltimore, 1989.

2 *The Musical Experience of Composer, Performer, Listener*. Princeton University Press, Princeton, 1950, p 31.

Chapter 20

The Translator as Actor

Lars Kleberg

Is the literary translation an independent creation or, at best, a faithful reproduction? Is the translator an artist or a craftsman? This chapter compares the translator to other interpretative artists, such as the classical musician or actor. Both the actor and the translator break down structures into smaller units and then re-assemble them, using building blocks from other languages. In the process, the personality of the translator/actor is explored and restructured by the original text. A key concept to be considered in both an actor's and a translator's work, is the *subtext*. The subtext is all that is not explicitly said in the dialogue: the underlying motivations (the situation, psychology, story) for the words, the web of significance to be found between the lines. The translator's presence in the text – unlike the actor's double presence (physical and fictional) on the stage – is in effect theoretical and almost invisible; a successful rendition of another text means that the translation itself appears completely transparent. The chapter speculates on the motivations behind the desire to become a translator or an actor. It is said, for example, that Diderot, forever vacillating between submission and rebellion finally "became himself" by hiding behind other people's speech. In order to extend the limits of culture, the translator/actor begins by exploring his/her own limitations. The resulting sense of freedom is at once the motor of creativity as well as its goal.

Is the literary translation an independent creation or, at best, a faithful reproduction? Is the translator an artist or a craftsman?

The discussion is as old as the translator's profession. An individual who has given clearer thought to this subject than most, the Czech scholar Jiří Levý, is of the opinion that translating should be regarded as an *interpretive art*, comparable to that of the musician or actor. The concert musician "translates" the work as clearly as possible from one language, that of the musical notation, to another, that of the sonic matter. The actor fills the text with life by transposing into a new context, that of his body, his voice, the context of his personality. According to Levý, the good literary translation is just such an interpretative art–simultaneously faithful and independent.[1]

Agneta Ekmanner's discussion of the actor's art in an interesting interview from 1986 shows, among other things, that the analogy between the work of the actor and the translator is very illuminating. This is how Ekmanner describes her work with a role:

> When I work with a part I chew it up into small pieces. I knead it until it finally fits me. But the work is really just as much in the opposite direction. The part chews me up into small pieces in order to be able to spit out whatever it does not need of me.
>
> To remold oneself into this person, to enter a person's language, way of expressing himself, way of relating to things, to transform oneself into this dramatic figure – that is the actor's art. It is not enough to just be natural and be able to set things up. You know, to have "a presence on stage", generally speaking. And have a "fantastic rapport with the audience". And handle the lines in a way that they sound, well, like you've heard them a thousand times before.[2]

Put "poem" or "novel" instead of "part", put "readable" instead of "natural, generally speaking" and you have a rather striking characterization of the translator's interpretive work.

To translate, it has been said, is to break down a structure into small pieces and then reconstruct it again, using building blocks from another language. Agneta Ekmanner's way of reasoning reflects another side of this process. It is not simply for the translator to "chew up" the original into small pieces – the original chews up the translator as well and takes advantage of certain sides of him in the formation of the new text. This, I think, is where one can find an important explanation as to why the translator's arduous and ill-paid work still has such an attraction for some people.

In his already classic essay[3] Eric Mesterton talks about two general tendencies in the art of translation: to bring the original closer to the reader or to bring the reader closer to the original. The first tendency concentrates on readability – compare Ekmanner's "fantastic rapport with the audience". The other tendency is marked by the translator's desire to transform the reader's linguistic horizon and at the same time be himself transformed (if only for the moment) – compare Ekmanner's "to remold one's body into this person, to enter a person's language, way of expressing himself, way of relating to things".

A key concept in the actor's work with his/her part, which Agneta Ekmanner discusses in the interview, is the *subtext*. Even here there are striking and interesting parallels with the way in which the translator works. The subtext is all that is not explicitly said in the dialogue: the underlying motivations (the situation, psychology, story) for the words, the web of significance to be found in between the lines. Just as there are role performances which lack subtexts and are simply represented by the lines, there are translations in which only the words, not the underlying circumstances, have been translated.

The notion of subtext was introduced into the theory of acting by Konstantin Stanislavsky but has gradually acquired a general validity. Today, some 50 years after Stanislavsky's death, quite a lot has been said and written about the work with the subtext. If the discussion of an analogy between the actor's art and translation is tenable, it ought to have consequences for both the theory and criticism of translation.

What does Diderot's *Paradoxe sur le comédien* have to say, if you regard it as a comment on the translator's art?[4]

The work of the translator is in many ways even more intuitive and isolated than that of the actor. It will no doubt have to remain that way to a great extent. But the translator's anonymity must be further alleviated. The double presence of the actor on stage, as a physical person and as a character, is quite obvious. The translator's presence in the text, very close to the author, is still theoretical and in effect almost invisible. Many a naively naturalistic reader – and critic – never question whether or not the Russian poet Marina Tsvetaeva actually writes like this:

> I had direct communication with the Devil ever since my birth, a direct line. Among that which provoked my secret fears among the fearful secrets most of all in my childhood was: 'God–Devil!' God–with the silent, lightning-like, irrevocable addition of Devil... 'God, make my prayer into: God–Devil!', and as if interrupted in my train of thought, I hurried on:" God–Devil!, God–Devil!, God–Devil!', and back again, like Hanon's sixth exercise: 'Devil-God! Devil–God! Devil–God!' up and down one's spine and the chilling keyboard of fear.
>
> There was not the slightest crack between God and the Devil, into which one could force one's will, not the slightest space into which one could stick one's consciousness in like a finger in order to stop this terrible fusion. God, out or whom the Devil flew, the Devil who spliced himself into 'God', who with his ending d already was–the D.[5]

It is difficult to imagine a closer and more daring reconstruction of the dualistic word magic in Tsvetaeva's prose than that produced by Annika Bäckström.[6]

Of course, when it comes to interpretations of poetry it is more difficult to ignore the presence of the translator. I still believe that many translators (at least if they are not renowned poets) have had to grin and bear the compliments aimed only at the translated poet, for instance, for his "explosive imagery" or for his ascetic style, "in which no syllable is superfluous". The work of the translator, his more or less successful rendition of another text, remains completely transparent. Not until we have translation criticism worth the name is the hood of invisibility going to be removed.

But the translator is also to blame for his own invisibility. I am not proposing that the translators should "dominate" the original in happy egocentricity;[7] but I do believe that they are unnecessarily afraid of doing just that.

For the sake of practice, try to translate Jonas Cornell's provocative reformulation of the relationship between the role and the actor: "We want to see the Baron as Frej Lindqvist and not the reverse performance".[8]

Why does anyone become a translator? Why does anyone become an actor? Jean Starobinski presents a hypothesis in his analysis of Diderot, who "became himself" by hiding behind other people's speech.[9]

Diderot had difficulties with the authorities, from his strict father the cutler in Langre, to Louis XV. He was oppositional and rebellious but also sensitive to the reprimands of the authorities and to public humiliations, not to mention his imprisonment in 1749. He criticized tyranny but accepted the company of Katherine the Great in St Petersburg. He hovered between submission and rebellion, often simultaneously, although in different directions; the authorities never gave him any peace of mind.

In Starobinski's view, Diderot found a way out of the conflict with the authority of his father by appealing to a higher authority, by becoming the latter's spokesman, borrowing his voice, "even identifying with him". Thus he becomes a translator, paraphraser, compiler. Ego extinction, submission to new authorities? Not simply. Protected by the new authorities, Diderot's behaviour becomes bolder than ever, he even dares an attack on the Creator himself. At the same time, hiding behind everything and everybody, he just about assumes the place of the latter. He hides not behind just anything but behind the gigantic universal project: *The Encyclopaedia*!

Assumed authorities to replace the Father? Submission and dreams of omnipotence? Without any statistical proof I would hazard the guess that impulses of that nature explain the professional choice of many translators and actors too, for that matter. Who is more sensitive to criticism than the actor and the translator, who complains more about the *personal plight* of this work than they do – and who is less inclined to do away with it?

When it comes to the actor's/actress's authoritarian conditioning, there may not be enough evidence for me to give an opinion. But doesn't the desire *to be someone else*, and thus the readiness to submit to the director's designs for the stage and the writer's words, no doubt belong to the same complex? Of the prominent translators I know I believe most – in spite of their unassuming manner (which perhaps confirms this even more) – have had a very authoritarian upbringing. Dreams of omnipotence behind the typewriter? All I need to do is look at myself.

If the authoritarian conditioning that Starobinski traces in Diderot might be a *necessary* precondition for a devoted translator, it certainly is not *sufficient*. What makes the translator continue? Philanthropic reasons are hardly the answer, even though the slight credit and meagre pay received could give that impression. There is something else involved. Neither is it the chance to dream about one's own brilliance in the face of one's own inability to create. It is a matter of hard and methodical work here, very similar to that in the carpenter Thomas Tempte's account of the reconstruction of Tutankhamen's chair:

> What then is the carpenter's achievement? Well, the existence of the chair. His contribution to the expression is all the proportions, the arrangement of technical solutions, but above all the amount of time he has spent on the work. *Conscientiousness* is probably the message reflected in the different parts of the chair and its developing forms, which have been molded over months of fitting and re-fitting in the process of making the chair. Does the chair possess any expression that can be traced to the person who made it with his hands and his presence of mind? I would maintain that it does. Because in order to materialize something that surely involved the directives of many people, a very special ability is required: a creative intellect.[10]

The translator expands the limits of culture, but he begins by expanding his own. The successfully executed translation is like the shedding of one's skin and it provides the translator with a very concrete sense of freedom, which is of a transient nature however. The years of practice and the numerous failures have, ideally speaking, taught him to shorten the path to that point of balance between necessity and arbitrariness, when he knows "to what extent force may be sacrificed for nobleness, flawlessness for lightness, or strict accuracy for the power of style".[11] This sense of freedom is simultaneously the motor of creativity as well as its goal.

Notes

1 Levý, Jiří (1969) Der literarische übersetzung, Frankfurt am Main.

2 Interviewed by Susanne Marko in *entré*, February 1986.

3 Mesterton, Eric (1985) Om möjligheten och omöjligheten att översätta. In: *Speglingar*, Uddevalla.

4 See my article "Skådespelaren och rollen" in *Dialoger*, no. 15 (1990) for a discussion of the "double presence".

5 Tsvetaeva, Marina (1981) *Min ryska barndom*, translated by Annika Bäckström, Stockholm p 34.

6 The Tsvetaeva/Bäckström word magic ("GoD, who with his ending D already was the D") has no direct correlation with the Russian here. The translation is thus "better than the original" here; but it is completely analogous to the way in which Tsvetaeva works in other places, where the interaction between linguistic expression and content is not as easily recreated.

7 Cf Karel Kraus's criticism of the actor, reported in my article "Skådespelaren och rollen", *Dialoger* no 15.

8 Cornell, Jonas (1973) Time in the theater *Ord och bild* 1/1973, p 34.

9 Starobinski, Jean (1990) Diderot och de andras tal (transl Jan Stolpe). *Dialoger* no 15.

10 Quoted from Göranzon, Bo (1990) *Det praktiska intellektet*, Stockholm, p 70.

11 Le Rond d'Alembert, Jean (1990) Iakttagelser rörande översättarkonsten (transl Anders Bodegård). *Dialoger* no 15.

Chapter 21

Translating the Self

Michael Robinson

This chapter examines the paradox of autobiography, a genre which attempts to construct a single, authoritative narrative by translating a multiplicity of past selves into the language of the present. Individual, lived experience passes into language and is mediated by the interrelationship between the signifiers, which stand in for the experience itself. The writer becomes a figure of the text, his past rooted in the present of its recall. Autobiographical story-telling elevates a temporal sequence into a causal one through the chronological enchainment of the text in which the writer inscribes himself. The narrative takes on the attributes of a plot which confers a line of intention and a portent of design upon the data it is processing. Identity is adapted from a plurality of texts and structured within and around the discourses available to it at any one moment in time. The autobiographer *is* his text, and as such constituted by the complex intertextuality of the discourses through which his identity is assembled. Like a good translation, an autobiography may resemble its primary text but cannot reproduce it exactly. This accounts for the self-reflexive nature of so many autobiographies. What an autobiographer writes supplements what he has lived and yet is an event in the life he is recounting. Like the actor, the writer has a capacity for the *dédoublement* of experience, for assuming, dissembling, or "representing" emotion in a manner that subverts the idea of a fixed, inviolable selfhood and the moral order with which it is often associated. In this, as someone who is his own spectator, he resembles Diderot's actor, at once his own subject and object, the player and first audience of his many roles.

The actor, it appears, lives a profusion of roles in other people's eyes just as (according to Rousseau, in the *Discours sur les sciences et les arts*) social man lives in the opinion of others, and presents himself to those around him in a series of (dis)guises. Consequently, Rousseau, who distrusted both these public arenas of display and dissembling, while at the same time entertaining grave doubts about his ability to present himself to others in public as he felt and knew himself to be, turned to autobiography in order to retrieve a just image of himself from the many misconceptions which he believed that other people held about him. His gaucherie and inability to improvise .a telling response in the course of general conversation made him unable to compose himself sufficiently in public in order to counter these misconceptions in person. Therefore writing an autobiography was for Rousseau the necessary substitute for the inadequacies and embarrassment of what he experienced in an interlocutionary situation, a domain where he might recompose himself in retrospect. "Le parti que j'ai pris d'écrire et de me cacher est précisément celui que me convenoit", he claimed;[1] unlike speech, which seems always to obscure his intentions and imprison him within the confines of the character with which he is endowed by others, writing will permit him to "rendre mon àme transparente aux yeux du lecteur".[2]

Like Rousseau, Diderot, in *Le Paradoxe sur le comédien,* also alludes to moments of personal experience during which he found it impossible to represent his true feelings directly to a conversational partner. He, too, frequently portrays himself as undone by sensibility and unable to negotiate the pitfalls of conversation, as inept and absurd when declaring his love or hesitant and struck dumb when unexpectedly meeting a friend after a long absence, and contrasts this with the great actor's sureness in rising to the occasion of every role by a controlled dissociation of the personality, which enables private experience to be translated into effective stage presence. For, as in his celebrated account of Mlle Clairon's performance in Racine's *Britannicus,* Diderot maintains that the great actress can, through emotional self-control, "se voir, se juger et juger les impressions qu'elle excitera" while apparently in the grip of her performance, thus making her in this instance at once "la petite Clairon et la grande Agrippine".[3]

In some respects Diderot's account of the actor's art anticipates the kind of *dédoublement* of experience often noted by the writers of a later generation, like Strindberg or Maupassant, whose Naturalism frequently evoked a division of consciousness wherein the writer "semble avoir deux âmes, l'une qui note, explique, commente chaque sensation de sa voisine de l'âme naturelle, commune à tous les hommes".[4] What it certainly also does is to suggest an affinity between the role-playing of the actor and the divided consciousness of the autobiographer, seeing, hearing, and judging not only his past self but the effect his present narrative will have on its readers. Just as the autobiographer seems to possess a double consciousness of himself as he was in the unfolding sequence of his experiences and as he now is at the moment of recording them, so the actor can look on at the emotion he or she is producing on stage.

This in turn might well be linked to the idea of the actor or actress which emerged during the nineteenth century as someone essentially devoid of personality, as indeed a void or "vacancy", the word used in Henry James's generally underrated novel *The Tragic Muse,* to describe the chameleon-like figure of the actress Miriam Rooth.[5] "What's rare in you", Miriam is told by her admirer, Sherringham, "is that you have – as I suspect, at least – no nature of your own... Your feigning may be honest, in the sense that your only feeling *is* your feigned one".[6] This is after he has concluded that "the expression that came nearest to belonging to her ...was the one that came nearest to being a blank – an air of inanity when she forgot herself, watching something".[7]

In short, performers like Miriam are nothing in themselves, but merely who or what they pretend to be, a conclusion which the ultimately irremediably bourgeois Sherringham clearly finds disturbing:

It struck him abruptly that a woman whose only being was to 'make believe', to make believe that she had any and every being that you liked, that would serve a purpose, produce a certain effect, and whose identity resided in the continuity of her personations, so that she had no moral privacy, as he phrased it to himself, but lived in a high wind of exhibition, of figuration – such a woman was a kind of monster, in whom of necessity there would be nothing left to like, because there would be nothing to take hold of.[8]

Like much else in his fiction, James's study of the actress clearly owes a great deal to a French tradition in which the arguments of Diderot's *Paradoxe,* though rarely mentioned by name, remain an evident point of reference. By 1890, when *The Tragic Muse* appeared, the idea of the actress as an impassive yet parasitically histrionic monster who preys upon the lives of those around her had become almost a commonplace. Edmond de Goncourt, for example, had deployed it in his anatomy of an actress, *La Faustin,* in 1882, by which time it had already been frequently exploited by Balzac in the *Comédie humaine.* If, on the one hand, this notion was closely related to many other male images of *fin-de-siècle* woman, as depicted in Munch, Zola, Wedekind, Huysmans and Mallarmé, it also echoed received ideas about the essential characterlessness of the writer, who is sometimes portrayed (by Balzac, Strindberg, and James himself) as a vampire, preying upon others and himself. Like the actor, the writer has a capacity for assuming or dissembling or "representing" emotion which seems often to be allied with a characteristic coldness, or *impassibilité,* and his incarnations, too, subvert the idea of a fixed, inviolable selfhood and the moral order with which it is almost invariably associated.

Nevertheless, James might also have found his portrait of Miriam Rooth endorsed by the comments of Janet Achurch (the first professional English Nora in *Et dukkehjem*), who was conscientiously reported by William Archer in *Masks or Faces?* (his 1888 riposte to Diderot's *Paradoxe*) as saying: "It is impossible for me to help it. Everything that comes, or ever has come, into my own life, or under my observation, I find myself utilizing, and in scenes of real personal suffering I have had an under-consciousness of taking mental notes all the time. It is not a pleasant feeling".[9] For it is of course Diderot who mounts a defence of what even the actress herself seems to have found dubious in her behaviour. Where Rousseau, in his *Lettre à d'Alembert sur les spectacles* of 1758, had inveighed against the actor's art on the grounds that to counterfeit, be inconstant, and prey upon others was immoral, Diderot regarded the variety of the great actor, with his ability, like Proteus, to assume a multiplicity of guises, in a positive light. "Le grand comédien est tout ou n'est rien" he affirmed, in *Le Paradoxe,* and again:

On a dit que les comédiens n'avaient aucun caractère nature leur avait donné, qu'ils devenaient faux, comme le médecin, le chirurgien et le boucher deviennent durs. Je crois qu'on a pris la cause pour l'effet, et ils ne sont propres à les jouer tous que parce qu'ils n'en ont point.[10]

Once again the similarity with the Keatsian paradox in which it is precisely a lack of identity which characterizes the writer is clear: "The poetic character", Keats wrote, "has no self... Not one word I ever utter can be taken for granted as an opinion growing out of my identical nature".[11] But in the context of autobiographical writing this, like Diderot's paradox, assumes a peculiar resonance, and may cast doubt on traditional notions of the genre. For if, in playing all his different roles, the actor is nevertheless consistently himself, his ability to assume a multiplicity of roles makes him an exemplary instance of the *multiplicité du moi* which an autobiographer, like Strindberg, observes in himself and recognizes in others, and hence suggests a possible parallel between their respective role playing, and the paradoxical lack of identity which is often the final sum of the autobiographer's endeavours.

As Barrett J. Mandel has observed, the major problems of autobiography as a genre usually arise from the unquestioned notion that a person's life is recoverable, that it is all somehow "there" ready and waiting to be simply unearthed and transplanted.[12] Moreover, it is also presupposed that the discourse in which the life is written is not a part of the life being recounted but a transparent medium through which that life can be seen. However, as St. Augustine pointed out at the time of the genre's inception, "with regard to the past, when this is reported correctly what is brought out from the memory is not the events themselves (these are already past) but words conceived from the images of those events".[13] These words are thus a translation, and though the life to which they refer may seem anterior to and outside the language in which it is recounted, the autobiographer's identity is constituted in the words he writes, which designate what is absent.

Autobiographical writing therefore entails alienation as well as identification. "Je" is always "un autre" since the remembered self with whom the writer identifies in the present (with whom the continuity of a perfect translation is claimed) is also a "he" (or "she"), the "third party" of Beckett's supposedly fictional narrators, whose appearances are always put in "by other parties" elsewhere, and whose unending story is told by "another".[14] Hence the paradox of the autobiographical narrator who is at once himself and yet not himself, continuous with his past and yet isolating that past in the act of writing about it, although like translation again, autobiographical discourse maintains the fiction of identity, of being a faithful rendering of a primary text.

It is, of course, Roland Barthes who drew attention to this dilemma in "To Write: An Intransitive Verb?": "When a narrator (of a written text) recounts what has happened to him", Barthes remarked, "the *I* who recounts is no longer the one that is recounted".[15] Moreover, even this recounting I, the seemingly stable discursive I of the narrator who is telling the story now, is not the self who is writing now when this self is taken to be "an interiority constituted previous to and outside language".[16] But from the perspective of autobiography the situation has perhaps been most acutely illuminated by Freud in his analysis of Screen Memories, where he elaborates upon the inevitable rupture between the acting and the recollecting self:

> In the majority of significant and in other respects unimpeachable childhood scenes the subject sees himself in the recollection as a child, with the knowledge that this child is himself: he sees this child, however, as an observer from outside the scene would see him... Now it is evident that such a picture cannot be an exact repetition of the impression that was originally received. For the subject was then in the middle of the situation and was attending not to himself but to the external world.[17]

This is true of all writing, including even so immediate a transcription of experience into language as certain entries in the diaries of Anais Nin, where she sought the instantaneous capture of experience "before it is altered, changed by distance or time".[18] But it clearly has a particular pathos in the case of autobiography, where the author claims to be the unique authority on the story he has to tell, and seeks to become his own progenitor. Confronted by the common patrimony of the language into which he is forced to translate himself, and which he inherits at birth, the autobiographer sometimes even speculates on the possibility of a means of utterance that is wholly his own. Thus, in seeking to communicate his own singularity, Rousseau sees a need for "un langage aussi nouveau que mon projet",[19] and his role as the model autobiographer is perhaps nowhere more apparent than in this desire to secede from common discourse and inaugurate his own. But as Roman Jakobson has pointed out, "La propriété privée, dans le domaine du langage, ça n'existe pas".[20] The language in which the autobiographer seeks to identify himself not only antecedes him; it is also held in common with other individuals as a shared circuit of exchange where he finds the available words already inhabited by the collectivity of speakers, of which he is only one voice. Moreover, if the language at the autobiographer's disposal is embedded in the conventions of his time, beset by the contingent emphasis of the moment, and permeated by the social and intellectual inferences of the age, it is exactly through this continual search for self-definition that he seems to vanish into the text of which he nominally is the master, where he becomes not transparent, as Rousseau wished, but a property of the language into which he translates himself. Individual, lived experience passes into language; it is mediated by the interrelationship between the signifiers, which stand in for the experience itself; they displace the past of the person they are nominally representing (and the notion of presence is ironically evoked by the faculty of language as representation, the fabrication of a copy that replaces the original); the empirical facts of the autobiographer's life are transformed into artifacts; sequence is endowed with meaning and condensed into design; and the writer becomes what for the reader he must remain, a figure of the text. For it is through the language to which the writer commits himself that the reader discovers the writer's identity; his self is actually formed under the eyes of the reader, in the latter's interpreting consciousness. Moreover, this written self emerges out of what Hume, in his reflections on personal identity in *A Treatise of Human Nature*, terms the "perpetual flux and movement" of an identity whose continuity we "feign",[21] and comprises a series of structuring choices and narrative strategies through which that self is composed. Further, every word employed to recover the traces of this buried past is also (like the tale which Alrik Lundstedt learns to tell about his past in "Den romantiske klockaren på Rånö") a matter of covering them over again with words. It is an essentially formal rather than substantial identity, and as Hume observed, "all the nice and subtle questions concerning personal identity... are to be regarded rather as grammatical than as philosophical difficulties".[22]

The autobiographer is therefore confined to a life in language, according to criteria which are often sustained by the conventions of he alternative, dominant literary genre, the novel, where language also fabricates character, and narrative condenses a life into a destiny. As Lacan writes, of the analogous discourse of the patient in analysis, by recounting a past event "he has made it pass into the *verbe*, or more precisely, into the *epos* by which he brings back into present time the origins of his own person. He creates a kind of exemplary fiction, told by the imaginary self in order to defend its illusory sense of autonomy. And he does so in a language which allows his discourse to be understood by his contemporaries, and which furthermore presupposes their present discourse".[23]

But the origin of an autobiography is not the remote past which the autobiographer normally proceeds to investigate, and which conventionally forms the opening chapter of his story, but its end, namely the act of writing itself. As Mandel, again, writes, "We experience our memories only in the present; it is the present moment which allows the past to exist for us",[24] and as in the case of *Tjänstekvinnans son*, the impulse to write an autobiography is frequently a response to present pressures rather than the allure of the past. Indeed, while it appears by definition to be concerned with the past, autobiography is in fact determined by the present, as a response to the moment in which it is written, and which is often everywhere present in the writing of a work that is its own conclusion. Hence it is tied to the vantage point from which the text of the past is being translated into the language of the present – the writer's past is in fact rooted in the present of its recall. It represents the writer's attempt to elucidate his present rather than his past, even though a common strategy is for the autobiographer to write of himself as if he were dead. (Thus Sartre sees *Les mots* as his obituary, Hume calls his memoir "this funeral oration of myself", and Darwin explains, in the preface to autobiography he wrote in 1876, how he has "attempted to write the following account myself, as if I were a dead man in another world looking back at my own life",[25] while Strindberg frequently insists that his autobiographical fictions are written "inför döden".) Nevertheless, the autobiographer creates his past rather than merely remembers it in the present, and in that respect his account is not something other than his life, not simply a secondary text into which he translates the primary text of his life, but an integral part of the life he is living and currently recording.

The problems raised by the medium in which the autobiographer seeks, like Rousseau, to convey "moi, moi seul"[26] are compounded by the recurring identifications, both literary and ideological, in the light of which he monitors and organizes his experience. For as a genre, autobiography expresses what Hayden White has called "the apparently universal need not only to narrate but to give to events an aspect of narrativity,"[27] and alongside the translation of the self into the general circuit of linguistic exchange, it is the teleology of narrative, which posits identity where there may only be at best a random contiguity, that endows the life of its subject with what Strindberg (in "Karantänmästarns andra berättelse") calls "en följd och ordning".[28] It is in the generally chronological process of autobiographical story-telling, where a temporal sequence is elevated into a causal one through the seemingly continuous and uninterrupted enchainment of the text in which the writer inscribes himself, that the autobiographer shapes his life and overcomes the contingency and evanescence of experience. The latter, following what Hume calls the inveterate human predilection "to suppose ourselves possessed of an invariable and uninterrupted existence thro' the whole course of our lives",[29] takes on the attributes of a plot which confers a line of intention and a portent of design upon the data it is processing, and thus holds out the promise of a progress towards meaning.[30] For the very act of narrating confers direction on the material which the text enchains, and it is this which allows Rousseau to date the unbroken consciousness of himself to his earliest reading and the discovery, in Mme la Tribu's lending library, of exemplary plots by means of which he could create a kind of specular image of himself through identification and reverie. Similarly, Ivar Lo-Johansson records the transition, at around the age of six or seven, from a time when memories were not yet enchained, and the past had not yet become a narrative composition, to a more consciously structured existence when he "började med minnets hjälp som ett slags byggklossar stapla upp sammanhang av större händelser som jag förut inte ens hade brytt mig om ... Jag 'författade' medvetet människor och inträffanden och jag gjorde ett slags dikter eller skisser av dem".[31]

Moreover, the translation of the subject into narrative is itself part of the interpretative process, and is conducted according to the codes and conventions which allow the autobiographer to make his singular experience intelligible to his readers. These obviously entail what Georg Misch, in his *A History of Autobiography in Antiquity*, calls "the different forms with which different periods provide the individual for his self-revelation and self-portrayal"[32] and which, for a nineteenth-century writer like Strindberg, would include the discourses of the *Bildungsroman*, the *roman intime*, the case history, journal, and confession. But they also encompass numerous more diffuse models, which in Strindberg's case included the structures of thought and feeling offered by what, in *Tjänstekvinnans son*, he calls the "kvadron av romantik, pietism, realism och naturalism",[33] the family romance of the patriarchal family, the constellation of the recurring image of himself as "tjällets och hyddans son – Tjänstekvinnans Son – Hagars",[34] and the metaphors for recuperating experience provided by (among others) Kierkegaard and Swedenborg.[35] Identity, as Strindberg recognizes himself in a letter to Bjørnson, in which he inventories his own "gamla råttbo till själ, der trasor af gammal kristendom, lappar af konstdyrkande hedendom, spånor af pessimism, flisor af allmänt verldsförakt ligga huller om buller",[36] is adapted from a plurality of texts and structured within and around the discourses available to it at any one moment in time. Hence it also entails an ability on the autobiographer's part of being able to read and interpret his self, of discovering and decoding the language in which he or she is written. For, as Strindberg suggests, in the preface to *Fröken Julie*, the self is an unstable mosaic of "konglomerater av förgångna kulturgrader och pågående, bitar ur böcker och tidningar, stycken av mänskor, avrivna lappar av helgdagskläder, som blivit lumpor",[37] an identity composed, in short, out of the discursive formations and determinacies of an often lacunary unconscious.

In recuperating this identity it is not the life as a succession of natural events that possesses meaning but the interpreted series into which it has been translated. The life is therefore a text to be read, interpreted, and hence re-written, and this extended transposition of the writer's lived experience into a written narrative brings with it a recognition that a life may be as much a work of fiction – of guiding narrative structures – as the novels from which these are often taken. (Hence Strindberg's remark, in a letter to Torsten Hedlund: "Mitt lif har ju haft den egenskapen att gestalta sig som romaner, utan att jag kan säga rätt hvarför",[38] and his delighted recognition, in a world so insistently shaped and designed by his own needs and desires, of plots and scenarios already imprinted upon the otherwise inchoate multiplicity of events in which he was both actor and spectator.) Like Mme Bovary or Don Quixote, the autobiographer lives the set of stories he or she inherits and invents; they all organize experience to provide a configuration of significance through which it can be viewed and offer an available corpus of narratives whereby it can be interpreted and retrieved. In short, they allow the autobiographer to create himself. The autobiographer *is* his text, and as such constituted by the complex intertextuality of the discourses through which his identity is assembled.

Like a translation, then, an autobiography is always less, or other than, its original. Hence the dissatisfaction which many autobiographers (Rousseau, Strindberg, Ivar Lo-Johansson, Gibbon, Leiris) seem to feel for the works which appear under their name, and which leads them to produce more than one account of a life which is, by definition, singular. Their repeated attempts upon their own lives, which suggest that no one version ever wholly accommodates the original, provide eloquent testimony to the fact that like a good translation, an autobiography may resemble its primary text but cannot reproduce it exactly. Indeed, an autobiography is always in one sense provisional, a prelude, since even when undertaken from a posthumous perspective, it does not include its author's death as an accomplished fact and an effective moment of closure, giving point even to a life cut off in mid career, as is the case with biography. Hence the manner in which autobiographical writing is often self-reflexive in a double sense: it is aware both of the self it is seeking to recover on the writer's behalf and of the terms of its own process. Indeed, many autobiographies reflect upon their own nature and provide a critique of the medium in which they are caste, although if they do raise doubts about the task in which the autobiographer is engaged, this often takes the form of a kind of *concessio* designed to validate his enterprise by recognizing its pitfalls and limitations. Thus, where the conventional notion of autobiography envisages its writer attaining "a sense of perspective and integration" in a work that, as literature, "achieves a satisfying wholeness",[39] the situation is more accurately reflected in Strindberg's interim account of his life in *Tjänstekvinnans son*, which ends, not with the customary climax of an identity discovered and sealed in writing, but in the paradoxical recognition of his textual multiplicity, recoverable (if at all) in the totality of his writing:

> Men resultatet, sammanfattningen? frågar man. Var ligger sanningen han sökte? Den ligger här och där i de tusen tryckta sidorna, sök upp dem, samla dem och se efter om de kunna sammanfattas; se efter om de äro giltiga längre än ett år, fem år, tänk efter om de ens ha utsikt att bli giltiga, då därtill fordras ett flertals erkännande. Och glöm ej att sanningen icke kan finnas, emedan den befinner sig som allt i en beständig utveckling.[40]

The autobiographer is condemned to the multiplicity of becoming rather than the singleness of being. His account resists the static dimension of singular definition that it may initially have been devised to satisfy, and raises the possibility that the autobiographer will lose, or (like Rousseau, Strindberg, Ivar Lo, or Leiris) disperse himself the more he multiplies himself.

However, while identity may be forever deferred in the play of the text, in mastering its inscription the writer-subject is somehow distinct from the chronology he calls his life while nevertheless adding to it in a double sense: what he writes supplements what he has lived and yet is an event in the life he is recounting. In this, as someone who is his own spectator, he resembles Diderot's actor, at once his own subject and object, the player and first audience of his many roles. Surrounded by all his numerous autobiographical texts, it is this that Strindberg has in mind when he tells his old friend, Leopold Littmansson: "...jag kan objektivera mig sjelf jag, hvilket åsnorna och – innorna med fålar kalla min subjektivitet, som skulle vara liksom något dåligt."[41] So can the actor, which is why he is at once morally suspect and dangerously creative. As Sherringham responds to Miriam's question, "And do you think I've no character?" – "Delightful being, you've got a hundred!"[42]

Notes

1 *Oeuvres complètes*, Gagnebin, Bernard and Raymond, Marcel, 4 vols. Paris, 1959–69, I, p 118.

2 *Oeuvres complètes*, I, p 175.

3 *Oeuvres*, Billy, André (ed). Paris, Gallimard, 1951, pp 1007–1008.

4 Maupassant, Guy de (nd) *Sur l'eau*. Paris, pp 115-116.

5 *The tragic muse*, Penguin edition, Harmondsworth, 1978, p 88. Cf Miriam with Diderot's portrait of Mlle Clairon: "'I wish you could see yourself,' Sherringham answered. 'My dear fellow, I do. What do you take me for. I didn't miss a vibration of my voice, a fold of my robe.'" (*The tragic muse*, p 230.)

6 *The tragic muse*, p 145.

7 *The tragic muse*, p 131.

8 *The tragic muse*, p 130.

9 Archer, William (1888) *Masks or faces?* London, pp 101–102.

10 *Oeuvres*, pp 1030, 1037.

11 *The letters of John Keats 1814–1821*, 2 vols. Cambridge, MA, 1958, I, pp 386–387.

12 Autobiography – reflection trained on mystery. *Prairie Schooner*. 46, 1972–73, p 324. Hence, too, the various recording instruments for logging the past which writers have put forward, from Locke's notion of the pre-mnemonic mind as a white page, devoid of all characters, and Diderot's soft substance of the brain as a mass of sensitive and living wax, capable of receiving new impressions while retaining and reviving the old, down to Freud's mystical writing pad.

13 *The confessions*, transl Warner, Rex. New York, 1963, p 118.

14 *The unnamable*. London, 1959, p 296.

15 In: *The structuralists: From Marx to Levi-Strauss*, De George, Richard and De George, Fernande (eds). Garden City, 1972, p 163.

16 Barthes, p 162. Cf Mikhail Bakhtin's observation in "The forms of time and the chronotopas in the novel". *PTL* 1978, 3: 3: "Even if he is the author of an autobiography, or of the most truthful of confessions, the writer nevertheless remains, as their creator, outside the world depicted in them. If I tell of (or write about) an event which has just happened to me, I, as the *teller* (or writer) of this event am already outside that time-space in which this event has occurred. It is impossible to identify absolutely myself, my 'I', with that 'I' of which I am telling as it is to lift myself up by the hair" (p 526).

17 *Standard edition of the complete works of Sigmund Freud*, Strachey, James (ed) 24 vols. London, 1953–73, III, p 321.

18 *Journals of Anais Nin*. London, 1973, I, p 6.

19 *Oeuvres complètes*, I, p 1153.

20 *Essais de linguistique générale*. Paris, 1963, p 33.

21 *A Treatise on Human Nature*. Penguin edition, Harmondsworth, 1969, p 302.

22 *A treatise*, p 310.

23 *Ecrits*, transl Sheridan, Alan. London, 1977, pp 46–47.

24 Autobiography – Reflection trained on mystery, p 325.

25 Hume, David (1966) My own life. In: Hendel, Charles W. (ed) *An inquiry concerning human understanding*. New York, 1966, p 3: Darwin, Charles and Huxley, Thomas Henry (1983) *Autobiographies*, de Beer, Gavin (ed). Oxford, p 8.

26 *Oeuvres complètes*, I, p 1149.

27 The value of narrativity in the representation of reality. *Critical Inquiry* 1980, 7: 8.

28 *Samlade skrifter*. Landquist, John (ed). 55 vols. 1912–20, XXXVII, p 114.

29 *A treatise*, p 301.

30 Brooks, Peter (1984) *Reading for the plot*. New York, passim.

31 *Pubertet*. Stockholm, 1978, p 137.

32 *A history of autobiography in antiquity*, 2 vols. London, 1950, I, p 4.

33 *Samlade skrifter*. XVIII, p 92.

34 *August Strindbergs brev*. Eklund, Torsten and Meidal, Björn (eds). 17 vols to date. Stockholm, 1948–, XIV, p 144.

35 Not to mention the multitude of identities, including Ahasverus, Asmodeus, Christ, The Flying Dutchman, Hercules, Jacob, Job, Jonah, Joseph, Merlin, Napoleon, Robert le Diable and Satan, in which Strindberg perceives some aspect of his experience incarnated.

36 *August Strindbergs brev*. IV, p 144.

37 *Samlade skrifter*. XXIII, p 104.

38 *August Strindbergs brev*. XI, p 224.

39 Buckley, Jerome (1984) *The turning key: autobiography and the subjective impulse*. Cambridge, MA, p 40.

40 *Samlade skrifter*. XIX, p 278.

41 *August Strindbergs brev*. X, p 350.

42 *The tragic muse*. p. 146

Section VIII:

On the Two Cultures

Chapter 22

One Culture, Two Cultures, Three Cultures

Jon Cook

The university's corporate culture is conditioned by the duality of its intellectual culture. The opposition of science and the humanities fuels a logic of "either/or" rather than "both/and", and encourages the two disciplines to compete for authority within the university's authoritative structure. A university's importance is defined by its exclusiveness, an exclusiveness maintained, historically, by the exclusion of different social groups. This attitude is mirrored in an attitude towards knowledge – the cult of .the expert and of specialization, the belief that specialized forms of knowledge require esoteric codes and, therefore, that any advance in knowledge will be expressed in such codes. Distinguishing between the informal, practical and collaborative practices of "community knowledge" and their negation in the formal structures of "university knowledge", the chapter argues that the interactions across this boundary are an important concern for any group considering the future of universities. The sciences and the humanities share a capacity for problem-solving. Problem-solving is not a skill that can be learnt in isolation from the historical and philosophical context which is its necessary condition, nor is it a skill that can be taught by learning a set of specific rules. Problem-solving is an attempt to mediate between skill and knowledge. Narrative may be seen as one form of problem-solving which pervades social life. The chapter advocates a history of knowledge as an integral subject, available to students in both the humanities and the sciences and thereby holding the two cultures in a single frame. The history of knowledge stimulates intellectual curiosity by rejecting the idea that knowledge is monolithic. The sciences and the humanities can also be held in the same frame by the study of information theory, a subject which may provide the component of a common language for the exchange of experience and ideas across the boundaries of the two cultures. The chapter argues for a form of intellectual opportunism, for cultivating the capacity to experiment with a difficult language in a way that produces a hypothesis useful to the learner. For these proposals to be effective, we need to revise the metaphor of the university itself. The metaphor of the university as an encyclopaedia is suggested, a metaphor intended to evoke "the whole circle of learning", an environment, the play of chance and invention, consultation and participation. The technological basis for this new encyclopaedia would be the computer as an instrument capable of providing an arbitrary, flexible system of classification which would offer large-scale access to – and rapid updating of – the knowledge base of the encyclopaedia. The encyclopaedia would develop the potential of its eighteenth century forbear as a focus for information, debate, group thinking, and reflection.

Introduction

In this chapter I shall offer some analyses of the culture of the university and the culture or cultures that interact with it. The analyses are presented in schematic form and their purpose is to promote further debate about the current and future state of university culture and how it affects our image of knowledge and its availability. What is offered here is not a comprehensive view of the problems involved, but a set of perspectives on the embedded and often unacknowledged assumptions about what universities have been and what they are now. My main reference will be to universities in the United Kingdom, although I hope that this will open up the possibility of international comparison. My concern with cultural analysis means that I shall not directly address the formal relations of the university to the political state, or the details of the university's internal organization. What does concern me is the way the university's formal status, its structure as an organization, and a history of attitudes towards knowledge implied by both of these, all find expression in the relatively informal attitudes, beliefs and assumptions about the boundaries that mark out the mental and institutional spaces within the university, boundaries that establish an everyday understanding of what and who the university is for.

The title of the paper indicates some dilemmas and some opportunities. One of the dilemmas comes in the form of an echo of the title of C.P. Snow's Rede lecture, *The Two Cultures and the Scientific Revolution* given some 30 years ago. In that lecture Snow noted what is still the case: that the fundamental cultural fact about universities is their division between scientific and humanist disciplines and that this division, in turn, expresses a range of attitudes towards modernity and tradition, the image of technology and the image of literature. Attempts to overcome this division remain rare, and are usually regarded as eccentric or misguided. The division is functional in so far as it allows the creation of images which sustain corporate morale on either side of it. For the scientist the humanist scholar is a whimsical speculator spinning webs of discourse that can neither be verified nor refuted. This image of the humanist permits the scientist a self-definition by antithesis as the serious seeker after serious truth. For the humanist, the scientist is a "philistine" whose narrowly focused pursuit of ever-more specialized forms of knowledge is premissed upon an ignorance of what the humanist knows: a realm of human truth and history which is not available to the quantitative methods of science. Each side secures its authority at the expense of the other. The culture of the university is not one but two, or, to put it more accurately, the unity of its corporate cultures is constantly conditioned by the duality of its intellectual culture and the ignorance and suspicion that this promotes.

I doubt that Snow's lecture has very much to offer by way of a solution to this problem, But the debate provoked by the lecture revealed the reality of the dilemma Snow addressed in so far as it led to a vigorous re-assertion of the boundary between the humanities and the sciences. It was significant, too, for what it revealed about how universities in England might be imagined. Snow's lecture was provocative, within a highly limited circle, because the underlying direction of its argument was at odds with its ostensible rhetoric. Snow promotes himself as a mediator between the two cultures, but the sharpness of his attack on the existing forms of humanism, suggests that he wants a science-based culture to become the central culture within the university, because, in his view, that kind of culture is more flexible, democratic and outward-looking than the insular and nostalgic humanities.[1] F.R. Leavis, Snow's principal antagonist in the debate that followed, responded to the implications of Snow's lecture, and he did so in terms of an attack on the fragmentation of the university that he believed was the consequence of a science-based university:

> Unlike Snow, I am concerned to make it really a university, something that is more than a collection of specialist departments – to make it a centre of human consciousness: perception, knowledge, judgment and responsibility. And, perhaps I have sufficiently indicated on what lines I would justify my seeing the centre of a university in a vital English School .[2]

Leavis's justification of the English School as "the centre of a university" is set out at an earlier point in his argument against Snow:

> "But there is a prior human achievement of collaborative creation, a more basic work of the mind of man (and more than the mind), one without which the triumphant erection of the scientific edifice would not have been possible: that is the creation of the human world, including language [3]

Leavis's language in these two quotations works upon a set of assumptions that will be important for arguments later in this chapter. One is that the development of scientific knowledge is equated with specialization, and that this undermines the university's responsibility to develop a unified knowledge (scientific specialization is therefore the condition of a familiar paradox: the more you know, the less you know). Another is that science is a second-order activity, dependent upon "the creation of the human world, including language". This creation is, in part at least, the responsibility of the English School, and hence gives it its priority over the sciences. But Leavis's language at this point is peculiarly charged and worth analysing in some detail. It is not just that science is denied the status of a creative language by Leavis and relegated to the role of an edifice. The "triumphant erection" figures science as a phallic masculine power which is both opposed to and depends upon the maternal and female creativity of language in the human world. The figuring of science in this way is, of course, well established.[4] It reminds us that the opposition of science and the humanities constantly draws upon other terms (in this case the terms of gender) for its articulation, and in doing so, it promotes an understanding of those other terms as opposed. It fuels a logic of "either/or" rather than "both/and".

But, if these terms mark out Leavis's opposition to Snow, it is important to note an assumption that they have in common: a coherent university must have a central subject or group of subjects, and this central subject must be either identified as science or as humanities. My contention is that this idea of a university's coherence is at one with an idea of its authority in the culture at large. In order to be authoritative a university has to be a university of this kind: with a subject at the centre which is more important, and subjects at the periphery which are less. In order to understand why this should be thought an authoritative structure in the first place, we have to enter the realm of metaphoric and analogical thinking which shapes our everyday conception of the world. This realm is also often that of the self-evident, the obvious, "what-goes-without-being-said". Its propositions take on the form of tautologies and circular arguments. In the particular case that concerns us it seem to me that the idea of an authoritative structure is traced through with an historical and even archaic conception of the sovereign power – deity, monarch, or dictator – whose authority depends upon subordination, where the absence of subordination indicates the absence of authority, where the presence of authority is indicated by something withheld and something excluded.[5]

Exclusion

The imagination of authority sketched above finds a particularly powerful exemplification in the history of English universities. Their authority in the culture has been repeatedly defined in terms of a power to exclude, and we need to see the workings of two cultures within universities in terms of this long-standing historical context. The forms of exclusion have been variable, and they have been variously contested. Different social groups have been excluded from universities on the grounds of religion (the debarring of Catholics and Dissenters from Oxford and Cambridge from the sixteenth to early nineteenth centuries); of social class (only within the last hundred years, and then only with considerable difficulty, has it been thinkable that members of the working class might want or need a university education); or of gender (the centuries long exclusion of women which began to break down about 150 years ago). Today the form of exclusion is paradoxical and centres on qualification. To get to university, not only do you need to pass examinations but pass them well. Only a small percentage of the school population take these examinations and therefore they are perceived as the opportunity of an élite. Therefore what permits one group access to universities effectively debars another larger group. Again, the narrowness of this conception of qualification has been recently challenged, and many universities are ready to recognize less formal kinds of qualification as a basis for admission. But those who enter university without formal exam qualifications are still in a minority, and are still regarded in the university system as people who need a special exemption from the normal rules of entry.

My concern here is not to protest about this state of affairs, or to analyse its historical causes, but to trace its cultural effects. The exclusions of the past live on in the shaping of values in the present: what makes a university important both to its own members and to the outside world is its inaccessibility. A university's *amour propre* is defined by a sense of all the people who are absent from it. This social exclusiveness of universities is mirrored in an attitude towards knowledge. Social exclusions from the place of knowledge sustain an image of knowledge as itself exclusive, esoteric, the property of an élite. Again we enter the tautologous cycles of the self-evident: the knowledge that is valuable is held by a few because what is valuable cannot be the property of a majority. This perception is reinforced by a number of phenomena in contemporary society: the cult of the expert; the presumption that *all* significant advances in knowledge, whether in the sciences or the humanities, are the result of specialization; the belief that specialized forms of knowledge require esoteric codes, and, therefore, that any advance in knowledge will be expressed in such codes.

The problem can be stated another way, by reference to theory of positional goods. This theory holds that in order for certain things to be valuable they have to be scarce: a beautiful beach is beautiful when used by a few, but ceases to be beautiful for anybody if thousands of people decide to sunbathe on it all at the same time. I am not concerned here with some general refutation of the theory, but with its applicability to knowledge. There seems nothing, *prima facie*, which requires knowledge to be a positional good, yet many of our attitudes and practices seem to give it that status. As a result we may have lost sight of what one historian has described as a "democratic epistemology".[6] The fundamental tenet of such an epistemology is that knowledge is in principle open to anyone, although it does not logically follow from this that knowledge has to be easy to understand. Historical analysis suggests that belief in the possibility of a democratic epistemology is scarcer now than it was in the nineteenth century.

We seem, then, to be confronted with another, specifically historical paradox. Societies which have increased educational provision, and encouraged access to education, through the activities of the political state, have at the same time produced an image of knowledge as something difficult of access, the preserve of an élite. Although more people are educated they do not as a result define themselves as possessing a right or a need to know. In the terms of this self-understanding, knowledge is always elsewhere, in the university that I am not in, for example.

Community Knowledge/University Knowledge

The analysis so far has been deliberately one-sided, and I want now to turn to another way of telling the story. To do this I shall elaborate a distinction in educational theory between "educational knowledge" and "common sense knowledge" or what, for the purposes of this chapter, I want to call "community knowledge" and "university knowledge".[7]

Community knowledge can be characterized as fluid, informal and practical, such that a knowledge of something is closely connected with a knowledge of *how to do something*. The people who hold this knowledge do not often recognize it as being worthy of the name (this indicates a more general problem about the way that the knowledge that is embodied in a skill is often not recognized as such). Where questions of accreditation or qualification arise they have to do with success or failure in acquiring a particular skill, not with defining somebody as intelligent or not. It would fit nicely with this description if community knowledge was defined both by its accessibility and by its character as a shared rather than an exclusive property. In practice the picture is not quite so simple. Community knowledge is cellular in character: a multiplicity of overlapping expertises, sometimes strongly bounded, sometimes not, constantly shifting into new configurations as well as having that traditional character which is designated as "common sense". Thus community knowledge might be exemplified at one point by the knowledge of a housewife, at another by apprenticeship into craft skills, and at another by the form of a work-place culture which enable people to learn how to work in a particular environment. Then we need to distinguish another form, which might itself be a cell within community knowledge or something distinct from it: the practice of the intellectual coterie or the avant garde group which defines its importance in part at least, by its distinction from university knowledge.

University knowledge can be defined dialectically as the negation of most of the qualities represented by community knowledge. It is formally maintained, demarcated into faculties and domains each with its own requirements of entry. It promotes a special consciousness of itself as a knowledge-bearing institution, set apart from others by its privileged relation to knowledge. Its system of qualifications indicates not just whether a particular person possess a certain kind of skill or not (indeed it may be definitional of a university education that you learn no skills from it), but whether they are "intelligent" or not. This power is part of the mystique of the university; the power, that is, to judge the quality of a person by their degree. What social utility this process serves is not altogether clear, unless it has to do with that exclusiveness which is an important feature both of university knowledge and those who possess it. Then the equation of qualification with quality of person becomes an index of a potential to join a social élite.

The distinction between university knowledge and community knowledge is crudely sketched here because my main purpose is to draw attention to the fact of a distinction between the two, and to the boundary that has built up around the distinction. My contention is that the interactions across this boundary are an important consideration for any group concerned with thinking about the future of universities. This is so for at least two reasons. Firstly, innovation in universities has occurred historically through the appropriation by universities of forms of community knowledge. Various subjects now taught in universities had a lengthy if differently recognized existence before they became established parts of the university curriculum. In the humanities, literary criticism, art history and drama would all be cases in point: in the sciences, engineering and geology are specific examples, but there are general themes in the history of science which are relevant here, such as the importance of technological change to the development of experimental method.[8] In each case what we find is the development of a subject, or method, or practice outside the university which is then taken in and, in some cases, taken over by it. I suspect that, historically, there are fluctuations in the intensity of the interaction across the boundary between university knowledge and community knowledge. I am also proposing a hypothesis which cannot be explored here: that periods of intellectual innovation in universities are systematically related to the intensity of negotiation across the boundary between the two kinds of knowledge. Put more simply universities, despite appearances to the contrary, have often without wanting to avow the fact, depended on outside sources for their own intellectual innovation.

But the boundary between university and community knowledge is also a site of transformation. What the university takes over it also changes. We might think of this, initially, as a process where value is both added to and subtracted from the kinds of knowledge that make this transition from one realm to another. At its most obvious, knowledge in the university gains a kind of prestige, but it often does this by becoming useless. A particular kind of embeddedness in a practical or professional application is lost or diminished, as knowledge becomes "pure" or "disinterested". But, of course, there is a powerful presumption that the knowledge that is "pure" or "disinterested" is itself more valuable than the knowledge that is not. A variety of popular stereotypes and narratives help to sustain this presumption, sometimes by parodying it: the "absent-minded professor" for example, is a paradoxical conception in so far as the professor's pursuit of "things of the mind", "pure" "disinterested" knowledge, produces a loss-of-mind when it comes to practical skills, living in the world. The more you have of mind at one level the less you have at another. On the other hand, the popular stereotypes of the professor finds its counter in the professor's stereotype of the popular: the "ignorant" or "mindless" masses, incapable of reason. These stereotypes occasion both fascination, suspicion and laughter but they rarely call into question the distinctions that made them possible in the first place.

We can trace the emergence of these distinctions historically. They go back at least as far as a deeply influential taxonomy proposed by Aristotle. In *The Politics*, for example, Aristotle discusses with what may now seem a brutal explicitness, the qualifications necessary for a man (the gender emphasis is intended) to become a citizen. Artisans and "mechanics" are excluded from the necessary qualifications on a number of grounds. Their work confines them to a particular activity, and to the interested promotion of that activity, so that if they were allowed access to the government of the state, their judgment would be swayed by the need to promote that interest. Their work confines the range of their experience, and therefore forbids them from acquiring that range of experiences which can become a basis for a knowledge of society as a whole. Because they work on one kind of thing, because they are immersed in the production of material objects, they do not develop the capacity for rational abstraction, the knowledge of kinds and classes as well as particular instances, which is necessary to a comprehensive or "disinterested" view of the social good. Only with this capacity for reason, Aristotle argues, can a person take part in the government of society.[9]

Although much has changed since Aristotle formulated his arguments, I do not think they are simply archaic. Aristotle does not, of course, claim that "disinterested" knowledge is useless. In fact his argument makes valuably explicit what is often hidden: the link between the claim to possess rationality and the right to govern. The distinction that he makes between the interested and particular knowledge of the "mechanic" and the comprehensive and "disinterested" knowledge of the free man is both repeated and transformed in subsequent philosophical and cultural arguments: in the Kantian claim, for example, that the highest knowledge of an object comes when it is perceived from a point beyond appetite or interest; or in Matthew Arnold's argument for the value of culture as a means of enabling its possessor to "see things steadily and see them whole". As the context of the arguments in Arnold's *Culture and Anarchy* makes clear this means seeing things outside the interests imposed by membership of a particular social class or political party. What replaces those interests and affiliation, in Arnold's argument, is the "disinterested" allegiance to culture, and he looks to the university as the place where this allegiance can be promoted.

This history of attitudes to knowledge still conditions the culture of universities today. What it means to know is intimately linked to the image elaborated by this history of the person who can know. Knowledge is intimate with power, if only because the knowledge that is thought to be most valuable ("pure", "disinterested", "objective") turns out to be what the powerful know. The culture of the university plays an important role in both sustaining and producing the equation. It confirms existing alliances between power and knowledge, and negotiates new alliances, not least through its capacity to include or exclude certain kinds of knowledge and certain kinds of people. But these powers of recognition and accreditation are not necessarily exercised with confidence. On the one hand there is the traditional image of the university at the apex of institutions of knowledge. On the other hand the university can fall in love with its traditional image and lose its capacity for response and innovation. This danger seems particularly acute at times when knowledge is undergoing revolutionary change.

The hierarchy of knowledge defined by Aristotle and many others has another quite specific effect. It defines the knowledge that is most valuable as the knowledge that is distinct from the manual skills of the artisan or "mechanic". Another boundary and another history come in to view. It would certainly be quite wrong to suggest that what lies on one or the other side of the boundary between the mindful knowledge and manual skill is rigidly fixed.[10] But it is a distinction that gets endlessly replayed, and in such a way that the kinds of knowledge that are embodied in many manual and physical activities occupy a low place in the hierarchy of knowledge. They are, as the vocabulary of this chapter suggests, given the lesser title of a skill. This distinction has, of course, shaped the culture of the university so that the introduction within it of a form of knowledge that is directly connected with a manual or physical skill, and with its accompanying technology, is initially perceived as a pollution of the "pure" activity of mind.[11] The technologies that make knowledge operational within the world are felt to threaten the contemplative and reflective stance of the "pure" reasoner. This perception is sustained by a particular image of technology which places it on the side of manual or physical activity. Technologies either replace or enhance forms of physical labour. But it is unlikely that this image can any longer be sustained given the existence of computer technologies which, however crudely, simulate mental activities. We are still at an early stage in understanding the cultural effects and possibilities of this technology, but, as with other, earlier technologies, it may well have consequences for our image of the activity of knowing, not least in the challenge that it offers to the view, powerfully at work in the culture of the humanities, that the knowledge which is most valuable is the knowledge that rises above the technological or mechanical [12].

Work/Leisure

Aristotle assumed that the exercise of reason appropriate to the free citizen required leisure as one of its conditions. The participants in Plato's *Symposium* are members of a leisured élite: Socrates' account of ideal forms occurs in an interlude between one bout of drinking and another. Hence, perhaps, one powerful assumption about philosophical speculation, that it occurs at a remove from the experience of labour, that the world of getting and spending is inimical to the leisurely unfolding of philosophical discourse and the knowledge that it brings.

The connection between philosophy and leisure has persisted, at once a curse and a privilege to philosophers. But the connection is not confined to philosophy alone. It extends to many other subjects that are grouped under the humanities heading. Reading books, watching films or plays, looking at paintings are, and have been for some long time, classified as the activities we engage in when we are at leisure. Once these activities become subjects in schools and universities they are re-classified as work, and subject to the demands that are felt to be appropriate to work. But the suspicion and embarrassment remains that to engage in the study of these subjects is to remove oneself from the world of "real" work. Recently the suspicion has taken on the character of a stark accusation: students of the humanities disqualify themselves for the working life that comes after their education.

The history of scientific research does not indicate so obvious a divorce from the world of work: the workshop can and has been the site of scientific experiment. This finds its complement in an idea that scientific education is felt to be better preparation for working life. Science assumes a purposive rationality. It is concerned with explanation, problem-solving, achieving measurable results. It calls for team-work and the subordination of the individual to a collective purpose, as distinct from the narcissistic and indulgent individualism associated with the humanities; hence the presumption of a closer fit between scientific education and the working world. But the picture here is by no means stable. If scientific education is more closely associated with working life than education in the humanities, it is also the case that both scientific and humanist education fall under another suspicion. As intellectual work in universities becomes both more specialized and more professionalized the education afforded to students increasingly becomes a means of entry into the particular specialism defined by their subject. Academic literary critics educate their students to become academic literary critics; research biologists educate theirs to become biological researchers. Within this atmosphere serious thinking about the relation between advanced education and work is pushed to the margins.

These histories and ideas are at the base of some of the stereotypes which condition thinking about the relation between the two cultures within the university and the culture of working life that exists outside it. They are implicit in the antagonism that exists in this country between government and industry on one side and the universities on the other. They are also seriously disabling to any thinking about the future of universities. My contention is that we have reached a point where a legacy of attitudes towards the humanities, the sciences and the world of work is in danger of stifling growth and of ignoring the possibilities for a for a more creative practice.

We could begin to change the current order of the two cultures by thinking about the humanities more practically and the sciences more aesthetically. One consequence of the separation between the two cultures is the view that the humanities are concerned with the cultivation of individual subjectivity, whether through access to a cultural tradition or through acts of expression which enable individuals to realize themselves, to know who they are in expressing what they are. Whatever the value of this way of thinking one problem that confronts it is what to do with this individual cultivation once it has been achieved. There is a difficulty about translating it into a realm other than the one of its initial realization. Aesthetic cultivation turns in to a sweet trap, confining the individuals who find self-realization in art to a realm which is by definition opposed to the alienating worlds of work and everyday life. But some recent historical and theoretical work offers a difference account which gives a more pragmatic and collective definition of some recurrent concerns in the humanities. Narrative, for example, is seen as a form of problem-solving which pervades social life. Or works of art can be understood as ways of encoding kinds of information, necessary for our survival, which cannot be registered by scientific axioms or mathematical symbols.[13]

On the side of the sciences, we need to pay more serious attention to what some of the best scientists and philosophers of science have been telling us for some time. The claim of science to afford a true knowledge of the world is not simply refuted by accepting that those truths are partial and incomplete. Whatever we may desire as an image of scientific knowledge, it no longer provides us with the basis for an evolving mastery of the world as more of the world is scientifically known. What we now recognize through science is inexhaustible complexity, a form of knowledge without end, delivering a sense of the world which cannot be finally controlled either intellectually or technologically. We know too that scientific discoveries are not necessarily the result of a rigorous pursuit of method. They call upon intuition, play, a feeling for harmony and form. Good science is not necessarily the science that accords with the established rules for scientific enquiry. We simply would not know what we now know if science had been as methodical and rule-bound a form as its public image can suggest.

To recognize the pragmatism of the humanities and the aesthetics of science has implications for an understanding of their educational value, and then for the relation between education and working life. If, that is, we bring the two cultures closer together we are in a better position to see what they have in common and where they diverge. What they share is a capacity for problem-solving. An education in either or both of the two cultures could be an education in the history and the practice of problem-solving. That means knowing how problems have been recognized and how and why they have been solved, fudged or simply disregarded. It also means recognizing the paradoxical dimension to problem-solving, as the philosopher and scientist, Michael Polanyi, has pointed out:

... To see a problem that will lead to a great discovery is not just to see something hidden, but to see something of which the rest of humanity cannot even have an inkling. All this is commonplace; we take it for granted without noticing the clash of self-contradiction entailed in it. Yet Plato has pointed out this contradiction in the *Meno* . He says that to search for the solution of a problem is an absurdity; for either you know what you are looking for, and then there is no problem; or you do not know what you are looking for, and then you cannot expect to find anything."[14]

Plato, as Polanyi reminds us, came up with an implausible solution to this paradox: new knowledge was a form of remembering. When we discovered something new that we were in fact doing was remembering something from a previous incarnation. What Polanyi learns from the *Meno* is a different lesson, which does not require any commitment to a belief in the transmigration of souls:

... For the *Meno* shows conclusively that if all knowledge is explicit, i.e. capable of being clearly stated, then we cannot know a problem or look for its solution. And the *Meno* also shows, therefore, that if problems nevertheless exist and discoveries can be made by solving them, we can know things, and important things, that we cannot tell.[15]

The point of this detour into the paradoxical logic of discovery is to point out that problem-solving is not a skill that can be learnt in isolation from the historical and philosophical context which is its necessary condition. Nor, as Polanyi's argument makes abundantly clear, is it a skill that can be taught by learning a set of rules which provide explicit guidance on how to recognize and solve problems.[16] It does call for something that we clumsily call creativity, a confidence that the initial sense of a problem, however ill-defined, is nonetheless real and that we do not immediately have to reach for a book of rules in order to find a solution.

My concern with problem-solving connects with the current obsession with "transferable skills". In English this phrase has taken on the quality of a talisman. Once university teachers, both in the humanities and sciences have drawn the attention of their students to the skills of report-writing, public speaking, numeracy and team-work that they pick up in the course of their academic study, then the gulf between the world of work and of education will be bridged. The value of the idea of "transferable skills" is that it may help to remind students of the different things they might learn by being at a university. Its limitation is that, in trying to close one gap, it opens up another, between the knowledge of a subject and skills acquired in the process of learning it. Thus a student may transfer the skills she has learnt about preparing reports as a result of giving a seminar paper on *King Lear*. But what she knows about *King Lear* is not so readily transferable.

What I have called problem-solving is an attempt to mediate between skill and knowledge. The person who has the confidence to identify and solve problems is somebody with a valuable capacity for working life. This confidence can be gained through work in the humanities and the sciences as long as that work is embedded in a context which combines practice with historical and theoretical enquiry. A knowledge of how problems have been solved or evaded in the past can contribute to a capacity to solve problems in the present. Whether employers want this capacity is, of course, another question and one that cannot be dealt with in the chapter. It raises the problem of whether what employers say they want is the same as what they need. It points to a major issue about the world of work which helps to promote the current divisions between education and working life: the fact that, too often, working life is segregated from opportunities to relax, to learn, to reflect and to do research.[17]

Utopias

Despite some rhetoric to the contrary, the existence of two cultures is not a global disaster. It is insignificant by comparison with the threat of ecological catastrophe or the divisions between rich and poor. It may be that our capacity to engage with the problems that currently confront us is seriously compromised by the splitting of intellectual life into the sciences and the humanities. What is more certain, I think, is that the persistence of the two cultures has serious effects upon the capacity of universities to take the initiative in debates about their role, purpose and future. This is so for a number of reasons. It leads universities to underestimate the new kinds of knowledge that can be discovered at points of overlap, intersection or confrontation between the two cultures.[18] Politically, it provides the current opponents of universities with a gift: an institution divided by ignorance, suspicion, and battles over the allocation of resources. Educationally, it promotes a tendency to turn students away from knowledge by constantly reminding them of all they do not know rather than encouraging them to find out everything they might know.

In drawing out from the chapter some proposals about what might be done, I am going to make the dangerous assumption that something might be worth doing. It is a dangerous assumption because any proposals for change are likely to seem frivolous when they confront what is also expressed through the two cultures: the entrenchment of intellectual life into segregated professions which divide physicists from sociologists, historians from biologists, philosophers from engineers. There are, however, some signs that this segregation is being challenged. The signs are not strong, but they do compose some messages of hope which may be worth developing.

One proposal has to do with a question that seems to be often ignored in educational planning. The question concerns the attitude to knowledge that is likely to be promoted by a particular educational practice. How, that is, are students encouraged to define themselves by engaging in a particular study in a particular way? There are, of course, a number of available identities: the passive recipient of what is defined as knowledge by others, the apprentice, the novice, the subordinate, the terminally bored. My own preference, as will become clear, is for the intellectual opportunist, an identity that seems to be currently in short supply. But, for the moment, I want simply to stress the value of attending to the question. The attitude to knowledge is a significant part of the context in which any innovation in education occurs, and the assessment of the value of innovation needs to analyse the attitude to knowledge it promotes.

If the current divisions between the two cultures inhibit intellectual curiosity and capacities for problem-solving it becomes necessary to develop forms of study which will hold the two cultures in one frame. There are many ways in which this might be done and here I simply want to outline two. We need to develop a history of knowledge as an integral subject, available to students in the humanities and the sciences. There are plenty of resources available to develop the subject, but a great deal of work remains to be done on its design.[19] What I mean by the history of knowledge is neither the history of ideas nor the philosophy of science as currently practised, although both have much to contribute. As its name makes clear the history of knowledge takes knowledge as subject with a history, and one that is marked by mutation and revolution. It tests the hypothesis that there are historically conditioned ways of knowing, that these ways of knowing are affected by the interactions between the arts, technology and the sciences, that the issue of what it means to know is debated and contested in a multiplicity of ways. One value of the subject is that it will open up to its students the recognition that knowledge is historically variable, that what we know and how we know it is never finally resolved, however, many powerful bids are made towards an authoritarian resolution of all questions. The history of knowledge can act as a permission to intellectual curiosity by its criticism of the idea that knowledge is monolithic.

The second subject which would hold the humanities and sciences in a single frame is information theory: the analysis of what makes a message a message, of the processes of encoding and decoding, of the interactions between technology and information. The concept of code extends from the analysis of literary texts to genetic theory. The question of what constitutes a message preoccupies the historian working in an archive and the physicist working in a laboratory. The technological amplification of information is important to both film-makers and astronomers. What information theory could provide is the component of a common language for the exchange of experience and ideas across the boundaries of the two cultures.

Of course neither these nor any other proposals for linking the two cultures in the university environment is going to work if teaching and learning succumb to the already powerful tendencies towards routine and inertia. Paul Feyerabend's account of the history of science provides a valuable example of what might be the case, as well as a warning about how a conception of the subject can promote dullness:

> The history of science, after all, does not just consist of facts and conclusions drawn from facts. It also contains ideas, interpretations of facts, problems created by conflicting interpretations, mistakes and so on. On closer analysis we even find that science knows no 'bare facts' at all but the 'facts' that enter our knowledge are already viewed in a certain way and are, therefore, essentially ideational ... a little brainwashing will go a long way in making the history of science duller, simpler, more uniform, more 'objective' and more easily accessible to treatment by strict and unchangeable rules.
>
> Scientific education as we know it today has precisely this aim. It simplifies 'science' by simplifying its participants: first a domain of research is defined. The domain is separated from the rest of history (physics, for example, is separated from metaphysics and theology) and given a 'logic' of its own. A thorough training in such a 'logic' then conditions those working in the domain: it makes their actions more uniform, and it freezes large parts of the historical process as well.[20]

Feyerabend emphasizes an idea central to this chapter: that intellectual disciplines shape the identity of those who participate in them. His claim is that a current conception of scientific education radically simplifies and limits the identity (and the capacity to know) of those who are subject to it.

Roland Barthes provides a valuable example of what it might mean to be different:

> I went to a scientist's lecture on the problems of cellular biology. I was fascinated by his scientific language – euphoric for me precisely to the degree that I had no resistance to offer. I did not resist but I distorted: as the speaker went on talking, I filtered out and grabbed hold of what, in such utterance, could make metaphors and, thenceforth, concern me ... I came up with this undoubtedly familiar notion but one whose scientific vulgarizations – however abundant in the press – never expand: that the main problem of modern epistemology is complexity. Whether in science, in economics, in linguistics, in sociology, the present task is less to be sure of main principles than to be able to describe imbrications, relays, returns, additions, exceptions, paradoxes, ruses: a task which very quickly becomes a combative one, since it comes to grips with a henceforth reactionary force: reduction. [21]

Barthes acts here as an intellectual opportunist. He discovers a stance towards knowledge which most current educational practice discourages. He listens to the scientist's lecture as an "outsider", a literary and cultural critic, not a specialist in cellular biology. But instead of being intimidated by what is outside his speciality, Barthes finds it fascinating and seductive. He invents a language in response to the language that he hears and as a result he makes discovery for himself about modern epistomology, a discovery, moreover, which links subject ordinarily divided by the two cultures. The passage is interesting because it gives a rich description of an act of learning: what risks are involved (not running away from what is strange); what inventiveness is called for (filtering out and grabbing, making metaphors); what discovery results from risk and invention (the complexity of modern knowledge). But what this also involves is a falling away from a certain account of intellectual authority. Barthes abandons the security of main principles as the guarantee of knowledge and replace it with an image of knowledge that is at once tentative and no longer co-ordinated by a single discipline. Instead what is sought as knowledge is, amongst other things, "imbrications": the point where one form of knowledge overlaps with another.

A common-sense critic might find Barthes's act of learning little more than a self-indulgence. What, after all, has Barthes learnt about cellular biology as a result of attending the lecture? Certainly there does not seem to be any direct evidence in this piece of writing about learning anything about a specific subject. Viewed this way, his discovery about complexity might simply be a way of disguising the fact that he has learnt nothing, wasted an hour of his time. He might have made the same discovery without attending the lecture at all.

But these objections may simply miss the point. Bathes does not attend a lecture about cellular biology but about its problems. The subject is identified for him in those terms, and in the terms of a strange language which stimulates invention. As a result he learns something about cellular biology by discovering a relevant context for its language and because he has done this, we could argue that he is in a better position to learn more of the detail of the subject. What we mean by learning here is the capacity to tolerate a difficult language in a way that produces a hypothesis useful to the learner (the world makes more sense after the hypothesis has been produced). This, of course, is not the same thing as becoming the master of a subject like cellular biology.

My proposals, then, are for an alertness to the attitude towards knowledge implied by the ordering of an intellectual discipline, for the development of new subjects such as the history of knowledge and information theory, for encouraging people to be intellectual opportunists who are able to experiment with a variety of difficult languages. If these proposals are to have any effect within the university itself another change is needed: a revision in the metaphor of the university, and, therefore, in the attitudes which shape its use. Instead of thinking about universities as "ivory towers" or as separated and competing faculties, or as "two cultures", I suggest the metaphor of the university as encyclopaedia. This deliberately invokes the precedent of the eighteenth century Encyclopaedists and would certainly want to renew those aspects of their project which have to do with taking knowledge out into the world, and finding a form which would make it more widely available. But the metaphor invokes more than a historical precedent. It is also intended to indicate those dictionary meanings of encyclopaedia which have to do with "the whole circle of learning", those meanings which counter the assumption that valuable knowledge is specialist knowledge. As metaphor, the encyclopaedia does not indicate a set of books on a shelf but an environment and an institution where knowledge is conceived as the "play of interferences and interreferences, where knowledge is not thought of in terms of order and mastery, but in terms of chance and invention".[22] The technological basis for this new encyclopaedia would be the computer as an instrument capable of providing an arbitrary, flexible system of classification which would offer large-scale access to the knowledge base of the encyclopaedia. It would also permit the rapid up dating of what the encyclopaedia can hold. Another opportunity the university-as-encyclopaedia provides is that those who have access to it can be both users and contributors. There would be a more rapid exchange of roles between teacher and student, reader and writer, than is currently the case. The new encyclopaedia would develop the potential of is eighteenth century forbear as an exercise in group thinking, for making the kinds of intellectual connection that are beyond the solitary mind. It would be a focus for information, debate and reflection. A utopian speculation, of course, except that this utopia is already happening: the question is whether universities are prepared to go against many of the prevailing intellectual and managerial orthodoxies, to risk a radical reorganization of their existing structures, in order to help make the utopia a somewhere.

Notes

An earlier version of this paper was given in the form of a talk to a group of Swedish colleagues visiting the University of East Anglia as part of a study visit, organized by the Swedish University Board, on the question of the two cultures. The thoughtful and generous response given on that occasion has led to a number of revisions in the current form of the paper.

1 For the text of C.P. Snow's lecture see Snow, CP (1960) *The two cultures and the scientific revolution*. Cambridge University Press, Cambridge

2 Leavis, FR (1962) *Two cultures? The significance of* C. *P.Snow*. Chatto & Windus, London, p 29.

3 *Ibid*, p 27

4 For some of the history here see Eastlea, B (1981) *Science and sexual oppression*. Weidenfeld and Nicolson, London.

5 For the figure of the sovereign see Foucault, M (1979) *Discipline and punish* (transl Alan Sheridan). Penguin Books, Harmondsworth.

6 See Barrow, Logie (1986) *Independent spirits: spiritualism and English plebians*. Routledge & Kegan Paul, London.

7 For one formulation of the distinction see Bernstein, B (1971) *Class codes and control*. Routledge & Kegan Paul, London, especially chap 11.

8 For some detail here see the account of the development of geology in Porter, Roy (1978) Gentlemen and geology: the emergence of a scientific career, 1660–1920. *Historical Journal* 21: 809–836.

9 I am indebted to John Barrell's analysis in his *The political theory of painting from Reynolds to Hazlitt*. Yale University Press, New Haven and London, 1986.

10 For the debate about whether painting was a mental or manual skill see, amongst other discussion, John Barrell, *op cit*.

11 The history of engineering as a university discipline would be a relevant example here.

12 For some of the history here see Williams, Raymond (1958) *Culture and society*. Chatto & Windus, London.

13 See some of the work by Kenneth Burke, Frederic Jameson and J.-F. Lyotard for examples of pragmatic thinking about the humanities and the problem-solving functions of art.

14 Polanyi, M (1983) *The tacit dimension*. Peter Smith, Gloucester, MA, p 22. My quotation here is not intended to endorse Polanyi's implied notion of solitary genius, distinct from an ignorant "rest of humanity".

15 Polanyi, *op cit*, p 22.

16 *Ibid*, p 23.

17 My thanks to Julian Hilton for pointing out this problem.

18 For a detailed example see Pickering, C (1985) *Constructing quarks*. Chicago.

19 Some of the resources can be found in the work of Foucault, Serres, Skinner, Toulmin, Wilden and Bateson.

20 Feyerabend, P (1975) *Against method*. Verso Press, London, p 19.

21 For an English translation of Barthes's brief essay see Barthes, R Complexity. In: Blonsky, M (ed) *On signs*. Blackwell, Oxford.

22 The quotation comes from the introduction by J. V Harari and D. F. Bell to a selection a Michel Serres's writings, *Hermes: literature, science, philosophy*. John Hopkins University Press, Baltimore and London, 1982, p xxix.

Chapter 23

On From "The Two Cultures"

Stephen Toulmin

How do we establish cross links between the cultures of science and the humanities in the world of learning and the professions? Why did the "Two Cultures" division, as identified by C.P. Snow in his Rede Lecture, play an unusually large part in English society? Why is English higher education unusually elitist and exclusive? The chapter argues that European culture had *two* separate and distinct origins, and our two sets of contemporary disciplines (humanistic and scientific) derive from, and look back to either the sixteenth century Renaissance Humanists or the seventeenth century Natural Philosophers. Today, however, with all of industry and engineering open to environmental criticism and control, and all of medicine to a parallel critique in ethical terms, humanist and scientific disciplines will start to enjoy equal status. Matters of theory can no longer be wholly self-justifying. Theoretical explanations and concepts (*episteme*) will increasingly be exposed to a wider analysis, in terms of their general practical efficacy (*techne*) and the prudence (*phronesis*) of putting them to use in particular real life situations. It is one task of the Diderot Project to characterize the confluence, or union, of the two branches of Modern European culture, the "reasonable" Humanities and the "rational" Sciences. The author questions the viability of pursuing the "Encyclopaedia" project within the context of the university, as advocated in the preceding chapter. It is suggested that the greatest power of the Encyclopaedia might lie in its ability to work *outside* specific academic institutions, its potential to form "invisible" patterns of learning by means of electronic information networks. An Encyclopaedia for the third millennium, the chapter concludes, may well become a major intellectual force, but only if it circumvents the orthodox academic world, instead of trying to work within it.

The aims of the Diderot Project require us to face the issues stated but unresolved in C.P. Snow's Rede Lecture on "The Two Cultures"; about the cultural division in the English (and, though to a lesser extent, the international) world of learning and the professions, between people who think in literary or humanistic categories but find mathematics hard to handle, and people who think in mathematical or scientific terms but find the concepts of the humanities intangible, even suspect. Initially, Snow's argument was a comment on the English social system, which leaves less room than other European societies for technically skilled professionals to occupy positions of influence in government and higher administration. But, more recently, his thesis has been broadened, and has been widely interpreted as making a contribution to the philosophy of culture more generally.

How did this happen? Certainly, in the more general form, Snow's argument does not lack force or examples: It is not hard to recognize paradigmatic bodies of thought that fall more or less neatly on one side of the supposed cultural division or another. Snow may have wished that all members of the intellectual élite in England could discuss John Donne and DNA with equal facility; but even today, in most countries, those scholars, thinkers and writers who have a real grasp of (say) molecular biology or thermodynamics tend to be less well informed about poetics or moral philosophy, and those who are expert in literary theory tremble at the sight of a differential equation. The internal connections among humanistic disciplines make it comparatively easy for an historian to exchange ideas with a philosopher or poet, and the internal connections among the exact sciences make it comparatively easy for physicists to cross over into cell biology or statistics, but the cross links between these two internally connected sets of fields are harder to establish and maintain. Why should this be so? And how can we cultivate the common ground at the intersection of these cultural territories? Denis Diderot's example allows us to frame and explore such questions as these in new and fruitful ways.

Let me begin by placing the Two Cultures debate into its historical context. Taken in its broader sense, the division to which Snow draws attention is, indeed, older than the social facts about English life in the twentieth century on which he specially focused, and I shall have to return later to the question of why England above all gave vivid social expression to this deeper cultural division. My first argument is that behind the current social division lies a salient historical fact: European culture had *two* separate and distinct origins, not just *one*, and our two sets of contemporary disciplines (humanistic and scientific) derive from, and look back to, one or the other of those twin beginnings. To go beyond the division of the cultures, therefore, we must first try to understand why the Natural Sciences and the Humanities had independent births: only with the answer to that question in mind can we see clearly what will be involved in bringing the two sides back together, and creating conditions for their collaboration.

The first foundations of cultural modernity were laid around 1500, and solidified in the course of the sixteenth century: the second were the products of intellectual changes that began around 1620–30, and were solidly established only after 1648. The sixteenth century Renaissance Humanists focused on questions about the *goals* of human life in the modern world: they took their stimulus from the literature of classical antiquity, and reinterpreted it in relation to new modes of life emerging in their own times. From Gutenberg and Erasmus, by way of Michelangelo and Rabelais, to Montaigne and Shakespeare – or even that transitional figure, Francis Bacon – the Humanists taught Europe what it was to live, to act, and to feel, in ways appropriate to *reasonable* human beings. By contrast, the seventeenth century Natural Philosophers developed the intellectual *techniques* typical of the modern world, and generated the abstract theories (many, though not all, of which were mathematical theories) that were to become the eventual foundations of twentieth century science and technology. From Galileo and Descartes, by way of Pascal and Hobbes, to Laplace and Kant, these "New Philosophers" thus taught Europe what it was to reflect, to explain, and to argue, in terms appropriate to *rational* thinkers.

For the next 250 years, unfortunately, these two cultural programmes – the cultivation of the "reasonable", and the pursuit of the "rational" – were seen as in competition for the loyalty of European thought. From the "scientific revolution" on, Francis Bacon and Isaac Newton were the twin icons of modern science: Bacon with his practical vision of science in the service of human welfare, Newton with his religious vision of a physics that testified to the Wisdom of God the Creator. But, after 1690, Bacon took second place to Newton. The dynamics of Newton's *Principia* was initially valued, less for technological reasons, than as a rational underpinning for the respectable eighteenth century world view. (Nahum Tate, in the libretto for Haydn's *Creation*, put it clearly: "The Heavens declare the Glory of God: the Firmament itself shows forth His Handiwork.") The icon of Isaac Newton was thus elevated above that of Francis Bacon; and from 1690 on, in England above all, European intellectuals, with very few exceptions – Goethe is the most obvious one – were more anxious to *think rationally* than to *act reasonably*, more anxious to believe correct truths than to perform right acts. From then on, the claims of Rationality were valued above those of Reasonableness.

In the twentieth century, we have reaped the fruits of this change, good and ill. On the one hand, as Bacon foresaw, the theoretical work of the Natural Sciences has at last borne practical fruit: in agricultural chemistry to begin with, later in electricity, medicine and electronics. However we view the exaggerated claims on behalf of formal rationality that were made in the meanwhile, it would by now be churlish to deny the (often mixed) blessings that those novel techniques have brought us. In human affairs, on the other hand, most notably in social and political analysis, the overvaluation of "rational" techniques at the expense of "reasonable" goals has led to deep failures. The Communist Party of the Soviet Union (though not yet that of China) is now finally admitting the weakness of approaching the tasks of government in ways that are purely theoretical and doctrinal. Even in the physical and biological sciences, as is now apparent, the best of theories is incomplete, so long as the nature of its human fruits has not been analysed and understood.

In the industrial world, for instance, the public attitude to major technological projects has been transformed over the last twenty years. As recently as 1960, the US Army Corps of Engineers could still plan vast dams and canals, confident of going ahead with their construction on the evidence of their technical merits alone; and in clinical medicine a handful of theologians alone had begun to call for more discriminating use of new technological procedures and machines. Yet, by now, all of industry and engineering is open to environmental criticism and control; and all of medicine is open to a parallel critique in ethical terms. Nor will this change be easily reversed. On the contrary, as the population of the world continues to grow, and the poorer nations raise their level of consumption, we shall become more, not less, aware of the human limits to the practical application of new scientific ideas.

In these respects among others, we are changing our vision of what it is to be *intelligent*, and of what an *intellectual* can be, or should be. From now on, Francis Bacon will no longer play second fiddle to Isaac Newton, but will share the top billing with him. Matters of theory can no longer be wholly self justifying. Theoretical explanations and concepts (*episteme*) will increasingly be exposed to a wider analysis, in terms of their general practical efficacy (*techne*) and the prudence (*phronesis*) of putting them to use in particular real life situations. As a result, we are obliged to retrace our steps, go behind the "rational" changes associated with the seventeenth century scientific revolution, and win back for our time the "reasonableness" of the sixteenth century humanists.

From this point on, it will at last be important for us to *believe* the right and rational thing, only if this helps us to *act* in a reasonable way. The earlier idolization of technology can be avoided, if rational minded engineers, doctors and industrialists accept a responsibility to recognize and respect the reasonable wishes of those fellow human beings whose lives are most directly affected by the technologies that they employ. To the extent that they can do so, the two branches of modern European culture, the "reasonable" Humanities and the "rational" Sciences, will be more and more directed toward that confluence, or union, which it is one task of the Diderot Project to characterize.

At this point, let me turn and discuss Jon Cook's commentary on the Two Cultures. He recognizes both the special relevance of Snow's thesis to England, and the stodginess and exclusiveness of the English system of higher education, as contrasted with (say) the Danish Folk High Schools and the Swedish Center for Working Life. Nevertheless, he speaks of the "Encyclopaedia" project as something to be pursued within the context of the university, and seeks to define a strategy which might transform the English academic world (so to say) *from within*.

I agree with many things in his account, but I am sceptical about his strategy. To explain why, let me return to the questions that I deferred: viz., Why did the "Two Cultures" division play an unusually large part in English society? and Why is English higher education unusually élitist and exclusive? The crucial point to recognize is the close relationship between the collapse of the Commonwealth in 1660, and the balance of political power in 1688, at the time of that "Glorious Revolution" which bloodlessly placed on the throne first the House of Orange, in the person of William III and his English wife, Mary, and later the House of Hanover, which has reigned in England since the early eighteenth century.

The Restoration in 1660 of the Stuart Kings, Charles II and James II, repudiated the democratic ideals, and the lower class political power of Cromwell's Commonwealth years. From then on, the political and social battle in England was one between rival parties in an educated oligarchy, which agreed only to suppress the proletarian culture and nonconformist religion of the Commonwealth. The attempt by the later Stuart Kings to return England to Catholicism, and develop an alliance with the Bourbons in France, was anathema to the English after 1685, with the Revocation of the Edict of Nantes, and the renewed persecution of the Huguenots. After its frustration in the late 1680s, the British monarchy chose the constitutional, not the absolute route, relying on the support of gentry, merchants and the

Anglican clergy. The core of Anglican Churchmen that took a lead in this alliance were "Newtonians" by persuasion: they used Newton's world picture as a theoretical rationalization of their political and social system, seeing in Newton's *cosmos* an Order of the same kind that they sought to maintain in the British *polis*.

So, in England, the public mind linked the Newtonian world picture to the exclusivity of Oxford and Cambridge universities and the Anglican Church. (Not until the mid nineteenth century could Dissenters study at the "ancient" universities, or run for Parliament.) A Unitarian minister and scientist like Joseph Priestley studied at the Dissenters' Academy at Daventry, and worked in Birmingham, until his open support of the French Revolution exposed him to the attacks of a mercenary mob, and made it prudent for him to emigrate to Pennsylvania. In France, the eighteenth century situation was different. There, Newton's world picture was picked up by Holbach and the other Encyclopaedists as part of a radically emancipatory, *anti*-élitist project, conducted in opposition to the established alliance of the Bourbon Court with the Catholic hierarchy. Far from being linked with the universities, or with the politically conservative and socially exclusive system of universities, the *Encyclopédie* was an instrument for opening access to learning to all who could read; and the unsuccessful struggle of the French Establishment to censor or suppress it shows that its *social* potential was widely recognized. So, far from trying to work through the French universities, the Encyclopaedists circumvented them, and flourished independently, rapidly eclipsing them as an intellectual influence on the larger culture.

"Can a university be an Encyclopaedia?" Can a modern Encyclopaedia, animated by the ambitions of Diderot and d'Alembert, succeed in operating through the Universities, at any rate as these exist in Britain today? This seems to me very dubious. It is the good luck of the Diderot Project to be rooted in Sweden, with a long non-élitist tradition of education, and associated with such para-academic institutions as the Center for Working Life and the Royal Dramatic Theatre. The university expansion of the 1960s and 1970s in Britain was not designed to open learning to the majority of the "lower" classes, but coopted the brightest students into a privileged oligarchy: so seeking to embed a New Encyclopaedia within the British university system runs the same risks that Lech Walesa has seen in Solidarity letting the Communists keep the Interior Ministry in a coalition government.

Maybe the University of East Anglia – based in Norwich, with better lines of communication to Amsterdam and Europe than to London and the English "powers that be" – is isolated enough to protect an Encyclopaedia project from the dead hand of English academia, and its State control. Personally, I would not wholly rely on it. Nor is it clear to me that the highest priority for the Encyclopaedia project is to obtain a suitable *building*. On the contrary, one may inquire whether the greatest power of the Encyclopaedia does not lie in its ability to work *outside* the bricks and mortar of academia, and form an invisible college embodied in electronic communication networks, rather than neoGothic masonry. Like its eighteenth century forerunner, an Encyclopaedia for the third millennium may well become a major intellectual force, only if it circumvents the orthodox academic world, instead of trying to work within it.

Chapter 24

The Metaphor of Caliban in our Technological Culture

Bo Göranzon

The meeting of Prospero and Caliban in *The Tempest* depicts a contrast between the abstract and the practical intellect. Prospero was partly modelled on Giordana Bruno (1548–1600), an Italian philosopher who wanted to create an universal language which contained not only an encyclopaedic knowledge but which also thought for itself. Prospero's knowledge is abstract – based on book learning – whereas Caliban's is practical and therefore essential for Prospero's survival on the island. Prospero and Caliban become dependent upon one another; Prospero struggles for 12 years to realize the ambiguous, intuitive qualities of Caliban in his own character, while Caliban in turn learns Prospero's language and is thereby forced into a new way of thinking. The relationship is thus simultaneously creative and riven with conflict and violence. Knowledge requires that one becomes familiar enough with one's area of skills in order to be able to formulate rules and interpret them. Johan Gottlieb Fichte maintained that the man of learning (and the student) must "come through" concepts, form them from himself and for himself, thereby to arrive at an insight, and develop and form the self. The chapter concludes by citing Hojer, who argues for mastering concepts, rather than being mastered by them, for describing one's system and concepts, rather than submitting to the mentorship of others.

In *The Tempest,* Shakespeare's last drama, the meeting of Prospero and Caliban depicts a contrast between the abstract and the practical intellect. Prospero and Caliban become dependent upon one another. What happens in the exchange between these two characters may be seen as an underlying metaphor for a great many of the clichés we are fed about the so-called information society.

In his writings Witold Gombrowicz becomes engrossed in the conflict between people and what he calls "the form". To him this conflict is both constant and intense, and because he both fears and strives for a link between his "self" and the world around him, his personal attitude towards it is one of apprehensive ambivalence. In his novel, *Ferdudyrke,* he writes that in this world people create one another. He sees people as being dependent on other people, in a constant creative relationship with one another:

> Great discoveries will have to be made, great blows will have to be struck with our poor bare hands against the tough armour plate of form. Unparalleled cunning, great honesty of thought, and intelligence sharpened to a degree, will be required to enable man to escape from his stiff exterior and succeed in better reconciling order with disorder, form with the formless, maturity with eternal and sacred immaturity. In the meantime tell me which you prefer, red peppers or fresh cucumbers?

In Gombrowicz there is a constant struggle around form. Form which is at once perfection and restriction. He is drawn to form, yet at the same time he preaches rejection of it.

This contrast is expressed in the tragi-comic conflict between "maturity" and "immaturity". A "mature" person is someone who has found his form, while an "immature" person is someone who has yet to find his form and, clumsy, forward or shy, attempts to acquire the form he finds in others.

Everything must be regulated, everything must be spelt out, everything must be given explicit form, everything must be made to give utterance, to make a statement, to give a response. In this context, Katarina Frostensson talks about the violence of language. "It is a language that is noticeable by the absence of the Other, the vague, the ambiguous, the shadowy."

Cordelia's dilemma in *King Lear*, "Which of you, shall we say, doth love us most?" is that the question is impossible to answer. One aspect of the meaning of the crisis in the drama is in the realm of the philosophy of language. Shakespeare shows there can be two completely different perceptions of how to use language. King Lear's is an objectivistic view of language – the dream of the precise language developed by Leibniz and which in our time has Bertrand Russell and Noam Chomsky as its foremost advocates. Cordelia's is a subjective view: when faced with her father's question, she falls silent; she no longer exists for him. For Cordelia, silence is an ethical necessity, while for Lear it is nothing more than a threatening denial. "Cordelia's ethical silence" is a main theme of Wittgenstein's works.

Prospero was partly modelled on the Italian philosopher Giordana Bruno (1548–1600). Bruno wanted to create a *clavis magna*, a kind of universal language which contained not only an encyclopaedic knowledge but which also thought for itself.

Shakespeare was inspired by the French author, Montaigne. An English translation of his essays is the only book from Shakespeare's library which has been preserved. Montaigne maintained that one had to learn that values such as right and wrong and good and bad changed as the cultural and historical context changed. The name Caliban would appear to be derived from the word cannibal. One of Montaigne's essays, *On Cannibals*, attempts to demonstrate the application of relativism in an area which was brought to the fore by the great voyages of discovery from the fifteenth century onwards. Montaigne puts his finger on the extreme ethnocentricity shown by the Europeans here, the ready acceptance that European religion and culture would be forced upon the foreign peoples they encountered.

Prospero forced Caliban to be his slave. Caliban is the savage who inherited the island to which Prospero came. Caliban's wide range of practical knowledge makes him indispensable to Prospero, Prospero having developed an abstract intellect based on book learning. The basic conflict in *The Tempest* is Prospero's inner struggle to see the figure of Caliban in his own character. It is the vague, the ambiguous, the shadowy, the intuitive. When we meet Caliban in the play, Prospero has had 12 years of daily confrontation with these shadowy parts of his self.

It may be said that Prospero had spent 12 years as Caliban's apprentice. Without Caliban, Prospero would not have survived. His education, and his assimilation of the darker side, is a protracted and arduous struggle. It is not unusual to have to work for 12 years to acquire this additional knowledge. At the same time it is rather embarrassing for the superior, abstract intellect to be reminded of its dependency on the tangible, the practical.

But Prospero also trained Caliban. He taught him to speak. Then Caliban begins to resist. He says that Prospero stole the island where he was "king". At the beginning of the play he states his view of his captivity:

You taught me language: and my profit on't
Is, I know how to curse. The red plague rid you
For learning me your language!

The language Prospero gave him forced Caliban into a new way of thinking. He finds no associations of his own, and no personal meaning in the words used in his contacts with Prospero. He is in peril of being emptied of his earlier experiences. Together with the Rabelaisian figures of Trinculo the jester and Stefano the drunken butler, Caliban plans an offensive to regain the initiative.

Remember,
First to possess his books; for without them
He's but a sot, as I am, nor has not
One spirit to command: they all do hate him
As rootedly as I. Burn but his books;...

Caliban's plan fails and, his resistance broken, he will "be wise hereafter, And seek for grace".

René Girard, the French literary historian, has written about what he calls mankind's urge to mimic. This urge to imitate is not only creative and essential to all development and all formation of identity, but can also easily be transformed into aggression and violence when the Other, which acts as the imitator's model, has been equalled, thereby becoming a rival and an impediment. The relationship between Prospero and Caliban develops into this kind of conflict.

Hag-seed, hence!
Fetch us in fuel; and be quick, thou'rt best
To answer other business. Shrugg'st thou, malice?
If thou neglect'st or dost unwillingly
What I command, I'll rack thee with old cramps;
Fill all thy bones with aches; make thee roar,
That beasts shall tremble at thy din.

Around the turn of the last century there was a debate at the Royal Institute of Technology in Stockholm on the relationship between theory and practical work in the training of engineers. This debate was documented by Nils

Runeby, Professor of the History of Ideas. In a study called *More Speed. Forwards. On an Engineers World of Conception,* he drew attention to Erik Cederblom, the Professor of Applied Mechanics.

In his writings, Cederblom constantly refers to the theme of the position and tasks of engineers. The preface to his work on steam engines published in 1889 contains arguments of central interest on, among other matters, the necessity of science. Cederblom finds himself called upon to defend a text book which is not merely a crib with tables, but which also explains the underlying principles involved. In Cederblom's opinion it is dangerous for an engineer to apply formulae if he is totally ignorant of their origins. An engineer stands on firmer ground if he is familiar enough with his field to need no other rules than those he can create himself from his own knowledge. This is the first level of knowledge that makes it possible for the engineer to develop for himself the formulae he needs for each particular assignment. Without it he is constantly exposed to the risk of error. The requirement is that one must be familiar enough with an area to be able to formulate rules and interpret them.

The view which Cederblom develops on the future professional knowledge of engineers echoes the tradition of ideas outlined by Nils Runeby in his essay *On the Right of Self-Awareness,* in events which took place a decade before and a decade after the beginning of the eighteenth century.

During this revolutionary period there lived a restless soul called Johan Gottlieb Fichte. His Ideas (and those of Kant) were introduced in Sweden by an equally restless soul called Benjamin Höijer.

The university was responsible not only for the "continued search for truth"; research was also an important task. Fichte developed this idea in his inaugural address as principal at the University of Berlin in 1811, where he says that each epoch should pass on to the next generation the knowledge it has acquired. The students must then assume responsibility for its further development:

Fichte emphasizes that a person is only a man of learning when he has come through the learning of his time and has the ability to form it in his inner mind (ausbilden), otherwise one becomes merely something ambiguous, something in-between.

Fichte maintained that the man of learning (and the student) must "come through" concepts, form them from himself and for himself, thereby to arrive at an insight, and develop and form the self.

Runeby quotes Höjer, who states a variation on this theme. Höjer puts forward arguments for not attempting to tie down language with rules:

"If I can master my concepts, and not be mastered by them, be able to describe my system, to give an account of my concepts – then I am one of the initiated, an adept, a member of the Order of Philosophers, and have no need of the mentorship of others. I master them and the world.

Chapter 25

Leadership and Character, or a Little Touch of Harry

Allan Janik

For Neil O'Keefe

What can we learn from Shakespeare's *Henry V* concerning the nature of leadership in business studies? According to Albert Danielsson, contemporary discussions of leadership tend to view the subject almost exclusively from below – i.e. from the perspective of the led – an attitude which obscures the challenges of leadership, especially in an age of high technology. Leadership must involve guidance through coordination based on trust. Paradoxically, leadership is therefore institutionalized and yet requires individuals in order to institutionalize the requisite confidence in established procedures. Since the maintenance of credibility and trust is essential to leadership, it is argued that leadership cannot be institutionalized without qualities of character. This leads the author to identify elements relevant to the role of character in leadership in Shakespeare's tetralogy, *Richard II, Henry IV Parts 1 and 2, and Henry V.* The tetralogy, it is argued, can be taken as an epic of leadership to the extent that Henry comes to embody the virtues that were so clearly lacking in Richard and his father. His character incorporates the public and the private, the institutional and the personal in a seamless unity. Shakespeare presents us with an ensemble of example and counter-example for distinguishing real leadership from its counterfeits. The chapter contends that literary modes of presentation such as the tetralogy play an important role in showing us how to understand and represent such a nebulous phenomenon as character. The result of an absence of leadership/character qualities may be seen in certain damaging practices of the "post-business" society, such as the hostile take-over.

The idea that Shakespeare's *Henry V* could contain something important for contemporary discussions of the nature of leadership in business studies will doubtless strike many people as either frivolous or bizarre, if not outright absurd; but that on its own should not be allowed to obscure the fact that his tetralogy, Richard II, Henry IV (Parts 1 and 2) and Henry V, elucidates important aspects of the nature of leadership that social scientists neglect at their peril. The maverick business economist, Albert Danielsson,[1] has called attention to the way that contemporary discussions of leadership tend to view the subject almost exclusively from below as it were, i.e. from the perspective of the led. Danielsson goes on to lament this attitude inasmuch as it almost systematically obscures the challenges of leadership, especially in an age of high technology, i.e. in a situation in which individual leaders are not in a position to understand all or even many of the technical aspects of the enterprises they administer. For Danielsson this implies that leadership must be essentially something institutional rather than individual; it must involve guidance through co-ordination based upon trust. This in turn leads to what we might term the Paradox of Leadership: whereas leadership is institutional, it requires individual leaders in order to institutionalize the requisite confidence in established procedures. Here is where I suggest that Shakespeare comes into the picture; for a close scrutiny of his account of the development of *Henry V* reveals a profound confrontation with several of the most vexing problems relating to the institutionalization of leadership from a perspective that we are unaccustomed to assuming in our discussions but is nevertheless indispensable to understanding the phenomenon: the notion that leadership is essentially a matter of character as it forms the basis for institutionalizing confidence. In Shakespeare's work, naturally enough, the vocabulary in which this is expressed is hardly that of twentieth century business administration; for the keywords in this discussion are scarcely ones that come to our lips easily: majesty, honour, glory and responsibility. In short, Shakespeare's discussion of leadership emphasizes a number of notions that we are inclined to omit. However, this is hardly accidental nor is it a matter of mere oversight. Since Max Weber we are accustomed to think of any form of leadership incorporating image-building in a systematic way as mere propaganda, i.e., as charismatic, rather than as genuinely majestic, which is to say as sexual and irrational rather than ethical and rational.[2] Doubtless the twentieth century's experience with totalitarian propaganda machines has rightly contributed to our neglect of the majestic side of leadership; yet, our justified weariness with charismatic leaders should not be allowed to obscure the ways in which character can – and, I submit, does – function as a principle of leadership. We need "a little touch of Harry" to remind us of a dimension of leadership with which Shakespeare was well-acquainted but which we have sadly neglected. However, I must emphasize from the start that this is not an exercise in nostalgia. It would be absurd and anachronistic to want to set the clock back 400 years. What is anything but absurd or anachronistic is to insist that leadership cannot be institutionalized without character, so essential is building credibility and trust to it.

A brief summary of these elements in the tetralogy which are most relevant to the problem at leadership will serve as a helpful reminder to the reader. I offer it with the caveat that a summary of a literary work can never be taken to have anything like the value of the original: the distinguishing characteristic of the literary work, its form, will always be lacking. So the following should by no means be construed as exempting the reader from an encounter with Shakespeare's four plays. Although they are thematically related, it must be emphasized that they are independent as works of art but must be considered together for the "contrapuntal" way in which they handle our theme.

Richard II forms the prelude to the story of *Henry V*. It relates with magnificent lyricism the story of how Richard's vanity and, above all, poor judgment brings down the wrath of his cousin, Henry Bolingbroke, Duke of Hereford, upon him ultimately causing his deposition and death. In part 1 of Henry IV we are introduced to Henry V as the rambustious young Prince Hal (who significantly, immediately tells us that we should not take this side of him as seriously as we might, for he is but biding his time) carousing in the company of the irrepressible hedonist and irresponsible braggart, Falstaff, and his coterie. Those who had rebelled with Bolingbroke against Richard, the party around Harry Percy, Earl of Northumberland, have now themselves fallen out with their new King Henry IV. The conflict between the erstwhile conspirators forms the backdrop for the coming of age of Prince Hal, in battle with the son of his father's enemy, Hotspur. Hal's defeat of Hotspur is the first direct sign that he is not the wastrel that he appears to be but a man of strength. Part 2 of *Henry IV* presents the dying king tormented by memories of the wrongs that he inflicted upon Richard. Hal, now significantly referred to as Prince Henry in the stage directions, visits his father's bedside. Thinking him dead, the Prince puts the crown upon his own head. However, the King is merely asleep. As he wakes and misses the crown only to be told that the Prince has it, he fears that all of his worst assumptions about his son and successor are true. However, in explaining his actions to his father, Prince Henry reveals his true character in an eloquent speech that persuades the dying King of his love for him. King Henry V at first shows himself uncertain and in need of counsel. To that end he reconciles himself publicly with the Lord Chief Justice, an old enemy, who had once imprisoned Hal for striking him. This is also recognition of his need for wisdom and continuity in administration. Henry V further establishes his firmness of character in unequivocally rejecting Falstaff and all that he stands for in public, much to his old pal's puzzlement and consternation. The stage is now set for *Henry V*. This play tells the story of the young king's decision to press this claim for the throne of France. It shows him as the inspiring leader spurring his troops on to victory at Harfleur and again, against overwhelming odds at Agincourt. The play presents Henry above all as both magnanimous in victory and warmly human. Thus the play ends with his successful wooing of the French Princess Katherine, whose union with Henry promises to usher in the Golden Age of English glory prophesied by his grandfather, John of Gaunt at the beginning of *Richard II*.

The two parts of *Henry IV*, and *Henry V*, present us ostensibly with a picture of the development of the prodigal Hal into the awesomely majestic figure of Henry V, a king rightly esteemed for his courage and wisdom. Yet, as we have seen, Hal has warned us from the start that things are not what they seem to be (always an important theme in Shakespeare):

By how much better than my word I am,
By so much shall I falsify men's hopes.[3]

Hal's assertion here is sometimes taken to be a mark of mere cunning and insincerity, a sign that he is in fact consciously and deliberately treacherous in the grand Machiavellian manner. This interpretation of Hal's transformation takes the role of his acute self-awareness as king-to-be, i.e., as a model of majesty, all-too little seriously. In fact Hal's aside to the audience at the beginning of *Henry IV* Part 1 should be seen to emphasize by anticipating something that can only be seen fully later in the tetralogy, namely, that his strength to inspire others through his example of wisdom, which itself will become a principle of order for those around him. Hal is aware from the start of the importance of "showing" what he is made of rather than prattling on about it as Falstaff does. Thus he compares himself to the sun letting itself be hidden by clouds only to show itself later in all its splendour; this is little less than a Wittgensteinian point about the necessity of showing rather than saying the most important moral truths. Put differently, his character must manifest itself in the form of sound judgment. His role in the two parts of *Henry IV* would have "shown" this to Shakespeare's contemporaries (as I shall indicate) at least in three ways:

1. In the mercy he extends to "the brave Douglas" in his moment of triumph over Hotspur:[4] for Shakespeare's contemporaries, mercy, the ability to distinguish between those cases where the rule must be relaxed rather than rigorously applied was the clear sign of prudence or practical wisdom.

2. In his reconciliation with the Lord Chief Justice,[5] which I have already mentioned.

3. In the similarly mentioned rejection of Falstaff.[6]

Henry V's reconciliation with the Lord Chief Justice at once dispels fears that his donning the crown before his father's death inspire and also signify his recognition of legitimate authority and institutions. In fact it is the indispensable first step in his transformation into the embodiment of kingship that Shakespeare's tetralogy problematizes and that Henry V triumphant celebrates. Thus, based upon his earlier experiences, the Lord Chief Justice fears only the worst from the young rascal. He is therefore taken aback when the young king's first remarks to him – indeed, his first remarks as King – show Henry in a different light:

"This new and gorgeous garment, majesty,
Sits not so easy on me as you think.[7]

Henry's reconciliation with the Lord Chief Justice is intrinsically related to his recognition that he needs wise counsel. His repentance is a mode of showing that he has put his part behind him and his recognition (unlike Richard) that majesty involves responsibility is in fact the first manifestation of the majestic dimension of his character and his avowed goal:

No prince or peer shall have cause to say,
God shorten Harry's life one day![8]

It is the first step to the moral institutionalization of power that Richard's personal failings allowed to ebb away and his fathers subsequent usurpation could not achieve. Similarly his rejection of his old drinking buddy, Falstaff, is but the other face of his effort to embody virtue as a principle of leadership, i.e., to be a worthy example to his people. For that reason his break with carousing has to be complete: "I know the not old man... Presume not that I am the thing that I was".[9] All of this lays the basis for his role in the subjugation of France against overwhelming odds, which at once establishes and legitimates his glorious majesty.

Shakespeare's tetralogy can be taken as an epic of leadership (are epics ever about anything else?), then, to the extent that Henry comes to embody the virtues that were so clearly lacking in Richard and his father. His character comes to incorporate the public and the private, the institutional and the personal – virtues that were failing in his Henry predecessors – in a seamless unity. As an epic of leadership the tetralogy as a whole turns upon the contrast which *Henry V* makes with them. Richard was a dandy and a playboy, even in matters military, who was actually only concerned with the trappings of kingship without being concerned about being worthy of them. His story must, therefore, be the movingly lyrical tragedy of the aesthete over-reaching himself: he only really knows what it is to be king in the moment that he is deposed by Bolingbroke and awaits death. Like Lear, he brings this upon himself inasmuch as he has forgotten his responsibilities as leader:

I had forgot myself. Am I not king?
Awake thou coward majesty; thou sleepest.
... A puny subject strikes
At thy great glory.[10]

Again like Lear, Richard's fate, that of the irresponsible king, is loss of both realm and personal identity. He has played the part that fate has allotted to him thoughtlessly and thereby wrought havoc upon himself as well as his land. He has lived in a dream world from which he awakes only with enormous suffering. In this context Henry V's rejection of frivolity in his rejection of Falstaff, which he significantly compares to awakening from a dream, forms a sharp contrast with Richard's unwilling self-realization at the moment of his death. Henry IV too has lived in a kind of a dream world inasmuch as he cannot escape from the nightmarish guilt occasioned by his usurpation of the crown and Richard's murder. The famous line "uneasy lies the head that wears a crown",[11] is but the expression of the nightmarishly guilty existence – *Macbeth* is, of course, Shakespeare's definitive analysis of the psychological consequences of regicide and usurpation. The Machiavellian Henry IV can assert himself, establish and maintain power; but he cannot live with himself. In short, despite his considerable ability as a general and administrator, he lacks the true king's majestic second nature. Thus Henry V's task becomes nothing less than to overcome Richard's sorrow and his father's guilt. His very personality has to transcend their limitations in a celebration of legitimacy in which the man becomes an institution, if the garden that is England is to flourish.

In *Henry V* we have a representation of the leader of destiny as a responsible Christian king (such as that was understood in Shakespeare's day), whose authority rests ultimately upon his wisdom, which in turn is epitomized in the practical ability to temper justice with mercy and in so-doing through his very personality institutionalizing order as he overcome vanity in himself and violence in the world around him. This is what is means for Henry to assert, "we are no tyrant but a Christian king".[12] Given the differences between our values and those of the Elizabethan age it is not altogether easy to grasp all aspects of Shakespeare's way of exemplifying

Christian kingship; but his contemporaries would have recognized his picture of the virtues of the Christian king in Henry, for example, in his piety with respect to the memory of Richard, which parallels his reconciliation with the Lord Chief Justice as an acceptance of the sins of the past in order to create legitimacy in the present for the sake of future stability.

All of this seems to pale in our eyes because of Henry's pronouncedly imperialist frame of mind. But to see the matter this way would be anachronistic. In those days waging war was a duty of a king.[13] Moreover, the imperialist ideology, so odious to us today, was then a very new concept of the divine mission of the British ruler to spread British civilization throughout the world (it was after all the age of the discovery of the New World and of its colonization). Indeed, the inventor of that concept was none other than the remarkable John Dee, whom Shakespeare admired to the point of basing the character of Prospero and perhaps even Lear upon him.[14] In any case there is no question that Shakespeare was remarkably well-informed with regard to the latest ideas about these matters (no small part of his success as a writer and producer was tied to the timeliness of his productions). Nor is there any question that these values are hardly those of enlightened twentieth-century intellectuals. Be that as it may, Henry's practical wisdom is exemplified in his rejection of revenge as he pardons the drunken man who had railed against him.[15] His treatment of the drunk is to be compared with that of the flattering conspirator Cambridge[16] and his impartiality in ordering the execution of his old chum Bardolph for explicitly disobeying orders forbidding plundering the subdued French after Harfleur[17] (so movingly portrayed in the recent Brannagh film version). Henry's practical wisdom is further manifested in his mercy towards the conquered French after Harfleur[18] and in his interactions with his soldiers before Agincourt when the King's disguise lets his humanity radiate through his encounters with his soldiers.[19] Just as Henry's magnificently inspiring words before Harfleur, "once more unto the breach...",[20] embody his capacity to persuade in words, so those episodes embody his capacity in examples, whose aim is to persuade by moving the audience. So it is hardly accidental that the play concludes with the King's persuading Princess Kate to marry him and bear his children. The kingly function, the leadership function, is to displace war, faction and violence, with peace and unity based upon love and confidence. For that reason this epic of leadership must be an epic of persuasion, which is itself a contribution to the realization of England's inner greatness, a way of making the garden England thrive and flourish. Lest we in a more cynical, media-dominated age consider this all-too naive to be taken seriously, we should not forget that Winston Churchill, arguably this century's canniest political leader, enthusiastically supported Laurence Olivier's superb film production in 1945 for its morale-boosting effects.

All in all Shakespeare is clearly presenting us with an ensemble of example and counter-example for distinguishing real leadership from its counterfeits in his tetralogy: "yet sit and see, minding true things by what their mockeries be".[21] When I suggest that the ensemble of examples and counter-examples in the *Henry V* tetralogy can still serve to enlighten the social scientist with respect to just what leadership as viewed from the perspective of the leader is, I am not asserting that literature can take the place of social science but that such literary modes of presentation can play – and have played – a role in showing us how to understand the way in which a nebulous phenomenon like character can be grasped and represented in the form of moving examples. Till now I have continually made reference to things that Shakespeare's audience would have been familiar with that we are not. It is time to spell out my grounds for these assertions. There is nothing accidental about the fact that a concept of leadership as rooted in character should be at the centre of Shakespeare's conception of the world. Indeed, it would be mighty curious if it were not: for Shakespeare, like Montaigne, whom he is known to have read, was very explicitly espousing and exemplifying certain features of Neo-Stoic practical philosophy according to which the most important political truths can only be so represented. To understand why that should have been so it will be necessary to sketch the programme for philosophy that the Neo-Stoic revival espoused.

The Neo-Stoic synthesis was first developed in the writing's of the Flemish Humanist, Justus Lipsius,[22] Renaissance editor of Seneca and Tacitus, and in the view of his illustrious contemporary and fellow student of Mural, Michel de Montaigne, the most learned man alive. Born in 1547 and dying in 1606, Lipsius was an almost exact contemporary of Shakespeare (1564–1616). Lipsius was renowned for being one of the most erudite men in an age of erudition. So it is virtually impossible that someone like Shakespeare, who was abreast of the intellectual currents of the day, should not in one why or another been aware of the views Lipsius represented at least indirectly via, say, Montaigne. In any case there is no dearth of internal evidence that central terms from the vocabulary of Neo-Stoicism turn up at crucial junctures in Shakespearean discussions of leadership and character. A sketch of the main lines of Lipsius's Neo-Stoicism will help to make the parallels with Shakespeare clear. Neo-Stoicism is a synthesis of ancient stoicism with late-Renaissance Christianity; as such it contains elements in juxtaposition which had hitherto been foreign to both. For example, an ethics of Christian love foreign to ancient Stoicism coexists side by side with a metaphysical dualism equally foreign to it; whereas the Stoics' strict determinism was no less foreign to traditional Christianity. Moreover, the Neo-Stoic concept of politics institutionalized an elitist conception of society, according to which it was the destiny of the cultivated "best" to rule the "base" with the strictest of discipline on the principle that the kings complete possession of virtue warrants absolute submission on the part of the ruled, which, while often compatible with the practices of, say, mediaeval Christian kings, was totally foreign to traditional Christian ethics. In politics the Neo-Stoic view could be described as a "critical Machiavellianism" inasmuch as Lipsius, while accepting the Machiavellian principles that reasons of state override all others and that the rulers thus have the right to lie when it is in the public interest for them to do so, was nevertheless sceptical of Machiavelli's endorsement of unbridled, unscrupulous use of power – something that was difficult to support after the horror of the St. Bartholomew's day massacre. Indeed, for that very reason Lipsius insisted that majesty which is real and not in the least feigned must be the basis of political authority. Thus character and responsibility came to be the earmarks of legitimate authority for him. Here it is important to emphasize that Neo-Stoicism was above all a practical philosophy. Although it incorporated a number of metaphysical principles from ancient Stoicism, Neo-Stoicism eschewed theory in true Aristotelian fashion with the argument that a theory of practice is a contradiction in terms. Practical wisdom as the fruit of experience is only transmissible by means of examples; it is a matter of learning to catch the drift of those examples. Moreover, since the Stoics believed that vivacity was the primary quality of truth, prudence or practical wisdom inasmuch as it can be transferred at all, it is best transmitted in terms of examples that have the power to move us to a position of inner resolution or constancy in the face of Fate's fickle finger. With classical Stoicism, Lipsius assumed that all that occurs is determined and thus in principle reducible to causal analysis; however, in practice fortune always appears to us as she does to Fluellen in *Henry V*:

> Fortune is painted blind ... and she is painted also with a wheel, to signify to you, which is the moral of it, that she is turning, and inconstant, and mutability, and variation.[23]

The trick then is to develop sufficient inner stability to roll with the punches, as it were. In one of his most popular works, De Constantia, Lipsius developed the notion that it is only on the basis of constancy, steadfastness of character, that we can cope with the unforeseen situations Fortune, now baptized as Providence, has in store for us. The importance of constancy is emphasized twice in *Henry V*[24] and in a number of important passages in Shakespeare's condemnation of tyrannicide (itself a good Stoic theme), *Julius Caesar*. Lipsius's own mode of presenting practical wisdom was in the form of handbooks filled with examples culled from classical literature and history (most selectively I should add). History and literature, which Shakespeare and Lipsius would hardly have distinguished, were thus a repository of practical wisdom and an indispensable one at that. For that reason Lipsius insisted that a solid knowledge of literature was the most important prerequisite for philosophizing.

The view of politics and the state which Lipsius developed in his classic *Sixe Bookes of Politikes or Civil Doctrine*, which in fact contained what would become the model for the Baroque monarchy, was an absolutistic conception of the state as the only rational answer to the chaos that the wars of Reformation wrought. Just as the *logos*, the divine word, is the unity of creation, so the state too must be an absolute unity, but like the unity in Nature the unity in the state must be strictly hierarchical. Thus God is to the world as the king is to the state. However, the order in the universe is anything but arbitrary; it is a cosmos ordered by immutable laws of nature. So too must the state be above all a law-governed rational order. The kingly wisdom cannot ever be divine but it can share in the divine inasmuch as the king subjects himself to reason in (1) recognizing the limits of his finite intellect and (2) institutionalizing criticism in the persons of his minister and advisors. In return for the power to criticize the king freely ministers must be absolutely loyal to him (it is in this context that the Stoic injunctions against tyrannicide have their prime significance). Thus both Henry's reconciliation with the Lord Chief Justice and the condemnation of tyrannicide in Julius Caesar are stipulated on Neo-Stoic principles.[25] The principle that majesty accrues to wisdom, justice tempered with mercy as its principal manifestation, is a justification of aristocracy in the literal sense of a rule by the best in the sense of the wisest. In this scheme, society is to be divided into its rational "best" element which rules by nature and its irrational "base" element which by its nature demands to be ruled (the most radical consequences of such a notion of society that we find in Shakespeare are in *Coriolanus*). In this scheme, *pietas*, loyalty to the hierarchy in society, i.e. "my station and its duties" is the principle civic virtue.

It is not altogether accidental that all of this should have found embodiment in the works of the greatest of all playwrights; for the Neo-Stoic moral scheme like that of the ancient Stoics, was at bottom theatrical. It was based upon a form of "spiritual exercise" according to which each individual is required to learn to see his life and everything in it as happening necessarily. In practice this means learning to see ourselves as actors who are required to play a specific role according to what has been allotted to us. As a practical philosophy in the ancient sense its aim was not to understand the world better or to establish rational principles for solving moral problems, but to make people better citizens. Since it eschewed formulae for achieving that end, this could only be accomplished by offering us models or exemplars as role-models. We should meditate upon our exemplar and internalize his mode of thinking and acting. The Roman philosopher, statesman and playwright, Seneca, was exemplary for the movement as a whole (indeed, we forget at our peril that Seneca was so important to the Renaissance that there were even university chairs of Seneca studies such as that at Vicenza). As a philosopher, who devoted himself to determining the most satisfactory way of coping with an uncertain world – and a severe critic of the role of speculative philosophy's ability to be illuminating in that situation, a kind of Richard Rorty *avant le lettre* – as well as a civil servant obedient even to the point of taking his life when his emperor demanded it, and last but not least as a playwright, whose *Thyestes* is a remote ancestor of *Hamlet* (via Kyd's *Spanish Tragedy*), Seneca was all-but ideally suited to the exemplary role he came to play in the Renaissance in northern Europe. Moreover, he was also the father of a style of writing that has come to be named after him. The "Senecan style" came to rival Ciceronian Latin in the late Renaissance. The so-called Stoic or Senecan style, in contrast to the elaborate architectonic symmetry and balance of the Ciceronian period, was aphoristic, pointed, almost military, unbalanced, abounding in alliteration and assonance. It was in fact the literary counterpart to Mannerism in painting and sculpture. Its aim was less to edify on the basis of eloquent exposition than to jolt the reader. With his revival of Seneca in conjunction with Plautus and Tacitus, Lipsius created a revolution in prose stylistics. Francis Bacon, like Montaigne, is a well-known representative of this style; but we find it also in Shakespeare. Consider Gloucester's speech in Act I of *King Lear*:

> These late eclipses of the sun and moon
> portend no good to us. Though the wisdom
> of nature can reason it thus and thus,
> yet nature finds itself scourged by the
> subsequent effects: love cools, friendship
> falls off, brothers divide. In cities, mutinies,
> in countries, discord; in palaces treason; and
> the bond cracked 'twixt son and father. This
> villain of mine comes under the prediction:
> there's son against father; the king falls
> from bias of nature; there's father against child.

We have seen the best of our time. Machinations,
hollowness, treachery, and all the ruinous
disorders follow us quietly to our graves –
find out this villain Edmund, it shall lose the
nothing: do it carefully – and the noble and
true-hearted Kent banished! His offense, honesty!
'Tis strange.[26]

Briefly, those cadences which are so typical of Shakespeare as to be unmistakable – *Romeo and Juliet*, for example, abounds in them – are no less typically Stoic. Why, then, should it not be the case that this great man of the theatre, so eminently sensitive to his environment, also incorporated the Neo-Stoic conception of character as the principle of leadership par excellence into his celebration of the English spirit in creating his *Henry V*?

The purpose of this long digression has been to make it plausible that Shakespeare did indeed incorporate important Neo-Stoic notions about leadership into his most thoroughgoing exploration of the topic. The question that logically pops up at this stage is: have there ever been kings who have taken this ideal seriously? Certainly many people will be surprised to discover that nearly all of Europe's great monarchs from Shakespeare's day down to the French Revolution were conscious of this ideal. Consider only: Gustav. III Adolf of Sweden, Frederick the Great of Prussia, Henri IV of France, Leopold I of Austria and above all Lipsius,[27] chief disciple Maurice of Nassau, all in their way subscribed to the ideal that the Bard brought to life in his Henry tetralogy. However, this concept of leadership as rooted in character has been by no means the exclusive property of enlightened absolutisms; for even the American revolutionaries were not untouched by it: they very clearly considered the Stoic conception of virtue the basis of public life – and none of them took it more seriously than the most extraordinary figure in their number: George Washington.[28] Indeed, Washington tends to be an enigma precisely because he embodied the Stoic and Shakespearean concept of leadership so thoroughly that he made himself into a legend. Washington can lay claim to being the most remarkable leader ever inasmuch as he chose to retire when virtually presented with absolute power – and that but a few scant years before the self-style tribune of the people, Napoleon Bonaparte, took a crown from the hands of the Pope to crown himself Emperor of France in complete betrayal of the ideals of the revolution. Washington's refusal to stand unopposed for a third term was no isolated incident in his life; he steadfastly inspired absolute confidence in his countrymen precisely because he did not seek power. Indeed, it was typical of him to refuse it when offered. For example, when offered the command of the Continental army he first refused outright and only relented to the continued demands of his colleagues on the condition that he would not be paid for his services. In fact he accepted no remuneration whatsoever for his generalship during the eight long years of the American Revolution. Throughout his life, Washington carefully cultivated an image of himself as a gentleman of character and he scrupulously sought to live up to that image. Thus his ability to lead a volunteer army to victory over a professional force under the most adverse circumstances as well as to lay a stable political foundation for the new American republic was not in the least unrelated to his renown elegance as a horseman and dancer. That elegance leant him the aura of victory even in moments of defeat. So it is not altogether accidental that his favourite play should have been Addison's *Cato*, a work abounding in Neo-Stoic themes, which, if I am not mistaken, forms the bridge between his style of leadership and Shakespeare's *Henry V*. Here, indeed, was a brand of leadership based upon personality but *pace* Max Weber rooted in character rather than charisma. Thus there is much to be said for the thesis that Weber's rejection of an ethics based upon conscience (*Gesinnungsethik*) in favour of a utilitarian ethics of responsibility (*Verantwortungsethik*) is in fact a lens which actually distorts what it would magnify. In the end Weber's scepticism with respect to leadership based upon character has fed the cynicism which informs many contemptible business practices today.

In order to round out my discussion of the significance of Shakespeare's concept of leadership for our world I propose to look at management guru Peter Drucker's analysis of what he terms "post-business" society – or significantly "knowledge society" – as opposed to business society.[29] In making this distinction Drucker wants to call our attention to the way in which "professional" values as represented, say, by our current cult of management (with whose emergence Drucker himself has had not a little to do) have come to displace traditional business values. Drucker refers to post-business society as the knowledge society because knowledge itself has ceased to have a merely functional role in business but has came to be itself an important commodity. The most typical phenomenon, the very embodiment of the values of post-business society, is the hostile take-over; it represents a new Machiavellianism in business with "information" as its chief symbolic representation. Drucker sees the cult of management with its worship of information as essentially charismatic: thus he does not hesitate to use the word "sexy" to describe the hostile take-over. His thesis, then, is that in post-business society "sexy information" takes the place of traditional know-how in a curious wedding of glamour and brutality. The hostile take-over is in fact but a symptom of the irresponsibility that comes with the rejection of know-how for "information". Since management's function is now exclusively to "manage", i.e., to produce not products but profits, the rational structure that production brings to capitalism is lost, leaving management without internal constraints and thus irresponsible. The result is a financial reign of terror, which in the circumstances is the only way of introducing a kind of order into business affairs (shades of Hegel!). In the end the hostile take-over is a post-business phenomenon inasmuch as it is an anti-business phenomenon; it is anti-business inasmuch as it demoralizes middle management, as Drucker emphasizes, by threatening the people that actually get the work done. Thus post-business society as epitomized in the hostile take-over is characterized most profoundly as a rejection of the idea that work has an intrinsic value. For the business world it represents the ultimate in de-personalization, a situation in which an enterprise is reduced entirely to its cash value at a given moment and vertical dialogue ceases to exist, i.e., persuasion ceases to play any role whatsoever in the relationship between middle and top management. Thus we arrive at a situation in which precisely those qualities which Shakespeare extols in *Henry V* are entirely lacking.

If Drucker's view does not actually imply that there is more to the Shakespearean-Stoic notion of leadership based upon character than meets the eye it at least clearly reminds us of the price we pay for endorsing a conception of leadership divorced from character considerations. However, let us return to Albert Danielsson's problem with the most frequently encountered perspective on leadership, i.e., the view that principally approaches it from the point of view of the led. It is certainly understandable that as a century of fascism grows to a close there would be a strong tendency to look at leadership from below; however, this perspective does have its price too, namely that of focusing our attention away from the crucial question of how we are to institutionalize leadership. As Danielsson has rightly insisted, leadership is in the first instance not something that we should equate with individual leaders, however, the paradox is that leadership cannot be institutionalized except through individuals; it is something that has to be constructed. My suggestion – following Lipsius and Shakespeare – is that character plays a considerably larger role in that process than social scientists are inclined to think, that Shakespeare knew this very well, and precisely on that account constructed his analysis of leadership in those terms. For that reason our discussions of leadership are radically incomplete without "a little touch of Harry".

Notes

1 This paper was written after a number of stimulating discussions with Prof. Danielsson. It is intended to compliment the anthology on the subject compiled by Danielsson and his colleagues in Business Studies at Stockholm's Royal Institute of Technology. Danielsson, Albert et al (1986) *Samtal om Lederskap*. Ledning & Ledare, Stockholm.

2 On Weber's concept of "charisma" see Hughes, H Stuart (1958) *Consciousness and society*, New York, pp 288–290. On the genesis of this concept see Mitzman, Arthur (1970) *The Iron Cage*. New York. I have benefited greatly from discussions of Weber's concept of rationality with the late Eugène Fleischmann.

3 I refer to Shakespeare's play by name along with act, scene and line numbers" Henry IV Part 1, 1, 2,208–209.

4 *Henry IV* Part 1, V, 5, 26–31.

5 *Henry IV* Part 2, V, 2, 42–143.

6 *Henry IV* Part 2, V. 5, 50–62.

7 *Henry IV* Part 2, V, 2, 42–43.

8 *Henry IV* Part 2, V, 5, 144–146.

9 *Henry IV* Part 2, V, 2, 50–59.

10 *Richard II*, III, 2, 82.

11 *Henry IV* Part 2, III, 1, 3O.

12 *Henry V*, 1, 2, 242.

13 Hale, JR (1986) In: *Why there were wars. War and society in Renaissance Europe*, Baltimore, pp 13–45.

14 Yates, Frances (1975) *Shakespeare's last plays*. London, pp 87–126; cf Yates (1983) *The occult philosophy in the Elizabethan age*. London, pp 77; 156–157. Dame Frances is also of the opinion that King Lear is in part based upon the disgraced and impoverished condition in which Dee found himself after his return from Prague in the reign of James I.

15 *Henry V*, II, 2, 39.

16 *Henry V*, II, 2, 2.

17 *Henry V*, III, 6, 104–110.

18 *Henry V*, III, 3, 51–59.

19 *Henry V*, IV, 1; IV, 6.

20 *Henry V*, III, 1, 1. John Keegan emphasizes how the historical Henry V courted risk continually during the battle of Agincourt; see Keegan (1978) *The Face of Battle*. Harmondsworth, p 336. Keegan's work is also notable with respect to leadership discussion in that he emphasizes how "the naturally stronger character" comes to fulfil the leadership function, i.e., regardless of rank in actual combat situations: ibid, p 51.

21 *Henry V*, IV, Prologue, 52–53.

22 On Lipsius and Neo-Stoicism see Oestreich, Gerhard (1969) *Geist und Gestalt des frÅhmodernen Staats*. Berlin, as well as his (1980) *Strukturprobleme der Neuzeit*, Oestreich, B. (ed) Berlin. cf Kirk, Rudolf (1604) Introduction. In: *Tvvo bookes of constancie written in Latino by Justus Lipsius* (transl Sir John Stradling). London, pp 3–62. See also my (1989) "Justus Lipsius: le pere de la philosophie autrichienne?" *Austriaca* (Rouen) 198: 31–41. I have further argued that those virtues which serve to legitimate the white magic of Prospero and to distinguish it from the black magic of Sycorax in *The Tempest* are in fact Stoic – a point that Dame Frances seems not to have considered in her treatment of the last plays. See my "Caliban's revenge", chap 16 of this volume. On the Senecan or Stoic style and the literary and philosophical strategies it entailed see Lafond, J (ed) (1984) *Les formes breves de la prose et le discourse discontinu (XVI–XVII Siecles)*. For Montaigne's view of Lipsius see his (1965) *Essais*, Villy, P and Sulnier, V-L, (eds). Paris, II, 12.

23 *Henry V*, III, 6, 29–36.

24 *Henry V*, II, 2, 117: "constant in spirit, not swerving with the blood" is the English soul; II, 4, 35: "how terrible in constant resolution" is Henry as represented by the Constable to the French king.

25 The following references to constancy in *Julius Caesar* are worth noting:

II, 1, 224–228, Brutus:

Good gentlemen, look fresh and merrily;
Let not our looks put on our purposes,
But bear it as our Roman actors do,
With untired spirits and formal constancy.

II, 2, 229. Portia:

I have made strong proof of my constancy.

III, 1, 23, Brutus:

Cassius be constant.

III, 1, 58–60, Caesar:

I could well be moved, if I were you;
If I could pray to move, prayers would move me;
But I am constant as the northern star.

III, 1, 72–3, Caesar:

That I was constant Cimber should be banished
And constant do remain to keep him so.

It should be pointed out here that little in my argument turns upon Shakespeare's direct knowledge of Lipsius's texts. There is ample evidence for the thesis that the latter was among the most widely read and discussed authors of his day. His were the sort of view that one had to be abreast of if one wanted to be *au courrant* of the latest intellectual trends, i.e., just the sort of thing that a canny man of the theatre would want to build into his dialogues.

26 *King Lear*, I, 2, 105–17.

27 Oestreich, G (1967) Justus Lipsius als Theoretiker des neuzeitlichan Machtstaats. *Historische Zeitschrift* 192: 43–78.

28 On Washington see Wills, Garry (1984) *Cincinatus.* New York. A bridge between the late Renaissance to the American Enlightenment is the symbolic significance of the figure of Brutus condemning his own sons as traitors in the Enlightenment inter alia the subject of a play by Voltaire and then well-known painting by Jacques-Louis David. In Shakespeare's tetralogy the theme is echoed in the Duke of York's exposure of his son's treason (*Richard II,* V, 3).

29 See Edward Reingold's interview with Peter Drucker, "Facing the new and dynamic". *Time* 22 January, 1990: 42–43. Drucker's account of the role of "information" in post-business society needs to be complemented by Alasdair MacIntyre's account of "expertise" in *After virtue.* Notre Dame, 1981, p 72. MacIntyre argues that the sort of knowledge that management science claims to be based upon cannot exist; moreover he associates the "managerial revolution" with the appearance of a new "stock character" in our culture.

Chapter 26

Concluding Remarks Part II

Jon Cook

The chapters in Part II are connected by three main themes: Diderot, dialogue and translation. Diderot is discussed in terms of his exemplary force as a non-specialist, encyclopaedic intellectual. The importance of his contributions to an epistomology of skill and to an understanding of dialogue is stressed. The present chapter goes on to summarize the value of dialogue as a form which can tolerate incompatible perspectives in a way that deepens reflective understanding of why we have the beliefs we do. This has both political and educational consequences. Dialogue is presented as a basic form of democracy and as a crucial metaphor for understanding the nature of skills. The discussion of translation extends these themes, giving, an example of the relationship between identity and skill, both for the translator of texts, and for the other kinds of "translation" involved in acting. These are issues which are contributing to the development of an international PhD programme in Culture and Technology.

The chapters forming the second half of this volume give some indication of a new phase of thinking that has developed since the Culture, Language and Artificial Intelligence Conference held in Stockholm in 1988. In this new phase explicit attention to the question of artificial intelligence has been subsumed into a wider range of concerns with the history and the cultural embeddedness of attitudes towards knowing and acting – attitudes that, in their turn, inform our thinking about the social impact and use of technology. What these chapters represent is a metamorphosis, a new shape emerging, not a completed intellectual synthesis. They are explorations and testings, necessarily diverse in their starting points and interests. Running through this diversity are a number of recurrent concerns. These can be summarized in the form of a proper name and two nouns: Diderot is the name; the two nouns are dialogue and translation. In these concluding remarks I want to comment briefly on each.

Why Diderot? Why a Diderot Project? An answer to the second question can be given in terms of a local history. One result of the 1988 Stockholm Conference was an agreement amongst a group of international researchers, coming from different disciplinary backgrounds, to develop their work around four related themes: computers and knowledge, the social impact of technology, the value of work, and the relevance of aesthetic modes to understanding working culture. The first full meeting of the Project was held at the Centre Culturel Suedois in Paris in February 1989, and since then there have been further planning meetings held in London, Innsbruck and Stockholm, as well as a parallel series of Dialogue seminars held in Stockholm, Norwich and Vienna. Some of these seminars have taken very general issues as their starting point: the Arts and the Sciences, the Media, Word and Image. Others have focused on specific texts: Shakespeare's *The Tempest*, Diderot's *Rameau's Nephew* or his *Paradox on Acting*. The seminars work within a common and developing ethos: not a huddle of specialists confirming their own importance, but a diversity of participants testing the possibility of moving across disciplinary and epistemologlcal boundaries; not lengthy papers followed by nit-picking discussion, but brief focused statements as a stimulus to a dialogue which would make the seminar an occasion for inventing rather than repeating a discourse.

What brings people through fog, snow, frost and darkness to these seminars? Amongst a myriad of motives two are relevant here: an impatience with academic specialisms and a desire to move across intellectual boundaries. Biologists talk to playwrights about the nature of experiment; forestry evaluators discuss the nature of judgment with philosophers and software designers; literary critics analyse the nature of codes with physicists. These cross-disciplinary conversations create the conditions for serendipity, "the gift of finding valuable or agreeable things not sought for". Each seminar adds to the network of individuals and institutions with an interest in the Diderot Project's aims. One result is the creation of an "invisible college", an intellectual community working across and beyond current academic and professional divisions of labour.

This brief local history of the Diderot Project helps to explain why it has the name it does. The range and ambition of the Project's work, its concern to find a new constellation of knowledge, find an exemplary precedent in the figure of Diderot. This is most evident in the sheer range of Diderot's interests moving with seemingly insatiable curiosity across the intellectual concerns which are now separated out into the two cultures of the arts and the sciences, and then into yet further divisions within those cultures. The expansiveness of the Encyclopaedia seems the natural outcome of Diderot's curiosity and inventiveness. The assumptions about knowledge and its representation which go into the making of the Encyclopaedia, itself a remarkable eighteenth century experiment in information storage and retrieval, stand in marked contrast to the Cartesian method and its reductive obsession with that minimum of knowledge which can be secured from all doubt.

As a number of the chapters in Part II of this volume show, there is no simple answer to any question about what Diderot understood by epistemology, perhaps because his writing constantly transgresses the boundary between a knowing subject and its objects of perception which is the starting point of so much epistemological enquiry. Stephen Toulmin's "On from the Two Cultures" (Chap. 23), gives one historical context for understanding Diderot's place in the history of knowledge: a thinker in whom the tension between what is reasonable and what is rational, between phronesis and episteme, remains a productive tension. Diderot's fascination with questions of method is counter-balanced by his concern with practical reason. This is true in the ethical sense described by Toulmin: what it means "to live, to act, and to feel in ways appropriate to reasonable human beings". But there is another dimension to practical reason in Diderot's thinking, one that is referred to in a number of the chapters in this volume, and is most obviously the theme of Magnus Florin's reflections on the meaning of instinct (Chap. 17). The letter to Sophie Volland contains one of a number of vivid examples in Diderot's work of a form of reasoning embodied in and sustained by practice. Diderot's account of the instinct, or the accumulated learning, which enabled Michelangelo to design the dome of St. Peter's, without benefit of sophisticated geometry, anticipates a recurrent concern, in this and related volumes in the series, with the relation between tacit knowledge and skill.

Diderot subsumes and challenges an epistemological analysis centred on the solitary mind's perceptions in another way. Whether in *Rameau's Nephew*, *Jaques the Fatalist*, or *The Voyage to Bougainville*, knowing and communicating are comically or ironically implicated in Diderot's work. The idea of dialogue, both as a form in Diderot's writing and as a fundamental psychological metaphor, are clearly relevant here. Before commenting on this in more detail, another, political component of the connection in Diderot between knowledge and communication is worth noting. Per Sörbom's account of Diderot's plans for a Russian University (Chap. 18) valuably reminds us that Diderot, while committed to universal education, was not an educational egalitarian. His educational system is both functional and élitist, closely linking educational provision to the individual's economic and social role. But, if Diderot's educational system is not egalitarian, his manner of addressing his reader often is. He is not an intellectual bringing the latest tablets of stone down from the mountain for us to read and obey. Diderot's communication of what he knows (more especially as what he knows may be fundamentally paradoxical, knowledge without certainty) assumes the reader is an equal. The conclusion of Herbert Josephs' detailed analysis of *Rameau's Nephew* (Chap. 19) gives a vivid example of this aspect of Diderot's work. A further implication of the argument is that Diderot's imagination was attracted by the idea that social and economic power was not necessarily connected to communicative power: in *Jaques the Fatalist* Jaques can tell stories far better than his master; the socially despicable nephew in *Rameau's Nephew* commands a verbal and physical eloquence which exceeds that of the socially respectable philosopher.

Authority circulates with remarkable rapidity in Diderot's texts. No character or voice remains unquestioned or uncontested for long. This produces the energy and animation of his writing, the qualities that Schlegel referred to as the "impudence", the "incomparable impertinence" of Diderot's style. His imagination is attracted to the voice that will unsettle convention and propriety. These characteristics of Diderot's writing are intimately linked to his invention of forms which do not contain the energy of argument and impertinent questions within a perspective which is itself left unchallenged.

The contest of voices and perspectives arises from Diderot's commitment to dialogue, not as a superficial style for presenting thought, but as the fundamental form of thinking itself. The return to Diderot, evident in all the papers collected here, is the basis for a reflection on the nature of dialogue as an epistemological and ethical principle. To think about dialogue in this way establishes deep historical resonances. One is indicated by the quotation from Plato's *The Sophist*, cited by Herbert Josephs (Chap. 19). "It is the voiceless dialogue of the soul within itself and with itself that we call 'thought'".

The thinking of thought as dialogue tends to be ignored or suppressed by more institutionally powerful epistemologies, whether those which conceive of mental operations as a more or less accurate mirroring of external, "non-mental" realities, or the programming of mental behaviour according to the logical systems of the syllogism, deduction, and induction, or the other logical forms spawned by twentieth century mathematics and philosophy.

The chapters by Allan Janik, Herbert Josephs and Bo Göranzon all reactivate and extend the tradition which conceives of thinking as dialogue, a tradition which has itself been significantly renewed in the twentieth century by the work of the Russian literary and cultural critic Mikhail Bakhtin. What all these chapters share with Bakhtin is a stress on the open, heterodox, and provisional nature of dialogical thinking. Apart from this sharing of an ethos, there are three major emphases which are worth noting.

One is that dialogue is a form of inner mental action as well as a kind of public performance. The implications of this idea are developed by Herbert Josephs (Chap. 19) on the dramatization of philosophical thought in Diderot's writing. Diderot thinks by inventing otherness, "a fictionalized presence in whom was inscribed values and attitudes frequently resistant to those of the narrating subject". The effects of this upon our image of the mind and the purpose of thinking are considerable. Where Descartes thinks in order to put an end to doubt, Diderot thinks in order to create it. Where Descartes finds certainty in the immobile equation of thought and identity, Diderot finds uncertainty in the theatre of the mind, where identities are dispersed and multiplied. Out of these identities arise the dialogues between experience and observation, the analyst and the analysand, dialogues that can be imagined as going on within the mind and as performed outside it, Hence the division between mental and physical realities enforced by Descartes is bridged by Diderot. The dialogue between experience and observation, the actor and the spectator, makes a society of the mind, and a mind of society.

Diderot summarized the dialogical character of thought and action in the term *dedoublement*, which indicates that special kind of reflective awareness, most fully explored in this volume in the chapters by Allan Janik (Chap. 16) and Bo Göranzon (Chap. 24). Janik's reading of *Rameau's Nephew* demonstrates the importance of dialogue between incompatible perspectives. In doing this Diderot "challenges a central tenet in modern philosophy, namely that practical knowledge ultimately has a theoretical basis... In Diderot's view the practical and theoretical, the experiential and the propositional, sorts of knowledge are not only radically incompatible with one another, but actually in competition with one another in the social world". The dialogue explores the scope of these incompatibilities, revealing how each view is simultaneously coherent but limited. The classic purpose of Socratic dialogue, the exposure and refutation of error, is replaced by another: the experience of a difference in perspective which cannot be resolved into a new synthesis. Janik characterizes this state as a "sort of reflective tension", the condition for developing "a framework or perspective in terms of which we may conduct future discussions more reflectively than we otherwise might".

The tone here is necessarily tentative, opposed to the triumphant clatter of language announcing the latest breakthrough which in practice solves nothing. What Janik argues for is a revision in our understanding of the purposes of thinking. This underlines the second emphasis given to dialogue, its connection to a concept of reflection. This gives a touchstone for distinguishing between effective and ineffective dialogue. The nature of effective dialogue is rarely, if at all, based on asking questions whose form presupposes their answer. Following from the example of the incompatible perspectives articulated in *Rameau's Nephew,* Janik characterizes the conditions for genuine dialogue: "... it has to be a matter of two different positions posing problems for one another in a situation where we had not previously been inclined to consider that there were problems at all". Reflection, the moment when "we are prepared to reappraise some belief", arises out of dialogue of this kind.

These revisionary and reflective outcomes of dialogue are closely connected to an understanding of dialogue as a form which mobilizes creativity. Both Herbert Josephs and Allan Janik find in *Rameau's Nephew* a form of writing which calls for the reader's inventive participation. Janik compares the form of the dialogue to a rebus, calling on the reader to "supply the missing, but suggested, elements, the 'grammar' binding them together". Another comparison might be with metaphor, that form of utterance which calls on the listener to go beyond the literal or first order meanings of words in order to make sense of what is being said. As with dialogue, so with metaphor, we have to go beyond the routine application of rules in order to understand what is going on. At another level the movement beyond routine applications is evident in Allen Janik's and Bo Göranzon's use of literary works as a way of thinking about aspects of working culture. Shakespeare's *The Tempest,* for example, provides a metaphor, and therefore the potential for reflection about the relation between the theoretical and practical intellect. Or Cordelia's silence in *King Lear* becomes a compelling analogy for the clash between two different conceptions of language where the demand for explicitness and accountability takes destructive priority over the claims of tacit understanding and trust.

These connections between dialogue, creativity and inventiveness indicate the third major emphasis emerging from the thinking about dialogue in this volume. A continuing concern with the nature and development of skill is evident in many papers. Although the thought is not developed at any length by any of the contributions, it may well be that any highly developed skill is itself dialogical in structure. Skilled work seems to call for a dialogue between worker and material so that the wood begins to "talk to" the carpenter about the shape of a chair, or the stone speaks to the sculptor about the nature of a statue, or a character tells the novelist how the story is to develop. But the negative example is also instructive; the occasions when the absence of a dialogue between a technology and its users produces a depletion of skills. These concluding remarks are not the place for any detailed elaboration, but there does seem to be an emerging question in the papers collected here: how might our understanding or the nature and value of work be revised, even transformed, by considering it in terms of the concept of dialogue? Further work will fill out an answer to the question.

A concern with the nature of skill and creativity is evident in the chapters by Lars Kleberg (Chap. 20) and Michael Robinson (Chap. 21) on translation. Kleberg's "The Translator as Actor" is a prototype of a case study approach which, by comparing two kinds of skill, illuminates the nature of both. The comparison between the actor and the translator brings out the dialogical and paradoxical character of both activities. As the actor "chews up" the part into small pieces and gets "chewed up" by it at the same time, so the translator in breaking down the original text into smaller units, begins to be transformed by the process of translation. In both activities too there is an evaluative concern with a tacit dimension, all the unspoken assumptions, the sub-texts, which make sense of the words of the text to be translated or the part to be played. The capacity to bring the subtext to life, without rendering it banally explicit, is one characteristic of successful performance or translation.

Both Lars Kleberg and Michael Robinson link the idea of skill in performance to paradoxes about identity. Again Diderot's thinking is an important stimulus here. In his *Paradoxe sur le Comédien* he attempts an explanation of what it is that distinguishes the performance of a great actress and finds it in the capacity to be both inside and outside the role, a mental balance which permits a simultaneous absorption in performance and a monitoring of it. Robinson finds a parallel case in the situation of autobiographical writing. The impulse to truth-telling encounters the paradoxical character of the truth to be told; the double consciousness of the autobiographer "as he was in the unfolding sequence of his experience and as he now is at the moment of recording them". As Robinson points out this "double-self" has entered into cultural history as a series of reflections about the nature of genius, and accompanying moral anxieties about the absence of identity and emotional coldness in both writers and actors.

The paradox here is that the absence of identity becomes an identity, and vice versa: "the autobiographer's identity is constituted in the words he writes, which designate what is absent". The self created by autobiography is always a translation of some putative original self, and not the faithful transcription of an identity which is simply waiting to be written down.

Kleberg locates the same paradox in relation to ideas of authority, whether those are figured in terms of the father, the state, or same original text which must be faithfully translated. Diderot, like the actor or the translator, confronts authority by appearing to succumb to it. Each hides in a role or a text in order to achieve their aims. The conclusion of Kleberg's chapter raises the possibility that this kind of absorption of the self into another is the condition for the dedicated work that produces any significant achievement, especially those that go beyond the traditions they appear to succumb to.

The chapters by Lars Kleberg and Michael Robinson make clear a concern that is at work elsewhere in this volume: to establish the terms for a psychology of skill which is neither behaviourist or functionalist in form. The example, and the metaphor, of translation illuminates some of the complexity of what it means to follow a set at rules or instructions, whether these take the form of an original text, a part in a play, or the kinds of authoritative knowledge present in tradition or working culture. One understanding of skill suggests that it consists in following the rules exactly. The example of translation reminds us that following rules also means knowing how to apply them in new contexts, and that the skills of judgment here may have very little to do with following sets of explicit instructions, but rather acting in accord with what Diderot described as instinct in his account of Michelangelo: a sense of balance or measure acquired in one context is translated into another. The translator draws on a tacit understanding of language to make the good translation no dictionary could predict or dictate. An actress brings new life to a traditional role by making it speak within a context unforeseen by the tradition. The autobiographer writes a life by inventing it. Another paradox arises: the skilful performance of a rôle, a good translation or autobiography appears at one and the same time a unique invention and faithful to an original.

The proper name and two nouns – Diderot, dialogue and translation – indicate a complex and evolving perspective on the nature of skill and creativity. This necessarily has a speculative and critical aspect to it. But what is also evident is a concern with practical applications. The debate about the two cultures in Stephen Toulmin's chapter (Chap. 23) and my own (Chap. 22), the recovery of the educational power of vivid examples in Alan Janik's account of the Renaissance neo-stoics (Chap. 25), Per Sörbom's analysis of Diderot's plans for a Russian University (Chap. 18), all raise questions about the nature of education and its institutional form. A marked feature of Western cultures at the moment is a pervasive crisis in education. This ranges from anxieties about basic literacy to concerns about over-specialization and a break-down in the dialogue between education and working life. These in turn are symptoms of major cultural and economic change. It is doubtful that any quick solutions are available. The claim made for educational change in some of the papers collected here has to do with establishing a new balance between theoretical and practical reasoning, tacit and explicit knowledge, "knowing that" and "knowing how". A new international PhD programme is currently being developed at the Royal Institute of Technology in Stockholm, the Technical University in Vienna, and the University of East Anglia in Norwich. Its purpose is to respect the complex nature of skills and skilled individuals, while offering to develop those skills to a high level, one that will avoid any sterile contrast between the "academic" and the "vocational". A major innovation is in prospect and it seems appropriate to conclude these concluding remarks with this indication of work to come.

Bibliography

Abelson RP (1973) The Structure of Belief Systems. In Schank R and Colby KM (eds) *Computer models of thought and language*. Freeman, New York
AI and Society (1988), Vol. 2, Nos 1–4, Springer-Verlag
Archer W (1888) *Masks or faces*, London
Aristotle *The Nichomachaen ethics*. Book VI
Asimov I (1979) *In memory yet green*. Doubleday & Co, New York
Asplund J (1987) *Om hälsningsceremonier, mikromakt och asocial pratsamhet*. Korpen, Gothenburg
Augustine (1963) *The confessions*, transl Warner, Rex. New York

Bakhtin M (1978) *The forms of time and the chronotopos in the novel, P-T-L* 3: 3
Barrell J (1986) *The political theory of painting from Reynolds to Hazlitt*. Yale University Press, New Haven and London
Barrow L (1986) *Independent spirits spiritualism and English plebians*, Routledge and Kegan Paul, London
Barthes R (1985) Complexity (translation). In: Blonsky M (ed) *On signs*, Blackwell, Oxford
Beckett S (1959) *The Unnamable*. London
Bernstein B (1971) *Class codes and control*, Routledge and Kegan Paul, London
Berry D and Broadbent (1984) On the relationship between task performance and associated verbalizable knowledge, *The Quarterly Journal of Experimental Psychology*, 36A
Berry D and Broadbent S (1985) Human search procedures and the use of expert systems. *Current Psychological Research Reviews*, 5
Bleiler EF (ed) (1985) *Supernatural fiction writers: fantasy and horror*, vol 1. Scribner, New York
Boden M (1980) Social implications of intelligent machines. In: Forrester T (ed), *The microelectronics revolution*. Blackwell, Oxford
Bowman RM (1985) *Star wars: defense or death star*. Institute for Space and Security Studies, Chesapeake Beach
Breuner J (1986) *Actual minds, possible worlds*. Cambridge, MA, Harvard University Press
British Computer Society Code of Conduct (1981) *BSC Handbook No. 5*. British Computer Society Publications, London
Broadbent D, Fitzgerald P and Broadbent M (1985) Implicit and explicit knowledge in the control of complex system. *British Journal of Psychology, 77*
Brodner P (1988) In search of the computer-aided craftsman. *AI and Society, 2*
Brodner P (1990) *The Shape of Future Technology: The Anthropocentric Alternative*, Springer-Verlag, London
Brooks P 1984) *Reading for the Plot*, New York
Buchler J (ed) (1955) *Philosophical Writings of Peirce*, Dover, New York
Buckley J (1984) *The turning key: autobiography and the subjective impulse*. Cambridge, MA
Bundy A and Clutterbuck R (1985) Raising the standard of AI products, In: *Proceedings of the Ninth IJCAI*, Los Angeles

Cannataci JA (1988), Liability and responsibility for expert systems. *CompLex 5/88*, Norwegian Research Center for Computers and Law, Tano, Norway
Capek K (1973) R.U.R., adapted for English stage by Playfair, Nigel; (ed) Schefter. Washington Square Press
Capek K (1937) *War with the newts*
Carnap R (1942) *Introduction to semantics*. Cambridge, MA

Chekov A *Three sisters*
Cherry E (1952) The communication of information. *American Scientist*, 40
Churchman C (1985) Churchman's conversations. *Systems Research*, 2
Cohen RS and Schnelle T (1986) *Cognition and fact. materials on Ludwig Fleck. Dordrecht*
Collins C (1987) *English language dictionary*, London and Glasgow
Concepts and categories (1980), Oxford
Cook P, Ellis C, Graf M, Rein G and Smith T (1987) Project Nick: meetings augmentation and analysis, *ACM Transactions on Office Information System*, 5
Cooley M (1989) *European competitiveness in the 21st century: integration of work, culture and technology*. Brussels: EEC FAST Programme
Corbett J M, Rasmussen LB and Rauner F (1991) *Crossing the Border: The social and engineering design of computer Integrated manufacturing systems*. Springer-Verlag, London
Council for science and society (1981) *CCS report: new technology: society, employment and skill*. Council for Science and Society, London
Critical Inquiry, 7 (1980)
Cvetaeva M (1981) *My Russian childhood* (*Min ryska barndom*), Swedish transl Bäckström A, Stockholm

Dagens Nyheter, 28 December 1987
Dalyell T (1987) *Misrule*, Cecil Woolf, London
Darnton R (1979) *The business of the enlightenment. A publishing History of the encyclopédie* 1775–1800
Darwin and Huxley T H (1983) *Autobiographies*, de Beer, G (ed) Oxford
de Montmollin M and De Kayser V (1985), Expert logic v operator logic. In: Mancini G, Johannsen G and Martensson L (eds) *Analysis, design and evaluation of man-machine systems*, Oxford, Pergamon (IFAC Proceedings)
De George R and De George F (1972) *The structuralists from Marx to Levi Strauss*, Garden City
Defense Advance Projects Agency (1983) *Strategic computing, generation computing technology: a strategic plan for its development and application to critical problems in defense*
Dewey J (1920) *Reconstruction in philosophy* , New York
Dewey J (1916) *Democracy and education*, New York
Dialoger, Florin M, Göranzon B and Sällström P. (eds) Stockholm
Diderot D (1951) *Oeuvres*, Bill, André (ed). Gallimard, Paris
Dietz p (1986) Artificial intelligence: building rule-rased ES, *Design News*, 3 March
Din AM (ed) (1987) *Arms and artificial intelligence: weapon and arms control applications of advanced computing*. SIPRI, Oxford
Dretske F (1981) *Knowledge and the flow of information*. Cambridge MA MIT Press
Dreyfus H (1979) *What computers can't do. The limits of artificial intelligence*. Revised edition, Harper and Row, New York
Dreyfus H and Dreyfus S (1986) *Mind over machine. The power of human intuition and expertise in the era of the computer*, The Free Press, New York
Dreyfus H L (1972) *What computers can't do: A critique of artificial reason* Harper and Row, New York

Easlea B (1981) *Science and sexual oppression*, Weidenfeld and Nicholson, London
Ekvall, G (1988) *Förnyelse och friktion*. Borås
Eliot TS *The waste land*
Employment Gazette (1980) September
Employment Gazette (1986) March/April
Ennals JR (1979) *The European parliament in the classroom*, Essex European Resources Centre, Clacton
Ennals JR (1980) *Simulations and computers*, Teaching History, June 1980
Ennals JR (1985) *Artificial intelligence: applications to logical reasoning and historical research*, Ellis Horwood, Chichester
Ennals JR (1986) *Star wars: A question of initiative*. John Wiley, Chichester
Ennals R (1991) *Artificial intelligence and human institutions*, Springer-Verlag, London
Ennals R and Gardin J-C (1990) (eds) *Interpretation in the humanities perspectives from artificial intelligence*. British Library, London
Eriksson K (1987) *Vårdandets idé* Almqvist and Wiksell, Stockholm
Feigenbaum E and McCorduck P (1983) *Artificial intelligence and* Japan's computer challenge to the world

Feyerabend P (1975) *Against method.* Verso Press, London
Fleck L (1935) Entstehung und Entwicklung einer wissenschaftlische Tatsache: Einführung in die Lehre vom Denkstil und Denkkollektiv, Basel
Fleck L (1979) *Genesis and development of a scientific fact.* Chicago and London
Flores F and Ludlow J (1980) Doing and speaking in the office. In Fick G and Sprague R (eds) *Decision support systems: issues and challenges.* Oxford, Pergamon (Proceedings)
Forster EM (1928) *The eternal moment and other stories*
Forsyth R (1984) (ed) *Expert systems,* New York, Chapman and Hall
Foucault M (1979) *Discipline and Punish,* transl Sheridan, Alan Penguin Books, Harmondsworth
Freud S (1953-73) *Standard edition of the complete works of Sigmund Freud,* Strachey, James (ed) London

Gardin J-C (1989) (ed) *Artificial intelligence and expert systems case studies in the knowledge domain of archaeology.* Ellis Horwood, Chichester
Garson B (1966) *Macbird,* Penguin, Harmondsworth
Geyl P (1963) Shakespeare as a Historian. In: Geyl p (ed) *Encounters in history.* Collins, London
Gill K (1986) (ed) *Artificial intelligence for society.* John Wiley, Chichester
Gill K (1990) *Summary of human centred systems research in europe.,* SEAKE Centre, Brighton Polytechnic, Brighton
Gold E (1989) *Virtual theatre from Diderot to Mallarmé.* The Johns Hopkins University Press, Baltimore
Gombrowicz W (1937) *Ferdydurke,* Swedish edition, 1969
Göranzon B (ed) (1983) *Datautvecklingens filosofi. Tyst kunskapoch ny teknik.* Carlsson and Jönsson Bokförlag, Stockholm
Göranzon B (1992) *The practical intellect: skill and computerization.* UNESCO Springer-Verlag, London
Göranzon B (ed) (1982) *Job design and automation in Sweden,* Research Report no 36, Swedish Center for Working Life, Stockholm
Göranzon B (1990) *Det praktiska intellektet. Datoranvändning och yrkeskunnande,* Carlssons, Stockholm
Göranzon B and Florin N (1991) (eds) *Dialogue and technology: art and knowledge.* Springer-Verlag, London
Göranzon B and Florin M (1990) (eds) *Artificial intelligence culture and language.* Springer-Verlag, London
Göranzon B and Josefson I (es) (1988) *Knowledge skill and artificial intelligence,* Springer-Verlag, London
Gregory B (1986) Delimiting ES, *IEEE Transactions on Systems, Man and Cybernetics,* SMC-16
Gregory D (1987) Philosophy and practice in knowledge representation. In: Zeidner J (ed) *Human productivity enhancement,* Vol II, Praeger, New York
Grimen H (1987) *Aspects of act identification and intention-identification. An essay on identificatory practices in human life.* Vitskapsteoretisk Forum, University of Bergen

Harmon P and King D (1985) *Expert systems: artificial intelligence in business,* John Wiley & Sons, New York
Hart A (1986) *Knowledge acquisition for expert systems,* Kogan Page, London
Hayes C and Wheatley DE (1979) *Trends in apprenticeship in the European community*
Hegel GWF (1807) *Phänomenologie des Geistes*
Heidegger M (1978) *Being and Time,* transl Macguarrie J and Robinson E. Basil Blackwell, Oxford
Hume D (1966) My Own Life. In: Hendel CW (ed) *An inquiry concerning human understanding.* New York
Hume D (1969) *A Treatise on Human Nature,* Penguin, Harmondsworth

Illich I (1973), *Tools for Conviviality,* Harper and Row, New York
Ivanov K (1988) Expert-support systems: the new technology and the old knowledge. *Systems Research,* 5

Jakobson R (1963) *Essais de linguistique générale,* Paris
James H (1978) *The tragic muse.* Penguin, Harmondsworth
James W (1978) *Pragmatism and the meaning of truth.* Harvard University Press, Cambridge, MA
Janik A (1989) Justus Lipsius: Vater der österreichischen Philosophie? *Austraica* (Rouen) 198: 31–41

Janik A (1989) *Style, politics and the future of philosophy*. Klu.ver Academic Publishers, Dordrecht
Janik A and Toulmin S (1973) *Wittgenstein's Vienna*. New York
Johannessen KS (1978) *Wittgenstein's Later Philosophy*. Stencil series no 42, Dept of Philosophy, University of Bergen, Bergen
Johannessen KS (1985) *Tradisjoner og skoler i moderne vitenskapsfilosofi*. Bergen
Josephs H (1969) *Diderot's dialogue of language and gesture: Le Neveu de Rameau*. Colombus

Keats J (1958) *The letters of John Keats 1814–1821*. Cambridge, MA
Kraus K (1979) *Die letzten Tage der Menschheit*
Kuhn TS (1962) *The Structure of Scientific Revolutions*. Chicago. Revised edition with Postscript 1970

Lacan J (1977) *Ecrits*, transl Sheridan A. London
Leavis FR (1962) *Two cultures? The significance of CP Snow*. Chatto and Windus, London
Lerda F (1984) *Calcolatori e intelligenza umana, sul neopositivismo informatico*, Nuova Civiltà delle Machine, Anno II, no 1
Lerda F (in press) Some considerations on the relationships between Human and Artificial Intelligence. In Ricciardi LM (ed) *Biomathematics and related computational problems*. Reidel, Dordrecht
Levý J (1969) *Der literarische übersetzung*, Frankfurt am Main
Lewis M (1796) *The monk*
Lighthill J (1972) *Artificial intelligence, a paper symposium*, Report to SRC HMSO
Lo-Johansson I (1978) *Pubertet*, Stockholm

Mandel BJ (1978) *Autobiography–Reflection trained on mystery. Prairie Schooner*, 46, 1972–73
Maupassant G (nd) *Sur l'eau*, Paris
McDermott J (1982) R1: A rule-based configurer of computer systems. *Artificial Intelligence*, 19
McGuiness B (1988) *Wittgenstein: a life, young Ludwig 1889–1921*. Duckworth, London
Mesterton E (1985) *Speglingar*, Fyhr L and Hansson GD (eds). Anthropos, Uddevalla
Misch G (1950) *A History of autobiography in antiquity*, London
Mitchie D (1985) Current developments in artificial intelligence. *Zygon*, 20
Michie D and Johnston R (1984) *The creative computer: machine intelligence and human knowledge*, Penguin, Harmondsworth.
Molander B (1989a) Acting with good reasons. Knowledge and ignorance in human action, *Studies of Higher Education and Research*, 1
Molander B (1989b) *Philosophical essays dedicated to Sven Danielsson*. In: Lindström S and Wlodzimierz R (eds) In so many words. Philosophical Studies, Uppsala
Muneles O (1956) *Prague Ghetto in the Renaissance World*, State Jewish Museum, Prague

New York Review of Books (1983)
New York Times (1988)
Newell A and Simon HA (1976) *Computer science as empirical enquiry: symbols and search*. Communications of the ACM, March
Nietzsche F (1888)
Nightingale F (1897) *To the nurses and the probationers trained under the Nightingale Fund*. Jun 1897, Information Department of St Thomas' Hospital, London
Nin A (1973) *Journals of Anais Nin*, London

Östberg O, Whitaker R and Amick B (1988) *The automated expert: technical, human and organizational considerations in expert system applications*. Teldok, Farsta, Sweden (Via Teldock 12/88)

Parkin N (1978) Apprenticeships: outmoded or undervalued? *Personnel Management* 10(5)
Partridge D (1986) Will AI lead to a super software crisis? In: Gill K (ed) *Artificial Intelligence for Society*. John Wiley, Chichester
Pask G (1980) Developments in conversation theory. Part I *International Journal of Man-Machine Studies*, 13
Pask G and Gregory D (1987) Conversational Systems. In: Zeidner J (ed), *Human productivity enhancement*, vol II. Praeger, New York
Pickering C (1985) *Constructing quarks*, Chicago
Plank R (1968) *The emotional significance of imaginary beings*. CC Thomas
Plato *Gorgias*

Plato *Phaedros*
Polanyi M (1966) *The tacit dimension.* Routledge and Kegan Paul, London
Polanyi M (1978) *Personal knowledge. Towards a post-critical philosopy.* Routledge and Kegan Paul, London
Polanyi M (1983) *The tacit dimension.* Peter Smith, Gloucester, MA
Porter R (1978) Gentlemen and geology: the emergence of a scientific career, 1660–1920. *Historical Journal,* vol 21

Rosenbrock H (ed) (1989) *Designing human-centred technology: a cross-disciplinary project in computer-aided manufacturing.* Springer-Verlag, London
Rousseau J-J (1762) *Emile*
Rousseau J-J (1959-69) *Ouevres complètes,* Gagnebin B and Raymond M (ed.) Paris
Ryle G (1949) *The concept of minds,* Hutchinson's University Library, London

Schön DA (1983) The Reflective Practitioner. *How Professionals Think in Action,* Basic Books, New York
Schön DA (1987) *Educating the Reflective Practitioner,* Jossey-Bas, San Francisco
Scott A, Clancey W, Davis R and Shortcliffe E (1984) Methods for Generating Explanations. In: Buchanan B and Shortcliffe E (eds), *Ruse-based ES: the MYCIN experiments of the Stanford heuristic programming project.* Addison-Wesley, Reading MA
Serre M (1982) *Hermes: Literature, science, philosophy.* Johns Hopkins University Press, Baltimore and London.
Sessions R (1950) *The Musical Experience of Composer, Performing, Listener.* Princeton University Press, Princeton NJ
Shakespeare W *Henry IV Parts 1 and 2*
Shakespeare W *Henry V*
Shakespeare W *Measure for measure*
Shakespeare W *King Lear*
Shakespeare W *Richard II*
Shakespeare W *The tempest*
Sloman A (1984) *Towards a computational theory of mind. In: Artificial intelligence: human effects.* Narayan and Yazdani (eds), Ellis Horwood, Chichester
Snow CP (1960) *The two cultures and the scientific revolution.* Cambridge University Press
Starr CG (1982) *The Roman Empire 27BC–AD476. A study in survival.* Oxford
Stoker B (1897) *Dracula*
Strindberg A (1888) *Fröken Julie* (Miss Julie)
Strindberg A (1901) *Ett drömspel* (A Dream Play)
Strindberg A (1912–1920) *Samlade skrifter,* Landquist (ed)
Strindberg A (1948–) *August Strindberg brev,* Torsten Eklund T and Björn M (eds)

Taylor C (1985) Interpretation and the sciences of man. In *Philosophy of the human sciences,* Philosophical Papers 2. Cambridge University Press, Cambridge
Tempte T (1982) *Arbetet ära. Om hantverk, arbete, några rekonstruerade verktyg och maskiner.* The Center for Working Life, Stockholm
The Oxford and Cambridge Review (1909)
Tikhomirov O (1974) Man and computer: the impact of computer technology on the development of psychological processes. In: Olson D (ed) *Media and symbols.* Chicago, University of Chicago Press
Truesdell CA (1981) *Il calcolatore, rovina della scienza e minaccia per il genere umano,* La Nuova Ragione, il Mulino, Bologna
Tsvetajeva M (1981) *Min ryska barndom*
Turing AM (1936) *On computable numbers, with an application to the Entscheidungsproblem,* Proc London Math Soc 2: 42

von Wright GH (1971) *Explanation and understanding.* Routledge and Kegan Paul, London

Waismann F (1979) *Ludwig Wittgenstein and the Vienna circle.* Oxford
Wang H (1974) *From mathematics to philosophy.* Routledge and Kegan Paul, London
Waterman D (1986) *A guide to expert systems.* Addison Wesley, Reading MA
Wells HG (1905) *A modern Utopia*

Whitaker R and Östberg O (1988) Channeling knowledge: expert systems as communication media. *AI and Society*, 2
Whitby B (1988) *AI: a handbook of professionalism.* Ellis Horwood, Chichester
Wiig KM (in press) *Commercial applications. In: New technology and employment.* Bertold T (ed), North-Holland, Amsterdam
Williams R (1958) *Culture and Society.* Chatto and Windus, London
Winograd T (1987) A language/action perspective on the design of cooperative work. *Human-Computer Interaction*, 3
Winograd T and Flores F (1986) *Understanding computers and cognition: a new foundation for design*, Ablex, Norwood NJ
Wittgenstein L (1953) *Philosophical investigations*, Blackwell, Oxford
Wittgenstein L (1961) *Tractacus Logico-Philosophicus*, Transl Pears D-F and McGuiness BF Routledge and Kegan Paul, London (originally published 1921)
Wittgenstein L (1969) *On Certainty*, Blackwell, Oxford
Wittgenstein L (1974) *On certainty*, Transl Paul D and Anscombe GEM Blackwell, Oxford
Wittgenstein L (1975) *Philosophical remarks*, Blackwell, Oxford
Wittgenstein L (1978) *Remarks on the foundation of mathematics*, Blackwell, Oxford
Wittgenstein L (1980) *Culture and value*, Blackwell, Oxford

Yates F (1975) *Shakespeare's Last Plays*, Routledge and Kegan Paul London

Appendix

Skill and technology – a new research field in a series of five volumes:

Bo Göranzon and Ingela Josefson (Eds.): Knowledge, Skill and Artificial Intelligence, Springer-Verlag, 1988, 3-540-19519-X
Bo Göranzon and Magnus Florin (Eds.): Artificial Intelligence, Culture and Language: On Education and Work, Springer-Verlag, 1990, 3-540-19573-4
Bo Göranzon and Magnus Florin (Eds.): Dialogue and Technology: Art and Knowledge, Springer-Verlag, 1991, 3-540-19574-2
Bo Göranzon and Magnus Florin (Eds.): Skill and Education: Reflection and Experience, Springer-Verlag, 1992, 3-540-19758-3
Bo Göranzon: The Practical Intellect: Computers and Skills, UNESCO/ Springer-Verlag, 1992, 92-3-102757-3/3-540-19759-1

Name Index